Philippine Politics

Philippine political history, especially in the twentieth century, challenges the image of democratic evolution as serving the people, and it does so in ways that reveal inadequately explored aspects of many democracies. In the first decades of the twenty-first century, the Philippines has nonetheless shown gradual socio-economic "progress."

This book provides an interpretive overview of Philippine politics. It takes full account of the importance of patriotic Philippine factors in making decisions about future political policies. It analyses whether regional and local politics have more importance than national politics in the Philippines. Discussing cultural traditions of patronism, it also examines how clan feuds localize the state and create strong local policies. These conflicts in turn make regional and family-run polities collectively stronger than the central state institution. The book goes on to explore elections in the Philippines, and in particular the ways in which politicians win democratic elections, the institutionalized role of public money in this process, and the role that media play. Offering a new interpretive overview of Philippine progress over many decades, the author notes recent economic and political changes during the current century while also trying to advance ideas that might prove useful to Filipinos.

Presenting an in-depth analysis of the problems and possibilities of politics and society in the Philippines, the book will be of interest to those researching Southeast Asian Politics, Political History and Asian Society and Culture.

Lynn T. White III is Professor Emeritus and Senior Research Scholar in the Woodrow Wilson School, Politics Department, and East Asian Studies Program at Princeton University, USA.

Routledge contemporary Southeast Asia series

1 **Land Tenure, Conservation and Development in Southeast Asia**
Peter Eaton

2 **The Politics of Indonesia–Malaysia Relations**
One kin, two nations
Joseph Chinyong Liow

3 **Governance and Civil Society in Myanmar**
Education, health and environment
Helen James

4 **Regionalism in Post-Suharto Indonesia**
Edited by Maribeth Erb, Priyambudi Sulistiyanto and Carole Faucher

5 **Living with Transition in Laos**
Market integration in Southeast Asia
Jonathan Rigg

6 **Christianity, Islam and Nationalism in Indonesia**
Charles E. Farhadian

7 **Violent Conflicts in Indonesia**
Analysis, representation, resolution
Edited by Charles A. Coppel

8 **Revolution, Reform and Regionalism in Southeast Asia**
Cambodia, Laos and Vietnam
Ronald Bruce St John

9 **The Politics of Tyranny in Singapore and Burma**
Aristotle and the rhetoric of benevolent despotism
Stephen McCarthy

10 **Ageing in Singapore**
Service needs and the state
Peggy Teo, Kalyani Mehta, Leng Leng Thang and Angelique Chan

11 **Security and Sustainable Development in Myanmar**
Helen James

12 **Expressions of Cambodia**
The politics of tradition, identity and change
Edited by Leakthina Chau-Pech Ollier and Tim Winter

13 **Financial Fragility and Instability in Indonesia**
Yasuyuki Matsumoto

14 **The Revival of Tradition in Indonesian Politics**
The deployment of *adat* from colonialism to indigenism
Edited by Jamie S. Davidson and David Henley

15 **Communal Violence and Democratization in Indonesia**
Small town wars
Gerry van Klinken

16 **Singapore in the Global System**
Relationship, structure and change
Peter Preston

17 **Chinese Big Business in Indonesia**
The state of the capital
Christian Chua

18 **Ethno-religious Violence in Indonesia**
From soil to God
Chris Wilson

19 **Ethnic Politics in Burma**
States of conflict
Ashley South

20 **Democratization in Post-Suharto Indonesia**
Edited by Marco Bünte and Andreas Ufen

21 **Party Politics and Democratization in Indonesia**
Golkar in the post-Suharto era
Dirk Tomsa

22 **Community, Environment and Local Governance in Indonesia**
Locating the Commonwealth
Edited by Carol Warren and John F. McCarthy

23 **Rebellion and Reform in Indonesia**
Jakarta's security and autonomy polices in Aceh
Michelle Ann Miller

24 **Hadrami Arabs in Present-day Indonesia**
An Indonesia-oriented group with an Arab signature
Frode F. Jacobsen

25 **Vietnam's Political Process**
How education shapes political decision making
Casey Lucius

26 **Muslims in Singapore**
Piety, politics and policies
Kamaludeen Mohamed Nasir, Alexius A. Pereira and Bryan S. Turner

27 **Timor Leste**
Politics, history and culture
Andrea Katalin Molnar

28 **Gender and Transitional Justice**
The women of East Timor
Susan Harris Rimmer

29 **Environmental Cooperation in Southeast Asia**
ASEAN's regime for trans-boundary haze pollution
Paruedee Nguitragool

30 **The Theatre and the State in Singapore**
Terence Chong

31 **Ending Forced Labour in Myanmar**
Engaging a pariah regime
Richard Horsey

32 **Security, Development and Nation-Building in Timor-Leste**
A cross-sectoral assessment
Edited by Vandra Harris and Andrew Goldsmith

33 **The Politics of Religion in Indonesia**
Syncretism, orthodoxy, and religious contention in Java and Bali
Edited by Michel Picard and Remy Madinier

34 **Singapore's Ageing Population**
Managing healthcare and end of life decisions
Edited by Wing-Cheong Chan

35 **Changing Marriage Patterns in Southeast Asia**
Economic and socio-cultural dimensions
Edited by Gavin W. Jones, Terence H. Hull and Maznah Mohamad

36 **The Political Resurgence of the Military in Southeast Asia**
Conflict and leadership
Edited by Marcus Mietzner

37 **Neoliberal Morality in Singapore**
How family policies make state and society
Youyenn Teo

38 **Local Politics in Indonesia**
Pathways to power
Nankyung Choi

39 **Separatist Conflict in Indonesia**
The long-distance politics of the Acehnese diaspora
Antje Missbach

40 **Corruption and Law in Indonesia**
The unravelling of Indonesia's anti-corruption framework through law and legal process
Simon Butt

41 **Men and Masculinities in Southeast Asia**
Edited by Michele Ford and Lenore Lyons

42 **Justice and Governance in East Timor**
Indigenous approaches and the 'new subsistence state'
Rod Nixon

43 **Population Policy and Reproduction in Singapore**
Making future citizens
Shirley Hsiao-Li Sun

44 **Labour Migration and Human Trafficking**
Critical perspectives from Southeast Asia
Michele Ford, Lenore Lyons and Willem van Schendel

45 **Singapore Malays**
Being ethnic minority and Muslim in a global city-state
Hussin Mutalib

46 **Political Change and Territoriality in Indonesia**
Provincial proliferation
Ehito Kimura

47 **Southeast Asia and the Cold War**
Edited by Albert Lau

48 **Legal Pluralism in Indonesia**
Bridging the unbridgeable
Ratno Lukito

49 **Building a People-oriented Security Community the ASEAN Way**
Alan Collins

50 **Parties and Parliaments in Southeast Asia**
Non-partisan chambers in Indonesia, the Philippines and Thailand
Roland Rich

51 **Social Activism in Southeast Asia**
Edited by Michele Ford

52 **Chinese Indonesians Reassessed**
History, religion and belonging
Edited by Siew-Min Sai and Chang-Yau Hoon

53 **Journalism and Conflict in Indonesia**
From reporting violence to promoting peace
Steve Sharp

54 **The Technological State in Indonesia**
The co-constitution of high technology and authoritarian politics
Sulfikar Amir

55 **Party Politics in Southeast Asia**
Clientelism and electoral competition in Indonesia, Thailand and the Philippines
Edited by Dirk Tomsa and Andreas Ufen

56 **Culture, Religion and Conflict in Muslim Southeast Asia**
Negotiating tense pluralisms
Edited by Joseph Camilleri and Sven Schottmann

57 **Global Indonesia**
Jean Gelman Taylor

58 **Cambodia and the Politics of Aesthetics**
Alvin Cheng-Hin Lim

59 **Adolescents in Contemporary Indonesia**
Lyn Parker and Pam Nilan

60 **Development and the Environment in East Timor**
Authority, participation and equity
Christopher Shepherd

61 **Law and Religion in Indonesia**
Faith, conflict and the courts
Melissa Crouch

62 **Islam in Modern Thailand**
Faith, philanthropy and politics
Rajeswary Ampalavanar Brown

63 **New Media and the Nation in Malaysia**
Malaysianet
Susan Leong

64 **Human Trafficking in Cambodia**
Chendo Keo

65 **Islam, Politics and Youth in Malaysia**
The pop-Islamist reinvention of PAS
Dominik Mueller

66 **The Future of Singapore**
Population, society and the nature of the state
Kamaludeen Mohamed Nasir and Bryan S. Turner

67 **Southeast Asia and the European Union**
Non-traditional security crises and cooperation
Naila Maier-Knapp

68 **Rhetoric, Violence, and the Decolonization of East Timor**
David Hicks

69 **Local Governance in Timor-Leste**
Understanding development in postcolonial communities
Deborah Cummins

70 **Media Consumption in Malaysia**
A hermeneutics of human behaviour
Tony Wilson

71 **Philippine Politics**
Possibilities and problems in a localist democracy
Lynn T. White III

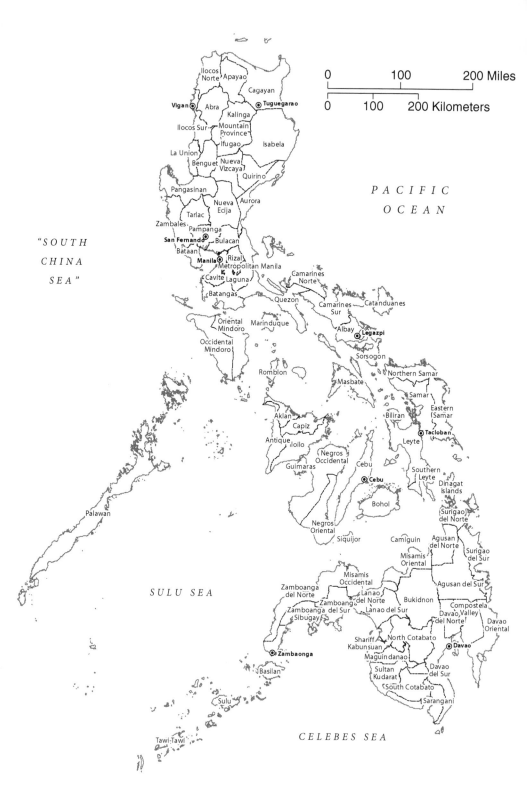

Philippine Politics
Possibilities and problems in a localist democracy

Lynn T. White III

LONDON AND NEW YORK

First published 2015
by Routledge
2 Park Square, Milton Park, Abingdon, Oxon OX14 4RN

and by Routledge
711 Third Avenue, New York, NY 10017

First issued in paperback 2017

Routledge is an imprint of the Taylor & Francis Group, an informa business

© 2015 Lynn T. White III

The right of Lynn T. White III to be identified as author of this work has been asserted by him in accordance with sections 77 and 78 of the Copyright, Designs and Patents Act 1988.

All rights reserved. No part of this book may be reprinted or reproduced or utilized in any form or by any electronic, mechanical, or other means, now known or hereafter invented, including photocopying and recording, or in any information storage or retrieval system, without permission in writing from the publishers.

Trademark notice: Product or corporate names may be trademarks or registered trademarks, and are used only for identification and explanation without intent to infringe.

British Library Cataloguing in Publication Data
A catalogue record for this book is available from the British Library

Library of Congress Cataloging in Publication Data
White, Lynn T., III
Philippine politics: progress and problems in a localist democracy / Lynn T. White III.
   pages cm – (Routledge contemporary Southeast Asia series; 71)
   Includes bibliographical references and index.
   1. Philippines–Politics and government–1946– 2. Democracy–Philippines. I. Title. II. Series: Routledge contemporary Southeast Asia series ; 71.
   DS685.W45 2015
   320.9599–dc23   2014030806

ISBN 13: 978-1-138-49233-2 (pbk)
ISBN 13: 978-1-138-82804-9 (hbk)

Typeset in Times New Roman
by Wearset Ltd, Boldon, Tyne and Wear

For Barbara-Sue

Contents

Acknowledgments		xii
List of abbreviations and acronyms		xiii
1	Local regimes: an introduction	1
2	Malay foundations and colonial semi-modernizations	12
3	Clan feuds localize political violence	27
4	Entrepreneurs as politicians	62
5	Marcos, failed centralization, and land from the tiller	100
6	Law of rule, power of separations	118
7	Populist rituals and elite reformism	135
8	Voting, pork, policy, and media	155
9	Corruption	176
10	PNoy, "Pacquiaos," and Philippine progress	207
	References	232
	Index	259

Acknowledgments

I could never have written this book without the loving encouragement of my wife, Barbara-Sue White, to whom it is dedicated.

Warm thanks go also to many scholars, some anonymous and many honored in a list below, who have read parts of this manuscript or have helped me by discussing its ideas.

I am grateful to Angela Leung and Hong Kong University's Institute of Humanities and Social Sciences for office space that was crucial as this book was prepared. Generous logistical help for my family has also come from Priscilla Roberts in Hong Kong. Sandy Flynn and Rita Alpaugh helped at Princeton. Thanks also go to my acquiring editor at Routledge, Jillian Morrison, to Senior Project Manager at Wearset, Amy Ekins-Coward, and to copy editor, Sally Quinn. Cartographer Tsering Wangyal Shawa expertly drew the map. For help with computers over many years, thanks go to Jimmy Wang and his colleagues in the Woodrow Wilson School information technology department.

It is a special pleasure to express my gratitude to those mentioned above and to: Aileen Baviera, Walden Bello, Alexander Brilliantes, Robin Broad, John P. Burns, Ricky Carandang, Ramon Casiple, Tom Christensen, Josephine Dionisio, Enrique Esteban, Raul Fabella, Gregory Felker, Mario Feranil, Tom Ferguson, Trina Firmalo, Leizl Formilleza, John Gershman, Linda Luz Guerrero, Carmen Jimenez, Ben Kerkvliet, Erik Martínez Kuhonta, Carlos Lazatín, Alexander Magno, Mahar Mangahas, Ma. Melanie R.S. Milo, Erik Mobrand, Francisco Nemenzo, Norman Owen, Pasuk Phongpaichit and Chris Baker, Maria Ressa, Temario Rivera, Joel Rocamora, Steven Rood, John Sidel, Julio Teehankee, Jorge Tigno, Jeanette Ureta, Geoff Wade, Wong Siu-lun, Deborah Yashar, and many others. I am also very grateful to the generous referee to whom Routledge sent this interpretive text.

I remain solely guilty as the perpetrator. The book in your hands contains many strongly stated views. The paradigms and definitions used in parts of it differ from those employed by other scholars. In particular, I apologize for having to include some material about impediments to Philippine progress. This is a matter of trying to be honest. I am in debt to the many researchers cited in notes, from whose varied and wonderful works I have learned a great deal.

Lynn T. White III
Princeton, October 2013

Abbreviations and acronyms

AC-DC	"attack, collect [money], defend, collect" blackmail (e.g., by journalists)
AFP	Armed Forces of the Philippines
AMRSP	Association of Major Religious Superiors of the Philippines
ARMM	Autonomous Region of Muslim Mindanao
ATM	automatic teller machine (literal, or "ATM" supplying "pork" funds)
BIR	Bureau of Internal Revenue
CARP	Comprehensive Agrarian Reform Program (originally of C. Aquino)
CARPER	Comprehensive Agrarian Reform Program Extension with Reforms
CBCP	Catholic Bishops Conference of the Philippines
CDFs	community development funds (one form of "pork")
CESO	Career Executive Service Officer
Comelec	Commission on Elections
CPI	corruption perception index
CPLA	Cordillera People's Liberation Army
CPP	Communist Party of the Philippines (see also NPA)
DAR	Department of Agrarian Reform
EDSA	Epifanio de los Santos Avenue, Manila (and political protests held there)
EJK	extrajudicial killings (a.k.a. "salvagings")
FDI	foreign direct investment
GMA	GMA News (by pure coincidence, sometimes Gloria Macapagal Arroyo)
GNP	gross national product
ICAC	Independent Commission Against Corruption (Hong Kong)
IFI	Iglesia Filipina Independiente (ex-Catholic)
ILT	"in lieu thereof" (non-monetary bribes)
ISI	import-substituting industrialization
IRRI	International Rice Research Institute (Los Baños, Laguna Province)
KBL	*Kilusang Babong Lipunan* (New Society Movement; Marcos's party)
KKK	Kapitunan (see Chapter 2; also used by anti-communist militias)

KMT	Kuomintang (Nationalist Party, now Taiwan; a.k.a. Guomindang)
Laban	Lakas ng Bayan (B. Aquino's anti-Marcos party, acronym means "fight")
Namfrel	National Citizens Movement for Free Elections
NBI	National Bureau of Investigation
NGO	non-governmental organization
NIC	newly industrializing country
NPA	New People's Army (armed Maoist/guerilla wing of the CPP)
MFN	most favored nation (whose exports enjoy minimal tariffs)
MILF	Moro Islamic Liberation Front (usually pro-independence)
MNLF	Moro National Liberation Front (pro-autonomy)
OFW	Overseas Filipino Worker
PC	Philippine Constabulary
PDAF	Priority Development Assistance Fund (called "pork" by critics)
PNP	Philippine National Police
PR	proportional representation
RAM	Reform the Armed Forces Movement (anti-Marcos, and later coups)
SMEs	small- and medium-sized enterprises
SWS	Social Weather Stations (foremost Philippine polling organization)
trapo	traditional politician (also Tagalog for "dirty washrag")
UNIDO	United Democratic Opposition (to Marcos)

1 Local regimes
An introduction

Democracies are hopefully designed to "serve the people." Liberal habits that tend to treat citizens as equals, if combined with electoral habits for choosing governors in national and local polities, are expected at least over long periods to become a self-reinforcing syndrome that promotes fairness. The democratic regime type also correlates internationally with high wages and entrepreneurial prosperity. There have, however, been sometime exceptions.

Philippine political history in the twentieth century challenged the rosy image of democratic evolution—and it did so in ways that reveal inadequately explored aspects of many democracies. This is a concern of Filipinos, not just of foreigners.[1] In the first decades of the twenty-first century the Philippines has nonetheless shown gradual socioeconomic "progress" as most people conceive such development. Many books about Philippine politics, especially those based on the era of President Ferdinand Marcos whose efforts at political centralization descended toward ineffective dictatorship, offer monotonic critiques of enduring political habits in the archipelago. Other books, often based on hopes after his demise, take the opposite tack, often showing either pan-gloss confidence about the country's future or patriotic pride that suggest occult causes of happiness for Filipinos.

President Marcos's propaganda from his 1965 democratic election to his 1986 downfall linked development and nationalism. So a "turn" of thought among many Philippine intellectuals has raised doubts about this linkage—albeit more doubts about development than about patriotism. As Resil Mojares has said, "Indeed, there is quite nothing like 'progress'—with the confidence and cosmopolitanism it brings—more conducing to an 'internationalizing' scholarship."[2] There is nonetheless evidence that most Filipinos really would like more progress in distributing both power and wealth.

The book in your hands argues that both the pessimist and optimist accounts, like both the patriotic and cosmopolitan accounts, are incomplete if they look at the Philippines as a well-unified political system. The main argument here is that the country includes many local polities, which are in conflict with each other and with "the state." Traditions of political personalism are especially powerful on these islands. They support institutions that may be evaluated as either "bad" or "good." However that assessment turns out, the rich variety of politics in the

Philippines trumps any attempt to define it in terms that are either modernistic or patriotic, or sad or glad. It is necessary to look at many sizes of institutions and informal power networks, and at the ideas these have fostered. Local patronism of a non-entrepreneurial kind continues to affect this political economy, despite waves of progress such as became evident in the decade after 2005.

It is usual to begin studies of a nation's politics with the central government, although that is barely a start on the subject in any country. What causes the Philippine state to be described by many scholars as weak relative to regional or local Philippine polities? In other countries, including some that have lower per-capita incomes, the ability of the central government to influence localities is greater. In some, such as China, surveyed popular trust of national leaders is combined with popular distrust of lesser cadres; but in the Philippines, democratic elections legitimate the local leaders. Weak states elsewhere have been explained by factors that are arguably inapplicable to the Philippines. Sharp ethnic or religious divisions, for example, have been said to account either for state weakness (as in Zaire/Congo at any period) or for state strength (as in Saddam's Iraq, which contrasted with Maliki's). Yet Filipinos, despite some relatively minor linguistic diversity, do not have such severe divisions. The Muslim–Christian split is exceptional, and it concerns a minority in just a part of far-south Mindanao. Philippine citizens' sense of nationhood is certainly not below par.

A country's large size is occasionally cited as a problem for governance, although this explanation may be challenged in many populous and relatively stable states (e.g., India). The Philippines, which now contains more than 100 million people, is among the dozen most populous nations on this planet. Its large size is neither a clear cause of political problems nor a clear advantage for the future.

Natural resource windfalls have sometimes been adduced to explain losses of public legitimacy in states ruled by kleptocrats. But the Philippines, despite fertile volcanic soil and plenty of sun for growing crops such as rice or sugar, has scant oil, gold, or diamonds. The "resource curse" may or may not explain authoritarian tendencies.[3] Either way, the evidence for it on these islands is mostly missing. The geographical sites of Philippine resources are not concentrated, as are many sources of mineral wealth that finance elites in other countries.

Another explanation of unsatisfactory governance cites international "bad neighborhoods." Several African and Middle Eastern states are weakened because of conflicts that slip over their borders from other countries (from Sudan to South Sudan or to Chad, from Rwanda and Burundi to Zaire, from Syria or Iraq to their neighbors). By a similar mechanism, Eastern European states may be developing better governance because of their European Union co-continentals. But the Philippines are islands. Some of the most reputed successful states on this planet, both authoritarian and democratic, are over adjacent seas in East Asia. This archipelago is not in a bad neighborhood.

Weak civil society is sometimes said to impede effective governance—but the Philippines has particularly strong traditions among electoral watchdogs, non-government organizations, investigative journalists and academics, clerics who express concern for the poor, and women's groups (although this country like many others has few effective trade unions). Nonstate institutions form readily in the Philippines to advocate for citizens who are seen to be underrepresented in government. Sometimes, as in the 1986 presidential transition from Marcos or the 2001 transition from Estrada, "civil polities" have been crucial (along with soldiers) for changing the chief executive. Nonstate political organizations have not been weak, although many Filipinos have been surveyed to perceive that democracy does not do much of substance for "the people," especially to raise their incomes.

Further often-cited causes of democratic unreliability are easier to document in the Philippines. Extensive violence and extensive poverty head this list of factors. Relatively frequent natural disasters, economic reliance on unstable international commodity prices, and legacies of colonial indirect rule contribute to Philippine problems. These factors can also be found in other weak states, although the Spanish and American bequests of frailty to Manila are particularly striking, as the next chapter will document. Comparisons with other countries can aid analysis of this book's main practical question: What reforms would make Philippine democracy serve the people better? But comparisons allow so many different conclusions that it makes sense mainly to study the place in its own right. An aim here is to see what this country's own trajectory can tell about modern governance elsewhere, not just what other nations' experiences suggest about the Philippines.

In the most recently published overview of politics throughout Southeast Asia, Richard Robison notes "three main ideological and scholarly traditions." The first he lists is "American political science ... especially as this is constituted within modernization theory." The second is "Political economy in the British and European tradition, especially ... Marxist." A third, which has actually not seen much application to the Philippines, is "Public choice/rational choice political economy and New Institutional Economics."[4] This book stands back from these somewhat fraught ideological-scholarly traditions, as from the rather abstract patriotic, elitist, and postmodern opposing ideologies that each of them has produced, to write about facts that anybody can observe in the history of the archipelago.[5]

Studies of the Philippine polity, and also of the economy, show a notable resilience of non-entrepreneurial localist patronism. Many scholars have documented the extent to which most local officials and judges outside Manila have been tools of family interests. Some of the clans have remained in regional power for generations. Studies of political clientelism have become controversial among some Philippine nationalist scholars.[6] But these ideas organize too much evidence to justify dismissing them on any existentialist grounds, even for would-be patriotic reasons. The central state remains weak; and local power networks have remained strong, even though that situation is slowly changing.

Historians such as Marcelino Foronda or Norman Owen have documented the autonomy of local affairs in the Philippines more carefully than most other social scientists have done, although some political scientists and activists such as Resil

Mojares and Joel Rocamora have also stressed the importance of place in Philippine affairs. They have tried to tell the stories of actors whose "stage was municipal or provincial, far from the national spotlight that focused on Rizal and Quezon."[7] Not just in a country of islands, local stories may be the main ones.

Lessons for democracies

The Philippines is procedurally democratic. Freedom of expression and other liberal norms are constitutionally enshrined, and they are often exercised. As in other democracies, the norm of liberty in stable eras tends to favor people who have wealth. For example, some journalists have asked, "Is the Philippine press free?" The standard joking answer is, "Yes, but it is not cheap."[8] Politicians there sometimes pay high prices for positive news coverage. Political and social NGOs flourish, as do chambers of commerce, and other "civil societies." Such organizations are important for governance anywhere, but their modal traits affect its democratic quality.[9] As Hutchcroft and Rocamora write, "No country in Asia has more experience with democratic institutions than the Philippines."[10] Yet the combination of voting and freedom for many decades did not generally serve the islands' people as much as they (and foreigners) expected.

Elections in the archipelago are occasions for fiestas, like those on village saints' days. Voter turnouts are much higher in the Philippines than in most democracies. Local races are often closely fought. Professionals—news anchors, movie stars, boxers, basketball players—join Congress along with representatives of famous political families (who now mostly have professional vocations too, often in law). Diverse Philippine elites do not all agree with each other on policies, of course; but a degree of formal courtesy can be documented among families of leaders who in the past have literally murdered each other. By contrast, surveys show a relative lack of trust among low-income Filipinos, rural farmers, and those who have scant education.[11]

Especially in a few regions, such as Bulacan or Pampanga, there have also been decades-old nonstate traditions of civil society movements for fair voting, for social justice, and sometimes against patronism. These have produced slow results. It is possible to explore why patron–client relations often dominate Philippine politics—and why such networks are sometimes less salient. Ideals of "people power" have occasionally become important, even though most of the people, when surveyed, believe they lack much national power. Later chapters will explain factors that catalyze the choices of Philippine elites, local or central, to be reformist or traditional.

Some foreign writers have suggested that Philippine political culture is irrevocably stagnant. James Fallows controversially speculated long ago that a lack of substantive results for most citizens in this democratic polity arises from some defect of Philippine nationalism:[12]

> When a country with extreme geographic, tribal, and social-class differences, like the Philippines, has only a weak offsetting sense of national

unity, its public life does become the war of every man against every man.... Filipinos pride themselves on their lifelong loyalty to family, schoolmates, compadres, members of the same tribe, residents of the same barangay ... total devotion to those within the circle, total war on those outside.

Fallows is wrong about weak national identity in the Philippines, even if he is right about strong identification with smaller groups. He overstates "tribal" (as distinguished from local) tensions, and he implies that differences of wealth will readily be articulated in politics. His report of "total war" is wildly exaggerated. All politics involve conflict, not just in this country. Yet many Filipinos are also distressed by the extent of sociopolitical violence, and they seek ways to reduce it.

At the same time, when foreigners look at the Philippines, they may see social disasters that worry fewer Filipinos. In a 2001 survey, a sample within the country was asked, "If you were to consider your life in general these days, how happy or unhappy would you say you are, on the whole?" The results reported considerable bliss (very happy, 31 percent; fairly happy, 53 percent; not very happy, 12 percent; not at all happy, just 4 percent). Filipinos were also offered the proposition: "People like me don't have any say about what the government does."[13] Apathy mixed with dissatisfaction in the responses: a plurality of 39 percent agreed or strongly agreed with the statement, and another tepid 33 percent neither agreed nor disagreed. Much later, in 2013, a follow-up survey found that Filipinos' "net personal optimism" and "net economic optimism" were both "very high."[14] Such polls have been repeated many times in earlier and later years, with similar results.

Few Filipinos thought they could affect national policy in Manila, but when they were asked, "How likely is it that you would be able to bring out some improvement in your local community?" a strong 64 percent in 2001 said this was "very or somewhat likely." This may just have been naïveté in an attitude poll, but a popular sense of political efficacy in local politics is stronger than is any sense that people can affect the national government.

Advice to Filipinos from foreigners has been extensive and often unflattering. As Michael Pinches points out,

> In a region of Tigers and Dragons, the Philippines has almost universally been portrayed as the exceptional failure, and has had to endure the label "sick man of Asia" as well as the condescending advice of regional leaders like Lee Kwan Yew.[15]

Urbanski called the Philippines a "non-substantive democracy." Kikuchi called the society "uncrystallized." McCoy and his colleagues produced very extensive evidence that the polity was "an anarchy of families." Yoshihara described the economy as "ersatz capitalism," and Hutchcroft described Philippine politics in terms of "booty capitalism."[16] It is understandable that Filipinos would tend not

6 *Local regimes: an introduction*

to like such descriptions, even when they too can see plenty of evidence for them. This book aims to find structural reasons for past Philippine problems, so that the future can be made brighter than the twentieth-century past. The twenty-first century has already seen some improvements that will be documented in later chapters, despite continuing issues deriving from the strength of the many regional Philippine political economies.

Localist institutions

An aim of this book is to provide an interpretative synthesis of information about the Philippine political economy that takes account of recent events such as the acceleration of economic growth after 2005 and the election of a reformist president in 2010 (while asking also whether the electoral structure is likely to make his successors reformist). Another aim is to provide a synoptic view of Philippine political history that treats factual data from the colonial and post-colonial periods together, looking for ways to design the democracy so that it serves ordinary people better. Filipinos, not foreigners such as this author, will of course make all the relevant decisions. The book should provide an overall introduction to Philippine politics for readers who may be newly interested in this very populous country that used to be a U.S. colony. It also relates Philippine problems and progress to universal hopes that Filipinos, like other people, generally inherited from the enlightenment. Political parties are crucial for translating ideas into action.

Stable parties with clear policy platforms have not formed in the Philippines because of "dependency relations embodied in patron-client networks, powerful regional elites, private landowner armies, and crosscutting social cleavages that constrain solidarity along class lines," Riedinger claims.[17] Without meaningful parties, according to Huntington, "elections are just a conservative device which gives a semblance of popular legitimacy to traditional structures and traditional leadership." Huntington distinguished "form of government" from "degree of government."[18] Erik Martínez Kuhonta, a younger scholar whose approach is similar, writes about his ancestral country as follows: "the advent of democratic elections throughout the archipelago, before the cementing of a bureaucratic core, weakened the potential for institutional development."[19] The forms of government in Manila and in many localities have for long periods been democratic, but time alone has scarcely changed state–society relations. The degree of government at the national level has been low, whereas the degree of power in local nonstate polities is high, especially outside Metro Manila.

Regime type is a collective choice, and the most usual list of types arranges them along a rather simple spectrum: totalitarian to authoritarian to democratic. This paradigm does not capture the degree of influence that relatively central regimes have over more local regimes, or vice versa. Governments that are authoritarian or totalitarian in terms of their ideals do not necessarily have extensive control—or even extensive information—about smaller polities within their countries.[20] Local power networks can just as well be called "regimes" too. Elites or followers at many sizes of collectivity use whatever situations and norms are available to them.

Philippine patrons may act as either godfather-warlords or else as politicians with a more "modern" public appeal. Patronism comes in many forms, and it can adapt to modern technologies and ideas.[21] Clients likewise can sometimes choose the extent of their obedience or indebtedness. Some even select the identities of their creditors or patrons. Regime types are chosen according to benefits that actors have in the structures they face—and these structures are by no means all at the size of a national state. They are also in families, villages, corporations, churches, and other political networks.

Alfred McCoy finds,

> a *local dimension* of free ports or outlaw zones, epicenters of contraband commerce that are detached from nation-state controls and known by evocative place-names.... Inside *individual nations* the interaction between the state's secret services and outlaw elements, whether rural warlords or urban gangsters, can define the character of an entire polity.

States are not the only power networks that can use force or have legitimacy. A modal local regime type can shape national politics at least as much as localities are shaped by a central government. So McCoy suggests "inverting [the usual] analytic framework to show not just the center's influence on these criminal and provincial peripheries but their role in shaping both political processes and actual administration at the epicenter of state power."[22]

Large countries contain relatively many sizes of polity. Each might be characterized by various regime-type adjectives. Most recent researchers have been so beguiled by the notion that the key to social truth is statistical, and so eager to use accessible national data from "large N" samples that include many small states, comparative analyses have been distorted by underweighting large nations such as China or India—or the Philippines—which include distinctively many sizes of power network. This critique applies equally to classic riches-lead-to-liberalism analyses that follow Lipset and to newer treatments of elite decisions about regime types that follow Rustow, Przeworski, Boix and Stokes, and others.[23] It also applies to analyses by economists such as Acemoglu and Robinson.[24]

When a modern country is extremely large, its size influences state structure as well as power structures "below" the "level" of the state.[25] Words such as "level" imply that larger polities always trump smaller ones, but the opposite is often demonstrably the case. Spans of control in large, dispersed countries can be tenuous; big countries can be difficult for central governments to monitor. Control of violence can be hard to monopolize in such a state, whether or not it aspires to a monopoly of force. Even when local elites vow abstract patriotic fealty to their larger nation—as they often have interests in doing—their benefit from controlling coercion near their own homes may be so great that they resist central efforts to coordinate the nation's police or army. To speak of an "elite decision" or "elite pact" in a large country, without distinguishing different kinds of elites at different sizes of collectivity that may be able to avoid each other, is to omit much political behavior. A populous but geographically fragmented nation such as the Philippines, which is divided into many islands and by volcanic ranges, may be misunderstood if only the whole nation is considered or if just one abstract type of regime is imagined to cover all of the terrain.[26]

Quick overview of chapters

This book is organized topically. Its main theses are that local Philippine politics has often trumped national politics, reducing substantive democratization for most of the people, and that this pattern is not fixed forever. Some chapter titles suggest specific periods or presidencies, and these may seem incongruous because they are bound by times rather than themes; but they are just shorthand. Themes that recur or change in different eras of Philippine history have been particularly salient at some times. Patronism and "unrepayable debts" can already be evidenced in early Malay traditions that the lightly staffed Spanish and American colonial administrations adapted for their own purposes. Clan feuds that localized the state (to use words from the third chapter's title) were important throughout the twentieth century—as were issues surrounding Chinese entrepreneurs—and these became particularly salient during the 1950s' economic boom that relied to a surprising extent on agricultural processing. Attempts to coordinate violence peaked under Marcos, who tried to centralize the state by binding rural to urban polities; but he failed by adopting counter-effective, non-sustainable policy in the field that might have had the greatest political effect, land reform. Problems of effective change became particularly obvious under Corazon Aquino, although partial solutions were implemented under Ramos. Estrada and then Arroyo became mainly famous for corruption. Hopes and achievements of progress are evident under the current President "PNoy" Aquino, although it is unclear that the structure of Philippine politics is likely to produce future elected leaders to continue even the policies of moderate reform that he has advocated; future elections might instead legitimate a strong conservative populist (the boxer Pacquiao is a possible future president, although the powers of that office are still somewhat limited no matter who holds it). Topics that span periods are discussed in order of the particular eras when they were most salient. The main theme in each chapter involves links between different sizes of polity, with particular attention to local strengths. Progress among periods, leading up to recent reform efforts and twenty-first century partial successes, creates the book's narrative.

Action possibilities to solve problems

This book is not a monograph. The author's intention is to offer a new interpretive overview of Philippine progress over many decades, noting recent economic and political changes during the current century while also trying to advance ideas that might prove useful to Filipinos. It would be especially presumptuous of an American such as the present author, who through no act of his own comes from a country that once claimed colonial sovereignty in the Philippines, to prescribe sure policy recommendations for Filipinos to follow—even when trying to write about issues that anyone whosoever may document. Philippine actors will naturally relate what they do to their identities, not just to the results that they envisage from their decisions. This book should help create a basis on which consequentialist thinking about such problems can proceed among scholars of any nationality.

Words such as "good," "ethical," or "recommendable" have two separate and in some respects opposite meanings. They can refer to actions taken by a person whose identity (or "ultimate values," to use a term associated with Max Weber) may determine what happens.[27] That kind of recommendation is not the forte of a foreigner. It would not be so even if the Philippines had never been a U.S. colony. But these words about ethics can also refer to actions taken because the economic, political, and social consequences are seen as desirable, as estimated by comparative models and values that many Filipinos and others deem universal. Evidence about the relevant objective situations, and comparative evidence to test those logics, is widely available. Existential positions do not negate it.

All of the chapters after this first one end with short sections on possibilities for progress, insofar as empirically derived consequentialist logics can justify them. This author has no certainty that these suggestions are always appropriate for the Philippines in cultural terms, although he doubts current social-science norms that shy away from showing ways in which "cultural" habits shape the live options that actors can conceive. Possibilities for progress, described in the final section of each later chapter, relate to the problems on which the relevant chapter concentrates.

Notes

1 Many Philippine authors share concerns for what this current book calls "substantive democracy": see Felipe B. Miranda, Temario C. Rivera, Malaya C. Ronas, and Ronald D. Holmes, *Chasing the Wind: Assessing Philippine Democracy* (Quezon City: Commission on Human Rights of the Philippines and United Nations Development Program, 2011), esp. the concluding chapter by Temario C. Rivera, "Rethinking Philippine Democratization," 182–99.
2 Resil B. Mojares, "Making a Turn: Thoughts on a Generation of Philippine Scholarship," Keynote Address at the Philippine Studies Conference, Kyoto, Japan, February 28 to March 2, 2014 (kindly supplied to the author by Norman G. Owen, originally distributed on Facebook by Vicente L. Rafael).
3 See Michael L. Ross, "The Political Economy of the Resource Curse," *World Politics* 51 (January 1999), 297–322—and for another view, Thad Dunning, *Crude Democracy: Natural Resource Wealth and Political Regimes* (New York: Cambridge University Press, 2008).
4 Richard Robison, "Interpreting the Politics of Southeast Asia: Debates in Parallel Universes," in *Routledge Handbook of Southeast Asian Politics*, Robison, ed. (Abingdon: Routledge, 2013), 5.

10 *Local regimes: an introduction*

5 Any epistemological or political tradition has a logical alternative, whose usefulness cannot be judged separate from its application. These alternatives can be organized by choices between methodological individualism or collectivism and by choices between evidence based on unintended situations or intended norms. To see how they have come up in practically all famous social theories, see the chart and notes in Lynn White, *Unstately Power*, vol. 1 (Armonk, NY: M.E. Sharpe, 1998), 58–67. But that is all abstract; more important are facts and people.

6 Later chapters will have to discuss Reynaldo Ileto, *Knowing America's Colony: A Hundred Years from the Philippine War*, esp. Lecture 3, "Orientalism and the Study of Philippine Politics" (Honolulu: Center for Philippine Studies, 1999) and John T. Sidel, "Response to Ileto: Or, I am Not an Orientalist," *Philippine Political Science Journal* 23:46 (2002), 129–38. Political families (Kennedy, Taft, Brown...) have been important in several democracies, and they are salient in the Philippines.

7 Norman G. Owen, *The Bicol Blend: Bicolanos and their History* (Quezon City: New Day, 1999), flyleaf; on Marcelino Foronda see p. 36, and on p. 181 Owen cites works of Mariano Goyena del Prado and Maria Lelia F. Realubit, albeit these too are about the almost-island of Bicol. Other localist scholars have studied parts of Mindanao, Negros, and other islands. Resil B. Mojares, "Making a Turn," refers to the "turn" toward local studies.

8 Chay Florintino-Hofileña, *News for Sale: The Corruption of the Philippine Media* (Quezon City: Philippine Center for Investigative Journalism and Center for Media Freedom and Responsibility, 1998), 91.

9 The now-classic treatment is Sheri Berman, "Civil Society and the Collapse of the Weimar Republic," *World Politics* 49 (April 1997), 401–29.

10 Paul D. Hutchcroft and Joel Rocamora, "Patronage-Based Parties and the Democratic Deficit in the Philippines: Origins, Evolution, and the Imperatives of Reform," *Routledge Handbook of Southeast Asian Politics*, Richard Robison, ed. (Abingdon: Routledge, 2013), 97.

11 Ricardo G. Abad, *Aspects of Social Capital in the Philippines: Findings from a National Survey* (Quezon City: Social Weather Stations, 2006).

12 James Fallows, "A Damaged Culture: A New Philippines," *Atlantic Monthly* (November 1, 1987), and www.theatlantic.com.

13 This Social Weather Station survey was large and stratified. See Ricardo G. Abad, *Aspects of Social Capital in the Philippines*, esp. 68–9.

14 The Social Weather Station found 39 percent of adults expecting their personal quality of life to rise by 2014, with only 6 percent predicting its decline. SWS Media Release, July 10, 2013.

15 Michael Pinches, "Entrepreneurship, Consumption, Ethnicity, and National Identity in the Making of the Philippines' New Rich," in *Culture and Privilege in Capitalist Asia*, Pinches, ed. (New York: Routledge, 1999), 275.

16 C. Urbanski, "Middle Class Exodus and Democratic Decay in the Philippines," *ANU Undergraduate Research Journal* 1 (2009), 71–8; Kikuchi Yasushi, *Uncrystallized Philippine Society: A Social Anthropological Analysis* (Quezon City: New Day Publishers, 1991); Alfred W. McCoy, ed., *An Anarchy of Families: State and Family in the Philippines* (Madison, WI: University of Wisconsin Center for Southeast Asian Studies, 1993); Yoshihara Kunio, *The Rise of Ersatz Capitalism in Southeast Asia* (especially the Philippines) (New York: Oxford University Press, 1988); Paul D. Hutchcroft, *Booty Capitalism: The Politics of Banking in the Philippines* (Quezon City: Ateneo de Manila University Press, 1998) (orig. "Predatory Oligarchy, Patrimonial State: The Politics of Domestic Commercial Banking in the Philippines," Ph.D. Dissertation, Political Science Department, Yale University, 1993).

17 Jeffrey M. Riedinger, *Agrarian Reform in the Philippines: Democratic Transitions and Redistributive Reform* (Stanford, CA: Stanford University Press, 1995), 13.

Local regimes: an introduction 11

18 Samuel Huntington, *Political Order in Changing Societies* (New Haven, CT: Yale University Press, 1968), quotations on 402 and 1.
19 Erik Martinez Kuhonta, *The Institutional Imperative: The Politics of Equitable Development in Southeast Asia* (Stanford, CA: Stanford University Press, 2011), 239.
20 For examples from another Asian country, see Lynn White, *Unstately Power*, 2 vols. (Armonk, NY: M.E. Sharpe, 1998 and 1999).
21 James C. Scott, "The Erosion of Patron–Client Bonds and Social Change in Rural Southeast Asia," *Journal of Asian Studies* 32:1 (November 1972), 6–37.
22 Alfred W. McCoy, *Policing America's Empire: The United States, the Philippines, and the Rise of the Surveillance State* (Madison, WI: University of Wisconsin Press, 2009), 48–9.
23 Seymour Martin Lipset, *Political Man: The Social Bases of Politics* (Baltimore, MD: Johns Hopkins University Press, orig. 1961, expanded ed. 1981); Dankwart Rustow, "Transitions to Democracy," *Comparative Politics* 2:3 (1970), 337–63; Adam Przeworski and Fernando Limongi, "Modernization: Theory and Facts," *World Politics* 49 (January 1997), 159–83; and Carles Boix and Susan Stokes, "Endogenous Democratization," *World Politics* 55:4 (2003), 517–49.
24 Daron Acemoglu and James A. Robinson, *Why Nations Fail: The Origins of Power, Prosperity, and Poverty* (New York: Crown Business, 2012) offers theses that are mostly compatible with those of this book—except that they overemphasize countries with relatively small populations that are strongly affected by neighboring states. These authors are fascinated by Botswana's "success," for example, as a sharp contrast to Sierra Leone's problems; but they scarcely mention Botswana's closeness to relatively affluent South Africa or Sierra Leone's closeness to several other economic and political "failures" in West Africa. They likewise neglect differences between places within "sovereign" states. Their book's 529 pages do not mention the Philippines—even though attention to localism in that more populous nation would refine their analysis.
25 Terms such as "level" are often used to describe political units that are "sub"-sovereign in a purely legal sense—but, of course, such terms falsely presume that behavioral power flows only "downward."
26 For comparison with another large East Asian country, see Lynn White, "Temporal, Spatial, and Functional Governance of China's Reform Stability," *Journal of Contemporary China*, 22:83 (May 2013), 791–811.
27 See Max Weber, "Politics as a Vocation," in *From Max Weber: Essays in Sociology*, trans. H.H. Gerth and C.W. Mill (New York: Oxford University Press, 1946), 77–128; and Reinhard Bendix, *Max Weber: An Intellectual Portrait* (New York: Doubleday, 1960), who interprets Weber's terms for existential *Wertrationalität* and purposeful *Zweckrationalität*.

2 Malay foundations and colonial semi-modernizations

A barangay, the most basic multi-family community in the Philippines, originally meant a "canoe," conceived as holding a group of early settlers. "The chief figure was the *datu*, generally a son or other blood relative of the founder [of] a kinship group," which could be mostly fictive.[1] When the Spanish, led by the Basque captain Miguel López de Legazpi, came to establish rule at Cebu in 1565, and in Manila by 1570, they gave inland chiefs the title *cabeza de barangay*. Every barangay was ideally centered on a patron's "house of stone," *bahay na bato*. There were "no kings or lords," but "many chiefs were recognized."[2]

Tagalog and Visayan settlements were often on riverbanks. Towns near the sea engaged in maritime trade, while upstream villages exchanged rice and forest products. According to Larkin:[3]

> All of the land and other resources as well as almost all of the labor belonged to a single *amo*, a quasi-patriarchal landlord who dispensed justice and favors in return for the complete subservience and total loyalty of his labor force.

The chief at the center of a settlement, taking the title *datu*, was presumed to own the land. He was supported by *timawa* warriors. They ruled over *tao* commoners, some of whom were slaves captured in wars, or debtors who accepted obligations of service as repayment.[4] A copper-plate document found in Laguna, south of Manila, and reliably dated to the year 900 CE, shows that the *datu* of Tondo released from their dues the descendants of a formerly indebted mid-level chief who had been especially loyal.[5] Traditional legitimate power derived largely from obligations that can be conceived as debt.

Anthropologist Frank Lynch writes about a "big-little distinction" between two types of people. He claims that it permeates Philippine history from pre-Spanish times to the present. In this view, society is not a spectrum; it is a natural dualism. Members assume either the big or the little identity. Lynch reported from Bicol:

> Men who wore white or good leather shoes were also men who never wore blue denim trousers or patched kahki shorts, who smoked cigarettes or

cigars but never chewed betel nut, and who did not hesitate—like the other kind of men—to invite me [a Westerner and Jesuit priest] into their homes ... of solid lumber roofed by galvanized iron in good repair.

But the big people were supposed to have natural human obligations to others:

When typhoons struck the Bicol region, before long the floors of the many smaller bamboo and *nipa* [stilt shack] homes were awash in rising waters. And where were the people who owned these little houses? Safely bedded down in the *salas* and bedrooms of their relatively wealthy neighbors.... "We are in trouble again, and here we are." When they were taken in without hesitation, they accepted the welcome as no more than their due. No fawning, no great show of gratitude, just a simple encampment.... On the other hand, people who lived in the big houses were at ease in asking favors of a manual nature from the *bakya* [clogs]-and-betel-nut set: to run an errand, slaughter and butcher an animal for a fiesta, take a newly acquired goat or pig to the farm and raise it there, carry a heavy package to or from the bus stop in the plaza, climb a coconut tree to cut down some young nuts, or make minor repairs on the house.... I frequently heard the labels "big people" (*dakulang tao*) and "little people" (*sadit na tao*) used in conversation.... For centuries, untold multitudes of Filipinos have found these terms of exchange both acceptable and desirable.[6]

Duties of the "big people" were supposed to be naturally reciprocated by their clients. Another anthropologist claims that anyone who failed to acknowledge a *utang na loób*, a "debt of gratitude," was "*walang hiya*, 'lacking in shame'.... In some regions, the worst insult you can give a person is to say that he lacks *hiya* (shame [or 'embarrassment']) or *utang* (obligation)."[7] The credit or shame of any individual was also imagined to extend to his or her community, especially kin.

Utang means "debt," e.g., of the monetary sort. *Loób* means "self," so that such debts are existential, "like those owed to one's parents, guilt-laden obligations which both parties understand can never be fully repaid. *Utang na loób* carries an ontological weight that is tied up with the debtor's sense of honor, self-esteem, and basic morality." Berlow also links this basis of clientage to the organization of large plantations on the island of Negros:

In its most ruthless incarnation, the hacienda is a complex maze of debts.... *Utang na loób* lies at the heart of the paternalistic system.... Frequently translated as a "debt of gratitude" or "lifelong debt," it is literally an "internal debt," the debt, *utang*, being tied to *loób*, a person's "inner being" or "inner self."[8]

The Philippine state, ever since 1565–71 when Legazpi founded it, has largely attempted indirect rule through nonstate patron–client networks. This has occurred despite the hopes of autocratic or reformist centralizers, as well as of patriotic writers who rue this description even when it can be evidenced.[9] The official government has never been emancipated from political "society." Its weakness is a positive construction. Elites that are linked to rural places, where most Filipinos live, gain from central state weakness; they sustain and tolerate it, in part so that rival elites have scant chance of displacing them on more local turfs. Such leaders, except in their Filipino-patriotic rather than family-loyal phases, usually support "informal" and local politics because that is the type they can control.

The Iberian metropole of Spain's East Asian colony was half a world away. In the two-and-one-half centuries from 1571 to 1821, Spain administered its distant colony not from Madrid but through Mexico City, capital of the Viceroyalty of New Spain where the Manila–Acapulco galleon docked. The first eastward galleon found the north Pacific winds to Acapulco already by 1565. On the westbound journey to Manila, the ships sailed further south and joined the route Magellan had pioneered.

Formal government within the Philippines extended down only to the provinces, whose capitals were supposed to be run by military officials (*corregidores*). In Spain's other colonies, bacteria and viruses to which Amerindians had scant immunity reduced the population the Spanish governed. But pathogens had travelled undocumented to Spain's Old World colony, where the people were more, relative to the administrators. For local governance in the colony that bore his name, King Felipe II assigned orders of Catholic friars to serve in smaller towns as official agents. Five orders of monks—Augustinians, Dominicans, Franciscans, Jesuits, and Recollects—were deputized to run settlements in specific groups of provinces. This "despotism of friars" lasted in some areas for more than three-and-a-half centuries, until the arrival of Americans—who, like the Spaniards, were very few relative to the large population of this distant Asian colony.

In 1576, just 269 friars had the task of trying to convert perhaps 750,000 natives (*naturales*), mostly scattered in small barangay villages.[10] The only solution was to convince as many *datu*-chiefs as possible to bring their flocks into larger settlements: district capitals (*cabaceras*) or towns (*poblaciones*). The *datus* gradually acquired state ranks, such as *gobernadorcillo* or *cabeza de barangay*. Relocating people helped the severely understaffed Spanish to establish two kinds of indirect rule. First, it farmed out to former *datu encomendero* leaders the jobs of organizing corvée labor and collecting taxes. Second, much of this labor went into the construction of stone churches and rectories (*conventos*) for friars, who were assigned secular functions alongside ecclesiastical duties.

Because *encomenderos* tended to abuse their tax-collection authority, they were sometimes criticized by friars who supposed that the main mission of the Spanish regime was to make religious conversions. This division in the system may have strengthened it politically by diversifying local interests—until the friar orders themselves became great landholders after 1700. By that time, the *encomiendas* system became less important, although it set precedents for later conflict between church officials (when they were reformers) and local secular authorities, who came to be called *principalia*.

Originally, Spain's policy had been to claim all land for the throne. But local *principalia* controlled much of the land, occasionally donating it to "friar estates" that over centuries also became extensive. The secular state was thin on the ground, though it was nominally in charge of the clerics in their non-church functions and of local landowners in governmental roles. The few colonial cadres or the more numerous friars, who over time increasingly were Filipinos (then called "Indios"), were the only official judges in each Philippine place during most of the Spanish period.[11]

The Spanish crown claimed a *patronato real*, a right to choose church officials and manage church revenues in exchange for royal support of Catholic activities—especially conversions of indigenous people. These procedures were legalized by concordats between the Vatican and Spain, although they were sometimes circumvented by religious orders—notably Jesuits before the royal expulsion of that order from the Philippines in 1768. A Jesuit excoriated Spanish administrators in the sixteenth century Philippines, saying that the secular officials did "not come to judge, but to rob."[12] The *caidas* (literally, "droppings") from prebends, licenses, bribery revenues, extortions, and fixed prices could bring big money. Officials who bought their posts needed the "droppings" to recoup their investments.

Outside Manila and Cebu, practically no Spaniards or other foreigners (except friars) were allowed to reside. Monks in most places became the colonial state.[13] Some Filipinos and their local leaders resented efforts by this largely ecclesiastical regime to settle them in villages that centered on churches. Some fled the Spanish policy of *reducción* and refused to live in the friar haciendas. They were called *remontados* (those who went "back" to the mountains). This word has long been in use, referring to people on the run from the state and its taxes—or from the American army, Japanese police, "lowland crop failures, local vendettas," and the Philippine constabulary.[14]

Yet most Filipinos in the colonial era were not *remontados*, and the small village polities that the Spanish created remain important. The main celebration in a Philippine town is normally the fiesta, held once a year on the village patron saint's day. It involves a planning committee headed by a *presidente*, contributions from rich citizens, games, religious services, and usually a ball at which a beauty queen is crowned. Civic officials may organize the secular events; priests organize a novena, nine days of prayer leading up to the saint's day.[15] Such fiestas are still important in the creation of local polities, not so much in Metro Manila but in the places where most Filipinos live.

By the 1820s, Spain lost its empire in Central and South America. A rebellion erupted among Philippine creoles who wanted to achieve independence following the Latin Americans. The Spanish strengthened their police and repressed it. The galleon trade with Acapulco had already ended in 1815 because of Mexico's independence war. The distant colonial government in Manila no longer reported through Mexico City, but now to Madrid—when before telegraphy they could report at all. Later, as liberal ideas spread in Iberia, especially by the 1860s, the tiny Manila government became less racist and incorporated more mestizo elites. Police compiled lists of subversives (*filibusteros*). The colonial state adapted by ruling indirectly through a greater variety of local Filipino elites.

Sangleys

The Spanish called the Chinese "Sangleys" and mandated a single *Capitan de Chinos* to maintain order and tax payments in that commercial community. This structure was normal in other Southeast Asian courts too.[16] A pirate adventurer named Limahong (a.k.a. Lim Hong, or Lin Feng in standard *pinyin* romanization) had attacked Manila as early as 1574, shortly after the Spanish established there. Limahong reportedly had 62 "war junks" and more than 2,000 in his company. South Chinese living in the Spanish city, however, were led by a merchant called Sinsay, another immigrant from Fujian who helped the Spanish drive Lim back. Lim was also wanted by the Chinese government for previous pirate attacks. He retreated to Pangasinan in west-central Luzon, whence a Spanish and local force under Juan de Salcedo eventually forced him away—but only after months of siege and war.[17] (Ferdinand Marcos claimed to be a descent of the pirate Limahong, perhaps to please local Chinese or to associate himself with a forceful ancestor.) Sinsay's help to the Spanish did not dispel their suspicion of Chinese, in part because Limahong's attack on Manila had nearly succeeded.

Nearly a century later, Zheng Chenggong (a.k.a. Koxinga, who took Taiwan from the Dutch) was expected in the Philippines too. This fear led the Spanish to conduct one of their periodic pogroms in Manila's Chinatown. Pirate kings such as Limahong or Koxinga came from South Chinese lineages; but they were outlaws in the view of Chinese imperial bureaucrats, who absolutely could not control them—and they had many Japanese and Southeast Asian connections.[18] They were subtropical Vikings.[19] Policies against Chinese became regularized, but they produced an unintended result: few Chinese women came to the islands. The *mestizo* offspring of Chinese men and local Filipina women slowly became an elite in the archipelago that was no less important than the children of Spanish *peninsulares*, Latino immigrants who came from Mexico, and native Philippine "Indio" elites with whom they intermarried.

Spanish laws required Chinese to have a written permit to travel more than two leagues from Manila. Chinese could not, on pain of death, stay in the fortified Intramuros part of the city after the nightly curfew. Chinese men could not marry Filipinas without converting to Catholicism and cutting off their queues—and if they took such a haircut, they could not safely return to China because of Manchu laws. "Mestizos-Sangleyes" paid twice the head tax of "Indio" Filipinos. The "Chinos puros" paid four times as much.

Spanish rulers restricted these South Chinese, but Sangleys ran most of the colony's export economy. Archbishop Ignacio Santibáñez of Manila wrote to

King Felipe II that Chinese were "coming to trade ... they have taken to the cultivation of gardens, resulting in the idleness of the Indios; they have become retailers, resulting in higher prices." As Weightman writes, "Throughout the Spanish era, the islands were economically worth more to the Chinese than to the Spaniards, a fact of which the latter and the Filipinos were aware, and which contributed considerably to communal tensions."[20] New World goods, especially silver, came on the Manila Galleons from Acapulco. Their further distribution throughout East Asia was mostly managed by traders from Fujian families.

Spanish officials and clerics sponsored major massacres of Chinese by Filipinos in 1603, 1639, 1662, 1686, and 1762. These pogroms, in which many Chinese were exiled or killed, were always followed by economic recessions—after which, some Chinese returned. They received no support at all from the Chinese government in Beijing, whose officials regarded them as unfilial for having absconded from the fatherland to make profits abroad. The Chinese state knew them as mere merchants (*shang*). In Confucian social theory, this placed them below scholar-officials (*shi*), peasants (*nong*), or artisans (*gong*); and they were absent-without-leave expatriates too.

The Spanish were no more generous to them. Weightman writes,

> Nowhere else in Southeast Asia did Chinese face more restrictions and cope with a more precarious existence (especially in the early centuries of colonial rule) than in the Spanish Philippines. Yet probably nowhere else in Southeast Asia (except independent Siam) was it more easy for them and their mixed-blood descendants to escape such restrictions and merge (often as the new elite) with the native society.[21]

Rich Fujianese businessmen often had multiple wives who might live together in the same households with their mistresses (*queridas*). Even when they maintained separate households, conflicts were common especially if one wife were Chinese and the other Filipina. Sangleys in the Philippines were a smaller part of the population than were South Chinese in other Southeast Asian lands, and because of the galleon trade they were more concentrated in the capital. According to an 1876 observer, Chinese mestizos were nearly a quarter of the people in Manila.[22] Triad secret societies formed in the Philippines, extorting protection money from Chinese shopkeepers. The affected salesmen might make pleas to the Philippine police, but Spanish and Filipinos mostly regarded this as a problem within the Chinese minority.

Noli Me Tangere, Rizal's most famous novel, contains sharp satire about both Filipinos and Chinese:

> The Pasig ... is known to some as the Binondo [Chinatown] River and like all the streams in Manila plays the varied roles of sewer, laundry, fishery, means of transportation and communication, and even drinking water, if the Chinese water-carrier finds it convenient.[23]

18 *Foundations and semi-modernizations*

Rizal's *El Filibusterismo* nearly approves pogroms. He describes a

> Chinese peddler who was there selling his outlandish mixtures and indigestible pastries. Crowds of boys surrounded him, pulled at his already disordered queue, snatched pies from him, haggled over the prices, and committed a thousand deviltries.... A whack would bring his face around smiling, and if the blow fell only upon is shoulders, he would calmly continue his business transactions ... receiving as caresses the light blows from their canes that the students gave him as tokens of farewell.[24]

This description may now be seen to discredit its *ilustrado* writer, who in other respects is an intellectual hero. It detracts from his outstanding literary distinction, but it could be understood in its international nineteenth century context. One of the ways of uniting a nation—as Rizal helped to accomplish for the Philippines—has always been to contrast it with others.

Rizal once called himself a "pure indio," based on his family's tax status. Actually, Rizal had Chinese as well as Malay-Philippine and Spanish ancestors.[25]

> Indios paid a base tax, mestizos de sangley paid twice the base tax, sangleys paid four times the base tax, and the blancos or whites (comprised of filipinos [Philippine-born children of "americano" Latinos from the New World]), and peninsulares [born in Spain] ... paid no tax.[26]

These labels also determined where people could live: blancos might reside in the walled city of Intramuros, Christianized sangleys (Chinese) and their offspring were in Binondo just across the Pasig River, non-Catholic Chinese sangleys lived in Parian, and indios lived everywhere else (except for a few non-indios in other large cities such as Cebu). Colonial Spain established a truly discriminating caste system.

"Many of the Filipino leaders who have attacked the Chinese interests most violently have had a Chinese father or grandfather," as Weightman says. Most Philippine heroes —Aguinaldo and others in addition to Rizal—have had Chinese as well as Philippine ancestors. The top Philippine elite has for centuries been disproportionately descended from Chinese (and Spanish or Latino-Mexican) forebears. Rizal had some of that background—yet in his novel *El Filibusterismo*, he "bitterly assailed the alliance of the friars and the Spanish mercantile elements, fictionally calling for the massacre of most of the Spanish Peninsulares and Chinese."[27] Racism has also affected a few more recent patriotic intellectuals, although none have combined it with Rizal's literary sharpness, his abilities to balance his views that were in tension with each other, or his personal commitment against brutality. The main controversy concerning his legacy centers on his elite status and on the usefulness of political non-violence.

Reformist independence?

Precursors of reformism in the Philippines go back for many decades into the Spanish period. Napoleon seized Madrid in 1808. This started a Spanish uprising (now remembered by many because of Goya's painting of a French firing squad) and the Peninsular War. This period of foreign-imposed change was followed by political reaction after the return of the deposed conservative Bourbon king in 1814. The Iberian metropole throughout the nineteenth century was washed by alternating waves of liberal hope and reactionary integrity. Each of these rippled off to Spain's most distant colony.

The end of the galleon trade required new bases for Manila's economy, which now needed fewer or different kinds of Chinese entrepreneurs. Mexico was independent by 1821. By the end of the century's third decade, all of Spain's colonies on the American continents were gone. The Philippines were affected, because the Spanish government took its Asian possession more seriously after losing so many profitable American ones. Within Spain, the regime became somewhat more secular despite its conservatism. In Manila, the bureaucracy remained tiny relative to the population it feigned to govern.

The office of *cabeza de barangay* had become elective in 1785, and that of *gobernadorcillo* became so in 1847.[28] The heads of these small governments were important locally along with various kinds of churchmen. Throughout the nineteenth century, bishops and non-monastic priests vied with friars in religious orders—and the non-monk clerics were increasingly successful. Free Masonry, the reformist "Propaganda Movement," and the pride of Philippine intellectuals grew in this era of hesitant and sporadic liberal reform.

The upper-class *ilustrado* who is now most famous, José Rizal, published *Noli Me Tangere* (*Touch Me Not*) in 1887. This remains the most important Philippine book, followed by his second novel *El Filibusterismo* (*The Reign of Greed*).[29] The Spanish executed him in 1896, during a would-be revolution that had been started not by Rizal but by the Katipunan secret society, most of whose members were from less elite families. Rizal's sharp, constantly critical style of thought was what got him into trouble. He appreciated and castigated both his own country and Spain with gleaming satire. The friars could not stand him, nor he them. But he did not advocate violence; his independence was mental.

The Kapitunan society was at first dedicated to expelling the Spanish. Its leadership included Andres Bonifacio, a former peasant, and the more elite Emilio Aguinaldo—who in 1897 proclaimed a "Dictatorial Government" of the Philippines, with himself as President-Dictator. This was planned as a temporary "government to be administered by decrees promulgated under my sole responsibility."[30] It was encouraged by the American Consul in Hong Kong, Rounsevelle Wildman, who opined that Aguinaldo "of course organized a government of which he was dictator, an absolutely necessary step if he hoped to maintain control over the natives."[31] It was soon opposed by Bonifacio, whom Aguinaldo's forces arrested, tried for treason, and after some hesitation executed. By that time, the Spanish–American War had ended in the Caribbean, and U.S. forces seized Manila with the help of Spanish who preferred not to surrender the city to Filipino forces. Aguinaldo, who is still regarded as the first Philippine president despite dubious credentials as a democrat, kept fighting for independence. As soon as the U.S. Army captured him, however, Gen. Arthur MacArthur granted Aguinaldo a pardon and recruited his officers for positions in the new colonial government, which like the previous Spanish regime was very thin on the ground.

The Katipunan secret society insurrectionists had opposed the Spanish and briefly the Americans, and they were also against self-identifying Chinese. Some in 1896 had called for anti-Chinese pogroms. Many Chinese left the Philippines until after the U.S. occupation had quelled the Katipunan. In the racist climate of the late nineteenth century, Americans extended Chinese exclusion laws to the Philippines (and Hawai'i, which the U.S. had seized in 1893).

American rule could not be very centralist because the imperial power's local resources were limited. The U.S. federation created no parallel federation in the Philippines, despite the archipelago's natural geographical separations. President McKinley nonetheless wrote in his 1900 orders to the Taft Commission which set up the colonial regime that, "In the distribution of powers among the governments organized by the Commission, the presumption is always to be in favor of the smaller subdivision."[32] Lack of U.S. staff required indirect rule through Philippine local elites.

The new U.S. administration confiscated Spanish monastic estates and allowed locally important clans to buy them. The American colonial regime took 400,000 acres of arable land from friars, selling it to regional social leaders—many of whose descendants still own it.[33] These clans were in many cases of partly Chinese ancestry, although they now self-identified as Filipino.

The Americans had an army; but like the Spanish earlier, they had too few civilian administrators to run local governments. So landed families were arbiters of order on most of the islands. Crucial clans governed in specific regions. A few of the most salient can be preliminarily listed, roughly north to south, although some had interests on more than one island. Singsons, Crisologs, Barberos, and Paredes were in north Luzon (a largely Ilocano region where Marcoses became dominant much later), Josons and Diazes in Nueva Ecija, Aquinos and Cojuangcos in Tarlac, Arroyos and Macapagals and other families in Pampanga, Ayalas and a much greater variety of mercantile families in Manila, Remullas in Cavite, Laurels in Batangas, and Basque and other lineages in conservative Bicol. South of Luzon were Roxas on Panay, Romualdezes in Leyte (and in Bulacan on Luzon), Montelibanos in Negros Occidental, Osmeñas and Duranos in different parts of Cebu, Dimaporos and many others on Mindanao. These clans and many others like them conflicted for dominance in particular parts of the Philippines.[34] Filipinos still say colloquially that someone is "DBF" ("*de buena familia*"), referring to such lineages.

William Howard Taft as Governor-General of the Philippines in 1901–03 (before he became U.S. Secretary of War and then President) had a "policy of attraction" to coopt Filipino elites. An early anti-sedition law made advocacy of

Philippine independence a capital crime. But *ilustrados* and less illustrious rural potentates were welcomed, along with urban professionals who were willing to go along with the colonial regime. A few joined a pro-American Federal Party (*Partido Federal*, naming itself in Spanish) even as pro-independence guerrillas were still fighting the U.S. Army in the bush.[35] The Americans' colonial regime ran municipal elections in 1901, and provincial governors were elected by 1902.

Many leaders of landed lineages did not fight the Americans, even though they wanted independence. This was the main platform of the Nacionalista Party, founded in 1907. Although the Nacionalistas had originally campaigned for immediate sovereignty, they later became gradualists. They won 72 percent of the vote in 1907, and this victory from the Philippine viewpoint expressed an clear elite consensus that the nation must not ultimately be a colony. From the American viewpoint, it was also a reply to the main question of the U.S. colonial period: how could so few Americans govern so many Filipinos? The answer was simple: they could not. Indirect rule was the solution.

In early Philippine voting, "gentry politicians were obliged to seek the help of petty landowners and prominent peasants living in the barrios, who were able to deliver the votes of their relatives, friends, neighbors, and tenants."[36] The Nacionalistas in 1907 won an overwhelming majority in the Philippine Assembly, a unicameral legislature with limited powers. Candidates for these offices in large constituencies built their support networks by combining their earlier mayoral machines, which survived from previous elections under both the Spanish and the Americans.

U.S. administrators had at first favored the Federal Party, but most Philippine voters cast their ballots for candidates who wanted an early revival of the short-lived republic that had declared Philippine independence at Malolos, Bulacan, in 1898. The Nacionalistas were led by young men such as Sergio Osmeña from Cebu in the central Visayan islands (the Assembly's first Speaker) and Manuel Quezon from Tabayas, near Manila in the Tagalog region. They trumped the Federal Party, which was closely associated with the American occupiers, concentrated in Manila. The Federal Party sent just two representatives to the 80-seat Assembly.

The policy of indirect rule was furthered in 1916, when the U.S. Congress passed the Jones Law, promising eventual Philippine independence. The Congress in Manila then became bicameral. Quezon and Osmeña respectively became Senate President and Speaker of the House, the two highest posts then available to Filipinos. Holding local elections—which local elites could buy—was an essential part of American colonial policy. Over the next two decades, many candidates of former Progresista families switched to become Nacionalistas (or else joined the smaller Democratic Party, which gradually lost members and was defunct by 1932). Osmeña and Quezon headed Nacionalista factions that sometimes cooperated and sometimes were rivals.

None of these parties or factions were mainly policy groups. They were coalitions headed by readily identifiable, locally connected leaders. To maximize their success in national elections, these most famous politicians tried to downplay their regional links, sending to their clients throughout the archipelago fiscal "pork" budgets that the American administrators readily approved. The top politicians of the early twentieth century were patriots in their way, even though they helped the U.S. colonial regime, which was familiar with similar money politics in the metropole.

When Osmeña and Quezon held together as Nacionalistas, the usual reason was threat to their power from opposition parties, at various times Federalists, Progressives, or Democrats. Nacionalistas maintained a legislative majority, but they were not a tightly unified party. In 1935, when the Philippine Commonwealth was established, planning to remain under U.S. sovereignty for ten years, Quezon became president and Osmeña was vice-president. These two leaders, then and later, were often in tension with each other, and they set a precedent of conflict between the two top Philippine officials that has been repeated in many later years.

Some members of Congress were from families that had owned extensive land under the Spanish. A few (including Quezon) were from Spanish families. Many other prospering clans (including the Osmeñas) were Chinese mestizo, though they seldom advertised that fact. Upwardly mobile people could buy land and display prestige in many ways, e.g., by running for offices or supporting political candidates. It was convenient for many politicians at this time to distance themselves from Chinese Filipinos—who, as in Spanish times, continued even after the galleons to make money in the Philippines, causing jealousy among most others on the islands. Until 1935, the U.S. colonial government did not let Chinese become Philippine citizens (although a mestizo could do so at age 21 if he or she had a local parent, almost always a Filipina mother who had not become legally Chinese at marriage). But the economic role of the small Chinese minority on the islands remained considerable. Identifiable ethnic Chinese investment in the Philippines before Japan's invasion almost equalled the American amount. Some Chinese invested in utilities, such as electricity. According to one report, 50 million pesos of this ethnic Chinese investment was in merchandising. Rice mills, which are not easy to concentrate in relatively safe cities, accounted for much less (16 million pesos). Banking accounted for just 12 million pesos, perhaps because of relative Philippine cultural legitimacy for unrepayable debts, which Chinese lenders had to distrust. But manufacturing enterprises were started by very few self-identifying Chinese. Sugar was the main primary product, and Americans and their Filipino local allies (including some who had Latino-Mexican family backgrounds) controlled most of the processing. Nonetheless, various reports from the post-war period put "Chinese" control of retail trade at 90 percent in Manila and 85 percent throughout the archipelago.[37]

Action possibilities against undemocratic traditional and colonial legacies

Pre-colonial Malay traditions, which presumed some equal dignity for "little people" but did not assure them much wealth or power, were not abandoned in the Spanish and American periods. The foreign administrators worked in their own states' interests. Resil Mojares understandably claims that, "There is a measure of bad faith in urging a country that has been colonized by foreign powers to 'globalize,' since by definition colonized is globalized." Yet he has immediate second thoughts too: "The imperative lies in whether it is being globalized in ways that people are critically aware of, and in terms that they can effectively negotiate with or command."[38] Legacies are most presentable when they are useful to people.

Habits of mind are created by situations that people have faced in their histories. It is unsurprising, for example, that in many Malayo-Polynesian communities, including places throughout the Philippines, settlements are conceived as "canoes," since they are imagined to have been started by ancestors who arrived by boat.[39] When the Spanish brought guns to establish a polity in Manila, but soon realized that the galleon winds and New World silver allowed Fujianese exile merchants to profit most from the colony's economy, it is hardly surprising that anti-Sangley discrimination grew. This situation promoted rakeoffs for the controllers of violence. It promoted *hidalgo* ("*hijo de algo*," "son of somebody") disdain for stateless traders. Most of the Filipino people, who were neither Spanish nor Sangley, had political or economic reasons to envy both. The Americans brought their preference for "professionals," especially lawyers, but these penchants did little for most Filipinos.

Residues of collective experience can be called "cultural." They tend to shape, without predetermining, much of the violence, corruption, local communalism, and lack of entrepreneurship (except near Manila) that later chapters of this book document for later times. But when cultures create problems, policies are weak tools to change them. A classic treatment of apparent problems in another modally localist political culture is Edward Banfield's attempt to describe "amoral familism" in southern Italy. He suggests Peace Corps visitors, antibiotics (to reduce fatalism), soccer teams, more "devoted teachers," even "Protestant missionary activity" to make his benighted town in southern Italy more like St. George, Utah.[40] These recommendations amount to a parody of trying to change culture through policy. The current book avoids such an attempt and will defer policy recommendations to later chapters that offer details about the situations that shape such norms, while admitting that "culture matters."[41] It is enough to notice that strong clan and regional solidarities emerged—often strengthening themselves in mutual conflicts. The Spanish and American colonial regimes, having weak central governments, depended on the local leaders of such families.

Notes

1 Quoted in Kikuchi Yasushi, *Uncrystallized Philippine Society: A Social Anthropological Analysis* (Quezon City: New Day Publishers, 1991), 9. Another very distant Malayo-Polynesian group, the Maoris, also define their lineages as having arrived in separate canoes (from an undefined "Havaiki" in the Tahitian part of Polynesia).
2 Relying on sixteenth century historian A. de Morga, in Kikuchi Yasushi, *Uncrystallized Philippine Society*, 8–10.
3 John A. Larkin, "Philippine History Reconsidered: A Socioeconomic Perspective," *American Historical Review* 87:3 (1982), also www.jstor.org/stable/1864158, 620.
4 Cf. the similar description of larger social polities on the mainland, in James C. Scott, *The Art of Not Being Governed: An Anarchist History of Upland Southeast Asia* (New Haven, CT: Yale University Press, 2009).
5 Patricio N. Abinales and Donna J. Amoroso, *State and Society in the Philippines* (Lanham, MD: Rowman & Littlefield, 2005).
6 Frank Lynch, S.J., *Philippine Society and the Individual* (Ann Arbor, MI: University of Michigan Center for South and Southeast Asian Studies, 1984), 95–8.
7 Fred Eggan, "Philippine Social Structure," in *Six Perspectives on the Philippines*, George M. Guthrie, ed. (Manila: Bookmark, 1968), 13.
8 Alan Berlow, *Dead Season: A Story of Murder and Revenge on the Philippine Island of Negros* (New York: Pantheon, 1996), 82.
9 Ferdinand Marcos is treated as a would-be centralizer in Chapter 5. A different kind of nationalist, also discussed below, is exemplified by Reynaldo Ileto in *Knowing America's Colony: A Hundred Years from the Philippine War*, Lecture 3, "Orientalism and the Study of Philippine Politics" (Honolulu: Center for Philippine Studies, 1999), 41–65. Ileto, p. 49, recognizes (as Lynch and anthropologists do) that modal Philippine "indebtedness is not simply a one-way repressive relationship but rather a reciprocal one."
10 Patricio N. Abinales and Donna J. Amoroso, *State and Society in the Philippines*, 53–7.
11 In 1861, a decree prohibited appointing as judges executives who had not been trained in law—but it was not quickly enforced.
12 Quoted in Greg Bankoff, "Profiting from Disasters: Corruption, Hazard, and Society in the Philippines," in *Corruption and Good Governance in Asia*, Nicholas Tarling, ed. (London: Routledge, 2005), 166.
13 Patricio N. Abinales and Donna J. Amoroso, *State and Society in the Philippines*, 67.
14 Fenella Cannell, quoted in Patricio N. Abinales and Donna J. Amoroso, *State and Society in the Philippines*, 69. Compare James C. Scott, *The Art of Not Being Governed: An Anarchist History of Upland Southeast Asia* (New Haven, CT: Yale University Press, 2009).
15 Frank Lynch, S.J., *Philippine Society and the Individual*, 209–23.
16 G. William Skinner, "Overseas Chinese Leadership: Paradigm for a Paradox," in *Leadership and Authority: A Symposium*, Gehan Wijeyewardene, ed. (Singapore: University of Malaya Press, 1968), 191–203.
17 George Henry Weightman, *Philippine Chinese: A Cultural History of a Marginal Trading Community* (Ph.D. dissertation, Sociology, Cornell University, 1960), 65–6.
18 Koxinga's mother was Japanese. Limahong's military adjutant was a Japanese named "Sioco." There is no reason to name such people in standard romanizations approved by modern national regimes. Unlike governments, these pirate kings were truly international; they established non-national states. For more on such traders' links to other Southeast Asian places, especially Ayutthaya, see works by the historian Yoneo Ishii.
19 The Vikings had similar multi-ethnic links and families, e.g., with Slavs and Celts and French, ranging from Kiev to Dublin to Caen.
20 George Henry Weightman, *Philippine Chinese*, 67.

21 George Henry Weightman, *Philippine Chinese*, 82, see also 311.
22 Patricio N. Abinales and Donna J. Amoroso, *State and Society in the Philippines*, 98.
23 Quoted in George Henry Weightman, *Philippine Chinese*, 267.
24 George Henry Weightman, *Philippine Chinese*, 269.
25 In Manila's Intramuros area, the recommendable "Bahay Tsinoy, Museum of Chinese in Philippine Life," presents a family tree for Rizal, detailing the names of his Fujianese and other ancestors. The exhibit tactfully omits any disrespect a caption below the chart might imply. Rizal's "pure indio" remark probably referred to Spanish taxation categories; it was untrue about his ancestry.
26 See http://aboutphilippines.ph/filer/spanish-colonial-caste-system-in-the-philippines.pdf.
27 George Henry Weightman, *Philippine Chinese*, 83–4, also 38.
28 Patricio N. Abinales and Donna J. Amoroso, *State and Society in the Philippines*, xxi–xxii.
29 See José Rizal, *Noli Me Tangere (Touch Me Not)*, tr. H. Augenbraum (New York: Penguin, 2006); also *The Indolence of the Filipino*, tr. Charles Derbyshire (Manila: Hard Press, 1913), and *The Reign of Greed (El Filibusterismo)*, tr. Charles Derbyshire (n.p.: Dodo Press, n.d.).
30 The announcement followed a meeting at his home in Cavite (Kawit) on May 24, 1898. The text of Aguinaldo's decree, in Spanish, is engraved on a stone outside his house.
31 Message from Consul-General Wildman to Washington, July 18, 1898, reporting Wildman's urging of Aguinaldo to establish such a government as a precursor, Wildman thought, to a U.S. choice either to assume sovereignty over the Philippines or to support that country's independence from Spain.
32 Quoted in Patricio N. Abinales and Donna J. Amoroso, *State and Society in the Philippines*, 136.
33 Benedict Anderson, "Elections and Participation in Three Southeast Asian Countries," in *The Politics of Elections in Southeast Asia*, R.H. Taylor, ed. (Washington, DC: Woodrow Wilson Center, 1996), 22.
34 James Clad, *Behind the Myth: Business, Money, and Power in Southeast Asia* (London: Hyman, 1989), 35, Benedict J. Tria Kerkvliet, "Contested Meanings of Elections in the Philippines," in *The Politics of Elections in Southeast Asia*, R.H. Taylor, ed. (Washington, DC: Woodrow Wilson Center, 1996), 138, and many other sources. See other parts of this book for more detailed lists.
35 Based on Paul D. Hutchcroft and Joel Rocamora, "Strong Demands and Weak Institutions: Addressing the Democratic Deficit in the Philippines" (essay provided by courtesy of Dr. Rocamora); see also Michael Cullinane, *Ilustrado Politics: Filipino Elite Responses to American Rule, 1898–1908* (Manila: Ateneo de Manila Press, 2004).
36 Carl H. Landé, "Party Politics in the Philippines," in *Six Perspectives on the Philippines*, George M. Guthrie, ed. (Manila: Bookmark, 1968), 86.
37 George Henry Weightman, *Philippine Chinese*, 140. This book quotes estimates by Catherine Porter, although the exactitude of such figures is admittedly chancy.
38 These are the last two sentences of Resil B. Mojares, "Making a Turn: Thoughts on a Generation of Philippine Scholarship," Keynote Address at the Philippine Studies Conference, Kyoto, Japan, February 28 to March 2, 2014 (kindly supplied to the author by Norman G. Owen, originally distributed on Facebook by Vicente L. Rafael).
39 This locution about "canoes" ranges widely from the Philippine archipelago, eastward to Rapa Nui (Easter Island), and westward to Madagascar (where Malayo-Polynesian Hovas/Merinos landed), including practically all of island Southeast Asia and Malaya in between.
40 Edward Banfield, with Laura Fasano Banfield, *The Moral Basis of a Backward Society* (New York: Free Press, 1958), 159–64 and 17. Banfield skirted the word

"immoral" and wrote in a colonial era, entering a line of political study that Tocqueville had begun. It later included Robert Putnam, *Making Democracy Work: Civic Traditions in Modern Italy* (Princeton, NJ: Princeton University Press, 1993). An earlier book that Banfield read, cited, and absolutely did not understand is Carlo Levi, *Christ Stopped at Eboli* (*Cristo si è fermato a Eboli*), tr. Frances Frenaye (London: Penguin, 1982). Levi sensitively tries to know Italian peasants in their own terms as well as modern outsiders' terms. Banfield's weak policy recommendations suggest the wisdom of trying to deal with situations, not just norms (to use words from Talcott Parsons, *The Structure of Social Action* [New York: Mcgraw-Hill, 1937]).
41 Lawrence Harrison and Samuel P. Huntington, eds., *Culture Matters: How Values Shape Human Progress* (New York: Basic Books, 2000).

3 Clan feuds localize political violence

Max Weber allowed that an organization is a "state" to the extent that it can "uphold a claim on the monopoly of the legitimate use of physical force."[1] The Philippine government has for decades had trouble making such a claim stick, because of the powers of regional and local regimes in extensive parts of the archipelago. Some current leading families, modernized *principalia*, maintain unofficial militias. Not all of these need to be active in order to influence local politics.

The Spanish and American governments, like that of the post-independence Philippines, have occasionally needed to rely on such forces. Spain used Pampanga mercenaries against rebels in other parts of Luzon. The U.S. Army, during the very violent Philippine–American War of 1898–1906, famously used soldiers from the Pampanga town of Macabebe as scouts, e.g., in the capture of the pro-independence leader Aguinaldo.[2] Alfred McCoy provides striking archival evidence of U.S. reliance on violent, clandestine, and criminal elements in the Philippines. The Americans coordinated their police with local coercive leaders to provide stability for the understaffed colonial state. The U.S. government learned from this experience how to save administrative resources in many places during later decades, whenever the state had aims that over-reached its capacity to sustain its coercive power—in parts of America itself, in Vietnam, and more recently in Iraq and Afghanistan.[3]

While the Japanese occupied the Philippines during World War II, collaborationist landowners hired private militias to protect themselves against anti-Japanese guerillas. After 1945, they continued such protection against the communist Hukbalahaps. Local elites established their own nonstate vigilantes whenever the state did not protect latter-day *principalia* interests. The Philippine state's army lost ground to warlords who had their own militias, such the Dimaporos of Lanao, the Duranos and Osmeñas and Cuencos of Cebu, and the Hukbalahaps of central Luzon.[4] Each clan or militia generally had a single clear leader.

Doronila claims that there is an "age-old Malay trait of extreme respect for authority," especially when this authority is personified in one man who is seen as strong.

> These authoritarian tendencies ingrained in the Filipinos the habit of submission to authority, as well as obsequiousness.... The family is built on

respect for authority of the father, and the feudal landlord–tenant relationship fostered landlord paternalism and dependence, as well as subordination by the tenants. The influence of the Roman Catholic Church, the dominant religion of the Filipinos which demanded uncritical acceptance of religious doctrine, contributed to the authoritarian milieu.[5]

Rizal wrote, "In the Philippines it is a well-known fact that patrons are needed for everything, from the time one is christened until one dies, in order to get justice, to secure a passport, or to develop an industry."[6]

If this authoritarian image of legitimate power on the archipelago is modal, why has leadership in the central Philippine state usually been weak? What (thus far) has prevented a populist dictator from centralizing it, as Marcos tried but ultimately failed to do with structurally lasting results? The likely answer is: because no domestic or international shock to the polity has spurred change of the modal pattern of local authority, and rivalries between or among local potentates tend to strengthen rather than weaken the usual pattern. Conflict *as such* attracts political interest.[7] The most enduring fights on these islands, within the last seven decades of living memory at least, have been local.

In many but not all localities, a dominant clan had a strong rival. Landé's description of traditional Philippine politics is a very broad claim, and it is that:

> two rival parties in each province ... are held together by dyadic patron–client relationships, extending from great and wealthy political leaders in each province down to lesser gentry politicians in the towns, down further to petty leaders in each village, and down finally to the clients of the latter: the common [people].[8]

This generalization about many sizes of polity can be documented by much (but not all) evidence, especially in the twentieth century.

The word "local," as used in this current book, can usually be interpreted as "regional and local." Often three sizes of polity (central, regional, local) are still not enough for adequate accuracy. Mina Roces, writing mainly about provinces, identifies

> certain families that have become inveterate rivals ... the Laurels and the Levistes in Batangas; the Cuencos, Duranos, and Osmeñas in Cebu; the Cojuangcos and Aquinos in Tarlac [some branches of these two clans feuded; others intermarried]; the Rodriguezes and Sumulongs in Rizal; and the Zuluetas, Lopezes, Ledesmas, Confesors, and Carams in Iloilo.[9]

This structure of clan rivalries prevails in many Philippine places; but from the viewpoint of most individuals, "bandwagoning" under a single clan's patron is more usual than trying to make gains by "balancing" rival clans. Roces claims there are two kinds of Filipinos: those who follow rules (being *mahina*, "weak") and those who confirm their proud positions by flouting norms arbitrarily (being *malakas*, "strong"). Ferdinand Marcos was a national example of the latter type. In his youth, he murdered a man and escaped punishment.[10] Not all Filipinos accept the legitimacy of such forceful *malakas* behavior, but its violence and unpredictability provide an image that some leaders in the archipelago have documentably chosen. Many authorities want to be understood by their publics as strong in this sense. They cannot prove they have such strength without exercising it. When they do so arbitrarily, they get attention.

This idealized, somewhat romantic description of one Philippine leadership tradition, to the extent it prevails, can create politics that are anarchic and "uncrystallized."[11] This cultural explanation is ambiguous—as all such accounts must be[12]—and is countervailed by other values of fair order. In the Philippines, as elsewhere, no single cultural principle wholly explains political behavior. As Roces admits, in her very apologetic book about the Lopezes of Cebu,

> It is not altogether impossible that the Lopez family's followers used violence. But, whether or not the Lopez followers resorted to violence, the more salient point is that the accusation reveals the public perception that violence is a possible weapon. It is widely believed that powerful families employ physical coercion and even murder in pursuit of their goals.[13]

Nonstate militias vary in their rhetoric more than in their behavior. The founder of a group called "Soldiers Against Communism and for the Oppressed" had earlier been a communist New People's Army officer. Some militias are simply composed of "armed bandits," according to the Philippine Alliance of Human Rights Advocates. Others are "fanatical cults" justified by religious ideologies, while yet others are "right-wing vigilantes."[14] These distinctions are less important than that they engage in private violence.

The footsoldiers were "little people," like those whom they usually attacked. Their leaders' leftist or rightist rhetorics varied, but the chiefs' goals were invariant: the maximization of client networks, money, and personal unconstrained power on local turfs. *Barkada* are gangs of young men who create conflictual social orders like that of Shakespeare's Capulets and Montagues. They are proud to attack similar *barkada* from rival barrios.[15] Private armies recruit soldiers among poor people, especially youths in *barkada* gangs. Visayan peasants, notably those who have migrated to Mindanao, have often joined militias simply for the sake of having an occupation and a patron. As May writes, "like other fanatical religious sects, their activities included elaborate rituals, a belief in the power of *anting-anting* [protective amulets], and a propensity for bloodthirsty attacks on perceived enemies, who were often decapitated or otherwise mutilated."[16]

Centralizers who cannot control militias nonetheless try to coordinate them. Marcos founded an "Integrated Civilian Home Defense Force" in 1976 to unite private and public armies of many kinds against communist guerrillas.[17] One such group, called Rock Christ, received support from the Philippines Benevolent Missionary Association as well as from the 125th Airborne Company of the

30 Clan feuds localize the state

Armed Forces of the Philippines. Later the army reorganized it as the *Kapunungan sa mga Kabus Kontra sa Komunista* (Organization of the Poor Against Communism). Some such armies claimed to be "Rizalista," although their hero would surely have despised their sadism.

Violence and threats of violence are crucial components of control in many countries (as Machiavelli noted) and in many Philippine localities. Muslim areas of Mindanao are particularly infamous in this respect. Anyone who has challenged the Ampatuan clan in Maguindanao has been in physical danger—notably anyone associated with another Muslim family named Mangudatu that has had limited electoral successes against the Ampatuans. In other areas too, the Duranos' rule of Davao City, like the Dimaporos' in Lanao, is especially firm. Relatively high frequencies of political violence in Luzon (especially Abra and Nueva Ejica), Samar, Negros Occidental, and more occasionally elsewhere have been part of normal Philippine politics.

Torres offers an international comparative perspective on local feuds:

> Depending on periods in history, this phenomenon has been documented in places such as the Balkans, Sicily, Corsica, the Caucasus region, the Middle East, and in the remoter past Scotland and the Appalachian region of the United States.... The Cordilleras in northern Luzon is famous for inter-village warfare and "revenge raids" caused by land and boundary disputes and competing economic interests over sources of water or firewood. Feuding also occurs among lowland Filipinos, a famous example of which was in the Ilocos in the early 1970s between the Crisologo and the Singson clans.[18]

In a 1987 survey of 127 vigilante groups, less than half (53) were in Mindanao, 41 were in the Visayas, and 33 were on Luzon (including six militias in Metro Manila).[19] Torres and his co-researchers documented feud killings of more than 5,500 people between the 1930s and 2005. Many thousands had to move their residences because of inter-clan violence. "The studies show that land disputes and political rivalries are the most common causes of *rido* [feuds]."[20] Sometimes the triggers of violence are small symbolic incidents that are seen to challenge a clan's honor: insulting jokes, cockfight losses, or minor thefts. Informal local norms in such situations trump any law of the formal government. Kinship groups often effectively enforce their claims to monopolies of violence. Such local families lead mini-states.

Philippine localities differ in the kinds of their political factions. Most cleavages are clan based, but some are ethnic. Zamora, an inland area in the mountains of Ilocos Sur, has for more than a century been divided between Ilocanos and coalitions of other ethnic groups (especially Itnegs and Igorots). Zamora "municipality" is not really a city; its main market is San Jose, outside the municipal borders. It "does not have anything resembling an elegant plaza," and the Catholic church in one of its two towns (Bato, the non-Ilocano center) overlooks a square although "typhoons have diminished its impressiveness." The other main town, Luna, is mainly Ilocano and has alternated with Bato for status as the *poblacion*, the center of official patronage. The Catholic church there too "shows signs of neglect" and is joined by Methodist and Church of Christ sanctuaries. Zamora is divided into 26 barrios, most of them either all-Ilocano or all-mountaineer. Shifting conflicts and alliances between the barrios determine most local politics. Non-Ilocanos have recently been dominant; and at earlier times, Ilocanos in the once-and-perhaps-future *poblacion* of Luna were more powerful.[21]

Bifurcated politics are normally based on longstanding rivalries between clans or lineages. Occasionally they are based on conflicts between rich and poor. Deaths can result from violence in either case. Combat in Bicol, for example, killed 25,000 people from 1969 to 2004—and displaced far more.[22] Many scholars of the Philippines, including Alfred McCoy, John Sidel, Joel Rocamora, and others from various perspectives have stressed the role of mafia-like violence in Philippine politics. Conspiracies that threaten killing are a long-standing topic of both rumor and reality in Philippine politics.[23] Informal conversations with reformist Filipinos reveal that some of them fear for the current President "PNoy," whom they like. They say they want him to protect himself from potential assassination. Violence and corruptions are common in the Philippines; so rumors about them seem credible, and some books on these subjects do not even try to distinguish fact from fiction.[24]

Types of militias

Private armies are run by many kinds of local leaders: political bosses in *trapo* clans, *jueteng* gambling organizers who use profits to pay private soldiers,[25] and religious sects (including the politically conservative *Iglesia ni Kristo* church, which has powerful "security forces").[26] Political uses of violence have been as important as economic uses among leaders in status-sensitive local polities. Forcefulness is seen by many as a virtue in a politician. This was especially true during Marcos's presidency, although (as data below on coup leaders will show) it was important in later times too. For Cavite Governor Juanito "Johnny" Remulla, bullets were important means of silencing and scaring political rivals. Gov. Remulla:

> dispatched armed goons, ordered the bulldozing of homes, and engineered the destruction of irrigation canals to expedite the departure of "squatters" and tenant farmers who were demanding compensation for their removal from lands designated for sale to Manila-based or foreign companies for "development" into industrial estates.[27]

This governor, no friend of labor unions, announced that his province was a "no-strike zone." Potential labor leaders tended to "disappear."

Governor Remulla was popular among many in Cavite, however. His local political machine collapsed not as soon as his friend Marcos fell, but only after the 1992 presidential election. Remulla opposed the presidential winner, Fidel

Ramos, but he also split his own supporters between Ramos's main rival candidates, Mitra and Cojuangco. So they both sent Remulla miniature coffins as appropriate gifts on his birthday.[28]

Nonstate militias were not all rural. In Metro Manila, Gen. Gemiliano Lopez, called the "Magic Eye," aimed to root out NPA supporters from urban barangays. Manila's Western Police District commander, Gen. Alfredo Lim, likewise used vigilantes against alleged communists in the Tondo slums.[29] Lim, also known as "Dirty Harry," had a slogan when he later was elected Mayor of Manila: "I don't shoot good men, only bad men."[30]

Manila and Cavite are relatively rich. Poor parts of the archipelago, where rents come more from land than from commerce, state, or international links, also suffer extensive violence. Alan Berlow's reportage on this phenomenon in Negros is especially harrowing.[31] It describes a cane-growing place that is devoid of any industry unrelated to this crop—but local violence has dominated politics in impoverished Negros at least as surely as in a more industrial, more centrally connected suburb such as Cavite.

Discussions of democracy that ignore the influence of coercion on voters' preferences and live options would be incomplete. Anyone who can affect public opinion, ballots, or leaders' reputations could become a target of violence. At least a dozen journalists were murdered in the late Marcos years. About 600 political prisoners at that time sat in military jails. Reports of tortures were numerous, as were dissidents' disappearances and "salvagings" (killings of non-combatants by Marcos's military).[32] Such extensive violence encouraged the growth of a Communist Party like Mao's, which organized a guerrilla army and a "National Democratic Front" that included labor unions. During Marcos's time, at least 2,500 people were extrajudicially "salvaged," i.e., killed. Another 709 "disappeared." But in the half decade after Marcos's demise through 1991, the monthly rate of disappearances was practically unchanged—6.45 persons per month under Marcos, as compared to 6.13 under Cory Aquino. The rate of "salvagings" was reduced, but only by one-third.[33] The violence of Marcos's time was not wholly unique.

Politics by other means

Clausewitz famously said that, "War is the continuation of politics by other means." He was describing international sovereignties, but among quasi-sovereign clans the same principle applies. Violence, including force and threats in local campaigns, can be part of politics. Elections are fights, and in the twentieth century balloting may have increased rather than decreased Philippine levels of local violence, largely because election winners receive "pork" funds. To judge from the experiences of other countries, this effect might be temporary. If rule of law accompanies democratic elections, voting may eventually help to decrease violence. But the rampages lasted a long time. They have not totally ended during recent bouts of voting. Reports of murders in electoral campaigns remain numerous.

Most Philippine elections in recent years have occasioned 100–200 deaths, including assassinations of candidates. The 2010 elections became notorious because of the mass murder in Maguindanao, Mindanao, of 57 journalists and rivals of the weaker of two Muslim families that had long ruled there. Goons with guns were sent by the Ampatuan clan to ambush campaigners for their rivals, the Mangudatus, and journalists who were covering the campaign. Yet the Ampatuans' violence did not prevent that clan from increasing their number of allies in Maguindanao Province mayoralties in the same election (even though their rivals took the governorship).[34] Voters, apparently from mixed fear and admiration of Ampatuan strength, supported a family they knew to be egregiously violent.

Aside from this much-publicized massacre in the 2010 vote, the rate of electoral killings that year was actually near the lower end of the usual number—about 100, mostly before the election. On the day of the poll, the number was about 20. Any democrat would wish it to be zero. Such killings show that elections are important for resource allocation in the Philippines.[35] Local democracy is powerful; if it were not, the murder rate would be lower.

Such violence is not distributed evenly over the archipelago. Police and Commission on Elections data from three polls in the current century (2001, 2004, and 2007) show some areas where killings have been frequent, as well as others where violence connected to voting is relatively rare.[36] Metro Manila and the central Visayas have less pre-balloting violence; the areas with relatively more of it are scattered.

This situation has improved along with the slow increase of non-landholding elected officials. By 1970, three-tenths of Philippine representatives and two-tenths of the senators "could be classified as businessmen," although the wealth of many still had largely agricultural roots.[37] Wurfel showed the continuity of interlocking wealth and power in Philippine elite families at least through the end of the 1970s.[38] Post-Marcos elected representatives nonetheless stayed in office on average longer than their recent successors, despite a three-term limit imposed by the 1987 Constitution. Nearly half of the House members as late as 2004 were kin of former Congress members. The portion of Congress from old political families rose slightly after Marcos's fall. Wives or children of incumbents could be elected as "breakers," after a representative's three terms were served.[39] A family head could skip one election—but then run again.

Elections Commission chair Jaime Ferrer as early as 1972 said he "knew all about the political warlords" and their private militias. He said at least six were owned by senators, 37 by representatives, and others by provincial governors, mayors, and "relatives of prominent politicians."[40] Fifteen years later, Ferrer was assassinated in a drive-by shooting; he was then serving in Cory Aquino's cabinet as Local Government Secretary.

Elections canvassers (*lider*) are general agents for local lords. They organize voting blocs and often double as barangay officials. Barangays are supposed to be parts of the national government—but now, with more than 50,000 of them, they are difficult to monitor. Mid-level "state" administration tends to be controlled by local bosses, and central control of most barangay activity is unfeasible.

A barangay captain may deputize any volunteer to serve as an auxiliary policeman, a *tanod*. This volunteer-with-local-coercive-powers is supposed to be legitimately part of the state. The inductee is sometimes given a gun (licensed or not) and in many cases carries a rattan stick too. Barangay elected captains and councillors receive budgets with which they compensate neighborhood watch volunteers.

City mayors in larger settlements appoint local top constables, albeit from among candidates proposed by the Philippine National Police. Municipal politicians (and local military commanders, at least in areas where communists are active) vet the appointment proposal lists first. President Marcos installed this system, which creates geographical diversity in the degree of medial or central control over choices of local police. In most inland or poor areas, Manila's writ is subject to veto by local lords.

Local communist pro-poor militias fit into this pattern. Mutual acknowledgement is evident among leaders of left and right who are violent. In part of Bicol, the Communist Party of the Philippines and its New People's Army have been "adept at playing the 'bourgeois' electoral game, for instance, supporting *trapos* who pay a 'revolutionary tax' or helping to unseat [rival non-leftist] *trapos* who have become too entrenched."[41] Factionalism is more important than ideology. Although some communist leaders have criticized voting, others find ways to participate in elections. The New People's Army has sold "permit-to-campaign" licenses in some districts. It reportedly has also killed leftist rivals outside its own organization.[42] The leftist front has been weakened by such assassinations, by disagreements about whether to form large or small military units in jungles, and by defections of effete revolutionaries who prefer urban insurrections to "country life."[43]

Violence in logging, farming, gambling, and prostitution

Economic generators of violence are probably as important as political ambitions. Exclusive attention to the financial uses of force would, however, neglect local leaders' existential self-images. Violence affects power and money together. Illegal businesses require forceful support. Local army and police have helped to maintain elites' economic activities, e.g., businesses such as illegal logging. Civilian politicians have used army help to sustain either the coercive or financial bases of their electoral victories.[44]

"Active auxiliaries" have received up to three-quarters of the revenue of the "Sugar Development Fund" run by planter elites on Negros. At Lubao, Pampanga, goons were paid by landlords to evict tenant farmers who violated laws against squatting. At Toledo, Cebu, vigilantes were hired by the Atlas Consolidated Mining Development Corporation to stamp out a labor union. Clergy were not exempt, if they were seen as leftists. At least ten priests were killed in the half decade after Marcos's demise at the hands of private gunmen hired by landlords, loggers, or businesses.[45]

Local violence in cities often protects illegal gambling profits. A reformist governor of Camarines Sur during Estrada's presidency, Luis Villafuerte, Sr., needed guns to quell "*jueteng* lords." These grandees reportedly included former security chief Renato de Villa, Gen. Romulo Yap, and others—who were closely linked to the Philippine National Police. Provincial Warden Ramon Y. Garcia, a civil servant appointed by Villafuerte, was able to provide the governor with firearms to help enforce laws against *jueteng*. President Estrada, as well as politicians such as Ramon Mitra, were said to support this effort, apparently because of grievances against de Villa and Yap rather than because of any personal distaste for *jueteng*. Estrada's and his friends were reported to have "monopolized the most lucrative gambling operations in the country, ranging from casinos to jai-alai and bingo." BW Gaming, a company owned by Estrada's friend Dante Tan, was reported by Alice Reyes, chair of the state gaming corporation, to have received an online bingo license because "it had the endorsement of the Office of the President."[46] This pattern is local, however, not just national. Garcia was the supplier of guns for the Camarines Sur governor who opposed gaming; so Garcia received death threats. In an attempt to find personal safety, he moved from Camarines Sur to an unadvertised location in Manila.[47]

Profits for pimps depend on their ability to hire goons who kidnap girls. Violence against women who are snatched by prostitution rings is extensively documented. But one nine-year-old girl, whose kidnappers "made their victims sniff a piece of cloth laced with a substance that sent them to sleep," out-smarted them. As she later reported (in Tagalog), "I see in movies that when strangers make you smell something, you fall asleep. So I just acted as if I went to sleep." Shanghaied in Tarlac, she was loaded with other girls on to a van for delivery to brothels in Manila. The truck stopped en route to pick up other victims. At one stop, "they were kept in an abandoned warehouse a few meters away from a police outpost.... Inside the bodega, she saw fifty other children guarded by men armed with firearms and knives." While the guards rested, she escaped and walked for hours to safety. A police superintendent admitted that, "The child-snatching syndicate has been operating here for some time now. Thanks to the street-smart girl, everyone is now on guard."[48] Yet nobody claimed that any of the pimps had been arrested, despite their proximity to the police station.

Nonstate militias: leftist, rightist, either

Whenever local leftists have challenged the ability of landowners to maximize rents, a standard response of patrons has been to create private armies. A barangay captain who was a Marcos supporter established the Masses Uprising (*Alsa Masa*) vigilantes in 1984 in a suburb of Davao, Mindanao, that is mostly inhabited by Visayan immigrants. The New People's Army murdered him in 1985. But ex-NPA comrades, led by a former communist, revived the anti-communist *Alsa Masa* in 1986. Violence led to "rents," no matter what political hue an extorting gang might assume.

The local Philippine Constabulary commander, who opposed this revival of lawlessness, was replaced by a hardline officer eager to see the anti-NPA vigilante group grow. As one of his supporters said, "We are tired of the Communists' taxation and killings. They have no respect for God." The new police superintendent claimed that, "In the fight between democracy and Communism, there is no way to be neutral. Anybody who would not like to join *Alsa Masa* is a Communist." Fearing violence, many settlers moved away from the rightist barangays. A local radio host who supported the *Alsa Masa* was "a confessed admirer of the tactics of Hitler and Goebbels"—although when he split with the chief of police, in order to create his own "Contra Force," "he seems to have shifted somewhat to the left."

Ideological positions were less important to these violence-prone local leaders than were their own demonstrations of personal power. As the local chief of police said in 1987, "There are almost no Communists left in Davao City today, just the priests and the nuns, and we'll go after them next."[49]

After Marcos's downfall the rhetorics of "people power," combined with on-and-off negotiations between communist rebels and the government, meant that rightist legitimations for nonstate violence gradually became less cogent. More of the vigilantes reverted into ordinary banditry, running local protection gangs. There was no need to bother with an abstract politics of policies, when armed thieving was the main goal. May asks crucial questions:[50]

> Why did vigilantism spread as it did in 1987, in the wake of the people power revolution, not only in rural areas and provincial towns but in Metro Manila, where even among the urban poor of Tondo prospective recruits volunteered in such numbers that they had to be turned away? Who in fact were these vigilantes, and why were so many "fanatical cults"—movements rooted in a "little tradition" of popular protest, the *tao* (ordinary people) seeking *kalayaan* (liberty)—fanatically anti-left?

He finds that the most straightforward answer can be found in groups that are "directly tied to landowner, business, or politician interests, or to organized crime." The relevant local leaders were innocent of ideology. They were simply kleptocratic patrons whose power depended on violence and threats of violence.

The power of the central government decreased after Marcos in an epidemic of *kudeta* (the Philippine version of *coups d'état*; Chapter 6 details this institution). But such a change is always relative; the power of local leaders rose. Some new militias adopted Catholic symbols; a Negros group called itself the KKK (*Kristiana Kontra Komunismo*, Christians Against Communism—although the same abbreviation is sometimes used for the Kapitunan).[51] Conservatives were able to appropriate symbols of commitment and sacrifice from peasant rehearsals of Christ's passion as readily as revolutionaries had.[52] President Corazon Aquino praised the activities of the rightist religious vigilante group *Tadtad* for fighting communists. She called this group an example of "people power." The name

Tadtad derives from a verb "to chop"—and the initiation ceremony for new members requires novices to

> kneel in prayer for several hours in preparation for the moment when their outstretched arms will be hacked by a bolo [machete]-wielding cult leader reciting Latin or Latin-sounding prayers known as *oraciones*. If the initiates' faith is strong, their limbs, it is said, will not be severed.[53]

Women are recruited into this organization to serve as shaman-like missionaries. Men are recruited to serve as soldiers.

The 1987 Constitution outlaws private armed groups, but they continue to be numerous. Many have been officially deputized as "Active Auxiliaries" or "Citizen Armed Force Geographical Units" or "Civilian Volunteer Organizations." But these are not really militias of the state. Most are armed and financed by businesses, politicians, churches, ethnic autonomists, landowning clans, and interest groups in fields such as gambling or traditionalism or socialism.

Citing the constitutional prohibition of private militias, the Commission on Elections is supposed to try to disband them because they affect voting. From the mid-1990s to 2000, Comelec identified about 150 private armies. It claimed by 2004 that the number was down to 115, and by 2007 down further to 93.[54] These figures are subject to interpretation, but the number of militias decreased only somewhat in the new millennium.

Just after PNoy's inauguration by 2010, the government announced that the Philippines contained 107 private armies. Armed Forces Chief Ricardo David and National Police Director Jesus Verzosa issued a joint order that these should be dismantled, starting with the provinces of Abra in north Luzon, Masbate in the Visayas, and Misamis Occidental in Mindanao. Secretary Rico Puno of the Department of Interior and Local Government said that, "all local executives were told to require their bodyguards, whether they are from the PNP or the Armed Forces or private security agencies, to be in proper uniform." He also said that his police were "assessing politicians who are maintaining private armed groups."[55]

Both the police and the army also have control of local coercive forces, and these sometimes conflict with each other. When police arrested a 16-year-old pickpocketer at a bus terminal in Pasay City, the boy said that he and other pocket "snatchers" were coordinated by army Captain Arnel Mariano—whom the police also duly arrested. Then "a dozen Army soldiers aboard a military pickup arrived" at the police station. The soldiers "positioned themselves in strategic places inside and outside" the building, and later they were relieved by another "heavily armed" contingent. When "it was time for filing the case against the Army officer, the arrested snatcher retracted his testimony reportedly out of fear, claiming that he was warned that a severe punishment awaited him." So the army captain was "released to the custody of his superior officers at Fort Bonifacio," and the boy was transferred to the Social Welfare Department.[56] This fracas occurred in 2000 in Metro Manila.

Rival coercive forces in further-flung places, such as the security troops of rival mining companies in Mindanao, are nonstate and can be very violent. A war broke out between the "guards" of JB Management and those of another mining firm called Helica. According to some reports, "The security men of Helica attacked the JB guards with guns and grenade launchers and also set their [mining] tunnel on fire." Police tried to arrest fighters from both sides, while hospitals dealt with the shrapnel wounds of 15 people.[57]

The state's army and constabulary are supposed to maintain security in such situations, but that work is sometimes beyond their resources. As a Bataan attorney Dante Ilaya put it,[58]

> To the soldiers, we would like to sound this appeal: if you sincerely take the interests of the ordinary people [to] heart, we would like to see you defending the small farmers, fishers, and workers instead of the landlords, the big fishpond owners, the big loggers, the big businessmen, and the big gambling lords. We look forward to the day when you shall be one with us in fighting the common enemy of peace and just development.

There are "enclaves of reform" in the security services, while other units remain dependent on local ruling clans.

The number of extrajudicial killings (bureaucratically called EJKs) reached a peak in 2006. This was an echo from the Marcos era, according to the Philippine Commission on Human Rights.[59] But extrajudicial killings continued at a high rate in 2010 even after reformist President PNoy assumed office. Radical nonviolent groups such as Bayan or the human rights NGO Karapatan recorded more than 20 killings in the first five months after the new president's 2010 inauguration. This was not an electoral season.

> The trend is truly alarming. There has been no let-up in the cases of extrajudicial killings even under the Aquino administration. Despite government claims that killings are being solved, there are fresh cases every month. The old policies and practices [under previous President Arroyo] remain, as far as the Armed Forces of the Philippines is concerned.[60]

In August 2013, shortly before local elections, three officials were killed in a Pampanga shooting "that could be linked to local political rivalries." The victims were in a government car travelling home; masked gunmen on motorcycles shot them, and all three died on the spot.[61] Electoral violence remained a local phenomenon even during the presidential reign of a reformer. In another instance, seven people were killed in mid-2013,

> after two families locked in a longstanding feud battled each other with guns in Lanao del Sur.... Many of the clan clashes are over political power, land, business, and past grudges in far-flung communities awash with guns and burdened by weak law enforcement.

Police said that violence between the Macugar and Capal families was nothing new, but "it was not immediately clear what the families were feuding over."[62]

Guns

There is no constitutional right to bear arms in the Philippines. The second amendment in the U.S. Constitution was not part of the archipelago's American legacy, because the colonial government hoped to monopolize arms. The island republic has strict gun laws. They are not enforced. Marcos made the illegal possession of firearms a capital offense. Guns, licensed and otherwise, have nonetheless for decades been widespread in all parts of the Philippines.

Warlords have sometimes run their own arms factories. Weapons manufacture is a famous and major sector of the economy of Danao City. Underground arsenals flourished against the Japanese during their occupation. Later Philippine national administrations legalized the making of some local guns but could not monitor all such manufactures. The Durano clan of Danao produced guns into the 1980s and probably later. When Marcos issued a presidential decree ordering all private armies to surrender their weapons, this did not disarm Ramon Durano who had his own arsenal.[63]

New guns also filter into the Philippines from abroad, and the army admits not knowing how they arrive. Six "brand-new AK-47 rifles" were captured by the military in a battle with a New People's Army unit in 2013, but the government had previously announced that "the NPA had stopped using AK-47s ... because of bullet and spare part supply problems." These Kalashnikov guns are standard issue for the infantries of China and other states. The army chief vowed to defeat the NPA rebels within three years, while admitting he did not know whence they got new foreign-made guns.[64]

The Philippine government has tried to buy guns from the population for many years. Nearly two-thirds of those it obtained in the post-Marcos period came from Moro rebel groups. The number garnered is thought to be a tiny portion of all firearms in the country. Many have been resold on black markets, and most are of poor quality. Guns are symbols of *malakas* strength; they are not owned merely for use. In some Moslem Philippine groups, such as the Tausug,

> men are not only providers but also, more importantly, protectors and defenders of the family's honor, the family itself, especially the female members, the home, the turf, and other possessions, and in a broad sense the clan.... For Tausug men, to fulfill the role of protector, which their society has imposed on them almost from the age of puberty, they must, first and foremost, have a weapon, formerly the *kris* (the Tausug [and general Malay] sword) but in modern times a gun.[65]

The Philippine National Police in 2005 reported that the country had "321,685 unregistered firearms." (It is not useful to imagine ways in which the government counted so exactly the number of guns on which it lacked records. It is more accurate just to say these weapons were many.) Most guns used during human rights violations in the Philippines are licensed—but 94 percent of the guns used in ordinary crimes are unlicensed.[66] Police and army guns have often aided organized local repressions by *trapo* families. Off-license guns are apparently the weapons of choice among less well-connected nonstate militias and individual criminals.

Communists in the late 1980s bought most of their bullets and ammunition from moonlighting members of the Philippines Armed Forces. According to one estimate, the usual price was about five pesos per round. The New People's Army was less interested in purchasing actual guns, however, because these main weapons were often available for free, after a soldier or policeman could be killed or threatened.[67]

Not all Philippine police carry firearms. PNoy presided at a ceremony to honor two officers who had shown personal bravery against armed robbers whom they were able to arrest even when the policemen had no guns. The president personally presented these officers with Glock 7 pistols, such as are "used by police forces in America, Europe, and Asia."[68] PNoy led a campaign to supply such guns to all Philippine police, reasonably expecting they would serve the public.

A 2010 estimate claimed that only 45 percent of registered guns were held by the state (36 percent by either the army or police). Another 15 percent were licensed to private security guards. A further third of the officially catalogued weapons were said to be "loose" firearms; the guns' numbers were on file, although state officials did not know who possessed them. The vast majority of weapons was not recorded at all. In 93 percent of "gun-related crimes" in 2010, the equipment was unlicensed.[69]

Members of elite families hire bodyguards and often carry personal pistols. These are usually registered. But licensing weapons does not surely prevent their arbitrary use. When "Noynoy" Aquino was in the Senate (before being elected President PNoy), his cousin Antonio "Tony Boy" Aquino got into a fracas with a woman at a KTV club; and

> while the two were in the lobby, [Antonio] Aquino was reportedly bumped accidentally by a security man of a certain David So, a Chinese businessman-lawyer. Aquino, who appeared already irate at his woman companion, allegedly drew his caliber .45 pistol and fired successive shots inside the lobby.

A KTV security guard was killed, and stray bullets hit three others. One witness said the battle was between the well-armed guards accompanying So and those accompanying Aquino. All agreed that Antonio Aquino "fled aboard a Mercedes Benz sedan," and Makati police searched for him although they "were reluctant to talk further about the incident."[70]

An additional gun law was passed in 2013, requiring all owners of firearms to renew their licenses every two years; but the penalty was merely that police could seize any unlicensed guns they caught. Repairers of weapons were also required to have certificates. "Professionals" could legally carry arms. Enforcement of the new law boded to be as spotty as of earlier gun legislation. Sources of new firearms did not disappear:

> The manufacturing of paltik guns, for instance, is common in Danao and Cebu. But most gun makers do not have licenses for their trade. Paltiks are guns made out of scrap metal and bits of angle iron manufactured inside home premises.[71]

Local Philippine police have broken rules against overuse of firearms, especially when the officers were involved in corruption. Fifteen police were present when they "rubbed out" two robbery gang leaders in Laguna on July 15, 2013. As a top superintendent said, "There was no firefight ... but we are completing the pieces of evidence so that [the charge against the policemen] can stand in court." The sister of one of the slain gangsters said her brother had "paid some policemen from Cavite to protect him after he escaped from prison last December." The head of the Philippine National Police admitted the possibility that the victims "were silenced to prevent them from revealing their protectors." The chief of all police in the Southern Tagalog Region (who had the rank of a military general) was "relieved," as were many of his minions. A presidential spokesman said, "This is something we certainly would have to look into."[72] PNoy condemned police trigger-happiness. NGOs to reduce the Philippines' high social "lethality" have emerged.[73] They have thus far created more hopeful recommendations than effective gun controls.

Maoists, Moros, and mountain people

The New People's Army movement is the longest-lasting Maoist insurgency anywhere. Its elite is recruited from cities, but its bases are in areas that no Philippine government has securely controlled. NPA guerilla strongholds are in Luzon, several of the Visayan islands, and northern and eastern Mindanao. The NPA is not secessionist; it calls for a revolution throughout the Philippines. By contrast, the secessionists among the Moros want a fully independent state in central-southwest Mindanao and adjacent smaller islands.

The areas these movements control have contracted during the reigns of several Philippine presidents and defense ministers, notably Magsaysay. In the late Marcos period, the NPA was able to recruit literate, high-quality cadres who were angry with the dictator. Since then, communist success has been somewhat reduced.

> Idealistic college students continue to join, though in much smaller numbers than in the 1970s.... The direction of conflict is dependent on the quality of democracy. If an inclusive, participatory democracy can be established, then the NPA's struggle will seem anachronistic to its potential members. Neither the government nor the NPA is likely to win a military victory.[74]

Recent presidencies have seen both fighting and ceasefires with communists, and the insurgent areas have fluctuated but have not disappeared.

Even at its peak in the mid-1980s, the NPA had only 6,000 soldiers, albeit their commitment to their cause was strong. The communist army makes links with local youths, peasants, and women, choosing "advanced" members to form "barangay organizing committees." A government report from Bicol opined that,

> The AFP cannot provide the services that the NPA provides to the villagers, such as land to till or lower land rent, the elimination of cattle rustlers, protection of peasants' rights, literacy lessons, health services, or even protection from domestic abuse. The pattern has been for the military to sweep a village free of insurgents and then leave. Civil government then fails to follow through with reforms, and the villages become vulnerable to rebel organizing once more.[75]

Sotero Llamas served for many years as the most effective Communist-NPA leader in Bicol—and this did not prevent him from running for governor of Albay Province in 2004. He lost that election but was honored by figures such as Panfilo Lacson (former head of the national police, and later a senator) for having fought poverty. Llamas was assassinated in a 2006 ambush that was of course "extrajudicial"—and was suspected by some to have been the work of President Arroyo's Malacañang, which wanted at the time to claim that the communists had severe divisions among themselves.[76]

The Armed Forces of the Philippines in December 2010 published the *AFP Soldier's Handbook on Human Rights and International Humanitarian Law*. This guide sets rules of engagement and aims to end complaints against the army. AFP Deputy Chief Reynaldo Mapagu said, "If we put our hearts and minds into it, and also practice it, people will see that we are serious, that we are upholding the law at all times."[77] The army now has a human rights office. Making humanitarian rights meaningful to a coercive force was (as Mapagu said) "dependent wholly on practice." High officers of the army by 2013 tried to keep track of soldiers' human rights violations. They probably underestimated the number, but at least they admitted that abuses of their coercive power sometimes still occurred.[78]

PNoy's election, and a possibility of more negotiations, did not mean that AFP–NPA conflicts ceased. In December 2010, the guerrillas caught a unit of the government's army in an ambush, killing nine soldiers and a young boy. The NPA spokesman explained that the army had trespassed in an area that was a communist base of operations. So, in his view, the ambush had been legitimate, because the NPA had followed the rules of war after a government incursion into its own territory.[79] His premise was that there was more than one state in the Philippines.

Ethnolinguistic and religious divisions in Mindanao, combined with government weakness so far south, created a situation in which private armies flourish. Many have been legitimated by Manila when they claimed to be anti-secessionist or anti-communist; and they are aided by the Armed Forces of the Philippines. One of the largest such groups, Masses Arise, has been discussed above and is largely composed of disaffected former communist guerrillas. Others such as Alamara and Alsa Lumad have been mostly composed of "indigenous communities" such as the Lumads. Any of these engage as bandits, cattle rustlers, and kidnappers against the New People's Army as well as others, whenever profits are available.

Visayan immigrants to Mindanao launch local operations especially against Moros and mountain people. Many private armies, such as the Ilaga Movement, are Visayan and anti-communist. Still others, such as Kuratong Baleleng and probably Nakasaka, are criminal gangs that acquired some state legitimacy when they began to kill communists. Yet others, such as Tadtad ("chop chop"), claim to be religious. One of its subgroups,

> formerly known as Sagrado Corazon Señor [Lord of the Sacred Heart] is a fanatical cult known for chopping up the bodies of its victims. It gained notoriety in the 1970s, when the military used its members in offensives against Muslim secessionist guerrillas.... Its members claim that their bodies have the power to repel bullets.[80]

The Bangsamoros (Philippine Muslims) are represented by three main political groups. The Moro National Liberation Front (MNLF) calls for autonomy. Under Cory Aquino's constitution, plebiscites on autonomy were held in 13 provinces, and four of these referenda passed. So Lanao del Sur, Maguindanao, Sulu, and Tawi-Tawi legally became the Autonomous Region of Muslim Mindanao (ARMM). Autonomist MNLF Muslims are still dissatisfied with the underfunded "Marshall Plan" development projects in their ARMM, but they usually maintain peace with the Manila government and with most other locals in Mindanao.

The Moro Islamic Liberation Front, on the other hand, has an "I" in its name that might as well stand for independence. In 2010, the MILF fielded about 12,000 combatants in central Mindanao (more than the communist NPA then had in the whole archipelago). MILF political leaders apparently realize they cannot for the nonce win against the government's army. So they remain armed but engage in ceasefires and peace negotiations. By 2014, these talks with Manila reached tentative agreement that a new and larger autonomous region, called Bangsamoro, would replace the Autonomous Region of Muslim Mindanao. But another part of the tentative bargain looked forward to MILF fighters laying down their guns, and implementation of that part was sure to be chancy because of existential links between weapons and masculinity in all Malay traditions. In addition, some MILF factions (including one called the Bangsamoro Islamic Freedom Fighters) rejected the peace proposal, which does not give full national sovereignty to Bangsamoro.[81] The MILF's most important political opposition among Muslims was the Ampatuan clan, which supports autonomists rather than secessionists and wins regular Philippine elections even when the Ampatuan chief sees fit to murder his (Muslim) electoral rivals.

44 *Clan feuds localize the state*

A much smaller group, Abu Sayyaf, is more radical, more concentrated on the islands separating Mindanao from Sabah, and more closely linked to international Islamists. Abu Sayyaf, like Al-Qaeda, calls for violence in the cause of establishing strict *shari'a* law in its area (on the string of islands from Basilan toward Sabah, and on adjacent mainland Mindanao). Its members have also used violence on behalf of more humdrum causes such as drug trading and ordinary thieving—which equally engage the interests of Philippine rightist militias.

The broader area that stretches from Mindanao's Zamboanga Peninsula to Sabah and Indonesia tests the limits of sovereignty of all three relevant electoral democracies (the Philippines, Indonesia, and Malaysia). Actors there tend to be "strategic hypocrites," using laws and norms of all three ostensibly sovereign countries in interests that are wholly local.[82]

Sporadic wars exist not only among and between Muslims and Christians, or between left and right, but also in other minority and majority ethnic groups. The Cordillera People's Liberation Army (CPLA) is a formerly communist group that in 1986 separated from the NPA. It is more ethnic than socialist. Its members come mostly from indigenous tribes in the north Luzon highlands. The leaders have called for a Cordillera Autonomous Region, which would be similar legally to the Autonomous Region of Muslim Mindanao. Plebiscites to establish such a region were held in 1989 and again in 1995—but they failed. Only a Cordillera Administrative Region was set up, no more or less autonomous than any other bureaucratic district of the country. The CPLA leaders once sent President Estrada a native dagger as a sincere token of their dissatisfaction.

Some areas, such as Abra Province in the cordillera of northwest Luzon, suffer particularly high levels of local violence driven by political rivalries. From 2001 to 2007, at least 13 barangay council members and 21 higher-level politicians were murdered in separate incidents. The national police by 2007 reported at least ten "partisan armed groups" in Abra, "most of which are in the service of local politicians." Warlordism has persisted in the highlands, where "a common assumption among locals [is] that the majority of politicians, from barangay captains to mayors, have private armies."[83] Feuding is existential and traditional between two particular clans, the Valeras and the Paredeses. Both of these Ilocano *trapo* families also fight, on their turfs, the communist NPA and the formerly communist Cordillera (indigenous) People's Liberation Army.

Mountainous terrain aids guerillas of any persuasion. Abra's population is divided between Ilocanos on lowlands, and Tingguians in the highlands. Hitmen are hired in, from neighboring provinces and among former convicts from Manila jails, for frequent paid assassinations. The "barefoot [saka-saka] assassins are often teenagers, but the killings are professional." A politician planning to run for Governor of Abra in 2004 "was shot in the head while watching basketball during his town's fiesta." Abra's representative in Congress, after having said in public that he feared for his life, was "killed by two motorcyclists in front of the church in Quezon City where his niece had just been married." A provincial legislator "was killed ... while jogging early in the morning."[84]

The Philippines is a land of volcanoes, intense typhoons, earthquakes, tsunamis, and flash floods. According to a particularly wary observer, this context promotes a climate of political fear and a "tenuous faith that victims—all victims—were guilty of something, an assumption that had the poisonous consequence of allowing people to excuse the death of ... just about anyone."[85] Cultural norms that accustom people to natural and man-made tragedies over centuries are not unique to the Philippines. They have been a subject of extravagant interest among social scientists of southern Italy, parts of Spain or Ukraine, and many other countries. Fatalism, to the extent it exists, affects people's sense of justice. It may also affect modal types of leadership.

Elections become occasions on which leaders can prove their *malakas* mettle, e.g., by using violence against rivals. Several politicians were reportedly planning to run for the Abra Province governorship in 2005 against Vicente Valera. He claimed to have reduced warlordism in the province. Valera apparently did so by making sure rival warlords were dead. His family and the Paredeses vied violently with other clans who formed a coalition (mainly Bernoses, Molinas, and Lunas). "When Valera was asked how private armies generated funds for their activities, he said, 'I can only surmise that they get their funds from the coffers of the government.'"[86] Abra's *trapos* fostered coercive and financial connections with the government in Manila, and also with the local infantry battalion commander. One of the Lunas filed murder charges against Valera. This "godfather" was eventually caught, along with one of his hit men, after an ambush in which a rival was killed. Police by 2013 explained that most of Valera's targets had been other Abra politicians. The helper assassin, who was apparently paid 50,000 pesos (about $1,200) for each major killing, "had been on the run for years, but the long arm of the law finally caught up with him."[87]

Clan dynasties' politics merge with professionals' politics

Violence gradually declines as local Philippine politics becomes less structured by public interests created in conflicts among families. Cory Aquino's 1987 Constitution, part II, sec. 26, hopefully provided that "the State shall prohibit political dynasties as may be defined by law." No legal definition of a dynasty, however, emerged during her presidency. (She was herself a "dynast" from the wealthy Cohuangco family that had earlier produced many politicians of various kinds.) Later, President Fidel Ramos supported a proposal from the Commission on Elections in 1993 that a "dynasty" be defined as a group of current "politicians having a third civil degree of consanguinity" or closer (i.e., spouses, parents, grandparents, children, grandchildren, siblings, nephews, and nieces, or the husbands or wives of any of these). They and their third-degree relatives by marriage would not, if this law had passed, simultaneously have been able to run for offices in the same legislative district, city, or town. Opposition to this plan was severe in the House, whose Rules Committee refused to allow debate of it. The Philippine Center for Investigative Journalism calculated that 17 of the 20 committee members actually had relatives who (at that time or earlier) had held political offices for which they would, under such a law, have been unable to run.[88]

Politicians from the same family often opposed each other. Marcos's main "crony" in Tarlac had been Eduardo "Danding" Cojuangco. He was first cousin of Corazon Aquino, who "is said to believe that Danding conspired with Imelda Marcos to order Benigno Aquino's murder."[89] The islands provide many other examples of *trapo* families that divide sharply. Different groups of Cojuangcos have run against each other, as have different factions of Osmeñas.[90] The Dy clan of Isabela Province, to take a later example, produced partisans of both Estrada and Arroyo during a period when those two were bitter rivals.[91]

When candidates who were not from *trapo* clans ran for congressional or mayoral posts in 1987–88, they received as many as half of the votes in very few parts of the Philippines (including Manila). In central Luzon north of the capital (Pampanga, Tarlac, and Nueva Ejica), a lower portion of votes went for candidates who were not in established clans—although many of the new faces represented old forces. In the southern Tagalog area, candidates without established names received only 30 percent of the ballots, in the Ilocos region 31 percent, and in southern Mindanao just 21 percent. These figures report the portions of all votes cast in those areas. Overall, during the 1987–88 elections of the "people power" era, contenders without well-established names won elections only 26 percent of the times they tried. Old clan incumbents won 50 percent of their campaigns. Their kin, upon first entering politics, already won 45 percent of the races they entered.[92]

A 1987 study showed that more than two-thirds of Philippine Congress members came from traditional clans.[93] Other representatives, who lacked such well-known family backgrounds, were politically affected by those who were more certifiable *trapos*. Many outside old families were proxies, supported by clan patriarchs who did not themselves want to run in political campaigns. This situation changed very slowly, as more candidates (*trapo* or not) were elected from white-collar professions.

Surveys showed that in 1992, fully 145 House members (a majority of the total 250) "belonged to old oligarchic families." This was slightly down from the 169 old-family congressmen in 1987.[94] Over half the representatives in the 1990s personally owned agricultural land.[95] Others were in professions; but they were not mostly "technocrats," who have never been many in the Philippines. "Professionals" are a wider group—and many of these come from old landed families that have supported or supplied politicians from landed estates for decades.

About one-third of the House members in the 1990s were "younger, middle-class professionals, bureaucrats, and entrepreneurs."[96] As a study by the Philippine Center for Investigative Journalism pointed out, "The *trapos* are not just landlords."

> The sources of most [Congress members'] wealth are more diverse, so that Congress can no longer be described as a "landlord-dominated" legislature. The *caciques* of old have been replaced by real estate developers, bankers,

stock brokers, and assorted professionals and business people.... Still, the reality is that a Congress of multimillionares makes laws for a poor country.[97]

Some politicians based their campaigns on urban wealth, which could come partly from renting out land within cities. "Oligarchic networks not only straddled the divide between Manila and the provinces according to the kinds of oligarchs prevalent in each sphere, but also through an urban–rural division of roles within major oligarchic families."[98] When *trapos* were not landlords, they nonetheless could maintain networks of clients like their predecessor rentiers. Patriarchic networks naturally used local–local and local–central connections. Politicians who started with wealth from sources as diverse as finance and boxing were nonetheless unified by an understanding that the modal style of politics was patronist. (The most prominent exceptions were a few party-list members in Congress; see Chapter 8 for more about these.)

A 1994 compendium of the backgrounds of all members of the Philippine Congress, including the Senate, nonetheless found that many were still from rentier families.[99] A decade later, an update found some increase in the number of members who came from newer economic groups. Some new politicians, e.g., from a family named Barber, were from non-rentier backgrounds—in that case, from the Manila Police Department. Several members of that clan advanced into politics at once, not from a traditional (or industrial) base, but in the same style as more traditional politicians, taking mayoral, senatorial, or congressional seats in the same election as a group. If party-list members are omitted from the count, then the percentage of "political clan" *trapos* in Congress was still two-thirds after the first elections of the new millennium.[100]

India, another populous democracy, shows contrasts with the Philippines regarding the occupations of elected legislators. Ashutosh Varshney argues from Indian evidence that when democracy precedes industry in a country, rural farmers can be strengthened despite the importance of urban wealth. Voters are mostly peasants, even in a modernizing economy. State policies would favor the countryside over cities, according to Varshney, if economic rather than identity interests motivated voters. But non-economic identity interests—religious, caste, or regional loyalties—limit the unity of rural power.[101]

Surprisingly few studies of Varshney's kind have been conducted in other countries, partly because "democracies" have often been defined as polities that maintain liberal systems over time, uninterrupted by coups or martial law. But the logic of Varshney's argument applies as well to countries such as Thailand and the Philippines, where coups and *kudeta* have occurred. A contrast between India and the Philippines is that, during the first half century of Indian independence, some of New Delhi's politicians, including some members of parliament, came from low-income rural backgrounds. Two-fifths of the Lok Sabha reported that their main family occupation was agriculture. Not all of these spend most of their time tilling fields, to be sure; but many reportedly self-identify with rural work (as well as with the ethnic and caste interests of their voters).[102] Their elections partly depend on such self-identification.

As Julio Teehankee has written concerning the Philippine Congress,[103]

> the interests of the marginalized sectors that include labour, small farmers, fisherfolk, the urban poor and women are hardly represented in the national legislature ... some scholars have argued that there is an observable shift in representation from elite landed interests to that of the more professional urban middle class. However, the shift is gradual and tenuous, as these new professional politicians tend to establish their own political dynasties.

This 2002 assessment might show slightly more inclusiveness if written a decade later, when economic and political changes became more evident in the Philippines. But many Filipino and foreign observers hoped for faster change in most parts of the country, where *trapos* remained dominant.

By the congressional elections in 2007, a survey suggested that:

> at least 76 percent of the incoming legislative districts representatives are members of political families [defined as those "with at least one relative who has been elected or appointed to office in the past," apparently at the same level], compared to their 83-percent command of the last Congress.[104]

Among the elected district representatives who were not members of such families, 38 percent had themselves been in the previous Congress. But among elected "clan" members in 2007, the rate was higher, 55 percent.

After the 2010 elections, three-quarters of the regular district representatives in the House still came from *trapo* dynasties. So did four-fifths of the Senate. University of the Philippines Professor Bobby Tuazon estimated that the strength of "political families ... has even increased, especially at the local level."[105]

Legislation to implement the constitutional prohibition of "political dynasties" (e.g., by defining the term) continues to be sharply resisted. Senator Miriam Defensor Santiago introduced implementing bills to the Senate, where they were stifled. Three other senators with historically prominent surnames immediately announced their opposition to Santiago's 2013 reintroduction of her anti-dynasty bill. "Bongbong" Marcos said, "You cannot restrain anyone from running for office." J.V. Ejercito asked, "If there is a qualified person, would you deprive him of running for office if he is part of a so-called 'political dynasty'?" Nancy Binay asked, "Why ban candidates from running? Why deprive the people of choice?" Other sitting senators with famous names (Aquino, Osmeña, two Cayetanos, Pimentel, Recto, Revilla, Sotto, Guinguna, Poe, and Villar) did not react immediately to Santiago's motion, but it would not have served their families. Together with those who expressed quick opposition, a clear majority of the Senate would vote against this effort to displace dynasties.

Former senator "Sonny" Angara opined that no such law was needed, because the Philippines had achieved an educated electorate. His paradigm did not address the notion that everybody might have equal rights regardless of education (or birth). Senator Santiago said that 80 percent of the Senate came from political families (which she numbered at 178 nationwide). So, by her count, did 74 percent of the House in 2013. On the basis of 2010 election results, she also said that such clans "rule over" 94 percent of the country's provinces.[106]

Trapo clan organizations do not want political modernization on their turfs. They want economic modernization if they can control it. They in any case receive revenue allotments from the central treasury because they run recognized local governments. Other sources of income for some clans are illegal gambling, drugs, and occasionally money from other criminal activities. The Philippines is a true democracy in the sense that elective offices are valuable. It is more extreme than most democracies in treating citizens unequally.

According to World Bank economists, Philippine "governance scores" declined significantly between 1998 and 2008 on two indices: "voice and accountability" and "political stability/absence of violence."[107] These political and economic measures relate to each other strongly. Economists have correlated Philippine places in which local dynasties rule with those in which poverty reigns.[108]

Action possibilities against undemocratic violence

Because of the close connection between clan solidarity and instances of political violence, an obvious policy recommendation for Filipinos would be to define the term "political dynasty" and to regulate elections so that the current trend toward a more diverse political elite might be strengthened. Such a law would reduce the institution of kin as "breakers," although it could hardly inhibit candidacies among new politicians who were not *trapo* kin but represented *trapo* interests. It would also not protect minorities against populist demagogues who could still be elected. A law inhibiting political dynasties is recommendable, even though its implementation would be somewhat difficult.

A more direct suggestion for reducing violence in the Philippines would be to enforce already-on-the-books laws regulating guns. Change in that direction seems practically prerequisite to other steps toward less intimidation in local politics. Any state is supposed to try to coordinate means of violence. Such centralization is opposed by groups that like "wild West" traditions. Their roots are diverse (Malay, Muslim, "Matamoros," and American too). The Philippine Constitution has no "second amendment" allowing guns, but many organizations and individuals oppose centralization of violence by the state. The Philippines is not unique in that respect.[109]

Control of force, like control of other resources, is seen as corrupt if it benefits a group that is perceived less worthy of benefit than is another group—which is usually larger. So the policy question becomes: what institutions might link less-inclusive communities with more-inclusive ones (including the nation that the state is supposed to represent) in ways that are tolerable to each size of collectivity? There may be no way to determine abstractly, separate from the effects on citizens, whether small groups and individuals should control means of violence or, instead, only the official state should. The real issue is whether smaller and larger networks can establish habits of mutual peace among each other.

50 *Clan feuds localize the state*

Some state institutions need to be armed, if only because some people anywhere are psychopaths. So President PNoy's policy of making sure that police and army officers have sufficient firepower is understandable, so long as the weapons they hold are used sparingly and are not later commandeered by non-state agents. Guns are still widely distributed in Philippine "civil" society. Diversifying new kinds of local leaders depends on security for their truly civil activities. Toward that end, more can be done to assure that the army and police actually hold on to their weapons and use them in public interests rather than private interests.

The most important of these private interests continue to be families. In any country, these are small polities. Edmund Burke famously claimed that,

> To be attached to the subdivision, to love the little platoon we belong to in society, is the first principle (the germ as it were) of public affections. It is the first link in the series by which we proceed towards a love to our country, and to mankind.[110]

This emphasis on linkage is crucial, and it applies to any nation.[111] In the Philippines, the main "little platoons" are families, or at least they are like families. They attract firm political loyalties from many. They are not necessarily sets of biological kin related by blood, but they are either trusting or intimidated sets of people who think they protect and provide for each other. In many places, prominent local lineages can be found at the centers of such groups.

A list of major political clans in Philippine regions, comprising most of the country, has been compiled for the mid-1980s, and practically all of these families are still active in politics. This book offers a list of political families that are important in particular provinces. Such a roster might also be divided into two sub-lists, related to past affiliations. In each region, it is possible to identify one or a few *trapo* clans that were associated by the 1980s with the Marcos–Romualdez KBL party, and a similar number in many regions that was aligned against Marcos.[112] But such lists are unstable. Clans can and sometimes do switch "parties." Each family is essentially independent. Loose national coalitions need them more than they need the parties. Socioeconomic preferences of the leftist or rightist kinds do not generally structure Philippine politics—and the main policy that could link families to social options would be the development of a stronger Philippine industrial economy. If more of the clan heads were interested in using their resources to start enterprises, stronger mutually reinforcing links might emerge between the state in Manila and the interests of local leaders.

Appendix

Reputed political clans in the Philippines

Many provinces have conflicting families. Anonymous analyst, reporting at www.philippinepoliticsismyreligion.blogspot.com compiled this list.

Clan feuds localize the state 51

Political clans	Provinces
Abad	Batanes
Abalos	Mandaluyong City
Abaya	Cavite
Abduraham	Tawi-Tawi
Acosta	Bukidnon
Adaza	Misamis Oriental
Adiong	Maguindanao
Aganon	Nueva Ecija
Agbayani	Pangasinan
Akbar	Basilan
Albani	Tawi-Tawi
Albano	Isabela
Alberto	Catanduanes
Alfelor	Camarines Sur
Almario	Davao Oriental
Amante	Agusan del Norte
Amatong	Compostela Valley
Ampao	Basilan
Ampatuan	Maguindanao
Andaya	Oriental Mindoro
Angara	Aurora
Angkanan	Sultan Kudarat
Anni	Sulu
Antonino	General Santos
Apostol	Leyte
Aquino	Tarlac
Armada	Iloilo
Arnaiz	Negros Oriental
Arroyo	Camarines Sur, Pampanga, Negros
Asistio	Caloocan
Astorga	Leyte
Atienza	Manila
Aumentado	Bohol
Bacani	Manila
Bacani	Quirino
Bagatsing	Manila
Balanquit	Northern Samar
Barbers	Surigao del Norte, Surigao City
Barroso	South Cotabato
Baterina	Ilocos Sur
Belmonte	Quezon City
Belo	Capiz
Biazon	Muntinlupa City
Bichara	Albay
Binay	Makati City
Bondoc	Pampanga
Brawner	Ifugao
Bulut	Apayao
Cabacang	Northern Samar

continued

52 Clan feuds localize the state

Political clans	Provinces
Caballero	Compostela Valley
Cainglet	Zamboanga City
Calingin	Misamis Oriental
Calizo	Aklan
Calo	Butuan City
Calumpang	Negros Oriental
Candao	Shariff Kabunsuan
Cappleman	Ifugao
Carag	Cagayan
Cari	Leyte
Carloto	Zamboanga del Norte
Catane	Misamis Occidental, Zamboanga del Norte
Cayetano	Taguig
Celera	Masbate
Chiongbian	Sarangani, Cebu, Misamis Occidental
Clarete	Misamis Occidental
Claver	Mountain Province
Climaco	Zamboanga City
Crisologo	Ilocos Sur, Quezon City
Cojuangco	Tarlac
Corvera	Agusan del Norte
Cosalan	Benguet
Cua	Quirino
Cuenco	Cebu
Cuneta	Pasay City
Cupin	Agusan del Norte
Dalog	Mountain Province
Dalwasen	Apayao
Dangwa	Benguet
David	–
Daza	Northern Samar
Defensor	Iloilo
Delfin	Antique
De La Cruz	Bulacan
De Leon	Misamis Oriental
De Venecia	Pangasinan
Del Rosario	Davao del Norte
Diaz	Nueva Ecija
Dilangalen	Shariff Kabunsuan
Dimaporo	Lanao del Norte
Dominguez	Mountain Province
Duavit	Rizal
Dumpit	La Union
Dupaya	Cagayan
Durano	Cebu
Duterte	Davao City
Dy	Isabela
Ecleo	Dinagat Islands
Emano	Misamis Oriental
Enrile	Cagayan

Political clans	Provinces
Enverga	Quezon
Ermita	Batangas
Escudero	Sorsogon
Espina	Biliran
Espino	Pangasinan
Espinosa	Masbate
Estrella	Pangasinan
Estrada	San Juan City
Eusebio	Pasig City
Famor	Zamboanga Sibugay
Fernandez	Pangasinan
Figueroa	Samar
Floriendo	Davao
Fresnedi	Muntinlupa City
Frivaldo	Sorsogon
Fuentebella	Camarines Sur
Garcia	Cebu
Garcia	Palawan
Garin	Iloilo
Gentuyaga	Compostela Valley
Gordon	Olongapo City
Guiao	Pampanga
Guingona	Bukidnon
Herrera	Bohol
Henson	–
Hofer	Zamboanga Sibugay
Imperial	Albay
Jalosjos	Zamboanga del Norte
Javier	Antique
Joson	Nueva Ecija
Kintanar	Cebu
Lacbain	Zambales
Lacson	Negros Occidental
Lacuna	Manila
Lagman	Albay
Lapid	Pampanga
Larrazabal	Leyte
Laurel	Batangas
Lavin	Northern Samar
Lazaro	Laguna
Lazatin	Pampanga
Ledesma	Negros Occidental
Lerias	Southern Leyte
Leviste	Batangas
Libanan	Eastern Samar
Ligo	Sultan Kudarat
Locsin	Negros Occidental
Lobregat	Zamboanga City
Loong	Sulu

continued

54 *Clan feuds localize the state*

Political clans	Provinces
Lopez	Iloilo
Loreto	Leyte
Lucman	Lanao del Sur
Luna	Abra
Maamo	Southern Leyte
Macapagal	Pampanga
Macias	Negros Oriental
Madrigal	Manila
Maganto	Bulacan
Magsaysay	Zambales
Malanyaon	Davao Oriental
Malinas	Mountain Province
Mandanas	Batangas
Mangudadato	Maguindanao
Marañon	Negros Occidental
Marasigan	Oriental Mindoro
Marcos	Ilocos Norte
Martinez	Cebu
Matalam	Cotabato
Matba	Tawi-Tawi
Mathay	Quezon City
Matugas	Surigao del Norte
Mayaen	Mountain Province
Mayo	Batangas
Mendiola	Occidental Mindoro
Mercado	Leyte
Miranda	Isabela
Misuari	Sulu
Mitra	Palawan
Molinas	Benguet
Montelibano	Negros Occidental
Montilla	Sultan Kudarat
Moreno	Misamis Oriental
Mutilan	Lanao del Sur
Navarro	Surigao del Norte
Nepomuceno	Pampanga
Nisce	La Union
Ocampo	Misamis Occidental
Olivarez	Laguna
Olvis	Zamboanga del Norte
Ople	Bulacan
Ortega	La Union
Osmeña	Cebu
Ouano	Cebu
Padilla	Camarines Norte
Pagdanganan	Bulacan
Palma-Gil	Davao Oriental
Pancho	Northern Samar
Paras	Negros Oriental
Paredes	Abra

Political clans	Provinces
Parojinog	Misamis Occidental
Pasificador	Antique
Paylaga	Misamis Occidental
Payumo	Bataan
Pelaez	Misamis Oriental
Pelegrino	Bohol
Perez	Pangasinan
Petilla	Leyte
Pichay	Surigao del Sur
Pimentel	Surigao del Sur
Pineda	Pampanga
Plaza	Agusan
Ponce de Leon	Palawan
Publico	Sultan Kudarat
Puno	Rizal
Punzalan	Quezon
Rabat	Davao Oriental
Rama	Agusan del Norte
Ramiro	Misamis Occidental
Raquiza	Ilocos Sur
Real	Zamboanga City
Recto	Batangas
Redaja	Western Samar
Remulla	Cavite
Relampagos	Bohol
Rengel	Bohol
Revilla	Cavite
Reyes	Marinduque
Reymundo	Pasig City
Reyno	Cagayan
Robredo	Camarines Sur
Romualdez	Leyte
Romualdo	Camiguin
Rono	Western Samar
Roqueros	Bulacan
Roxas	Capiz
Rodriguez	Rizal
Sahidulla	Sulu
Salazar	Eastern Samar
Salceda	Albay
Sali	Tawi-Tawi
Salipudin	Basilan
San Luis	Laguna
Sanchez	Cebu
Sandoval	Malabon, Navotas, Palawan
Sarmiento	Bulacan
Sering	Surigao del Norte
Silverio	Bulacan
Singson	Ilocos Sur

continued

Political clans	Provinces
Sinsuat	Shariff Kabunsuan
Siquian	Isabela
Soliva	Agusan del Norte
Sotto	Leyte
Sulpicio/Tupas	Iloilo
Sumulong	Rizal
Tañada	Aurora, Quezon
Tanjuatco	Rizal
Tatad	Catanduanes
Tan	Samar, Southern Leyte
Tanco	Capiz
Tolentino	Tagaytay
Teves	Negros Oriental
Trinidad	Compostela Valley
Umali	Nueva Ecija
Valentino	Marikina City
Valera	Abra
Velasco	Western Samar
Veloso	Leyte
Verceles	Catanduanes
Villanueva	Negros Occidental, Negros Oriental
Villar	Las Pinas, Pangasinan
Villafuerte	Camarines Sur
Villareal	Capiz
Villaroza	Occidental Mindoro
Villegas	Negros Oriental
Violago	Nueva Ecija
Yap	Tarlac
Yebes	Zamboanga del Norte
Yulo	Laguna, Negros Occidental
Ynares	Rizal
Yniguez	Leyte
Zubiri	Bukidnon

Notes

1 Talcott Parsons, *The Theory of Social and Economic Organization* (New York: Simon & Schuster, 1964), 154.
2 Soliman M. Santos, Jr. and Paz Verdades M. Santos, *Primed and Purposeful: Armed Groups and Human Security Efforts in the Philippines* (Geneva: Small Arms Survey, Graduate Institute of International and Development Studies, 2010), 188.
3 Alfred W. McCoy, *Policing America's Empire: The United States, the Philippines, and the Rise of the Surveillance State* (Madison, WI: University of Wisconsin Press, 2009).
4 Alfred W. McCoy, "An Anarchy of Families: The Historiography of State and Family in the Philippines," in *An Anarchy of Families: State and Family in the Philippines*, McCoy, ed. (Madison, WI: University of Wisconsin Center for Southeast Asian Studies, 1993), 19 and 22.
5 Amando Doronila, *The State, Economic Transformation, and Political Change in the Philippines, 1946–1972* (Singapore: Oxford University Press, 1992), 89–90.

6 José Rizal, from *El Filibusterismo*, quoted in Nathan Gilbert Quimpo, *Contested Democracy and the Left in the Philippines* (New Haven, CT: Southeast Asia Council, Yale University, 2008), 25.
7 This argument about conflict is indebted to E.E. Schattschneider, *The Semi-Sovereign People: A Realist's View of Democracy in America*, intro. by David Adamany (Hinsdale, IL: Dreyden Press, 1975).
8 Carl H. Landé, "Brief History of Political Parties," in *Foundations and Dynamics of Filipino Government and Politics*, Jose Abueva and Raul de Guzman, eds. (Manila: Bookmark, 1969), 156, quoted in Paul D. Hutchcroft and Joel Rocamora, "Strong Demands and Weak Institutions," 4 (draft provided by courtesy of Dr. Rocamora); also *Journal of East Asian Studies* 3 (2003), 259–92.
9 Mina Roces, *The Lopez Family, 1946–2000: Kinship Politics in Postwar Philippines* (Manila: De La Salle University Press, 2001), 31. A much longer 2007 list of *trapo* clans is at http://en.wikipilipinas.org/index.php?title=Political_Dynasties#List_of_Political_Clans.
10 Mina Roces, *The Lopez Family*, 35–40. Since Marcos's demise, remaining members of his family have continued to fare well in electoral politics.
11 Kikuchi Yasushi, *Uncrystallized Philippine Society: A Social Anthropological Analysis* (Quezon City: New Day Publishers, 1991).
12 The cockfight and the Brahmana ordination ceremony provide contrasting options in a classic account of "culture" by Clifford Geertz, "Deep Play: Notes on the Balinese Cockfight," in *The Interpretation of Cultures* (New York: Basic Books, 1973), 412–53. To be sufficiently adaptable and useful to its adherents as new situations arise, "culture" must be inconsistent. Past experiences provide different "rational" choices of types of action, apt in different situations. Culture comprises diverse memories that shape—but do not wholly determine the use of—concepts of viable options.
13 Mina Roces, *The Lopez Family*, 86.
14 Ronald James May, *Vigilantes in the Philippines: From Fanatical Cults to Citizens' Organizations* (Honolulu: Center for Philippine Studies, University of Hawaii, 1992), 8, see also 29–30.
15 Raul Pertierra, *Religion, Politics, and Rationality in a Philippine Community* (Quezon City: Ateneo de Manila University Press, 1988), 66.
16 Ronald James May, *Vigilantes in the Philippines*, 12.
17 Soliman M. Santos, Jr. and Paz Verdades M. Santos, *Primed and Purposeful*, 188.
18 Wilfredo Magno Torres III, "Introduction," in *Rido: Clan Feuding and Conflict Management in Mindanao*, Torres III, ed. (Manila: Asia Foundation, 2007), 7.
19 Ronald James May, *Vigilantes in the Philippines*, 29.
20 Wilfredo Magno Torres III, *Rido*, 112.
21 Raul Pertierra, *Religion, Politics, and Rationality in a Philippine Community*, chapter 3, 59–76, quotations on 71.
22 Soliman M. Santos, Jr. and Paz Verdades M. Santos, *Primed and Purposeful*, 49.
23 See Manuel F. Martinez, *Assassinations and Conspiracies: From Rajah Humabon to Imelda Marcos*, and his second volume *More Assassinations and Conspiracies* (Manila: Anvil, 2003 and 2004 respectively).
24 See Frank Chavez, *Blighted!* (Mandaluyong: Primex Printers, Fairnews Media, 2009)—fiction based on "verified and verifiable corruptions," according to the preface.
25 This suggestion is explicit in a sarcastic blog, allegedly from an "honorable Filipino bureaucrat" in answers.yahoo.com [November 24, 2011].
26 Interview with a senior and well-informed Filipino source.
27 John T. Sidel, *Capital, Coercion, and Crime: Bossism in the Philippines* (Honolulu: University of Hawaii Press, 1999), 76, see also 53.
28 Sicilians do not have a copyright on such intellectual property. John T. Sidel, *Capital, Coercion, and Crime*, 77–8.

58 *Clan feuds localize the state*

29 Ronald James May, *Vigilantes in the Philippines*, 36.
30 *Time*, December 22, 1997, 20–2.
31 Alan Berlow, *Dead Season: A Story of Murder and Revenge on the Philippine Island of Negros* (New York: Pantheon, 1996).
32 Lawyers' Committee for Human Rights, *"Salvaging" Democracy: Human Rights in the Philippines* (New York: Lawyers' Committee, 1985), 1–2.
33 The data are from G. Sidney Silliman, "Human Rights and the Transition to Democracy," in *Patterns of Power and Politics in the Philippines*, James F. Eder and Robert L. Youngblood, eds. (Tempe, AZ: Arizona State University Program for Southeast Asian Studies, 1994), 107–9 and 114. Most of the Marcos killings were in the 1983–85 era, after the assassination of Benigno S. Aquino, Jr.
34 Karen Tiongson-Mayrina, "Ampatuan Clan is the Biggest Winner in May 2010 Polls," *GMA News*, July 18, 2010.
35 Compare Benedict Anderson, "Murder and Progress in Modern Siam," *New Left Review* 181 (1990), 33–48.
36 See the map in Edna Co, Nepomuceno Malaluan, Artur Neame, Marlon Manuel, and Miguel Rafael V. Musngi, *Philippine Democracy Assessment: Rule of Law and Access to Justice* (Quezon City: Action for Economic Reforms, 2010), 132.
37 Amando Doronila, *The State, Economic Transformation, and Political Change in the Philippines, 1946–1972* (Singapore: Oxford University Press, 1992), 85.
38 David Wurfel, "Elites of Wealth and Elites of Power: The Changing Dynamic," *Southeast Asian Affairs* (Singapore: Institute for Southeast Asian Studies, 1979), 233–49.
39 Yvonne Chua, "An Expensive—and Unaccountable—Legislature," March 22–24, 2004, pcij.org/stories/2004/congress2.html.
40 Compare Anon., "Philippine President Orders Disarming of 'Private Armies,'" *Agence France Presse*, January 25, 2007, 5, with Filemon V. Tutay, "Who Me?" Philippines Free Press editorial, February 5, 1972, http://philippinesfreepress.wordpress.com/2007/02/05/who-me-february-5-1972.
41 Nathan Gilbert Quimpo, *Contested Democracy and the Left in the Philippines* (New Haven, CT: Southeast Asia Council, Yale University, 2008), 188.
42 Paul D. Hutchcroft, "Philippines," in *Countries at the Crossroads: A Survey of Democratic Governance*, in Sanja Kelly, Christopher Walker, and Jake Dizard, eds. (Lanham, MD: Rowman & Littlefield, 1978), 519.
43 Details about many such groups are in Soliman M. Santos, Jr. and Paz Verdades M. Santos, *Primed and Purposeful*, 261–325. Moro and indigenous Mindanao groups are similarly treated on 327–418.
44 For more, see Francisco Lara, Jr. and Horacio Morales, Jr., "The Peasant Movement and the Challenge of Democratization," in *The Challenge of Rural Democratization: Perspectives from Latin America and the Philippines*, Jonathan Fox, ed. (London: Frank Cass, 1990), 148.
45 G. Sydney Silliman, "Human Rights and the Transition to Democracy," 129–31.
46 Glenda Gloria, "Estrada and Associates Monopolize Gambling," Philippine Center for Investigative Journalism, www.pcij.org/stories/print/gamblingg2.html, 2000, contains many details.
47 Interview with Voltaire C. Garcia, December 17, 2010, and other sources.
48 Benjie Villa, "Street-Smart Girl, 9, Puts One Over Her Kidnappers," *Philippine Star*, January 13, 2000, www.philstar.com/headlines/86790.
49 Ronald James May, *Vigilantes in the Philippines*, 19–21.
50 Ronald James May, *Vigilantes in the Philippines*, 58.
51 This "Christian" KKK did not harken back to the Klu Klux Klan, but instead to the Kataas-taasang Kagaland-galangang Katipunan ng mga Anak ng Bayan (or just Katipunan), the 1892 secret society aiming at first for independence from Spain. On this twentieth century KKK, see Ronald James May, *Vigilantes in the Philippines*, 33.

52 On earlier intentional revolutionaries, see Reynaldo Ileto, *Pasyón and Revolution: Popular Movements in the Philippines, 1840–1910* (Quezon City: Ateneo de Manila University Press, 1979).
53 Ronald James May, *Vigilantes in the Philippines*, 2 and 14.
54 Soliman M. Santos, Jr. and Paz Verdades M. Santos, *Primed and Purposeful*, 198.
55 "Police, Military Vow Dismantling of Remaining 107 Private Armies," *Manila Times*, August 5, 2010, 6.
56 Jaime Laude, "Army Captain in Pickpocket Ring," *Philippine Star*, January 14, 2000, www.philstar.com/headlines/86802.
57 Edith Regalado, "Rival Mining Firms in Diwalwal Clash, 15 Injured," *Philippine Star*, January 14, 2000, www.philstar.com/headlines/86812.
58 Quoted from *National Midweek*, June 6, 1990, 36, in Robin Broad and John Cavanaugh, *Plundering Paradise: The Struggle for the Environment in the Philippines* (Berkeley, CA: University of California Press, 1993), 104.
59 Interview with an official in Manila who requested anonymity, August 2010.
60 See www.philstar.com/subcategory.aspx of November 16, 2010.
61 Agence France Presse, "Three Dead in Pampanga Ambush," August 4, 2013, also *Philippine Inquirer*, http://newsinfo.inquirer.net/458473.
62 Associated Press, "7 Killed in Lanao Clan War," *Philippine Star*, July 22, 2013, www.philstar.com/headlines/2013/07/22/997121.
63 Alfred W. McCoy, "An Anarchy of Families," 22.
64 Jaime Laude, "AFP Seeks NPA Supplier of AK-47s," *Philippine Star*, July 12, 2013 www.philstar.com/headlines/2013/07/12/964721.
65 Soliman M. Santos, Jr. and Paz Verdades M. Santos, *Primed and Purposeful*, 151–4, also quotation on 177.
66 Soliman M. Santos, Jr. and Paz Verdades M. Santos, *Primed and Purposeful*, 186, refers to a study in the middle of the first decade of the century. The oddly specific estimate of unregistered guns is on p. 204.
67 Alan Berlow, *Dead Season*, 171.
68 Cecille Suerte Felipe, "Noy Promotes 2 Hero Cops, Distributes Glock Pistols," *Philippine Star*, July 3, 2013, www.philstar.com/headlines/2013/07/03/960998.
69 Soliman M. Santos, Jr. and Paz Verdades M. Santos, *Primed and Purposeful*, 232.
70 Jaime Laude, "Solon's Cousin in Shooting Rampage," *Philippine Star*, January 10, 2000, www.philstar.com/headlines/86740.
71 Cecille Suerte Felipe, "New Law on Gun Control to Take Effect in September," *Philippine Star*, July 27, 2013, www.philstar.com/headlines/2013/07/27/1018291.
72 Cecille Suerte Filipe, "Ozamis Gang Paid Off Cops" and "PNP Sees Rubout in Ozamiz Slay," *Philippine Star*, July 19 and 24, 2013, www.philstar.com/headlines/2013/07/19/987331 and www.philstar.com/headlines/2013/07/24/1005861.
73 See Jose V. Abueva (former UP president), *Towards a Nonkilling Filipino Society: Developing an Agenda for Research, Policy, and Action* (Riverbanks, Marikina: Aurora Aragon Quezon Peace Foundation and Kalayaan College, 2004).
74 Soliman M. Santos, Jr. and Paz Verdades M. Santos, *Primed and Purposeful*, 18–19.
75 Soliman M. Santos, Jr. and Paz Verdades M. Santos, *Primed and Purposeful*, 46–8.
76 This accusation against Arroyo is unconfirmed, and other parties could also have been interested in killing Llamas. Presidential involvement has been rumored in other murders too (notably in the case of President Marcos and the killing of Beningo S. Aquino, Jr.), Soliman M. Santos, Jr. and Paz Verdades M. Santos, *Primed and Purposeful*, 51.
77 "AFP Launches Human Rights Book," *Philippine Star*, December 18, 2010, 5.
78 Xinhua, "AFT Admits to 7 Human Rights Violations in H1," *Philippine Star*, July 11, 2013, www.philstar.com/headlines/2013/07/11/964437.
79 *Philippine Star*, December 18, 2010, seen that day.

80 Soliman M. Santos, Jr. and Paz Verdades M. Santos, *Primed and Purposeful*, 199–202, quotation on 202.
81 "A Fragile Peace," *Economist*, 430:8872 (February 1, 2014), 33–4.
82 Justin V. Hastings, "Strategic Hypocrisy," in *Democratization in China, Korea, and Southeast Asia? Local and National Perspectives*, Kate Zhou, Shelley Rigger, and Lynn White, eds. (Abingdon: Routledge, 2014), is based mainly on evidence from Borneo/Kalimantan but also addresses adjacent islands in the Philippines. See also Maria A. Ressa, *Seeds of Terror: An Eyewitness Account of Al-Qaeda's Newest Center of Operations in Southeast Asia* (New York: Free Press, 2003).
83 Soliman M. Santos, Jr. and Paz Verdades M. Santos, *Primed and Purposeful*, 216–24, quotation 220, also 198, and 143–5.
84 Soliman M. Santos, Jr. and Paz Verdades M. Santos, *Primed and Purposeful*, quotations on 216. The current author, buying pants at a Sears store in New Jersey in 2011, noticed that the cashier spoke with a Philippine accent. She said she was from Abra. He mentioned reports of violence there. Yes, she said, an unknown man had been shot dead just the previous month directly in front of her family's Abra home. Such rumors are anecdotal, but even the statistics are incomplete.
85 Alan Berlow, *Dead Season*, 195.
86 Soliman M. Santos, Jr. and Paz Verdades M. Santos, *Primed and Purposeful*, 223.
87 Reinir Padua, "Abra Man Admits Involvement in Bursamin Ambush," *Philippine Star*, July 10, 2013, www.philstar.com/headlines/2013/07/10/963696.
88 Kent Eaton, "Restoration or Transformation: *Trapos* vs. NGOs in the Democratization of the Philippines," *Journal of Asian Studies* 62:2 (May 2003), 487, also 476 and 481.
89 James Clad, *Behind the Myth: Business, Money, and Power in Southeast Asia* (London: Hyman, 1989), 30–1.
90 Brian Fegan, "Entrepreneurs in Votes and Violence: Three Generations of a Peasant Political Family," in *An Anarchy of Families*, 49.
91 Anon., "Democracy as Showbiz," *Economist*, July 1, 2004.
92 Eric U. Gutierrez, Ildefonso Torrente, and Noli G. Narca, *All in the Family: A Study of Elites and Power Relations in the Philippines* (Quezon City: Institute for Popular Democracy, 1992), graphs on 34, 46, 57, 67, 98, 108, 116, 124, 132, 141, and 161 report the portions of votes for these posts that went to candidates who were (and were not) either old-clan incumbents or their kin. The Eastern Visayas saw new candidates do better than most other parts of the country (including the Central and Western Visayas) in the mid-1980s, but this may have been a temporary post-Marcos reaction against Romualdez influences. The "Yellow" (pro-Cory Aquino) complexion of candidates in other parts of the country apparently had no statistical effect on whether they won or not. In any case, by 1995 Imelda Romualdez Marcos was back in Congress representing her Visayan birthplace in Leyte—and, by 2010, she was elected yet again, that time representing the second district of Ilocos Norte. Her daughter Imee Marcos (whom this author knew when she was a student at Princeton) won the Ilocos Norte provincial governorship.
93 Eric U. Gutierrez, Ildefonso Torrente, and Noli G. Narca, *All in the Family*, 5.
94 Renato S. Velasco, "Does the Philippine Congress Promote Democracy?" in *Democratization: Philippine Perspectives*, Felipe V. Miranda, ed. (Quezon City: University of the Philippines Press, 1997), 290.
95 Jeffrey M. Riedinger, *Agrarian Reform in the Philippines: Democratic Transitions and Redistributive Reform* (Stanford, CA: Stanford University Press, 1995), 115.
96 Renato S. Velasco, "Does the Philippine Congress Promote Democracy?" 290.
97 Sheila S. Coronel, Yvonne Chua, Luz Rimban, and Booma Cruz, *The Rulemakers: How the Wealthy and Well-Born Dominate Congress* (Quezon City: Philippine Center for Investigative Journalism, 2004), quoted in Satur C. Ocampo, "Political Dynasties Still Dominate Congress," *Philippine Star*, October 1, 2011, www.philstar.com/subcategory.aspx.

98 John A. Larkin, "Philippine History Reconsidered: A Socioeconomic Perspective," *American Historical Review* 87:3 (1982), 619, is cited in Jeffrey A. Winters, *Oligarchy* (New York: Cambridge University Press, 2011), 197.
99 Eric Guttierrez, *The Ties that Bind: A Guide on Family, Business, and Other Interests in the 9th House of Representatives* (Pasig City: Philippine Center for Investigative Journalism, 1994).
100 Sheila S. Coronel, "How Representative is Congress?" *Manila Times* website, March 22, 2004, www.manilatimes.net/others/special/2004/mar/22/20040322spel.html.
101 Ashutosh Varshney, *Democracy, Development, and the Countryside: Urban–Rural Struggles in India* (New York: Cambridge University Press, 1998).
102 Ashutosh Varshney, *Democracy, Development, and the Countryside*, 192.
103 Julio C. Teehankee, "Electoral Politics in the Philippines," in *Electoral Politics in Southeast and East Asia*, Aurel Crossant and Marei John, eds. (Bonn: Fiedrich-Ebert-Siftung, 2002), 195.
104 Karen Tiongson-Mayrina and Allan Vallarta, "Clans Still Rule in 14th House but Fewer in Ranks," www.gmanews.tv, June 28, 2007.
105 Personal communication from Prof. Tuazon, November 23, 2011. His Center for People Empowerment in Governance also noted that two-thirds of the House was still *trapo*, if party list delegates are included.
106 Mario B. Casayuran, "Political Dynasty: Relevant or Not?" and "No Need for Bill Against Political Dynasty?" *Manila Bulletin*, July 30 and 31, 2013, http://mb.com.ph/News/Main_News/24641 and 24813.
107 On other indices (government effectiveness, regulatory quality, rule of law, and control of corruption), the Philippines showed no statistically significant *change* on these indices from 1998 to 2008, and it was relatively low. See http://papers.ssrn.com/sol3.papers.cfm?abstractt_id=1424591 [October 29, 2010].
108 Arsenio Balisacan, "Poverty and Inequality," in *The Philippine Economy: Development, Policies, and Challenges*, Arsenio Balisacan and Hal Hill, eds. (Manila: Ateneo De Manila University Press, 2003), 311–41.
109 The reluctance of many American individuals to abjure rights of gun ownership is well documented. Actually, the U.S. Constitution's Second Amendment has more state-communal aspects than U.S. courts admit; it says that "a well regulated militia" is "necessary to the security of a free state." The current author has been struck, in conversations with contemporary mainland Chinese, especially entrepreneurs, that some claim China would be better if a greater variety of agents (not just the Communist Party) had control of guns.
110 Edmund Burke, *Reflections on the Revolution in France*, paragraph 75 (seen at Bartleby.com, available in many sources).
111 The U.S. Constitution, especially in its Ninth Amendment, suggests a similar claim: "The enumeration in the Constitution, of certain rights, shall not be construed to deny or disparage others retained by the people." This is difficult to enforce because words such as "certain," "disparage," and "people" are purposely vague. But this and the Tenth Amendment say that national sovereignty is not the only kind; more local polities are legitimate too.
112 Eric U. Gutierrez, Ildefonso Torrente, and Noli G. Narca, *All in the Family*, 11–12.

4   Entrepreneurs as politicians

Industry was not a hallmark of Spain's Asian colony, or of America's. In post-independence years, the "regnant model of development alleged that the Philippines' comparative advantage was in the export of minerals and tropical agricultural products."[1] Industry was largely devoted to processing plantation crops. Commerce and services employed some people but took relatively little capital. On this limited basis, the Philippines once had a boom. Between 1949 and 1960, manufacturing production more than tripled, growing from 9 to 18 percent of national income. Most of the products, except from plantations or mines, were sold domestically.[2]

Who led this growth? A study that was confined to entrepreneurs with Philippine citizenship found they had "somewhat more Western and Chinese ancestry" than most Filipinos. Their non-Filipino forbears had immigrated earlier than the grandparental generation. Fully 61 percent of these entrepreneurs were Tagalog (as determined by the first language they learned in childhood—whereas just 19 percent of the nation's population at that time was Tagalog in that sense). Another 15 percent were Pampangan (whereas just 3 percent of the whole population was Pampangan). None of the other Philippine languages, as differentiated by academic linguists, accounted for more than 8 percent of the entrepreneurs.[3] Most of these sampled managers were in small and medium businesses; founders of large industries and plantations were fewer and more often foreign. The survey nonetheless shows the extent to which basic-level entrepreneurship was confined to the Tagalog area, in and around Manila.

Businessmen and businesswomen of this kind mostly got their start as rentiers, and they were a tiny portion of the whole country's population. Surprisingly many of the entrepreneurs reported in the mid-1960s that the first Western language they had learned was Spanish rather than English—although just 2 percent of the Philippine population in that period could still speak Spanish. Most Philippine entrepreneurs were from landed gentry families, and most grew up in or near Manila although their clan land might be far away. Some were urban Chinese–Filipinos. Especially for the others, rent money from inherited land was important along with entrepreneurship in making the contexts from which they started businesses.

A disproportionate number of entrepreneurs have hailed from specific towns not far from Manila. Malabon and Marikina in Rizal, or Meycauayan in Bulacan, for example, are close to railway lines that lead into the capital's markets. Regional variance in entrepreneurs' backgrounds was notable; the best study of this topic suggested that most Pampanga entrepreneurs were not "from landowning or milling families."[4] Entrepreneurship in that province north of Manila may have tended to come more from personal initiatives of the business people than from the availability of land-rent capital, relative to entrepreneurship that developed in other districts, even those nearer to the capital.

Some regions, such as the Ilocano area, are affected by wind patterns so that no rain falls for as many as five months in the year. Crops do not grow easily in that period, and people seek other occupations. In the central Visayas, by contrast, rain comes in all seasons. Rice can be double-cropped at least.[5] Such differences affect modal activities. Large industries other than agricultural processing are particularly scarce in the Visayas—and in most of the country outside the provinces near Manila.

Regional stereotypes are overgeneralizations that nonetheless last over long periods in many countries.[6] An anthropologist opined that, "The Ilocanos are very hard working; the Tagalogs are supposed to be intensely nationalistic; the Visayans are thought to be more internationally minded and are more prone to spend their money on dress and other visual evidence of affluence." Are Pampangans really more entrepreneurial, as they are sometimes reported to be, than Bicolanos who were arguably more influenced by conservative Spanish models of nobility? "Most of these stereotypes have a certain amount of truth and a good deal of fallaciousness."[7]

Economic startups may correlate geographically with revolutionary dissidence. Cavite and Batangas, which are now centers of entrepreneurialism just south of Manila, were at the turn of the twentieth century (from 1896 to 1905) sites of especially strong resistance against Spanish and then American rule.[8] Forming businesses and engaging in politics have correlated. In Pampanga, north of Manila, landowning classes faced electoral challenges in the 1930s and "full-scale agrarian revolt ... in Pampanga between 1946 and 1953."

> There is, in fact, a long tradition of social unrest in Pampanga, and we hear that as far back as 1660 "the people of Pampanga, driven to desperation by the repeated demands of the shipyards on their labor and by the continued inability of the government to pay for the goods it requisitioned, rose in revolt."[9]

Perhaps in part because of labor unrest, enterprises in sectors that need many employees tend not to be industrial. A "trader's mentality" dominates; most business people stay away from manufacturing. Factories often require more capital. In some sectors, they require the hiring of male workers who in practice demand higher wages than women can. The pro-labor Jesuit sociologist John Carroll found, however, that a disproportionately large number of former manufacturers—craftsmen and others—have entered craftlike industries which are relatively stable in their technology and have little need for engineers or research. Shoemaking and printing are probably the best examples ... there seems to have been considerable pressure on those who did begin with light processing and packaging operations, including many former merchants, for "backward integration" into somewhat more basic production.[10]

Many of the manufacturing entrepreneurs had already become rich from agriculture or logging. They were in land-based industries before they moved into fields such as "plywood, chemical, and cement manufacture,... they began their enterprises at a relatively sophisticated technological level, and their main drive is for expansion rather than for technological change."

The Philippines' 1950s temporary boom, to the extent it occurred, was largely in processing. GNP grew at 7.7 percent annually in the first half of that decade, with manufactures (which included the processing of agricultural products) growing at 12 percent. This high rate was aided by U.S. grants while Manila was fighting a communist rebellion in central Luzon. During the second half of the 1950s, total growth fell to 4.9 percent annually (and, for manufactures and processed goods, to 7.7 percent). The processing enterprises often employed heavy machinery rather than many workers. This situation was combined with patriotic policies of import-substitution and restrictions on Chinese in business, as well as Catholic support for high birth rates. The result was stagnant income per capita, even as the economy grew somewhat.[11] After a peak in 1961, later years of that decade all saw lower GDP levels per person.[12]

Agricultural processors and other industrialists had diverging interests. Two loose national coalitions conflicted politically from the 1950s. A "sugar bloc" sold to the U.S. under post-colonial (still semi-colonial) "free trade" arrangements. These processors wanted maximal free entry of American manufactures to the Philippines in order to justify politically their market share for agricultural exports to the U.S. But import-substituting industrialists wanted patriotic protection of Philippine products; so they favored tariffs, an overvalued peso, and rice imports that lowered food prices and were an implicit subsidy to the wages they paid to workers.[13] Neither the agricultural exporters nor the industrial protectionists showed much interest in exploring new technologies to create new sectors.

Foreign economists' predictions of Philippine growth were exceedingly hopeful. The World Bank in 1957 proclaimed that, "the basic economic position of the Philippines is favourable ... it has achieved a position in the Far East second only to Japan, both in respect to its level of literacy and to per capita production capacity."[14] These economists ignored the influence on the economy of local political factors. So their crystal balls were flat wrong. In 1960, the democratic Philippines was still widely seen as the most "advanced" country in the Far East outside Japan. (Half a century later, another group of economists remained almost as negligent of local factors, especially those that are difficult to quantify.)[15]

By the middle of the 1960s, the situation had changed. Philippine growth had slowed. The U.S. boycott of sugar from Castro's Cuba chased rice off arable Philippine land; so the archipelago soon became a rice importer. Yet sugar and other crops were increasingly processed by machines; so Philippine workers were chased off too. These evolutions might not have been disastrous—similar phenomena have occurred in many industrializing nations—except that the Philippines lacked enough entrepreneurs to set up firms that might have absorbed the ex-agricultural workers.

What kind of economic growth benefits most Filipinos? It is growth that increases the number of jobs in which they can raise their skill levels. Capital-intensive agricultural industries do this for relatively few workers. Small industrial and commercial firms collectively hire many more people. A Cornell economist in the 1960s hoped that,

> Those seeking encouragement in the Philippine scene must take comfort in signs that the entrepreneurial class as a competing political elite promises to displace the heretofore dominant reactionary *rentier* class. Filipino entrepreneurship is distinctively Filipino in its propensity to seek advantage through political institutions and processes. At the same time, this element in the society is the potential nucleus to which middle class elements—the bureaucracy, teachers, professional groups—may adhere in seeking political power.[16]

Fifty years later, the optimist discourse had changed only somewhat, as the strength of rentiers in the islands' political economy declined slowly. Too few Filipinos ventured the risks of founding industries or other firms that could hire workers. It is also possible that too many of the potential hires sought easy rides, although research on that latter point has not been done. The entrepreneurs who did found firms were disproportionately from the Chinese–Philippine minority that still felt some discrimination, especially when its businesses needed to have debts paid.

The long-term shortage of entrepreneurs had political correlates. Many scholars have asked whether the existence of a middle-income group is helpful to democratization. The eventual but not immediate answer to that question is almost surely yes. The middle-income group has been, during the Philippines' recent periods of some growth, a minority between rich elites and proletarians. Democracy requires a combination of rights for minorities with other decisions taken for the majority. So threats to democracy can come from either extreme, usually conceived as rich and poor. Too much power for either can overwhelm the other.

Yet if enough of the people are in the middle, they can join with a small rich elite to help maintain a system's integrity, or alternatively they can join with mass movements to push for an enlargement of justice. They are flexible and react to circumstances. A sizeable middle-income group, whether or not it is conscious as a "class," helps establish deliberative balance in a system, against either old monarchs or new demagogues. Aristotle first put forth this idea in his book on *Politics*, and Pareto and others have expanded that paradigm by describing leaderships of these social classes.[17] In the Philippines, the middle group is small. As this bourgeoisie becomes larger it may for a while support authoritarian demagogues rather than liberal democrats (as traders did under leaders like Marcos or the Shah in Iran).[18] In the long run, however, its interests lie in the economic stability that market liberalism, a reliable judiciary, and electoral legitimacy can promote.

Small economic organizations particularly support democratization. Their entrepreneurs need links to local government representatives who enforce or neglect regulations over them. But in the Philippines, small and medium enterprises (SMEs) are less important economically than in other countries with similar levels of wealth per capita. Large plantations have dominated production in Philippine crop-based industries such as sugar and coconut oil, whose processing and marketing requires considerable capital. Philippine SMEs participate in both the domestic and export economies even less than do the SMEs of other Asian economies, e.g., China's or Thailand's.

For whatever reasons, the Philippines did less well economically in the late twentieth century than several comparable Southeast Asian countries. From 1980 to 1985, the Thai economy grew at 5.1 percent annually, whereas the Philippine rate was negative, at –0.5 percent.[19] If a longer time period is considered, in the three decades after 1975, Philippine real GDP grew just 3.5 percent annually. Yearly population increase was 2 percent.[20] Living standards for Filipinos scarcely budged.

Entrepreneurs: Chinese and Filipino

By no means are all entrepreneurs on the archipelago "foreign," although many are resident ethnic Chinese. Temario Rivera finds "a long tradition of political leadership that distinguishes the landed capitalist segment of the manufacturing bourgeoisie from its newer non-landed corporate segment and Chinese-Filipino component."[21] Many wealthy businesspeople are "Tsinoy," i.e., Filipino-Chinese; they have had their own Chamber of Commerce and Industry and later similar organizations. Others, such as the Ayalas, are "Kastilaloy," from Spanish-Castilian (actually often Basque) or Spanish-Mexican family origins; and they join the Makati Business Club.[22] Tension has been occasional between these two elites, and its effect on Filipino-Chinese willingness to take investment risks is difficult to ascertain. Philippine leftist intellectuals, including some who are themselves partly Chinese by ancestry while downplaying that situation, have occasionally connived with a kind of nationalist racism even though it probably hurts the national economy. The small self-identifying Chinese and ancestrally part-Chinese group in the Philippines provides local services and subcontracting that are important for growth (similar entrepreneurs have run such firms in Thailand, Indonesia, and Malaysia, as well as Taiwan and China where they are not minorities).

Local and national government factors are important, along with ethnic factors, in promoting or discouraging entrepreneurial startups. Business people relate to official regulators at any size of polity, and politicians identify variously with managers and with farmers. Rural Filipinos who are not rich potentially have plenty of voting power to influence governments whose leaders are elected. Ashutosh Varshney argues from Indian evidence that when democracy precedes industry in a country, rural people can be strengthened despite the importance of urban wealth. Voters are mostly peasants, in any low- or medium-income economy. So state policies might naturally favor the countryside over cities, when economic rather than identity interests motivate voters. But non-economic identity interests—religious, regional, or caste loyalties—limit the unity of rural power.

Surprisingly few studies of Varshney's kind have been conducted, partly because "democracies" have often been defined as countries that must maintain stable electoral systems over time, with parties alternating in executive power uninterrupted by martial law. A contrast between India and the Philippines is that some of New Delhi's politicians during the first half century of Indian independence, including some members of parliament, have come from low-income (and "low" caste) rural backgrounds. Two-fifths of Lok Sabha members report that their main family occupation is agriculture. These do not spend most of their time tilling fields, but they reportedly self-identify with rural work as well as with the ethnic interests of their voters.[23] Most Philippine politicians, though not all, come from very rich families, often rentier when rural.

Every nation in the modern world, according to Barrington Moore, needs some group to accumulate capital. Otherwise, the country becomes weak and by Darwinian logic is subsumed into others. So the development of regime types depends on the way in which the capital-accumulating group (bourgeois, aristocratic, or communist) relates to the state. Early democracies, such as England, France, or America despite their differences, were led by bourgeois capitalists that evolved liberal regimes, either absorbing major non-bourgeois classes (e.g., aristocrats in England, peasants in France) or sweeping them aside (e.g., English peasants, French nobles). These nations had capitalist revolutions.

Countries with strong aristocracies and weak bourgeoisies, such as Germany or Japan, had "revolutions from above" led by old landed families. They flirted with the democratic regime type, but then they created expansionist dictatorships (until these were defeated in war). But this was just one of the authoritarian regime types, in Moore's view.

The third main itinerary to a regime-type that he describes was followed by Russia and China, whose state bureaucracies generally restrained the role of bourgeois entrepreneurs in modern strengthening. Peasants and workers could be organized by a few revolutionaries to seize power in these centralized states, creating communist regimes.[24]

Moore's paradigm logically allows further cases beyond these three. In the Philippines, for many decades there has been no bourgeois dominance over landed elites, no lasting creation of a unified dictatorship by landed aristocrats, no cohesive organization of the peasantry, and a perennially weak state. Relatively delayed development has ensued, rather than an objectively full social revolution either "from above" or "from below."[25] Sociopolitical change in the Philippines has tended, at least until recent times, to be relatively glacial.

Two "cultural" reasons for this slowness are commonly dismissed by social scientists who point out that "culture" is a concept broad enough to explain almost any social phenomenon. A first posited reason for a lack of development hastiness is discrimination against Chinese entrepreneurs such as have run most Southeast Asian economies. A second is the Philippine tradition of existential respect among males, who sometimes interpret their marketed service as slavery that insults them; so they avoid selling themselves regardless of the wage.

"Race-based interpretations of development" may ignore three factors.[26] First, when governments or cultures channel ethnic minorities into some kinds of livelihood while forbidding others, it is unsurprising that ambitious members of the channeled groups excel in those sectors. A famous example was the dominance of Jews in early European banking, when churches forbade Christians from lending money to each other at interest. Another example arose on Taiwan when the authoritarian Kuomintang under Chiang Kai-shek steered ambitious Taiwanese to try for wealth in small businesses so that they would not try for power in the government or military, which were for many years dominated by mainlanders rather than Taiwanese. Yet another occurred under the British, French, and Dutch regimes of Southeast Asia that allowed Chinese to immigrate and go into business. This account of some minorities' entrepreneurship points to external, structural incentives that ethnic groups faced, without considering the reasons for them taking up (or ignoring) such incentives.

A second objection to culture-based explanations of Chinese enterprise is that not all Chinese are alike. Some are demonstrably non-entrepreneurial. Many of these may have self-selected not to emigrate from China. More research could be done on the stay-at-homes. Many families in identifiable areas of Fujian or Guangdong during the nineteenth century, for example, did not send members to make money abroad. But once in Southeast Asia, the lineages and towns that sent people to cities like Manila tended to prosper, and local cultures of entrepreneurship grew in these emigrant communities.

A third objection points to the notable number of unprosperous Southeast Asian Chinese. Their rich cousins are very prominent but do not typify the whole Chinese diaspora. Some Chinese families in the Philippines (and other Southeast Asian countries) lead lives fairly similar to those of non-immigrants in the same places. Still, ownership of firms in the archipelago is disproportionately Chinese-Filipino.

This situation, even after Spanish discriminations against *sangleys* and American discriminations against Chinese, has led Philippine patriots to restrict both ownership rights and access to citizenship. "Dual allegiance of citizens is inimical to the national interest and shall be dealt with by law," according to Article IV, Section 5 of the current 1987 Constitution, which is like its predecessor on this point. In 1954, after the sweeping victory of Magsaysay's Nacionalista-Democratic coalition in Congress, apparently patriotic lawmakers presented bills to "nationalize" commerce.

Mayor Arsenio Lacson of Manila said, "We have come to meekly accept as inevitable the control of our domestic trade by the Chinese, our foreign trade by the Japanese soon, and our foreign policy by the Americans."[27] Congress passed a law that barred any new "alien" (including resident non-citizens) from owning stores. It provided for the liquidation within ten years of any retail partnership or corporation that was not wholly owned by Filipinos, and it prohibited alien heirs from buying land and from operating most firms. This Retail Trade Nationalization Act was not implemented efficiently. Chinese immigrants without Philippine citizenship could sometimes pay bribes for its non-enforcement. But the main effect was to inhibit or close small and medium provincial enterprises that resident Chinese had founded.

President Carlos Garcia (1957–61) continued this "Filipino First" policy.[28] Chinese could not easily get Philippine citizenship even if they had been born in the country. Small and medium enterprises were less often established in the Philippines. From 1956 to 1962, when Philippine overall growth was higher than in later periods, small firms' value-added *fell* 5.4 percent annually, while larger companies' value-added rose 10.0 percent per year.[29]

The Supreme Court in *Ichong* v. *Hernandez* (1957) upheld the Retail Trade Nationalization Act, opining that:

> Freedom and liberty are not real and positive if the people are subject to the economic control and domination of others, especially if not of their own race [*sic*] or country. The removal and eradication of the shackles of foreign economic control and domination is one of the noblest motives that a national legislature may pursue. It is impossible to conceive that legislation that seeks to bring it about can infringe on the constitutional limitation of due process.[30]

The law would not have presented Philippine-Chinese entrepreneurs with much problem if they could easily have become naturalized. The Philippine Constitution uses a *jus sanguinis* (law of blood) criterion, so that simply being born in the Philippines does not qualify a person for citizenship. From the 1940s through the late 1960s, only a few hundred Chinese were naturalized per year. Marcos, after his decree of martial law, changed this pattern by issuing a presidential decision that lowered the financial and language requirements for citizenship. In the 1970s, about 38,000 Chinese heads of households became legal Filipinos.[31]

The Federation of Filipino-Chinese Chambers of Commerce and Industry had been founded with the aim of countervailing the effects of the Retail Trade Nationalization Act. This commercial organization became the most prominent representative of self-identifying Chinese on the archipelago. Most Chinese-Filipinos prior to Marcos's decree still did not have and could not get local citizenship, even though their wealth gave them political clout. The Federation was closely aligned with Taipei. It had supported Diosdado Macapagal, Marcos's opponent in his first presidential election. But Ralph Nubla of the Chinese Tobacco Association and Chinese Textile Association had endorsed Marcos. The Federation, having bet on the wrong presidential horse, soon made Nubla its head because of his close links to the new president in Malacañang.[32] (A similar shift of loyalty among Chinese businesspeople occurred after Cory Aquino's victory, when the Chinese business group quickly elected her friend Domingo Lee as its president.) Chinese-Filipinos continued to suffer from Garcia-era restrictions until the early 1970s, when Marcos recruited them and their money by relaxing citizenship laws. Their enterprises quickly expanded. Marcos once remarked, "I have Chinese blood in me.... I am not ashamed to admit that perhaps the great leaders of our country all have Chinese blood."[33]

When Marcos in 1972 declared martial law, the army temporarily jailed and interrogated Nubla's successor as Federation president, Antonio Roxas Chua. But Marcos met Nubla and wanted Chinese-Filipino backing for his declaration of martial law. The Federation's board passed a motion of "unqualified support" of Marcos's legal basis for dictatorship—and then Chua was freed.[34] After this, the rate of Chinese kidnappings in the Philippines decreased for a while.

Marcos's wife Imelda led a trade delegation to Beijing in 1974. By the next year, Marcos himself went there to establish diplomatic relations with the People's Republic. Taipei was predictably furious, but Filipino-Chinese were told that Beijing wanted them to become Philippine citizens—and Marcos encouraged this process. The Chinese business federation's political functions shifted to a new organization, the Kaisa Para sa Kaunlaran.[35] After April 1975, when Marcos issued his presidential decree to expand Chinese-Filipinos' opportunities for naturalization, about three-quarters of the federation's members applied to become Filipinos under the new rules. Within the next five years, about two-thirds of their applications were approved.[36] The approval process was thus rather slow, and it is unclear the extent to which it required bribes. President Corazon Cojuangco Aquino did not reverse this Marcos policy toward Filipino-Chinese. As her maiden name made clear to everyone, she herself was mestiza (although many elites with less obviously Chinese family names are also mestizo). Past policies of discrimination against Filipino-Chinese, under the Spanish, American, and then independent Philippine regimes, have been slowly reduced. These had major effects on small enterprises, which could become large after their foundings. For larger companies, further policies were needed.

East Asia has generated at least two major "development models" for major industries, and neither of them has been extensively used in the Philippines. One, of which Japan and South Korea are the main exemplars, relies on central state guidance of large private enterprises, especially to promote exports. The other, which Taiwan and parts of east and south China best exemplify, especially allows nonstate small and medium enterprises to flourish.

The first pattern was an ideal of Marcos, one of his many concepts that he did or could not implement. He and his so-called "cronies" proved too inefficient or corrupt to make it work as it did in Japan or Korea. And Filipinos have scarcely tried to adopt the second, more labor intensive of the two models, relying more on SMEs. The entrepreneurialism of this second gambit would require new kinds of nonstate leaders in many parts of the country. Current local chiefs did not change their self-images and use their considerable capital to go into business. Modernized *hidalgo* norms may explain, along with situational factors, why this has not happened over many decades. The professions—lawyers, doctors, engineers, and teachers—were prestigious in both the Spanish and American colonial periods. These callings attracted away from entrepreneurial risk-taking many scions of ambitious families that started with wealth from rural processing or land rents.[37] Professional commitments relate to ethnic self-identifications.

People with both Chinese and Philippine ancestry, as well as others, have headed large companies. John Sidel argues that the Philippines, like Thailand, has successfully assimilated local Chinese.[38] There are some differences of degree. The process in both countries began centuries ago, but part-Chinese people in Thailand have more often identified openly with their Chinese ancestors than in the Philippines. Legal assimilation of immigrants in the archipelago is largely a matter of recent decades. In Thailand, open toleration of Chineseness is more common; and politicians there, who are mostly Sino-Thais, advertise their ancestries more often than Sino-Philippine politicians do.[39]

The percentages also differ; self-identifying Chinese have been estimated at just 1.2 percent of the Philippine population, while low estimates for Thailand are about 14 percent (and a majority in Bangkok). More than half of Filipino-Chinese live in Metro Manila. Most such families long ago adopted the Roman Catholic religion. Chinese-Filipinos report they are 70 percent Catholic, 13 percent Protestant, and only 2 percent Buddhist. At home, they normally speak Tagalog or English, not Chinese languages. Many have names that do not sound Chinese, although on the basis surnames and other traits many Filipinos guess which of their neighbors have Chinese ancestors. Now over 70 percent of Filipino-Chinese who acquire citizenship do so by having a citizen parent, usually a mother.[40]

"To the question 'Who are the new rich?' most Filipinos respond that they are the Chinese. Many Filipino-Chinese say the same."[41] "Social distance" surveys indicate that people of Chinese background are regarded by other Filipinos as "business-minded, good in mathematics, rich, industrious, thrifty ... exploiters, abusive employers, shrewd businessmen, and tax evaders ... economic animals."[42] Many Filipinos say Chinese control the Philippine national economy. Gen. Jose Almonte in the 1990s claimed that,

> Our so-called Taipans ... can pay our indebtedness, and that is about $30 billion. That's a lot of money. Now, it's all right if this was acquired through means acceptable to the national community, but they were not, and we must get them to show a greater responsibility to the community.... The problem of insurgency is no longer in the mountains of the Sierra Madres and the Cordillera but in the boardrooms of Binondo [Manila's Chinatown] and Makati.[43]

Entrepreneurs as politicians

Resentment against rich business groups, in the West notably Jews, is nothing new in politics. Surprisingly many intellectuals, and a less surprising portion of others, can find no border between patriotism and racism.

The heads of the five richest families in the Philippines during the new millennium all had Chinese surnames. They were, in order of wealth according to *Forbes* researchers: Henry Sy, Lucio Tan, Andrew Tan, Enrique Razon, Jr., and John Gokongwei. The sixth richest was "Jimmy" Ayala, whose family was established long ago by Latino immigrants. The richest major Philippine politician on the *Forbes* list was former senator Manuel Villar, only at sixteenth place.[44]

By 2000, a Constitutional Reform for Development ("Concord") proposal aimed to increase foreign investment by relaxing the constitutional ban against non-Filipinos' ownership of more than 40 percent of any company in utilities, media, education, or resources. But the mainly non-Chinese Makati Business Club liked this protectionism and warned of other dangers (limiting civil liberties, ending term limits) that any constitutional change might engender.[45]

During PNoy's presidency, his reformist camp was divided on whether to amend the constitution. Speaker Belmonte, shortly before his re-election in 2013, filed a "charter change" resolution in the House that would have reduced nationality restrictions on ownership of land and businesses, including media. Several senators joined Speaker Belmonte, wanting to raise investment in the Philippines by loosening the requirement that in crucial sectors foreign ownership of a local company could not exceed 40 percent. But the basis for this provision had been enshrined in the Constitution. Although the sponsors claimed that they only wanted the economic amendment, PNoy's spokespeople suggested that opening up constitutional revision could lead to many further changes—and patriotic support for keeping Philippine ownership laws remained strong.

PNoy claimed the restrictions were "not detriments to getting foreign investment"—although many in Congress disagreed. Congressman Magtanggol Gunigundo supported the economic amendments but wisely warned that any such change would be "handicapped by local government units that fail to streamline procedures [for] issuance of business permits, building permits, transfer of real property, and payment of real property taxes."[46] Local corruptions deter foreign investors, no matter what the national constitution may say.

PNoy was wary of appearing to favor any amendment, regardless of its topic, because his predecessor Arroyo had used various potential needs for amendment in an effort to open the possibility of extending her presidential term. Senator Franklin Drilon, a PNoy ally, explained that there "is always doubt that a president wants to extend his term when he touches 'cha-cha' during his last three years in power."[47] (For more on "charter change," see Chapter 6.)

Filipino-Chinese investors run many small businesses and some large ones, but Japanese, American, and Korean money is now also flowing into the Philippines. Foreign investment has spurred much of the twenty-first century prosperity. In automobile manufacture, for example, many foreign companies now make cars in the Philippines. In electronics, the north Luzon city of Baguio has a Texas Instruments factory that provides the world's largest output of digital signal processing chips, used in Nokia and Ericcson cell phones. Baguio also manufactures aircraft parts used in both Boeing and Airbus planes. It is still unclear to what extent foreign-owned firms subcontract to local-run SMEs for value added (as multinationals did during Taiwan's or East China's eras of halcyon growth). Expansion in some fields, such as shipbuilding, would involve more local entrepreneurship. Recent increases of manufacturing have improved the islands' economic numbers. So has the growth of international services such as telephone call centers, which also depend largely on non-local entrepreneurs. The increased wealth is welcome news for Filipinos; its origins are mixed.

The government of business

Starting an enterprise in the Philippines has, in the eyes of business people, practically always required government help. In other Asian places such as Thailand, Taiwan, Fujian, or Zhejiang, many small entrepreneurs were able to found their firms with no government financing and few official licenses. Interviews with early Philippine entrepreneurs reported, however, that they considered lack of state help "the main problem in getting started." They deemed import licenses, official loans, and tax exemptions to be crucial. One manager said it was necessary for business people to spend 10 to 20 percent of their time cultivating bureaucrats. Another said, "The best connections are under the table."[48] Starting an enterprise requires numerous permissions, and thus numerous bribes.

The process for registering a typical small business in the Philippines recently required 36 items of information (often accompanied by money) for government approvals. Reformers vow to decrease the number. One proposal for streamlining would still saddle new entrepreneurs with 15 or 20 necessary approvals and potential bribes.[49] Also, this was merely a proposal. Nobody imagined it would be easy to convert such recommendations into practice among bureaucrats, whose jobs were to help entrepreneurs but who were also used to helping themselves.

Manufacturing startups have, over long time periods, been particularly few. A knowledgeable scholar of central Luzon, publishing in the 1980s, reported that, "During the past decades not one factory, large or small, has been established in Nueva Ecija," which is a large province.[50] A few entrepreneurs nonetheless founded firms without benefit of government. As late as 1993, 40 percent of the archipelago's economy was estimated to be "informal," unmonitored, and often illegal.[51] When Philippine entrepreneurs were asked how they set up manufacturing businesses, they gave a great variety of answers. About half cited economic opportunities—but often they also referred to politically generated factors such as tax exemptions or preferential tariffs against imports that might compete with their products. Just one-tenth mentioned enthusiasms about technologies, and one-eighth suggested large communal motives, such as creating new national industries. Life-style incentives were crucial for these managers:

a modern air-conditioned office; membership and frequently elective office in the Lions' Club or Rotary, a golf club, and one or more business associations; a large and very modern home in one of the suburbs of Manila, air-conditioned and often with a swimming pool; a summer home in the mountain city of Baguio; a prestige school in the Philippines and/or education in the United States for his children; frequent travel abroad; two or more automobiles and a great variety of fine clothes for the entrepreneur and his family. Occasionally—and the [Jesuit] writer has no way of knowing how common this is—it includes a *querida* or mistress.... Few of the interviewees gave evidence of the compulsive need to work and to amass wealth, which appears in [G.W.] Skinner's description of the self-made Chinese business leaders in Bangkok.[52]

This group was less hardscrabble than "pillow and mat capitalist" entrepreneurs elsewhere in Southeast Asia, where the Chinese diaspora was more numerous and a larger portion of the national populations.[53] The Philippine business ethic has been generally more relaxed than in other Asian countries.

The coercive context of doing business, however, has occasionally been unrelaxed. Local threats and violence can affect profitability even in relatively modern parts of the country. "Manila newspapers frequently feature articles implicating town mayors from various parts of the Philippines in murder, extortion, robbery, illegal gambling, illegal logging, and land grabbing." Officials can do this when "the local political economy lends itself to enduring monopolistic or oligopolistic control."[54]

Only a small part of such violence is leftist. In Bicol, "The fear of NPA revolutionary taxes limits investment and employment opportunities."[55] But most political control of profits is institutionalized and rightist. One writer argues that,

> a political élite grants to members of an economic élite monopoly concessions, normally in domestic service industries, that enable the latter to extract enormous amounts of wealth without a requirement to generate the technological capabilities, branded corporations, and productivity gains that drive sustainable development.[56]

Marcos franchised satraps to take charge of specific Philippine industries: "there was a 'sugar king,' a 'banana king,' a 'drug king,' and so on [including a 'car king']. According to the buttons on the intercom system at Malacañang Palace, Ferdinand Marcos was simply 'the King.'"[57] This president created state-run companies for banking, oil, transportation, fertilizer, and electric power. He was a centralizing president, and he socialized major industries. Some technocrats whom he appointed to run economic and other agencies of the government at first delivered efficient results. The first year in which the independent Philippines enjoyed an international trade surplus was 1974. National income rose largely because of new export processing zones.[58] Marcos advertised that he ran a technocratic-professional government—but his gestures to do so were trumped by his kleptocratic patronism and bureaucracy.

Infrastructure development requires particularly long time horizons for planning. For example, Marcos's Minister of Energy, Geronimo Velasco, was a technocrat who envisioned nuclear plants to generate electricity. Plans at that time were aided by an expectation that martial law would continue. But this expensive state-run effort was reversed after the dictator's fall. Marcos's demise also led to state purchases of firms that had been acquired by his political cronies. Who was a "crony?" A journalist explained that a crony was simply "someone on the other side of the political fence, who has the misfortune of not having moved his assets out before February 1986." So José Campos was a crony, because he "had the supreme bad luck to leave behind a list, showing all his dummy business operations for Marcos."[59]

A cadre of professional Career Executive Service Officers (CESOs) was established during the Marcos period. The Philippine Development Academy that graduated them still exists in Tagaytay, south of Manila. Senior civil servants receive tenure, and most of them at middle levels do not want to be challenged by other executive technocrats who are appointed to high posts. So the Cory Aquino administration abolished this system.

Also, the CESO-status officers generally did not serve throughout the country. Most were in central ministries—in Manila. Unlike postings of the Indian Administrative Service, which has been famously successful helping to hold together another large developing country, prestigious generalists from the Philippine Development Academy could avoid being sent to district officerships outside the capital. Central government departments are supposed to run their provincial branches throughout the archipelago. But whenever the heads of these agencies have resources (e.g., in police or military roles), such appointments are first vetted with governors or mayors, who are strongly legitimated in democratic elections and tend to serve local stakeholders—in many cases, *trapos*. So the central state of the Philippines, which is not constitutionally federal, continues to run a system of indirect administration. Marcos failed to change that pattern. When the state recruits talented people, it still keeps many of them in the capital, although this nation of more than 100 million is not a small country.

Marcos's administrators tended to keep their budgets near their offices. By 1987, the three-year congressional election cycle became the main political timekeeper for infrastructural investment plans. Few Filipinos in business or in government were given economic incentives to look far into the future. By Ramos's time, it became evident that many of the companies Marcos had nationalized were net drains on state assets; so the government sold them. Often they were "reacquired by their former owners (such as the Lopezes) or by former Marcos cronies such as Lucio Tan (who purchased Philippine Airlines)."[60]

Entrepreneurs care who runs the government, but they care even more for political stability. Business support, along with military support, was important in the public oppositions that brought down both Marcos and Estrada, who were almost surely the most corrupt two presidents (in terms of asset amounts acquired) in the republic's history. Many entrepreneurs disliked Estrada's presidential successor Arroyo too, but they disliked turmoil more. Economic activity

76 Entrepreneurs as politicians

has been "shielded from political crisis by ... remittances and heavy government borrowing." As Rocamora writes,

> business leaders know that what needs changing is not just a Marcos or an Estrada or an Arroyo, but the political system that spawned them. Yet for many business people, an unsatisfactory *status quo* is better than an uncertain future.[61]

This status quo has been no guarantee of prosperity. An unsympathetic foreigner wrote of Philippine manufacturing that,

> There were not many viable sectors to begin with, and most of them were taken over by cronies. The industrial sector is used to guaranteed monopolies and high tariff protection. It's inward-looking and believes it cannot compete.... Union organizing has run far ahead of productivity. It's a poor country, but an expensive place in which to produce.[62]

Monopolies and oligopolies in large industries have depended on government "rents," and SMEs cannot prosper in most rural places without *trapo* agreement and "rents" to local officials.

Small firms may have a greater cumulated effect on economic growth, and certainly on hiring, although large firms' fortunes are easier to document. Clans' links to major plantations and industries remained strong after Marcos. Tadeco was the Philippines' "number one agri-based company," owned by the Antonio Floirendo family "whose business interests range from fresh fruits to automotive dealerships."[63] Other major Filipino conglomerates have also been associated with particular families: San Miguel with the Sorianos, Purefoods with the Ayalas (who developed real estate in the Makati business district of Manila), General Milling with the Uytengsus, Republic Flour Mills with the Concepcions, and Universal Robina with the Gokongwei Group.[64]

The central government of the Philippines affects large companies, not just because it owns some of them. President Ramos (and later PNoy) encouraged some reductions of these monopolies and oligopolies. One of the clearest cases of Philippine industrial decentralization was the 1991 breakup of the long distance telephone company. This is an unusual industry, because it is inherently inter-local. Reformist presidents have favored "public–private partnerships" for infrastructure investment. Their supporters have hoped for fewer politicized regulations in utilities such as water and power.

Economic export zones have also now been established at the former U.S. military bases at Subic Bay and Clark Field. Laguna and Batangas provinces in the southern Tagalog region developed export zones. A "Technopark" in Greenfield City, Laguna, boasts electronic investments by Panasonic, as well as outlets for Toyota and Nissan cars. It is surrounded by condos and gated communities such as few Filipinos can afford. American suburbia is the model for Greenfield City and upscale places like it, which boast malls, parking lots, Home Plaza do-it-yourself retailers (whose advertisements copy Home Depot), as well as factories for producing Coca-Cola and Alaska yoghurts. This is an atypical part of the archipelago.

In more typical places, wealthy families own multiple firms and farms, in some cases scattered on different islands. Many clan members are usually absentee, living in provincial capitals, in Manila, or abroad. Foreign corporations also own factories and plantations. Government agencies own land, as do churches (though less than in Spanish times). Managers or majordomos commonly administer estates for distant owners, but they seldom funnel the local resources that they control into new enterprises. If the owner is from a political family that needs votes, the local manager also may be an election canvasser (*lider*). Attempted "long distance" or "remote control" management of business decisions is common in the Philippines.

Entrepreneurs as marginal men—and especially women

Local markets can operate on either of two opposite principles: impersonal or personal. Sellers and buyers in the Philippines who do not have frequent exchanges with each other trade in economics textbook form: the vendor sells at a price that assures a normal profit, and the buyer receives the commodity after paying. But if a seller and a purchaser deal with each other often, they can establish a "*sukî*" relationship. Then the store expects regular business from a particular customer, who in compensation can ask a lower price and can often buy on credit. If a *suki* buyer is caught purchasing a product that the usual vendor also sells at a similar price, however, the store will break off the relationship and demand payment of the account. Most local trade occurs between *suki* partners. Credit may occasionally be extended outside this kind of understanding, but it is offered in such cases only by sellers who can claim repayment.[65] "Maintaining one's *suki* buyers and suppliers is the principal device for optimizing predictability and minimizing risk in Philippine exchange."[66]

These are social links, not just market relationships. "*Compadrazgo*" connections are made between people who expect each other to be reliable. A buyer who asks a vendor to step in as godfather or godmother, for example at a baptism or wedding, may hope the honor of the godparent title will encourage the store to offer a line of credit. It may in practice do so. But an anthropologist in Benguet claimed it was often hard for a seller "to collect his debts in a very efficient way.... It may even involve the delicate use of a go-between, since it is extremely embarrassing for one *kumpare* [*compare* or personal friend] to approach another on the subject of money."[67]

Women are often more effective entrepreneurs than men, because they can demand payments with less violation of *compadrazgo* norms.[68] In the late nineteenth century, an American observer wrote that, "more often than not, the women are the financiers of their families; and I have frequently been referred to by the head of a household to '*mi mujer*' when I wish to make a bargain."[69] Substantial parts of the Philippine population, especially women in poor suburbs, are "buy-and-sell" traders on a small scale, retailing goods sometimes after processing them slightly. Roces claims that, "The Filipino family unit itself is basically very enterprising. Most wives hold purse strings and they are involved in one way or another in a small business 'on the side' to supplement the family income."[70] But few of these make much money.

The sociologist Frank Lynch, has argued that a Philippine value is "smooth interpersonal relations," going along with others (*pakikisama*), often achieved by willingness to yield to a leader, to avoid shaming others by using euphemisms, and to rely on go-betweens in any situation that might involve conflict.[71] Any such tradition is changeable, of course, and this one does not apply on all occasions. James Anderson nonetheless did research in Pampanga and Manila markets, claiming that,

> Filipino economic personalism provides the social cement which helps overcome lack of trust and weakness of institutional facilities.... Economic success depends importantly on social alliance, technical competence is less crucial than social competence, and legal-rational "efficiency" is subordinate to personal loyalty and trust.[72]

According to many anthropologists, there is a particular Philippine norm that poor people must be helped by others who have assets. Wealthy Filipinos are expected to share with those who are less well-off. This does not mean that trust or "social capital" is necessarily high; it means that many people frown on stinginess toward the poor. Cristina Blanc Szanton, for example, writes about a fishing boat returning to port that is accosted by a trader-boarder who wants to buy the fish at a low price before they reach the market:

> If he finds an unwillingness to sell, he may argue and insist on at least a small sale, on the basis of his right to make a gain or to feed his family. Even the outfit [boat] owners usually give in to such requests. If they regularly refused, they would become known as tightfisted and stingy and would lose prestige in the eyes of the community. There is also a real danger of violence.[73]

Destitution and coercion affect such markets. As a seller said, "One has to be patient with [buyers demanding credit]. They have no money and might get violent." But female creditors are safer than are males to whom money is owed. So bazaars are usually run by women.

> Vegetable vendors found the notion of a man joining their ranks on a regular basis as a source for great mirth.... Likewise, men clearly dislike having women join them in fish dealing, because of the great difference in their styles of business operation and the sanctions that can be pressed against them. As they put it, "Women fight with words," which circumvent and nullify threats of physical violence, the basis for controlling business transactions among men.[74]

Entrepreneurs as politicians 79

Practically all studies of Philippine entrepreneurship ask whether it depends more on such normative-cultural factors, or instead on situational-unintended factors. That mind/matter distinction so beguiles Western epistemologies of social science, authors address it as crucial. When faced with empirical evidence, practically all conclude that (while the fad to exclude "cultural" factors is very strong), both kinds of causes are required in order to explain what happens.[75] Culture matters, and matter also matters. Either can change.

"Culture" (Chinese, Philippine, or other) also has at least some effect on the success or failure of family firms. The influence is probabilistic and shaping, rather than sure or determinative, and it is not constant. Ann Swidler shows that culture shapes "a repertoire or 'tool kit' of habits, skills, and styles from which people construct 'strategies of action.'" But culture guides behavior differently in different situations. The "tool kit" can recommend one policy for calm times, and in chaotic times it may be abandoned.

> In settled periods, culture independently influences action, but only by providing resources from which people can construct diverse lines of action. In unsettled cultural periods, explicit ideologies directly govern action, but structural opportunities for action determine which among competing ideologies survive in the long run.[76]

This model can be applied fruitfully to many cases of economic prosperity or stagnation in East Asia. It suggests that entrepreneurs take opportunities to use the resources available to them—or demur to do so—depending on whether their surrounding contexts, including governments, encourage such action. States are particularly important in such contexts, although they are not the only surrounding situations (other factors range from typhoons, to knowledge of export market languages, to the existence or absence of transnational networks—but states are usually discussed in example cases because they are imagined to make all policy).

An instance is Taiwan from 1947 into the 1950s and 1960s, when the KMT had every incentive to urge ambitious Taiwanese into business rather than politics. So foundings and expansions of the island's small and medium enterprises flourished, with legendary good effects on Taiwan's growth and equality.[77] The Taiwan boom came at a time of considerable tension between mainlanders and Taiwanese. The freedoms or limits of both businesses and government were relatively clear. They combined to produce economic and social change such as the Philippines started to see much later, in the early twenty-first century. Documentable tendencies of Taiwan's family firms (high savings rates, trust among kin co-workers, and existential desires of workers to become their own "*laoban*" bosses) contributed to that island's boom.[78] They did so in the context of a particular time and politics. Modal Chinese traits at other times have had other results.[79]

Conditions somewhat like those on Taiwan in the KMT period also apply to some of the relatively liberal "models" of growth in some mainland China regions during the 1970s to 1990s era. Examples are the varied economic-political "models" of Sunan (under local governments in southern Jiangsu), the Pearl River Delta (where Hong Kong capital was especially important), or Wenzhou in southern Zhejiang (where free-wheeling capitalism went further than at any other place else in China). In the Philippines, the political factors for entrepreneurship documentably gave rise to fewer startups.

Cultural habits, activated or not at different times or places, affect the extent to which entrepreneurs take opportunities to use the resources that are available to them.[80] Filipino families are probably as solidaristic as Chinese ones, although their goals seem less often to be economic and more often to be local-political.[81] In business, as in local politics, Philippine family members have often cooperated with each other. But relatively few, wealthy or not, have taken entrepreneurial risks, and some studies find low levels of trust among Filipinos with few years of schooling (as contrasted with more educated ones).[82] This may not generally apply to the Chinese-Filipino minority. If firms are not founded, habits of family closeness, especially in rural areas, can repress entrepreneurship rather than fostering it.

So why do not more Filipinos take the plunge into business? Anthropologist David Szanton describes two kinds of business people in the islands. The first kind, who are almost entirely Filipino men, are patrons who organize other Filipinos as laborers. They create networks of clients, to whom they are supposed to give provision and protection. Minor employees who remain for long periods of time tend to develop a moral sense of unrepayable debt to their patrons. They may act as if they were legitimately enslaved. Business patrons who rule such networks become rich by exploiting labor.

A more modern kind of business person uses fewer laborers and makes money mainly from markets. Bargainers of this type need not live up to the obligations of a traditional patron. Minority Chinese and Protestants, who are marginal to the main Roman Catholic community—as well as some entrepreneurial Filipina women—have been found to be more adept than male Filipino patrons at establishing profitable trade relations with the wider world. Anthropologists have detailed how these marginal-person entrepreneurs linked a Panay fishing town, for example, with markets in Manila and beyond. Income among Protestant families in this fishing town averaged 125 pesos, but the average was 97 pesos in Roman Catholic families. When Chinese, Protestant, or woman entrepreneurs gave loans, they expected repayment on time. Their networks of clients were small, and they seldom participated directly in local politics. But they were important in the local economy.[83]

Other kinds of Philippine entrepreneurs had multiple occupations. One of a person's jobs might be mainly designed to make money, while others might offer social status:

> A physician is also a *hacendero* (estate owner), politician, and owner of a bus company; a lawyer maintains a practice, teaches law, and operates several commercial fishponds; a bureaucrat holds offices in two government

agencies and owns property in a rice mill; a high-school principal operates a small transportation company and acts as a tobacco buyer seasonally.[84]

Philippine entrepreneurship might be greater, if keeping big profits were socially more acceptable in rural areas. But when "small-scale buy-and-sell-dealers" come into major money, for example because market prices rise,

> While it is acceptable to use such windfalls to repay outstanding debts or redeem pawned properties, the man who has gained sudden wealth is greatly pressured to spend the remainder for the immediate benefit of his relatives and companions, who in their turn would do likewise. In fact, these persons often feel *entitled* to a share in such unanticipated gains, and if they are not directly distributed to them as gifts, they will press for a drinking party or "blowout," which may consume the total sum. Failure to respond to these pressures, to show that despite sudden wealth he is still "one of the boys," will bring bitter accusations of being *maimut* (stingy) and "aristocratic," or *esnab* (snobbish). Very few of the small-scale dealers are able to withstand these socioeconomic levelling mechanisms. As a result, small-scale dealers ... do not tend to organize corporate economic ventures which require savings and long-term planning and investment.[85]

Crewmen on a fishing boat are clients (and employees) of absentee patron-owners, whom they may nonetheless cheat.

> The outfit owners have had varying success in their attempts to limit [low-price] sales at sea. Some are apparently unable to prevent the loss of large quantities of fish. Others close their eyes, as long as the amounts remain reasonably small. A few attempt to limit the men to their normal shares.... These more businesslike owners are openly resented by the crewmen, who often develop elaborate strategies for rendezvous at sea to escape detection. They justify this by what they consider to be a fundamental prerogative, "the right to live," or in concrete terms, to have enough fish to feed their families and a little left over to cover the cost of the other basic commodities.[86]

These ethics crucially affect labor relations. "Being fired is a reflection upon the individual, and it is further a reflection upon his family," according to an anthropologist. "One way around this is to have many activities done on a piecework basis ... rather than as wage work. This is an adaptation to the fact that once someone is hired, it is almost impossible to fire him directly."[87]

Barriers to industrial unions

Increasing numbers of Filipinos are linked to trading systems or engage in cottage processing. They are no longer full-time farmers, but their products tend to use local materials and handicraft skills.[88] The formal, large-company industrial portion of Philippine gross domestic product declined from 35 to 32 percent between 1990 and 2002. Industry of that kind employs less than one-sixth of Philippine workers.[89] But family-scale enterprises are many, and they are important sources of work for people even though they seldom expand.

In the first decade of the 2000s, agriculture still absorbed 45 percent of Philippine labor, and the service sector another 40 percent—leaving just 15 percent for other activities, including all industrial manufactures.[90] Registered unemployment at the end of 2012 was high, at 25 percent of the workforce over age 18 who were surveyed as seeking jobs.[91] No less an authority than Karl Marx praised exploitation by the "bourgeoisie [that] put an end to all feudal, patriarchal, idyllic relations [and] rescued a considerable part of the population from the idiocy of rural life."[92] Marx's insight is expanded by the non-Marxist classical economics of Arthur Lewis, who shows that controllers of assets and technology enjoy a financial windfall, so long as they can put their capital alongside a supply of workers who are still willing to work at wages near subsistence.[93]

If unions demand high compensation for unskilled work long before this supply of near-subsistence-wage labor dries up, their labor movement is eroded and controllers of capital invest less. This slows economic growth.[94] It likewise slows the development of modern politics. This has been a problem in Philippine workers' unions. Jane Hutchison, in the most comprehensive recent overview of the history of these unions, documents the extent to which, "Rather than attempt to mobilise labour support,... emerging elites moved to contain the disruptive potential of workers' collective activism ... parliamentary oppositions did not emerge to reflect socioeconomic cleavages within the polity."[95] Unions did not create a Philippine left. Their links to parties, to the state, and to unorganized workers were not robust. They also had internal frailties.

A group of Philippine analysts has written that a "gerontocratic class" runs the trade unions, based on "family dynasties,... where family members inherit positions.... This may be regarded as an anomaly of union democracy."[96] Leadership in unions, as in the civil service and elective politics, often takes the form of prebends. This pattern has now been allayed somewhat in the National Federation of Labor through union bye-laws that limit the terms of the federation's General Secretary and President. The secretary explained, shortly after the turn of the millennium, that term limits should bring new talent and ideas into the federation. The main problem of the Philippine workers' movement, however, is still a shortage of entrepreneurship that shifts laborers from agriculture into jobs that can finance higher wages. Improving the internal governance of unions would not balance this relative lack of lucrative industries, which accounts for workers' weakness.

As Quimpo writes, "A major factor in the resilience of the Philippine left is that capitalism in the Philippines has not been as successful as in the other modern countries of Southeast Asia."[97] In most contemporary nations, the democratic left depends on workers. But no major industrial union movement has emerged in the Philippines—and such a development would correlate with having more factories. Especially outside the Manila region, these are relatively few. Slow development of industry has made for slow development of the left too.

The decline of unionism has been recent and rapid. Union membership in the Philippine public and private sectors dropped by half—by 48 percent—from 1995 to 2006. By 2006, union members were just 9 percent of all full-time employed workers. Even among union members, only 14 percent were covered by collective bargaining agreements. Many such contracts were minimal, providing no more benefits than were legally required. Health care was often completely omitted. Unions' bargaining power has been low because "there is a large mass of marginalized workers, workers in the informal sector, women, and the unemployed—people outside the reach of the trade union movement who have no means to protect their ranks from exploitation and abuse."[98]

Trade unions worldwide, not just in the Philippines, were eroded during the last decades of the twentieth century when pressures for "competitiveness" affected labor more than capital. Political-economic elites raised their own profits. Technological innovations to save labor and reduce employers' costs were quick during this period, raising unemployment without inspiring much new Luddism. National repression of unions has been less severe in the Philippines than repressions by local networks. "A weakened state role in industrial relations is not good for union revitalization," scholars in Manila have argued.[99] The main hindrance to Philippine industrial unionism is not the state. It has been repression of both entrepreneurship and workers in parts of the archipelago that have few industries.

Many global companies such as Procter and Gamble once manufactured products in the islands but later moved elsewhere, leaving behind only their sales departments. Textile firms during the Marcos era shifted their operations often to China and then to countries such as Bangladesh—taking only a few experienced Filipino foremen with them to other parts of Asia. These defections were partly caused by extensive strikes that Philippine workers could organize illegally even in the martial law period. The May 1 Movement (*Kilusang Mayo Uno*) of that time and the present could be cited as evidence of freedom, patriotism, and democracy. Its main unintended effect has been to cost workers their jobs. Unionization of workers is almost surely a requirement of solid, lasting democratization.[100] Unions require industries or sizeable service firms, however, and capital chases profits across borders—unless the state is able to keep it at home.

"Immiserating growth"

It is possible for average incomes to rise while greater portions of the people become poorer. Economists such as James Boyce call this phenomenon "immiserizing growth."[101] Rising tides do not always lift all ships.

The richest 10 percent of Filipino families, according to the World Bank, received 27 percent of the nation's total income in 1956. By 1985, the top 10 percent got much more: 37 percent.[102] The 50 richest Filipino families were estimated in 2013 to control more than one-quarter of the GNP.[103]

The portion of Philippine households living in poverty (according to a standardized definition of poverty) dropped slowly—just 0.9 percent per year—in the 15 years before 2000. Econometrics can involve various methods of surveying such an issue. From 1990 to 2002, the annual rise of the United Nations Development Program's "human development index" for the Philippines was less than four-tenths of 1 percent.[104] The portion of Filipinos living in poverty (having less than $1 per day) by 2005 exceeded similarly impoverished portions in China, Indonesia, or Vietnam. This situation improved somewhat in the post-2005 decade, but regional diversity of poverty rates within the country remained salient. The estimated percentage of poor people was ten times higher in Bicol or Western Mindanao than in Metro Manila.[105]

The upper and middle classes of the Philippines (which are defined in standard A, B, and C categories) became smaller between 1998 and 2007, from 10 to 7 percent of the total population. Upper-poor groups also declined, but the most impoverished category rose from 18 to 25 percent of the people.[106]

The Philippine economy grew slowly until about 2003 or 2005—but after that, GDP accelerated. The United Nations Development Program estimates annual GDP per capita growth from 1990 to 2005 at just 1.6 percent (while that of non-"tiger" Laos was 3.8 percent, Cambodia 5.5 percent, and Myanmar 6.6 percent). Walden Bello has mooted alternative explanations for the late-twentieth-century stagnation, dismissing most of them.

An often-cited candidate factor is the archipelago's high population growth. This affects the denominator in a changing GDP/capita index. But poverty partly causes the high birth rate, not just vice versa. Women's lack of jobs and careers makes more of them relatively young mothers. Other economies (e.g., Taiwan, just north of Luzon) have had simultaneous high growths of population and product. Some Philippine political forces, notably the Catholic bishops, prefer on other grounds to neglect that the high birth rate contributes to unemployment, low wages, and poverty. But change of GDP/population has both a numerator and a denominator; attention to either alone is insufficient. So is neglect of the additional time denominator in change of GDP/births-minus-deaths/year, the rate at which generations turn over, which is affected by a typical mother's age when her first child is born. If the workforce grew more slowly, capitalists would have to offer workers higher wage hikes. If more entrepreneurs founded prospering companies, more people could find income to increase the GDP. High birth rates reduce wages and raise poverty, although their effect on production is less clear.

Corruption is a similarly ambiguous explanation, because poverty almost surely correlates with corruption, not just vice versa. Other sections of this book stress that corruption has many aspects. Rich economies are usually less corrupt than poor ones, but the mutual causation is a two-way street. Levels of wealth are also different from rates of change in wealth.

Yet another factor is national protectionism. The current author believes that competition-suppressing tariffs have played some role in slowing Philippine growth—but countries such as Thailand, which has fared better economically than the Philippines in recent years (and boomed before 1997), have had higher rates of protection for manufactures.

A further possible explanation is that Philippine democracy protected labor more than did the polities of Asian comparator countries, thus discouraging international investment. The present author gives somewhat more credence to this factor than Walden Bello does, although the sociologist Congressman offers many reasons for the "crisis of investment." Relatively little new capital has come to the Philippines from foreign sources. Inbound capital plummeted (from about 30 to 20 percent of GDP) between 1990 and 2010. Bello sees that the lack of domestic investment in public infrastructure, such as roads and transport, discouraged foreign companies from bringing their capital, for which the missing infrastructure would have provided "external economies" and raised profitability.

The Philippine government followed IMF and World Bank directives to pay down its debts. Many other developing countries have defaulted, later having those bills reduced or canceled. Bello argues that the Philippines should have done that too. This explanation for slow growth may downplay the deficit of domestic entrepreneurialism in most of the country, but it convincingly discredits the international community's inconsistencies on "moral hazard." It criticizes the Manila government's impulse to obey foreign technocrats.

Payments to the government's creditors fluctuated. During the last five years of the 1990s, debt service as a portion of national government revenues varied between 27 and 43 percent. After 2000, debt service soared, rising to 86 percent of revenues in 2004.[107] By 2005, Manila was putting 29 percent of all state expenditure toward interest payments on foreign and domestic debts—and just 12 percent into capital projects.

The Manila government's payments on debt by mid-2013 were running at a rate of 2.17 billion pesos per day. The total outstanding debt was slightly less than half of annual GDP. But most of the creditors were rich Filipinos. Seven-tenths of the interest payments went to domestic rather than foreign creditors, and repayments of principal were about 84 percent of the outflow. Interest was decreasing as a portion of debt service.[108]

The Philippines has ranked well below the Asian mean on a "global competitiveness index," and it ranked 71 among 131 countries worldwide (followed largely by national basket cases among economies in Africa).[109] Both domestic and foreign investment were insufficient to sustain rates of growth such as occurred in other populous Asian countries.

Aside from the impulse to prioritize repayments over infrastructure, an apparent factor that slowed growth in the late twentieth century was a relative disinclination by Filipinos to take risks and start companies. To the extent that languid growth cannot be explained except by reference to cultural factors, especially the existential motives of managers, they do not determine what happens but point to options that Filipinos find to be attractive or uninteresting in their current contexts. That reason for slowness does not dismiss other reasons, such as counter-effective unionization and more attention to foreign debts than to infrastructure. But without a modern economy, the nation lacked modern prosperity.

Usual neoliberal economic theories have not explained the Philippines' era of GDP stagnation. They also provide no clear insight to account for the much better news that has followed: by 2012–13, real product in the Philippines was growing at 7 percent annually (up from 4 percent in the first three years of the millennium).[110] This is the good news, and it could well continue whether or not the economists can explain it.

Overseas Filipino workers

Past Philippine governments have encouraged the outflow of Overseas Filipino Workers. This is arguably created a "brain drain"—and some drain of entrepreneurs. Yet OFW remittances have seldom gone into capital construction or to start new companies in the many Philippine places from which the emigrants came. OFW departures, at least of educated Filipinos, have apparently reduced the supply of domestic entrepreneurs.

Sociologists Walden Bello, Frank Lynch, and Perla Makil as early as 1969 published an analysis of "brain drain" in the Philippines and urged the government to improve conditions so that Filipinos going abroad would want to return.[111] For many decades that followed, nothing of the sort was done, although Manila's policies changed after 2010.

About one-tenth of all Philippine workers are abroad. Some are low-paid construction hands, ship crew members, or household servants. But the portion of emigrants who are professionalized, leaving the islands permanently to take up well-paid technical jobs abroad, is a majority—and an increasing majority.[112] Many are medical doctors, computer gurus, news reporters, property brokers, or certified nurses. A minority of emigrants have menial jobs (seamen and amahs in Hong Kong are particularly obvious). These return to the Philippines after their foreign contracts end; often they may not legally stay after that in other countries. The well-paid majority of emigrants creates a "brain drain."

In 1980, one-eighth of all Philippine workers had some college education—but half of OFWs had been to universities. Most of these did not return, receiving residency or citizenship in higher-income countries. By the 1990s, the number of Philippine professionals who emigrated was greater than the number of professionals who joined the islands' workforce. In just six years, from 1997 to 2003, a government study showed that the "middle class" (using a broad definition of that group) was reduced from 23 percent to less than 20 percent of the domestic population.[113]

Remittances sent back by OFWs (after they have met their own expenses in foreign lands) are about one-seventh of the Philippine GNP.[114] Manila governments before 2010 encouraged OFW emigration, because these remittances are important for the nation's foreign exchange reserves. By 2013, money coming into the country from OFWs exceeded $1.8 billion per month. More than four-tenths came from the U.S., and about three-tenths came from workers at sea. Because of this unusual source of national income, the Philippine balance of payments since 2005 has been in surplus, providing enough money to pay foreign creditors.[115]

Having many relatively ambitious and skilled people leave the country, however, also involved incalculable costs. Ricky Carandang, a journalist and press secretary for reformist president PNoy, estimated that half of the Philippine middle class lives abroad.[116] So PNoy changed the previous administrations' policy on OFWs and has insisted that going abroad is an individual choice, not a goal of policy. Middle-income Filipinos' commitment to political or economic change is almost surely weakened because so many of them and their kin have moved elsewhere. As Sheila Coronel put it, "You don't join a political organization; you line up at an embassy."[117]

It is very difficult to estimate the loss of domestic entrepreneurship because of OFW emigration, partly because the relatively professionalized migrants are in a limited number of specific fields. Nurses, valued internationally, became a particular shortage in the Philippines. PNoy's advisors supported proposals to raise nurses' monthly salaries in government hospitals, "to prevent them from seeking other jobs abroad."[118]

Remittances had a tendency to become "dead capital" when sent from workers who stayed overseas. As a report from another country suggests, such capital is "immobilized into purchases of apartments, houses, or luxury cars.... This money does not circulate, does not serve the local businesses."[119] The most enterprising members of recipient families in the old country are those who leave. The emigrants have enough get-up-and-go to try their luck abroad, but they or their homeland relatives have not generally used remittance money to reproduce itself—although the recent upturn in the Philippine economy might change this pattern.

To encourage entrepreneurship and local job creation by OFWs who had foreign jobs but then returned to the Philippines, a potential policy lies in microfinance. A mutual fund could be established to advance loans in the style of the Grameen Bank. If it were conceived as independent from political rake-offs, and if it showed local economic successes, it might spur new industries and use OFWs' capital more productively. Such ideas have been discussed—but have not yet been widely implemented.

Because of OFWs, Filipinos are scattered widely around the world. So the country might be expected to rank highly on an index of "globalization." But surprisingly, the country's "economic globalization," according to an index that attempted to measure trade and capital connections, was just below that of Fiji; it ranked 101 among 187 countries. Philippine international "political connectivity" was higher, at rank 43 (just behind Ukraine). "Social globalization," reflecting "the extent of the dissemination of information and ideas," was ranked at 127 (just behind Cuba).[120] These measurements can be doubted; but they suggest that, for better or for worse, there is less Philippine globalization than most observers would guess. The archipelago remained isolated, even though many of its citizens were not.

Infrastructure gaps: Manila transport and housing as examples

A crucial economic role of modern government is to provide infrastructure that creates external economies for both official and nonstate investments. The Philippine state has traditionally put little money into infrastructure. Roads are a major example. In Metro Manila, a barrier for many years separated lanes of cars going in opposite directions on the main auto route between Quezon City and downtown. It was extended to close off most cross streets. Traffic on the main road thus ran faster without the public expense of an elevated highway. This "Filipino freeway," as locals sardonically called it, had a disadvantage: vehicles needing to travel at 90 degrees to the main road could not do so except at a few widely spaced crossings that had traffic lights.

Such problems have existed for a long time, and Marcos's minions made some progress against them. Manila's elevated rail lines date from that era, as do a state-owned bus company that the Cory Aquino administration privatized. The capital's slow transport system still discourages both international and domestic businesses from investing in the Philippines, even though more capital in labor-absorbing sectors would help to reduce poverty.

Manila traffic jams have been especially severe in the 7–9 a.m. and 5–8 p.m. periods of any weekday—and increasingly, outside those hours too. Depending on the last digit of its license plate, a car may not legally be driven on Manila streets during rush hours on at least one of the five weekdays, or in many areas on even- or odd-numbered days. This policy encourages wealthy Filipinos to buy multiple cars (or multiple counterfeit plates).

A team of Japanese transport experts estimated the total implicit costs of Metro Manila's traffic jams were 2.4 billion pesos daily. To lessen these losses, PNoy's government and the Manila City Council declared plans to rehabilitate main roads, especially Epifanio de los Santos Avenue (EDSA) between the business center of Makati and Quezon City. Construction plans were mooted, as were plans that "targeted street vendors" who were perceived to block traffic. A "total daytime truck ban, allowing trucks on main roads in Metro Manila from 10 p.m. to 5 a.m." was also mooted—but it "met strong opposition from trucking companies and other stakeholders."[121] The government by 2013 was trying to relieve Manila's debacle on thoroughfares. If the proposed laws were passed, and if police enforced them, such traffic problems (common though they are in large cities) might become less costly.

Policies to loosen traffic jams could offend some stakeholders such as current taxi and jeepney drivers. Bus companies or politicians associated with them in Metro Manila's many separate cities might also be discomfited. The political engineering that is necessary to make the capital's traffic move has begun, but there are many would-be "veto players" for any relevant decision. So people remain inconvenienced, and informal conversations suggest that many are fatalistic. Filipinos do not always expect good results from government.

The basic problem is lack of road space per traveller. Ways to face it include higher taxes on new private car purchases, expensive annual license fees for plates valid in Metro Manila, and a better train system. Air-conditioned buses might be used (in preference to jeepneys or tricycle sidecars) during rush hours by people who demand more commuting comfort and are rich enough to buy cars that take more road space per passenger. High-frequency minibuses might appeal to that same middle-income group (as they do in crowded but rich Hong Kong). Extra revenues from such policies could finance paving better roads not just in cities but between them. Presuming the Philippine economy accelerates nicely, as it has done in the past few years, such solutions may become needed.

Until recently, the Philippines has produced only some of the vehicles that the country uses. A former jeepney factory in Sarao, just south of Manila, ceased most operations in 2001; it is now devoted only to reconditioning old vehicles. It resembles a carriage museum more than a factory.[122] But the recent economic upturn has already involved a sharp increase of vehicle production. The foreign companies Ford, Toyota, Mitsubishi, Nissan, Honda, Kia, and Suzuki have now all invested in the growing Philippine automobile market.

Non-transport kinds of infrastructure are arguably underfunded too. Major Philippine cities, if compared for example with large cities in some other Asian countries, have far less public housing. Urban immigrants from the countryside settle on land they do not own. Many squat on public land, often reclaimed from swamps, building shacks on stilts often above water. Local officials post signs promising they will be "responsible" (the word *responsableng* appears often in political ads) for improving these slums. But most impoverished residents resist redevelopment. They know they could not afford the prices of new flats that would later be built in the same places after renewal. Legal procedures exist for giving one-year notices prior to evictions, but the squatters are stakeholders. They have votes.

The government has tried to distinguish "informal settlers" from "professional squatters." The latter group, opposing plans for redevelopment of land where the "informal settlers" live, are apparently just the leaders or more politicized members of the former group. The Department of Social Welfare and Development in 2013 offered 18,000 pesos (about $400) to any family willing to move away from riverside *esteros* of Metro Manila. Mayor Joseph Estrada met with developers "to thresh out plans."[123] It was unclear what would happen to "professional squatters" who refused inducements to leave, but it was clear that they had at least some local power.

PNoy's government tried to move "informal settlers living in dangerous and high-risk areas to decent housing sites."[124] Many squatters did not want to move. Compensation was in view, but on a periodic basis: "the relocated families can only receive the monthly stipend as long as they stay put in their new homes." As PNoy ally Sen. Franklin Drilon pointed out, removing "informal settlers" from waterways in Metro Manila "would depend on the cooperation of all the stakeholders, particularly local chief executives." He said that the government's plan to relocate 100,000 families were good. But actually, an initial program was proposed to cover only 4,000. Drilon clearly expected resistance not just from the "settlers" but also from local politicians whom they elected.[125]

Existential motives of entrepreneurs

Adam Smith wrote that, "It is not economic motivation that prompts a man to work, but status, esteem, moral mettle, qualities which would allow him to be a man of worth and dignity."[126] Briones and most other economists, forgetting Smith's wisdom, claim that "institutions," which they distinguish from actors' cultural habits, are the main hindrances to Philippine long-term growth. Institutions reflect the accumulation over time of such customs. Norms are institutionalized as surely as are situational unintended constraints or incentives. Briones, showing both patriotic and professional preferences, calls for more long-term optimism, "less hand-wringing over Filipino culture and corruption." But he moves from this appeal immediately to call "above all, [for] focussed and sustained development of functional capitalistic institutions." Economists are insufficiently curious to ask why such development has not already occurred. Neoclassical theories suggest it should have happened in a country like the Philippines, which maintains an apparently free market economy. They discount the economic results of having political constraints on local startups, a weak state, and a high degree of oligopoly.[127]

The economists' main objections to cultural explanations are two. First, culture does not cause behavior, because its inconsistent components as understood by actors merely shape action without determining which road will be chosen among those that cultural maps suggest. But when there has been scant growth, i.e., scant change on a major "dependent variable" as well as weak traditions of entrepreneurship, this result suggests a need to look at normative differences between the Philippines and other countries that have similar assets where growth has actually occurred. Most economists simply say that such investigations are not part of their discipline. This means their economics has been unable to account for factors that sharply affect the performance of economies.

Second, cultural variables are often less easy to quantify than are nonnormative unintended situations. If the only convincing kind of social truth is presumed to emerge from statistical correlations (skill in which is now the least-common-denominator basis of academic careers in most social science), this difficulty of quantification practically excludes norms as means of understanding. The objection to citing cultural variables is unpresentable in intellectual terms, since enumerated items are not always easier to understand than others, and there is no reason to throw out evidence before testing its relevance. But the allergy to "culture" has affected economic studies of the Philippines—and of other countries whose long-term trajectories economists have failed to predict (Japan's and China's and India's among others). Many economists blithely advise good market and enterprise policies but fail to show why Filipinos have until recently adopted such policies less often than people in neighboring countries that have prospered better. Cultural causes are important preferences.

Other social scientists, favoring a different epistemology but faced with the same choice of evidence types, downplay the possibility that changing contexts can alter norms. Anthropologist Filomeno Aguilar, for example, claims that Philippine "social existence is powerfully perceived and lived as a gamble: stratification is the outcome of *dungan* [spirit] rivalries that confound kin relations."[128] Filipinos sometimes talk about a fictional Juan Tamad, "Juan the Lazy," who hopes that wealth will befall him through a good marriage or lucky bets. Work is not seen as the road to riches. By contrast, Chinese sometimes criticize themselves for being too nervous, too "fearful of losing" (*pashu* in Mandarin, but far more famous in the South Fujian language as *kiasu*). They are not content unless they are worrying. These opposite self-criticisms are of course just anecdotes. Such stereotypes are static, not allowing results from structural change. The actual situation, however, is changing. The Philippine present and future are almost surely brighter than the late twentieth century generally was, in both economic and political terms.

More wealth has recently come from manufacturing. Past and recent economic growth has certainly not been uniform over the whole Philippine territory; change is geographically uneven in all countries. The only official large "region" of the Philippines in which industry accounted for more than three-fifths of gross product by 2012 comprised the provinces just south of Metro Manila (Laguna, Cavite, Batangas, Rizal, and Quezon). Some provinces north of the capital also did well by this criterion (although their statistics were administratively conflated with other poorer provinces in the Central Luzon Region).[129] In Metro Manila, four-fifths of GDP came from services. In the country as a whole, just a third of product came from industry, while half came from services. A third of all Filipinos in 2012 still lived below the official poverty line, and unemployment in modern sectors was 7 percent.[130] But in comparison with previous decades, the years after 2003 showed that the Philippine economy could prosper.

Crystal-ball gazers have grouped the Philippines with Thailand and Indonesia as "tiger cubs." HSBC seers predicted the Philippines would have Southeast Asia's largest economy by 2050. That might happen. But neither professional economists nor journalistic gurus have track records of prediction that inspire absolute confidence in their accuracy. The archipelago's economy is faring better in the new millennium, quite separately from any future news they sell.

Action possibilities against undemocratic wages

The Philippines is now slowly developing a more modern economy. If this process accelerates in sectors that absorb labor, wages can rise for Filipinos who have skills. Politics is the main factor of economic growth. Some economists such as Acemoglu and Robinson have now recognized the primacy of politics for economics, even though professional fads for regressions of national statistics have led them to neglect the effects of local power networks—and all economists' allergy to the word "culture" causes them to neglect the non-material incentives of both workers and entrepreneurs.[131] Policy recommendations of interest to Filipinos might include measures that encourage local stakeholders to allow more startups and capital in low-wage rural areas outside cities. Until the nation fosters more firms that will hire laborers, wages will remain low and many talented Filipinos will continue to work abroad.

Various kinds of regulations, including anti-trust laws, can contribute to local economic democratization. So can administrative reforms. Resurrecting the prestige of Career Executive Service Officers, and assigning more of them outside Manila, might help reduce poverty—if these elite civil servants were empowered to become effective agents of the central government in low-wage rural areas that are still dominated by *trapos*. Executives in the Indian Administrative Service have shown that such mediators can link central to local powers sensitively, even in low-income areas. A "law of avoidance" can rotate officials among localities where they would somewhat balance *trapos*. In particular, they could report independently on coercive forces (police, military, and illegal private militias). They could be assigned special responsibility to urge that local revenues be used for infrastructure such as roads, to provide external economies for future investments, both public and private, especially for labor-absorbing sectors.

Measures that aid local political transparency will also aid economic enterprise. The "action possibilities" described in the conclusions of most other chapters of this book are also relevant for reducing poverty. Clan feuds have localized most of Philippine politics as Chapter 3 shows, for example; but if incentives from the central state could help new firms to establish in sectors that hire workers, this would expand the range of actors in local politics. Serious land reform (as mooted in Chapter 5) would distribute more income to tillers, increasing income equality and consumption. Fairer law-abiding judges would encourage firms to compete for labor (if Chapter 6 is right). Independent media and transparency about corruptions could yield similar results (see Chapters 8 and 9). The suggestions at the ends of each of these chapters are complementary and mutually reinforcing, if Filipinos undertake them. None of the aims here is more important for substantive democracy than raising the average wage rate.

Such reforms would probably face political resistance in the Philippine places where they would most help to reduce poverty. Nonetheless, even old-style leaders can have new ideas. Reformist politicians, if elected, would benefit from attempting such changes. Economic modernization is a collective hope of many citizens, who would support serious ways to accelerate it.

Notes

1 Gary Hawes, "Marcos, His Cronies, and the Philippines' Failure to Develop," in *Southeast Asian Capitalists*, Ruth McVey, ed. (Ithaca, NY: Southeast Asia Program, Cornell University, 1992), 148.
2 By 1949, at the start of this boom, Philippine output was already near pre-war levels. John J. Carroll, *The Filipino Manufacturing Entrepreneur, Agent and Product of Change* (Ithaca, NY: Cornell University Press, 1965), 37–8.

Entrepreneurs as politicians 93

3 The other first languages of entrepreneurs, in order of rounded percentages, were Ilongo-Hiligaynon 8 percent, Bicolano 5, Cebuano just 2, Pangasinan 0, and Ilocano 0—despite the stereotype that Ilocanos are entrepreneurial. John J. Carroll, *The Filipino Manufacturing Entrepreneur*, 46.
4 John J. Carroll, *The Filipino Manufacturing Entrepreneur*, 54.
5 Fred Eggan, "Philippine Social Structure," in *Six Perspectives on the Philippines*, George M. Guthrie, ed. (Manila: Bookmark, 1968), 18–19.
6 For example, Wolfram Eberhard, "Chinese Regional Stereotypes," *Asian Survey* 5:12 (December 1965), 596–608.
7 Fred Eggan, "Philippine Social Structure," 6–7.
8 Alfred W. McCoy, *Policing America's Empire: The United States, the Philippines, and the Rise of the Surveillance State* (Madison, WI: University of Wisconsin Press, 2009), 133.
9 John J. Carroll, *The Filipino Manufacturing Entrepreneur*, 54, also quoting Horacio de la Costa from the fifteenth century.
10 John J. Carroll, *The Filipino Manufacturing Entrepreneur*, 175–6.
11 George L. Hicks and Geoffrey McNicoll, *Trade and Growth in the Philippines: An Open Dual Economy* (Ithaca, NY: Cornell University Press, 1971), as reviewed by Martin E. Abel in *Journal of Asian Studies* 32:2 (Spring 1973), 384–6.
12 World Bank, http://data.worldbank.org/iondicators/NY.GDP.PCAP.CD.
13 Brian Fegan, "The Philippines: Agrarian Stagnation Under a Decaying Regime," in *Agrarian Transformations: Local Processes and the State in Southeast Asia*, Gillian Hart, Andrew Turton, and Benjamin White, eds. (Berkeley, CA: University of California Press, 1989), 129.
14 Michael Pinches, "Entrepreneurship, Consumption, Ethnicity, and National Identity in the Making of the Philippines' New Rich," in *Culture and Privilege in Capitalist Asia*, Pinches, ed. (New York: Routledge, 1999), 105, quoted from the World Bank.
15 See Dante B. Canlas, Muhammad Ehsan Khan, and Juzhong Zhuang, eds., *Diagnosing the Philippine Economy: Toward Inclusive Growth* (Quezon City: Anthem Press, 2011).
16 Frank Golay's introduction in John J. Carroll, *The Filipino Manufacturing Entrepreneur*, x.
17 Vilfredo Pareto adopted Machiavelli's terms, contrasting "lion" and "fox" leaderships, in *The Rise and Fall of the Elites: An Application of Theoretical Sociology* (New York: Arno Press, 1979; orig. 1901).
18 Misagh Parsa, "Entrepreneurs and Democratization: Iran and the Philippines," *Comparative Studies in Society and History* 37:4 (October 1995), 803–30.
19 Jamie Mackie and Bernardo Villegas, "The Philippines: Still an Exceptional Case?" in *Driven by Growth: Political Change in the Asia-Pacific Region*, James Morley, ed. (Armonk, NY: M.E. Sharpe, 1993), 116.
20 Anon., "Democracy as Showbiz," *The Economist*, July 1, 2004, www.economist.com/printerfriendly.cfm?story_ID=2876966.
21 Temario C. Rivera, *Landlords and Capitalists: Class, Family, and State in Philippine Manufacturing* (Quezon City: University of the Philippines Center for Integrative and Development Studies, 1994), 39.
22 Joel Rocamora, "Estrada and the Populist Temptation in the Philippines," in *Populism in Asia*, Mizuno Kosuke and Pasuk Phongpaichit, eds. (Kyoto: Kyoto University Press, 2009), 51.
23 Ashutosh Varshney, *Democracy, Development, and the Countryside: Urban–Rural Struggles in India* (New York: Cambridge University Press, 1998), 192.
24 Barrington Moore, Jr., *Social Origins of Dictatorship and Democracy: Lord and Peasant in the Making of the Modern World* (Boston, MA: Beacon, 1966). The Philippines was not during early modernization the only "null case," with no strong bourgeoisie, no strong state, and no unified aristocracy—although its landed elites

94 *Entrepreneurs as politicians*

might have allowed a figure such as Marcos to conduct a "revolution from above," if they had not been so disorganized nationally. India is the largest "null case" in Moore's terms. Varshney argues that, "India's peasantry ... has penetrated state institutions and has sustained mobilization on an impressive scale," but this could not be said of the Philippines. See Ashutosh Varshney, *Democracy, Development, and the Countryside*, 27.

25 The period near the turn of the twentieth century, when Philippine patriots fought Spanish and then American foreigners, is often said to be a revolution—and this term is more respectful of Filipinos' feelings than calling it an "insurgency" would be. It was a major violent war, albeit with limited long-term effect on local sociopolitical structures. Large social revolutions are often associated with central dates of change (e.g., China in 1949, but 1850–65 or 1910 or 1966 are relevant too; or Russia in 1917, but 1825 and 1905 are relevant too). Was the English revolution under William and Mary or instead, as Lawrence Stone argues, under Cromwell? Was the American revolution in 1776–83, or did it also involve those English earlier events and especially the greater violence and social change of 1861–65? Was Mexico's revolution only in 1910? Revolutions often come in ripples before and after big waves. The current author guesses the main Philippine hero of the relevant period, José Rizal, might have criticized concrete (if not normative) exaggeration of what happened. For better or worse—probably for better—the Philippine nation has not experienced as much violence as occurred at the peaks of other populous countries' revolutions. Consider Reynaldo Ileto's claim for "The Philippine Revolution of 1896," in Lecture 1, *Knowing America's Colony: A Hundred Years from the Philippine War* (Honolulu, HI: Center for Philippine Studies, 1999), 1–18. Has this event shaped the national consciousness for greater change in the future? That hope may be its vector, but questions about the future are even harder than questions about the past.

26 Cf. Joe Studwell, *Asian Godfathers: Money and Power in Hong Kong and Southeast Asia* (New York: Atlantic Monthly Press, 2007), xv–xvii.

27 George Henry Weightman, *Philippine Chinese: A Cultural History of a Marginal Trading Community* (Ph.D. dissertation, Sociology, Cornell University, 1960), 179, also 180–1.

28 See Wikipedia on Garcia, the only Philippine president who identified with the Visayan island of Bohol. His predecessor presidents Aguinaldo, Quezon, Osmeña, and probably others had at least some Chinese ancestry.

29 Small firms were, in this survey, those with five to 19 workers, and the larger ones had more than 20. In the same period, the small firms' value added *per worker* (at constant prices) was higher (3.3 percent per year) than in larger firms (2.5 percent)—but their employment was down 2.2 percent. For the data only, see Arnulfo F. Itao and Myrna R. Co, eds., *Entrepreneurship and Small Enterprises Development: The Philippine Experience* (Quezon City: University of the Philippines Institute for Small Scale Industries, 1979), 15.

30 Yoshihara Kunio, *The Nation and Economic Growth: The Philippines and Thailand* (Kuala Lumpur: Oxford University Press, 1994), 37.

31 Derived from Yoshihara Kunio, *The Nation and Economic Growth*, 31 and table on 7, see also 22.

32 Theresa Chong Carino, "Chinese Chambers of Commerce in the Philippines: Communal, National, and International Influence," in *Chinese Populations in Contemporary Southeast Asian Societies*, M. Jocelyn Armstrong, R. Warwick Armstrong, and Kent Mulliner, eds. (Richmond: Curzon, 2001), 97–122.

33 See http://en/wikipedia.org/wii/Filipinos_of_Chinese_descent.

34 Theresa Chong Carino, *Chinese Big Business in the Philippines: Political Leadership and Change* (Singapore: Times Academic Press, 1998), 46–9.

35 Teresa Chong Carino, *Chinese Big Business in the Philippines*, 2–5.

36 Theresa Chong Carino, *Chinese Big Business in the Philippines*, 55–6.
37 Cf. John J. Carroll, *The Filipino Manufacturing Entrepreneur*, 65, which also relies on work by Edward Tiryakian, *The Evaluation of Occupations in a Developing Country: The Philippines* (New York: Garland, 1990).
38 John Sidel, "Social Origins of Dictatorship and Democracy Revisited: Colonial State and Chinese Immigrant in the Making of Modern Southeast Asia," *Comparative Politics* 40:2 (2008), 127–41.
39 G. William Skinner, "Chinese Assimilation and Thai Politics," *Journal of Asian Studies* 16 (February 1957), 237–50, reprinted in John T. McAlister, ed., *Southeast Asia: The Politics of National Integration* (New York: Random House, 1973); and G. William Skinner, "Change and Persistence in Chinese Culture Overseas: A Comparison of Thailand and Java," in Skinner, ed., *Change and Persistence in Thai Society: Essays in Honor of Lauriston Sharp* (Ithaca, NY: Cornell University Press, 1975).
40 Teresita Ang See, "The Ethnic Chinese as Filipinos," in *Ethnic Chinese as Southeast Asians*, Leo Suryadinata, ed. (Singapore: Institute for Southeast Asian Studies, 1997), 158–210.
41 Michael Pinches, "Entrepreneurship, Consumption, Ethnicity, and National Identity in the Making of the Philippines' New Rich," 275–301.
42 Teresita Ang See, "The Ethnic Chinese as Filipinos," 169.
43 Ibid., 172.
44 Chino S. Leyco, "Sy, Tan still lead Forbes PH Rich List," *Manila Bulletin*, August 2, 2013, http://mb.com.ph/News/Main_News/25147/.
45 Des Ferriols, "Business Declares 100-Day 'Honeymoon' with Estrada [who opposed 'Concord']," *Philippine Star*, January 11, 2000, www.philstar.com/headlines/86742.
46 Louis Bacani, "House Speaker Files Cha-Cha Resolution," *Philippine Star*, July 9, 2013, www.philstar.com/headlines/2013/07/09/963461.
47 Louis Bacani, "Solons Still Support Cha-Cha Despite Aquino's Opposition," *Philippine Star*, June 17, 2013, www.philstar.com/headlines/2013/06/17/955033.
48 John J. Carroll, *The Filipino Manufacturing Entrepreneur*, 179, 181–2.
49 Interview with a Philippine cabinet member, 2010.
50 Willem Wolters, *Politics, Patronage, and Class Conflict in Central Luzon* (The Hague: Institute of Social Studies, 1983), 35.
51 Filipe V. Miranda, "Political Economy in a Democratizing Philippines: A People's Perspective," in *Democratization: Philippine Perspectives*, Felipe V. Miranda, ed. (Quezon City: University of the Philippines Press, 1997), 162.
52 John J. Carroll, *The Filipino Manufacturing Entrepreneur*, 131, quotation on 134–5. Compare G. William Skinner, *Leadership and Power in the Chinese Community of Thailand* (Ithaca, NY: Cornell University Press, 1958), 45. (Also, G. William Skinner, *Chinese Society in Thailand: An Analytical History* [Ithaca, NY: Cornell University Press, 1957]).
53 See Pasuk Phongpaichit and Chris Baker, *Thailand's Boom!* (North Sydney: Allen & Unwin, 1996). Among the 37 million self-identifying Chinese in the diaspora by 1990, 20 percent were in Indonesia, 16 percent in Thailand, 15 percent in Hong Kong, 15 percent in Malaysia, then only 6 percent in Singapore, 5 percent in Vietnam, 4 percent in the US, 4 percent in Myanmar, and just 2 percent each in Canada and the Philippines. All other countries had less than 1 percent self-identifying Chinese, and they supplied the remaining 10 percent of the total diaspora. Dudley L. Poston, Jr., Michael Xinxiang Mao, and Mei-Yu Yu, "The Global Distribution of the Overseas Chinese around 1990," *Population and Development Review* 20:3 (September 1994), 631–45.
54 John T. Sidel, *Capital, Coercion, and Crime: Bossism in the Philippines* (Honolulu, HI: University of Hawaii Press, 1999), 25 and 27.
55 Soliman M. Santos, Jr. and Paz Verdades M. Santos, *Primed and Purposeful: Armed*

96 Entrepreneurs as politicians

    Groups and Human Security Efforts in the Philippines (Geneva: Small Arms Survey, Graduate Institute of International and Development Studies, 2010), 49.
56 Joe Studwell, *Asian Godfathers*, xiii.
57 See Mark R. Thompson and Philipp Kuntz, "After Defeat: When Do Rulers Steal Elections?" in *Electoral Authoritarianism: The Dynamics of Unfree Competition*, Andreas Schedler, ed. (Boulder, CO: Rienner, 2006), 120.
58 Patricio N. Abinales and Donna J. Amoroso, *State and Society in the Philippines* (Lanham, MD: Rowman & Littlefield, 2005), 211.
59 James Clad, *Behind the Myth: Business, Money, and Power in Southeast Asia* (London: Hyman, 1989), 39.
60 Patricio N. Abinales and Donna J. Amoroso, *State and Society in the Philippines*, 246.
61 Ibid., 21–2.
62 James Fallows, "A Damaged Culture: A New Philippines," *Atlantic Monthly*, November 1, 1987, and www.theatlantic.com. This extremely controversial essay has stirred many discourses.
63 Antonio J. Tujan, Jr., ed., *Contract Growing: Intensifying TNC [Transnational Corporation] Control in Philippine Agriculture* (Manila: IBON Foundation, 1998), 39.
64 Antonio J. Tujan, *Contract Growing*, 41.
65 This is an anthropologist's report from a fishing village market in Panay, but *suki* relations are also documented in Benguet (north Luzon) and many other parts of the archipelago. See Cristina Blanc Szanton, *A Right to Survive: Subsistence Marketing in a Lowland Philippine Town* (University Park, PA: Pennsylvania State University Press, 1972), 97–108.
66 James N. Anderson, "Buy-and-Sell and Economic Personalism: Foundations for Philippine Entrepreneurship," *Asian Survey* 9:9 (September 1969), 653.
67 Quoted from William G. Davis in Cristina Blanc Szanton, *A Right to Survive*, 114.
68 See David L. Szanton, *Estancia in Transition: Economic Growth in a Rural Philippine Community* (Quezon City: Ateneo de Manila University, 1971), and Cristina B. Szanton, *A Right to Survive*.
69 Quoted from Rosanne Rutten, *Artisans and Entrepreneurs in the Rural Philippines* (Amsterdam: VU University Press, 1990), 31.
70 Mina Roces, *The Lopez Family, 1946–2000: Kinship Politics in Postwar Philippines* (Manila: De La Salle University Press, 2001), 29.
71 Frank Lynch, S.J., *Philippine Society and the Individual* (Ann Arbor, MI: University of Michigan Center for South and Southeast Asian Studies, 1984), 31–4.
72 James N. Anderson, "Buy-and-Sell and Economic Personalism," 642–3.
73 Cristina Blanc Szanton, *A Right to Survive*, 131–2.
74 Ibid., 139.
75 See Eric Vincent Batalla, "Entrepreneurship and Philippine Development," *Canadian Journal of Development Studies* 31:3–4 (2010), 341–65.
76 Ann Swidler, "Culture in Action: Symbols and Strategies," *American Sociological Review* 51:2 (April 1986), 273.
77 For more, see Lynn White, *Political Booms: Local Money and Power in Taiwan, East China, Thailand, and the Philippines* (Singapore: World Scientific, 2009), chapter 2.
78 Shieh Gwo-shyong, *"Boss" Island: The Subcontracting Network and Microentrepreneurship in Taiwan's Development* (New York: Lang, 1992).
79 The most famous treatment, written a century ago and now outdated, is Max Weber, *The Religion of China: Confucianism and Taoism* (Glencoe, IL: Free Press, 1951). Weber deserves great credit for asking the crucial question, even if with resources then available he gave a flawed answer. A treatment more in line with the ideas of this present book (or of Swidler's approach) is Susan Greenhalgh, "De-Orientalizing

the Chinese Family Firm," *American Ethnologist* 21 (1994), 746–75, based on empirical work in 25 Taiwanese enterprises.
80 The author benefitted from a November 3, 2010, lecture on "Chinese Enterprise: Resources and Opportunities" by Australian scholar Jack Barbalet, although there is clearly overlap between the concepts in that subtitle. Barbalet notes that family enterprises have been more important in Western development than is generally appreciated. He "distinguishes between objective patterns of opportunity, the specification of which permits differentiation of enterprise cultures, and cognitive opportunity structures which function in terms of schemata relating to anticipations of and responses to change." Although his original intention was to apply his model to East Asian economic "dragons" only, his response to a question changed that: he now hopes to look at the Philippines too. The lecture was at the University of Hong Kong Centre of Asian Studies, which is part of the Hong Kong Institute for Humanities and Social Sciences.
81 See the article (which is comparative both internationally and between two Philippine provinces, Cavite and Cebu) by John T. Sidel, "Economic Foundations of Subnational Authoritarianism: Insights and Evidence from Qualitative and Quantitative Research," *Democratization* (2012), 1–24.
82 Ricardo G. Abad, *Aspects of Social Capital in the Philippines: Findings from a National Survey* (Quezon City: Social Weather Stations, 2006).
83 David L. Szanton, "Contingent Moralities: Social and Economic Investment in a Philippine Fishing Town," in *Market Cultures: Society and Morality in the New Asian Capitalisms*, Robert W. Hefner, ed. (Boulder, CO: Westview, 1998).
84 These are real cases documented in American Field Service reports by Alfred Ravenholt, quoted in James N. Anderson, "Buy-and-Sell and Economic Personalism," 646.
85 David L. Szanton, *Estancia in Transition*, 64.
86 Ibid., 49.
87 Fred Eggan, "Philippine Social Structure," 14.
88 Rosanne Rutten, *Artisans and Entrepreneurs in the Rural Philippines*, 1–6.
89 Patricio N. Abinales and Donna J. Amoroso, *State and Society in the Philippines*, 246.
90 Ibid., 16.
91 The Social Weather Stations refer to "joblessness" rather than "unemployment," because its sample is aged over 18 rather than over 15. The statistic fell (improved) in 2012, and job seekers were surveyed to be optimistic it would fall further; but it was still considerable. See www.sws.org.ph/index_pr20130220.htm.
92 Karl Marx and Fredrick Engels, *Manifesto of the Communist Party*, tr. Samuel Moore [1888] (Beijing: Foreign Languages Press, 1970), 33–6.
93 W. Arthur Lewis, "Economic Development with Unlimited Supplies of Labour," *Manchester School of Economic and Social Studies* (1954), 139–91.
94 Walter W. Rostow, "The Take-Off into Self-Sustained Growth," *Economic Journal* 66 (March 1956), 25–48. Rostow styles his analysis as an "anti-Communist manifesto," but major factors in his account of development are actually consistent with Marx's. Most of his logic could as easily be adopted by socialist regimes.
95 Jane Hutchison, "Labour Politics in Southeast Asia: The Philippines in Comparative Perspective," *Routledge Handbook of Southeast Asian Politics*, Richard Robison, ed. (Abingdon: Routledge, 2013), 50.
96 Marie E. Aganon, Melisa R. Serrano, Rosalinda C. Mercado, and Ramon A. Certeza, *Revitalizing Philippine Unions: Potentials and Constraints to Social Movement Unionism* (Manila: Friedrich Ebert Stiftung and UP School of Labor and Industrial Relations, 2008), 20, based on research by Rudolf Traub-Merz. See also 42–3.
97 Nathan Gilbert Quimpo, *Contested Democracy and the Left in the Philippines* (New Haven, CT: Southeast Asia Council, Yale University, 2008), 69.

98 Whether all "full-time employed workers" were accurately counted may be a question; but see Marie E. Aganon, Melisa R. Serrano, Rosalinda C. Mercado, and Ramon A. Certeza, *Revitalizing Philippine Unions*, 2–3.
99 Marie E. Aganon, Melisa R. Serrano, Rosalinda C. Mercado, and Ramon A. Certeza, *Revitalizing Philippine Unions*, 17.
100 Dietrich Rueschmeyer, Evelyne Huber Stephens, and John D. Stephens, *Capitalist Development and Democracy* (Chicago, IL: University of Chicago Press, 1992).
101 James K. Boyce, *The Political Economy of Growth and Impoverishment in the Marcos Era* (Quezon City: Ateneo de Manila University Press, 1993), 6.
102 Richard J. Kessler, *Rebellion and Repression in the Philippines* (New Haven, CT: Yale University Press, 1989), 18.
103 Anon., "Richest Pinoys' Wealth c. 2.8 Trillion, More than a Quarter of GDP," August 1, 2013, *Philippine Star* www.philstar.com/business/2013/08/01/39191.
104 Estimated in Benedict J. Tria Kerkvliet, "Political Expectations and Democracy in the Philippines and Vietnam," *Philippine Political Science Journal* 26:49 (2005), 10–11.
105 Philippine GDP per capita in that year was still higher than in Indonesia or Vietnam, but it was growing more slowly. These measurements of poverty and GDP are in "purchasing power parity" U.S. dollars. See Arsenio M. Basilican, "Why Does Poverty Persist in the Philippines?" in *Whither the Philippines in the 21st Century*, Rodolfo C. Severino and Lorraine Carlos Salazar, eds. (Singapore: ISEAS, 2007), 204–5.
106 Mark R. Thompson, "After Populism: [Arroyo's] Winning the 'War' for Bourgeois Democracy in the Philippines," in *The Politics of Change in the Philippines*, Yuko Kasuya and Nathan Gilbert Quimpo, eds. (Pasig City: Anvil, 2010), 26–7.
107 By 2004, government spending minus interest payments was just 13 percent of GDP. Joel Rocamora, "From Regime Crisis to System Change," in *Whither the Philippines in the 21st Century*, Rodolfo C. Severino and Lorraine Carlos Salazar, ed. (Singapore: ISEAS, 2007), 36–7.
108 Anon., "Philippines to Pay 2.17 Billion Daily for Debt—Recto," *Philippine Star*, August 9, 2013, www.philstar.com/headlines/2013/08/09/1071081.
109 Bello's condemnation of "foreign forces" almost expands the concept of unrepayable debt (*utang na loób*) to the national scale. His policy prescription is to stop repayments without making the creditors into patrons. This strikes the current author as good advice. Bello does not explore what Philippine entrepreneurs would then do, if better infrastructure supported their expected profits and employment opportunities. Foreigners surely created some Philippine problems but are unlikely to solve them all. See Walden Bello's important analysis, *The Anti-Development State: The Political Economy of Permanent Crisis in the Philippines* (Manila: Anvil, 2009), xv–xxiii.
110 This is based on Philippine National Economic Development Authority official statistics. Mainstream economic theories also failed to predict China's growth since the early 1970s, Taiwan's from the mid-1950s, Thailand's before 1997 (or the crash at that time), and many other booms and busts. They neglect politics, national and local, which is the main factor of economic growth.
111 Frank Lynch, S.J., *Philippine Society and the Individual*, 417–49.
112 C. Urbanski, "Middle Class Exodus and Democratic Decay in the Philippines," *ANU Undergraduate Research Journal* 1 (2009), 74.
113 C. Urbanski, "Middle Class Exodus and Democratic Decay in the Philippines," 74.
114 A red carpet and special OFW immigration lane at the Manila airport welcome them back because of their major monetary contributions, but they seldom get red-carpet treatment in the foreign places where they work. Jason DeParle, "A Good Provider is Someone who Leaves," *International Herald Tribune*, April 21, 2007, 2.
115 Prinz Magtulis, "Remittance from OFWs Up by 5.3%," *Philippine Star*, July 16, 2013, www.philstar.com/headlines/2013/07/16/975181.

116 Ricky Carandang, "Shrinking Middle Class," *Newsbreak*, April 12, 2004. Also C. Urbanski, "Middle Class Exodus and Democratic Decay in the Philippines," 71–8.
117 Quoted in C. Urbanski, "Middle Class Exodus and Democratic Decay in the Philippines," 71.
118 Anon., "P25k Salary for Nurses Sought," *Philippine Star*, August 5, 2013, www.philstar.com/headlines/2013/08/05/1054701.
119 From a reference in Eugenia Markova, *Economic and Social Effects of Migration on Sending Countries: The Cases of Albania and Bulgaria* (Geneva: OECD, 2006), 49. The author thanks Irishman Ray Thornton for this reference. The Philippines is by no means the only country to have experience with its overseas workers and their remittances, although comparative research on these situations is scarce.
120 See http://globalization.kof.etz.ch, estimated by the KOF Swiss Economic Institute (Konjunktur-forschungstelle), Zurich, March 1, 2013.
121 Aurea Calica, "Gov't to Decongest Metro Manila," *Philippine Star*, July 7, 2013, www.philstar.com/headlines/2013/07/07/962529.
122 The author visited this former factory.
123 Cecille Suerte Felipe, "Legal Moves Eyed vs Professional Squatters," *Philippine Star*, July 3, 2013 www.philstar.com/headlines/2013/07/03/961016.
124 Louis Bacani, "Noy Asks Roxas to Lead Relocation of Informal Settlers," *Philippine Star*, August 5, 2013, www.philstar.com/headlines/2013/08/05/1055071.
125 Marvin Sy, "Drilon: Success at River Rehab Efforts Rests on Local Chief Execs," *Philippine Star*, July 7, 2013, www.philstar.com/headlines/2013/07/07/962527.
126 Cited from another source in Alastair Iain Johnston, *Social States: China in International Institutions, 1980–2000* (Princeton, NJ: Princeton University Press, 2008), 84.
127 Roehlano M. Briones, *Asia's Underachiever: Deep Constraints in Philippine Economic Growth*, CEM Working Paper (Los Baños: UP College of Economics and Management, 2009).
128 Filomeno V. Aguilar, *Clash of Spirits: The History of Power and Sugar Planter Hegemony on a Visayan Island* (Honolulu, HI: University Press of Hawaii, 1998), 228.
129 The Muslim Mindanao and Bicol regions have lower per-capita GDP than any of the Philippines' other 15 regions, while the Metro Manila, Cordillera, and south-of-Manila areas have the highest per-capita products among the regions, according to government statistics.
130 For a summary and further documentation, http://en.wikipedia.og/wiki/Economy_of_the_Philippines.
131 Daron Acemoglu and James A. Robinson, *Why Nations Fail: The Origins of Power, Prosperity, and Poverty* (New York: Crown Business, 2012). A 1933 Nazi theatrical play also included a sentiment that rational actionists in social science often reproduce: "When I hear the word 'culture,' I reach for my gun." Economists are not good at comprehending concepts that must involve internal inconsistencies; see chap. 3, fn. 12 and Geertz's references to the (radically contrasting) cockfight and Brahmana ordination ceremony that are both "like Bali."

5 Marcos, failed centralization, and land from the tiller

Landownership was, at least until 2000, the first basis of political power for most leaders in the Philippines. This country probably has the most polarized land distribution in any populous Asian nation.[1] Four-fifths of land in the archipelago is owned by one-fifth of the population. Seven-tenths of the farmers own no land.[2]

Average land holdings tended to become larger during the Spanish period because of "repurchase agreements." When a peasant needed money, he usually went to kin and "sold" land, on a theoretically temporary basis with presumed rights to buy it back at the same price. Such an agreement (*pacto de retroventa*) was in many cases difficult to liquidate; it could become long-lasting, socially acceptable, and normal for both parties. If the debtor needed more funds, for example to pay interest, the creditor might loan more, deepening a debt that both guessed would never be repaid in money. Eventually, everybody recognized that ownership of the land had permanently changed. The debtor often stayed on as a tenant tiller.[3]

Land policy in the Philippines, as in other developing countries, is for most of the people absolutely the most crucial matter. What would an effective land reform look like? Would it divide estates? Would it involve new technology? Who would run it? In the 1970s, many who believed that the country needed a serious land reform saw Ferdinand Marcos as a president willing to fight well-established landowning families—and indeed, he fought some of them. He presented himself as a pro-poor populist, even as he announced a land reform, hired technocratic economists, and promised the Philippines "new industrializing country" status.[4]

The Marcos family was marginal-*trapo*. Ferdinand's father Mariano Marcos had twice lost National Assembly elections in Ilocos Norte to a man named Julio Nulundasan. A court in the 1930s convicted Ferdinand of Nulundasan's murder. So the future president studied law while in jail and finally persuaded the Supreme Court to acquit him. He was a top student of law, as well as a boxer and wrestler, at the University of the Philippines.[5] He claimed that a Chinese pirate had been one of his ancestors. He said that during World War II he led a sizeable guerrilla army against the Japanese (although a U.S. military investigation cast doubt on this assertion). Marcos's penchant for forcefulness recommended him to some Filipinos who thought their country needed stronger central leadership.

Marcos was so eager to be president in 1965 that he abandoned the Liberal Party (which nominated the incumbent Diosdado Macapagal to be re-elected). So Marcos switched to become Nacionalista, received that party's nomination, and defeated Macapagal, winning 52 percent of the votes. As president, Marcos soon launched public works projects on roads, bridges, waterworks, and electricity infrastructure. He said he would fight corruption and would cleanse the judiciary. He appeared at first to be a reformer strong enough to get things done.

By 1969 the opposing presidential candidates, Ferdinand Marcos and Serging Osmeña, both had very tough pasts. "One [Marcos] was indicted for political murder, the other [Osmeña] for treason. Both were authoritarian in temper, skilled manipulators of complex organizations, naturally introverted, and highly motivated."[6] Like many other would-be presidents of the Philippines, perhaps to some extent Benigno Aquino, Sr., these leaders were flawed liberals. In the 1969 presidential race, Marcos was re-elected with 61 percent of the vote (up from his 1965 showing). He is the only president of the independent Philippines to have served more than one term.[7]

Philippine democracy temporarily ended after the 1971 senatorial campaign. A grenade attack on August 21 at the Plaza Miranda in Manila killed nine and injured hundreds, including most of the Liberal Party's anti-Marcos candidates for the Senate.[8] The wounded included many famous Philippine political names: Magsaysay, Salonga, Estrada-Kalaw, Mitra, Pendatun, Singson, Ilarde—and Serging Osmeña. Benigno Aquino, Jr., would have been hurt or killed, except that he was late to the meeting. He suggested that Marcos was behind the attack. Perhaps communists launched it. However that may be, Marcos benefitted. The main effects were two. The violence was cited to justify a presidential declaration of martial law. It caused important anti-Marcos politicians, notably Osmeña, to retreat from politics because of shrapnel wounds and consequent psychological depression.

The old Commonwealth Constitution, still in effect in 1972, provided that:

> In case of invasion, insurrection or rebellion, or imminent danger thereof, when the public safety requires it, [the president] may suspend the privilege of the writ of *habeas corpus*, or place the Philippines or any part thereof under Martial Law.

Marcos cited this clause and took full control of the national government—which was not in practice all local governance in the Philippines, even though he tried to make it so.

Malakas means "strong" in Tagalog, and it also means "well-connected"—echoing terms such as Chinese *guanxi*, Arabic *wasta*, or Russian *blat* (with more differences of denotation or connotation than of practical usage). Such concepts are frequent in the common speech of all these places. Clout and connections are important in politics everywhere, and they are especially stressed in diverse political cultures where patronist networks rule. As *malakas* means "strong," *maganda* means "beautiful" or "pretty." This dualism is of a type common in cultural constructs. Other examples include the literary vs. military (*wen* vs. *wu*) dualism in China, or the opposite symbolisms of cockfight and brahmana ordination ceremony that Geertz found to be both "like Bali" despite their diametric differences.[9] In each such case, neither half of a dyad determines behavior; the other half is culturally just as available. Each has been useful for the cultural community in different past situations. Each makes specifiable, non-universal options live for actors, displacing other options that actors are less likely to conceive. Culture shapes behavior without fixing it.

The Marcoses, Ferdinand and Imelda together, are still described by some Filipinos as having covered the *malakas*-to-*maganda* waterfront. Ferdinand nearly advertised his taste for arbitrary violence; he never hid that he had killed a man in his youth. Such *malakas* strength is supposed to demand that subordinates make links with the leader. Imelda was a certified beauty queen, though in her elder years she has become a target for insults on that same basis.[10] Such categories do not foreclose possibilities of cultural innovation. They describe terms in which many actors indicate that they think.

Some Philippine intellectuals, even during Marcos's early martial law era, had become so alienated by Congress members' greed and inability to reform Philippine political institutions, they applauded the 1972 abolition of Congress and its replacement by Marcos's Batasang Pambansa. This National Assembly was elected from relatively large districts that sent multiple members to Manila. The structure was designed to nationalize, under the dictator-president, clientelism that had previously been more local. But mere constitutional change did not end the sociopolitical power within their turfs of many *trapo* families.

Marcos's land reform

Marcos's "Masagana-99" ('Prosperity-99') program mandated that participating farmers plant short-stalk rice. Seeds for this had been crossbred at the International Rice Research Institute (IRRI) in Los Baños, Laguna Province. By 1980, three-quarters of Philippine farms were planted with high-yield rice varieties; a dozen years earlier, the portion had been only one-fifth.[11] In a Bulacan Province village, the new short-stalk varieties covered "all but a tiny fraction" of paddy.[12]

These seeds produced nice yields in years of good weather. But they hurt poor farmers locally, at least until they were re-hybridized into "semidwarf" varieties that lodged less often, because they raised tillers' costs for fertilizers and machines such as pumps.

Under sharecropping arrangements that had been widespread prior to Marcos's campaign, a landlord usually paid for most agricultural inputs. But with leasing, which increased during the Masagana reform, tillers only got land and were responsible for all non-land factors of production. This entitled the farmers who rented land to keep larger portions of the crop—but leasing also entailed unrecoverable expenses. If heavy rains fell and short-stalk varieties were flooded, tillers could lose value from their fertilizer and machinery investments as well as the value of their labor. The Philippines are often hit by typhoons. Tillers' indebtedness rose over multi-year periods. The Green Revolution commercialized traditional agriculture, but as a peasant said, "Rice farming these days is akin to gambling."[13]

A Manila NGO found that high-yield varieties "reduced real farm income as much as 52 percent within an eleven-year period from 1970 to 1981"—even as rice volume rose 72 percent.[14] Costs to farmers grew 51 percent, but the prices they could get fell 46 percent. The new seeds increased both production and poverty. The new technology converted farmers into defaulters.

Local patrons went into local finance. Rent increasingly came from owning debt, rather than owning land. "Smart landlords ... joined the ranks of the commercial elites."[15] The livelihoods of relatively rich rural families improved, but landless households often went into clientage. New acres were brought under the plow. But "no villager has bought land from farm profits."[16] Growing rice yielded lower net returns. This was a singular accomplishment for an Asian government.

The effects of Marcos's policies on the Philippine economy were arguably good in the short run and destructive in the long term. Presidential Decree No. 27, which had the force of law because Marcos arrogated all legislative power to himself, converted from share tenants into leaseholders tillers of rice and corn fields greater than seven hectares. Land growing other crops was exempt. Marcos's state banks loaned farmers money to buy the "miracle rice" seeds, and the fertilizers, and water systems that short-stalk rice required. In most years, the output effects were positive. Traditional seeds did reasonably well, on average, in only three out of five years. Because short-stalk rice is relatively subject to drowning, whole harvests could be wiped out by a storm. Fertilizers could be easily washed away.[17]

As an economist writes, "for Filipino rice producers, the green revolution began well and ended badly."[18] The rice price fell, while the prices of their inputs to agriculture (especially fertilizer) rose. Less genetic variety in the IRRI rice types also created risk of plant epidemics; and in 1971, the "tungro" virus hit central Luzon, reducing the crop by one-third.

Tenants in flood-prone places were particularly vulnerable, and they resisted the financial risks of becoming leaseholders, who were responsible for making the new agronomy profitable. Lowland farmers might be able to supplement their rice incomes with shrimp, fish, bamboo, or vegetables; but this did not fully compensate for occasional loss of the rice harvest as a major source of livelihood. Patronage systems may earlier have been no stronger in lowlands than in middle-elevation ecologies, but Marcos's reform strengthened them by tending to raise clients' debts.

Medium-altitude areas that use pump irrigation got somewhat better results from the IRRI rice varieties that the Marcos government subsidized. In these places, "the transfer to leasehold is attractive, in the abstract, to most farmers."[19]

Deforestation, which was also rife under Marcos, nonetheless raised the portion of land subject to flooding. Average rice yields rose in non-riverine areas of Luzon, but the ties that bound farmers to their rural patron-creditors became stronger.

At still higher altitudes, where land is steep and generally less fertile, crops are largely rain fed. Some new rice varieties, especially one called IR-5, did well in highland environments. Farmers there tend to be poorer than at lower altitudes, but they signed up for lease arrangements partly because the tiller's control of expected crop size was somewhat more weatherproof in highlands.

The Philippines suffers "more natural hazards than any other country, having had more than ten a year, affecting at least 65 million people severely."[20] Typhoons sweep these islands from June to November every year. When the intensity of the storms is exceptional, news of the damage spreads internationally (as it did in 2013 during Supertyphoon Haiyan, known nationally as Typhoon Yolanda, hitting Samar and Leyte and the regional capital Tacloban very hard). But lesser storms can also be destructive. In addition to heavy rains, seismic hazards also afflict this archipelago that would not exist without crustal uplift as the Philippine Sea Plate crunches westward beneath the islands. More than 20 volcanoes are active in the country, and earthquakes are frequent. The Philippines is estimated to lose up to 2 percent of its GDP, as an annual average, to natural disasters—especially tropical storms.[21]

The botanists at Los Baños were slow to realize that some of their seeds were increasing local political and economic inequality. Their main response was intellectually stubborn, still mainly natural-scientific and neglectful of social science: they bred better short-stalk rice that could survive submersion in flood water for somewhat longer periods. They also developed seeds that required somewhat less fertilizer and fewer pesticides. These adjustments had good effects; but by that time, many farmers had lost enthusiasm for new seeds and had switched back to older rice varieties.

Multiple cropping also expanded during the Marcos reforms. Average landholdings increased. Displaced sharecroppers were left with fewer sources of livelihood. Patrons tended to become financiers, having more tenuous links to land and to the work of their clients. Rice production rose, while tillers became poorer.[22]

Empirical research on many developing countries shows that smaller farms often produce more output. Economists generally believe that farmers grow more if they are given secure ownership of land. This depends, however, partly on farm size.[23] It also depends on whether land titles are established by government policy (sometimes resulting in larger plots owned by relatively wealthy families), or instead by the farmers themselves. Collective land when transferred to large owners, ranging from *encomienda* lords to local elites in various countries, may later become either efficient or inefficient depending on the incentives to farm entrepreneurship and on technological changes.

Settling land titles on small owners allows distress sales, which increase the average size of holdings after droughts, floods, or migrations of active rural people to urban industrial jobs.[24] Tillers' security of ownership *over time* probably raises production (as classicists like Smith or Locke guessed). Tenancy hinders efficient agricultural production, as Alfred Marshall argued. Tenants, able to keep only a share of the crop for themselves, have insufficient incentives to commit labor and capital to the fields. And landlords lack full incentives to do so too, if they receive small portions of the crop.[25] Fields are best maintained by agents who can reap major rewards from them.

Philippine sharecroppers might shift from tenancy to leasehold status under Marcos's reform—but generally the landlord had to agree. Patron approval is "probably the single most important factor" for converting tenancies into leaseholds, giving tillers more control of land and higher incomes in good years.[26] Philippine governments for years passed laws that were supposed to encourage such conversions, but without funding or enforcement. The effect of Marcos's seed-change reform, combined with his pro-leasing reform, was to make tillers more dependent on their local patron-creditors, later forcing more farmers back into tenancy. If landlords disliked what the Masagana reform asked of them, they could exempt themselves by having their tenants plant crops such as sugar.

Machines that saved labor were subsidized by Marcos's program. Surveys in Laguna and central Luzon showed that the worker-days that were required per hectare of rice declined after the late 1970s. Unemployment became especially severe among former sharecroppers, rather than among tillers in families that still owned some land. Machines lowered wages among the remaining agricultural workers, because of the hunger for work of those who had been made redundant. As Boyce writes, "Labor was not pulled from rice agriculture by more remunerative employment in other sectors. It was pushed out."[27] The green revolution for rice was, at least in these years, wondrous technology in the unintended service of disastrous development for the poor.

Agricultural technology in the Philippines is now more helpful to more people, but in crucial regions arable land is decreasing. Because Philippine laws exempted cash-crop land from reform, owners continued to shift acreage from rice to plantation exports. Coconut products (especially coco oil) have remained a leading Philippine export during all the decades this book covers. In provinces that developed or boded to develop factories, especially the relatively prosperous south Tagalog regions such as Laguna or Batangas, owners could hold on to land by keeping it out of rice cultivation. They correctly speculated that its value would increase later.

Overall, at least during Marcos's time and for many years later, as Fegan shows,

> rice production under the terms of trade and natural risks prevailing in the Philippines in the [1980s] has been unprofitable. Mobile capital has sought other investments ... capitalist entrepreneurs stay out of farming, finding niches upstream and downstream of the farm.[28]

Landless tenant peasants seldom have savings. A patron who hires them to work his land may also allow them to build shacks, usually with materials they buy. Ownership of the buildings they put up is generally presumed to be the landlord's. They usually also have small yards for chickens or hogs, and these sidelines produce some sustenance but scant income. Land ownership, while still important in many localities, is not the only way to control clients. Rural administrators are surprisingly many, in comparison to the number of tillers. Hierarchy among overseers at different levels can cause conflicts whenever it is unclear who is in charge of serving an absent owner. The patron–client relationship has become more seldom face-to-face (except perhaps at occasional election rallies). In practice, layers of patrons and sub-patrons have multiplied.

Tillers have faced complex rural hierarchies, each of whose layers charged various kinds of rents. Latifundismo in most of the rural Philippines has remained relatively stable. It made money reliably for landowners who had large tracts, for their majordomos who could maintain stable local jobs, and increasingly for owners of debt. It is unlikely to change much until new economic factors come into play.[29] This pattern does not benefit most Filipinos or the country as a whole. Industrial and commercial entrepreneurship has affected the country slowly; so local-political change has likewise been slow. The main result of Marcos's reforms in the countryside was to strengthen clientelism through indebtedness.

Democratic *trapo* stability

Where most people are farmers and democratic elections are the accepted means of legitimating government, state redistribution of land from elites to tillers might serve most voters. But land reform of this populist sort requires sufficient leftism in the state to make democratization meaningful as a syndrome that reinforces itself over time. Where this process has been lacking (as in Guatemala or the Philippines), political modernization has scant local basis. Where it has been present (as in Costa Rica), democracy is better sustained.[30]

Progress in either the Philippines or Latin America, according to Ernest Feder who studies both, depends on distributing agricultural resources to promote social change. Feder contrasts two approaches to this issue: "technocrats" want to alter agricultural production systems by using more capital for machinery, management, irrigation, clearing jungles, "magic" seeds, and education of peasants on ways to adopt new cropping techniques. Because the money to finance such changes is usually controlled directly or indirectly by current latifundista landowners, any improvement for tillers is a "trickle down" effect. Feder calls the technocrats "elite-oriented."

"Reformers," on the other hand, are "peasant-oriented."

> [They] see in the existing agrarian structure an almost absolute barrier to an efficient use of technologies.... Hence, as a prerequisite for a rapidly expanding agricultural sector able to distribute much greater benefits to the peasants, they propose to do away with the existing agrarian structure.... It is probable (although of course not certain) that the Reformers' approach to agricultural development is the correct one.[31]

Feder knew that despite his hopes, "the latafundio is firmly entrenched."

Where socioeconomic development has actually occurred in the Philippines, its main factor has been non-agrarian change that sometimes has agricultural progress as a side result. Greater involvement of ex-peasants in manufacturing and selling, rather than changes of agronomy, may be more beneficial in the long term for most people than either technocratic fixes for agricultural productivity or reformist hopes for changing local or national politics. A major value of land reform for some tillers might lie in the possibility that they could administer it (rather than having landowners control it). Eventually many of these quit farming for higher-paid pursuits.

The Philippines has been more oligarchic than most other nations. Even Marcos, strong dictator though he wanted to be, could not totally destroy his rivals. (Hitler, Mao, and especially Stalin were far more thoroughgoing in their despotic projects.) Neither Marcos nor his political enemies permanently changed the local structure of Philippine politics. The country lacked any reliable "protection pact" among elites; so (in Slater's words) it has also lacked "the strongest coalitional basis for authoritarian regimes both to *extract* resources from elites and to *organize* their most powerful allies."[32]

Marcos tried to destroy the political family of Eugenio Lopez, Sr., who had started as a potentate in Iloilo, Panay, for example. Lopez by the early 1970s had become the wealthiest man in the republic. He was head of the Manila Electric Company, a sugar magnate, director of the largest media conglomerate—and an ardent opponent of Marcos. So after declaring martial law, Marcos had Lopez's son imprisoned on capital charges. He forced Lopez to give up major business interests.[33] But the would-be centralist president could not abolish local power, and after 1986 the Lopezes returned to prominence on their traditional turf in Iloilo.

In northern Cebu, Marcos received support from the Durano patronage network—but the dictator tried to hedge his bets, appointing a non-Duranista as governor to counterbalance local Durano power. After Marcos was defeated in 1986, his successor Cory Aquino was able to remove a pro-Marcos Durano from the mayoralty of the major north Cebu island city, Danao. Even then, "policies allowed the Duranos to retain the coercive mechanisms they had built up over nearly forty years of political dominance."[34] The strongest Philippine president could weaken, but seldom could totally destroy, resilient local power networks.

The dictator's violence obscured his government's infirmities. Doronila argues that the Philippine state became "highly interventionist" from the time of independence into the Marcos period. He says this led to a "transformation of the class structure, with the appearance of new classes" and to "conflict of interest among segments of the dominant class affected by change."[35] In comparison with the Spanish and American colonial regimes, which were glosses on the greater power of local nonstate networks, this description of a more "interventionist" post-independence state is accurate. Marcos was more forceful in trying to strengthen his own government. But the Philippines, to a greater extent than other countries with which it is usually compared, had and has a weak central state.

Marcos claimed his "New Society" would end the Philippines' "Old Oligarchy." But he merely created a new oligarchy, alongside the clans he had weakened but not destroyed. An advisor later said that Marcos thought "he could have a vision for society ... and still loot it."[36] The dictator's political demise was gradual. His rival Salvador Laurel's nephew had been able in 1980 to win the governorship of Batangas, the Laurel home province, despite an attempt by Marcos's soldiers to abscond with ballot boxes. Laurel became the center of an anti-Marcos coalition of traditional families that included former Liberals (such as Diosdado Macapagal and Gerardo Roxas, respectively a former president and son of a former president) as well as Benigno Aquino, Jr., who moved to exile in America. Although their United Democratic Opposition (UNIDO) could win few elections, this union of heads of well-known clans maintained the political hopes of the many gentry whom Marcos had disaffected.[37]

Non-Ilocanos in the military resented that Marcos mainly promoted members of his own linguistic group to officerships. Together with Chief of Staff Fidel Ramos, a Protestant Ilocano from Pangasinan, they they started a Reform the Armed Forces Movement, "RAM." This group was not openly anti-Marcos at first, as UNIDO was. But together, the influence of UNIDO and RAM (and Defense Minister Enrile, also an Ilocano) showed that President Marcos had not effectively suppressed alternative elites. One of the anti-Marcos leaders' main concerns was the possibility of their unattributable assassinations. The level of violence in the Philippines is high; and for politicians there, it remains a greater worry than foreign democrats generally want to realize.

Benigno S. Aquino, Jr., was murdered at the Manila airport on August 21, 1983, as soon as he returned from exile. Marcos denied complicity and mandated the "Agrava Commission" to investigate. Evidence implicated his chief of staff and close associate Fabian Ver, who resigned.

Marcos faced the expiration of his six-year term in 1987. He knew that he was losing ground to potential oppositions in UNIDO and RAM. So with studied nonchalance, he announced plans for a "snap election" on the TV program *This Week with David Brinkley*. Elites in UNIDO and in the Laban Party (Lakas ng Bayan, whose acronym means "fight") correctly surmised that Corazon Aquino, widow of Marcos's assassinated rival, would be an effective campaigner for the presidency—and Salvador Laurel was willing to run on the same ticket as merely the vice-presidential candidate perhaps because of his own pre-1980 close connections with Marcos.[38] Centralizer-president Marcos apparently thought he had succeeded in dominating local politics in most of the archipelago.

At election day, the National Movement for Free Elections gathered data for a "quick count" on the basis of exit polls at three-quarters of all Philippine precincts. Namfrel announced on the day after the election (February 8, 1986) that Aquino had won with 52 percent of the vote. But Marcos's National Assembly, together with the Marcos-dominated Comelec as well as many media, said that he had won on the basis of returns from a more complete set of precincts. Scattered evidence of vote-stealing and other coercions created a widespread public impression that Corazon Aquino should have taken the presidency. Whether she won at the polls or not—she probably did, but nobody surely knows—many by that time gave her the benefit of doubt. Defense Minister Juan Ponce Enrile and Gen. Fidel Ramos on February 22 switched to the Aquino side and gave military backing to the dramatic "people power revolution" that television broadcast. The impression of Cory Aquino's win was domestic within the Philippines, and it was also international. This was a messy, constitutionally questionable, but effective way of deciding a very important presidential election. Marcos's apparent futile violence was really the deciding vote.

Ramos and Enrile had withdrawn with soldiers to Camp Aguinaldo and then to Camp Crame on EDSA Boulevard in Manila. Marcos on February 24 had himself sworn in for a new presidential term—but Corazon Aquino also took the presidential oath at an almost simultaneous ceremony in the Club Filipino near Camp Crame. Marcos eventually realized that the army would no longer obey him. Telephone calls from U.S. diplomats and politicians invited him to board American aircraft, first to Clark Air Base and then to Hawai'i, where in 1989 he died.

Marcos was defeated in stages: first by the political ineptness of his henchmen who assassinated Benigno Aquino, Jr., then by the reaction of career military officers who led the February 1986 *kudeta* because Marcos had promoted many officers on ethnic or factional grounds rather than merit, by fraud in the disputed presidential election, and thereafter by the "people power" rally at EDSA. The military aspect of his departure was as important as the populist aspect.

"People power" was loosely organized. The anti-Marcos coalition was as diverse as Marcos's own slow, even "gentle," early introduction of martial law had been, imposed at first only on obvious rivals of the president. Marcos's "recurring pattern of reform and crackdown originally demobilized most moderates and radicalized others." As Boudreau says, this dictator's repression had been limited in speed and strength, and the resistance it engendered was "revolution-*esque*" rather than revolutionary. Incomplete repression brought an incomplete sequel. A "complex of movement organizations" rather than a single party brought Marcos down.[39]

Land non-reform and political fragmentation after Marcos

The Philippines is by no means the only country in which liberal democratic procedures have been restored after a wave of dictatorship. Many others, e.g., Argentina, Guatemala, or South Korea, have shared this experience.[40] Later strengthenings of democracy in some of the others encouraged cautious optimism about the Philippine future. An analyst of the "third wave" and its ebbs wrote that, "In contrast to durable authoritarianism in Egypt and Malaysia and a squandered opportunity for democratization in Iran, the Philippines provides a test case of authoritarian breakdown and democratization."[41] This was almost everyone's impression after 1986. Such a paradigm captures some aspects of Philippine politics. It would capture more if attention were paid to the foundations of national state forms in localities—in any of these countries.

President Cory Aquino quickly tried to install new local officials. For example, Aquino wanted Ruben Umali as Mayor of Lipa City, Batangas, to replace a Marcos supporter in that post. Two weeks of negotiations were required to persuade the outgoing mayor to give up physical possession of his desk in Lipa City Hall. Aquino's man, Umali, promised in his inauguration speech to retain civil service employees—or at least to observe their "performance" before firing them. Many of the posts were openly advertised but then filled in closed political meetings of Umali's advisors. Some civil servants from the old regime simply "switched their loyalty to the new mayor," and this was accepted.[42] The potentially lucrative post of City Engineer, in charge of contracting to build roads, went to a relative of Mayor Umali. Barangay captains, who by law are supposed to stand for elections on a nonpartisan basis, flocked to Umali's office, asking to join his UNIDO party.

Newspapers soon claimed that "cronyism" made way for "Coryism." The new president's Cojuangco clan and their fair-weather friends took over some assets that had previously been controlled by friends of Ferdinand Marcos. In many such cases, Marcos had previously appropriated them from families that managed to retrieve them after 1986.

Some peasant leaders had joined the anti-Marcos movement. They hoped Cory Aquino would be more populist; so they organized a rally at Mendiola Bridge across the Pasig River in Manila, where they had previously conflicted with Marcos's troops. After several days of attempting to negotiate with Aquino's advisors for better land policies, they marched toward Malacañang. Police and marines opened fire, killing 13 and injuring hundreds.[43] Leftist agrarian guerrilla leaders immediately withdrew from peace talks with government. By 1987, Aquino made a speech at the Philippines Military Academy, vowing she had "unsheathed the sword of war" against the communists. Faced with several threatening *kudeta* led by rightist generals, she abolished the Presidential Committee on Human Rights that had been investigating abuses by soldiers during Marcos's time.[44]

Cory Aquino's land reform was a mirage. As an Australian economist wrote,[45]

> This government is simply not going to cause a revolution in the social structure. Just before the new Congress convened, as her near-dictatorial powers were about to elapse, Aquino signed a generalized land-reform-should-happen decree. Most observers took this as an indication that land reform would not happen, since the decree left all the decisions about the when, where, and how of land reform to the land-heavy Congress.

Trapo oligarchs have been ideologically divided. A few, represented for example by the Aquino and Cojuangco families, have sometimes supported moderate land reforms for the purpose of heading off electoral or guerrilla defeats by radical leftists. (This situation is comparable to that in Costa Rica after that country's 1948 civil war. It contrasts with the Guatemalan pattern since the mid-1950s.)[46] In the Philippines, at most times, the landowning oligarchy has been monotonically opposed to any serious land reforms.

The main alternative, which landowners feared, came from the Communist Party of the Philippines in its "September Thesis" of 1988. This document advocated open rather than clandestine collective action, mainly on plains rather than peripheral hilly fields, recruiting several different kinds of leaders, and adding a peasant component to the urban "people power" movement of 1986.[47] Squatting on land and other forms of "everyday resistance" were promoted by the communists, but they insisted that protests should not be hidden.

Corazon Aquino's "land" reform encouraged some corporations, including that of her own Cojuangco family, to offer non-voting minority stock shares to their workers—but not land.[48] Her administration's "Comprehensive Agrarian Reform Program ('CARP'), begun in 1988, was dominated by *anti*-reform policy currents and marked by nepotism, corruption, repression, and the non-participation of several rural social movements."[49] Fidel Ramos's election later temporarily improved the performance of this CARP as a land reform. By 1996, the World Bank was financing it better. But by the late 1990s and early 2000s, after Estrada and Arroyo became presidents, the Bank discouraged its implementation in small and medium farms (five to 24 hectares). So "market-assisted" reform was thereafter dominated by people who already had land and money.

The Comprehensive Agrarian Reform Program was ineffective because nine-tenths of the targeted land did not change ownership. The irrigated portion of Philippine arable had expanded during the Marcos era, but not afterward. As a newspaper reported, this amounted to "failure of a land reform whose aim was merely to distribute land to the tillers without the attendant technical and financial support." The stock redistribution option scheme, in which farmers were supposed to get partial ownership of plantations they worked, was reported to have its "own set of failures.... So both schemes can be considered back to zero."[50]

Therefore a new "Comprehensive Agrarian Reform Program Extension with Reforms" (CARPER) was proposed by party-list Congress members in 2009, to extend the time in which land could be redistributed and to allocate more pesos of support for agriculture. But it was difficult to pass this law, because most members of Congress and their wealthiest constituents are fond of continuing to control land. A watered-down version passed. The new law required that private lands could be redistributed from recent owners (who were often rich) only if the original CARP had previously handed out nine-tenths of its local target land. The Department of Agrarian Reform was very slow to release implementing rules. The delays were both in law and in enforcement. Local authorities were usually unwilling to implement the state's land regulations.

Many Philippine clans regard land as existential rather than economic, but they especially wanted to keep suburban agricultural land that might later be developed as urban. For example, the Manotoks, who owned a valuable 34 hectare property next to the gated community of Ayala Heights, left their land undeveloped because, "land was for the family—and noone else—to take care of, to live on, and to earn from. Business ventures with real estate developers were something new." When a fire in the Quezon City Hall destroyed land records, two other clans challenged the Manotoks' possession. Their ownership was confirmed in many lower and superior court cases involving multiple agencies, especially the Land Registration Authority of the Justice Department as well as the Land Management Bureau of the Department of Environment and Natural Resources. These units' functions overlap in practice. When the case went to the Supreme Court, the Manotoks hired a former justice as their lawyer. "It apparently helped that Feliciano was once part of the brethren." But televangelist "Mike" Velarde, head of the Catholic evangelical sect El Shaddai, is also in the real estate business; and he openly lobbied a justice whom he had supported for appointment to the Supreme Court, hoping (without success) that the Supreme Court would decide against the Manotoks. Ownership involved politics, not just law.[51]

A similar case, also apparently decided on political bases in large part, was *People of the Philippines* v. *Benjamin "Kokoy" Romualdez* (brother of former First Lady Imelda Romualdez Marcos, from a major *trapo* family in Leyte). The question was whether statutes of limitations protected Benjamin Romualdez from punishment in numerous corruption cases that dated from 1962 to 1985. After many iterations in lower courts, the Supreme Court (with all 15 justices meeting unusually *en banc*, rather than in one of their five-justice panels) voted against Romualdez—but later reversed itself after a pleading "on a different ground." As a dissenting justice, Arturo Brion, wrote: "We cannot blame an adversely affected litigant who asks: 'Why was Benjamin 'Kokoy' Romualdez given exceptional treatment, while I was not?'"[52]

Yet another land case in which the Supreme Court's decision seems to have been politically influenced was occasioned by an expansion of Batangas Port in the early 2000s. Many small owners had rice fields that Enrique Razon, Jr., wanted for this second-largest port in the Philippines (after Manila's). Justice Angelina Sandoval-Gutierrez, herself from Batangas, wrote a decision that gave mainly agricultural owners of 1.2 million square meters of land 5,500 pesos per square meter (after lower-level hearings had valued the land down to a government offer of just 400 pesos/sq.m.). But after Sandoval-Gutierrez retired from the court, two of the other justices "flip-flopped" and acceded to a new decision, compensating the farmers at a rate of just 425 pesos. Was Razon's political influence the reason? A seasoned observer found "unsettling questions" about whether the Supreme Court treated all Philippine citizens equally under law.[53]

Assessing Philippine land reform more broadly, Kerkvliet reported by 2005 that, "Land redistribution has been barely perceptible."[54] CARP funds worth 200 million pesos in 2007 and 2008 were "granted to questionable nongovernment organizations." An Ombudsman started investigations—five years later. The money was said to have gone into "dummy NGOs, reportedly for ghost projects."[55]

The CARP law, including its CARPER amendment, expired in 2014. PNoy and many landlords favored its further extension. A pro-poor peasants' group, however, petitioned the Catholic Bishops' Conference to "reconsider the position" of supporting the government on this, in order to make a "new, genuine, and truly redistributive land reform program." A leader of these farmers pointed out that CARP and CARPER had distributed more public land than landlords' land. "In particular, Hacienda Luisita [owned by the Aquino-Cohuangco family] is a testament to CARP's failure in addressing landlessness, poverty, hunger, social injustice, oppression, and deception in the country."[56]

Three years after PNoy's election, his family's Hacienda Luisita sugar plantation decided to sell 6,600 square meters to more than 6,000 "farmer-beneficiaries." Many of the latter, however, were reportedly planning to sell their small farm lots once they received titles to the land. The total size of Hacienda Luisita is much larger. Leaders of some farmers' groups suggested to the Supreme Court that they should get the whole plantation and that the Department of Agrarian Reform (DAR) should be held "in contempt for violating its order to distribute the 4,915-hectare farm owned by the family of President Aquino." They also objected to the procedure of having a raffle-draw system to determine which tiller got which Lot Allocation Certificate for a specific small plot of land. "Who in his right mind would accept this? President Aquino is making land reform a mere lottery affair. This is total mockery of land reform and contempt of us farm workers," according to the head of one tillers' group. She also said that the Department

> has excluded land claimed by the Rizal Commercial Banking Corp, Centenary Holdings, and SCTEx [Subic-Clark-Tarlac Expressway]. DAR is planning to shrink down the size of land [allocated] by about 400 hectares, which would result in the reduction of an average 0.66 hectare to be awarded to each beneficiary.[57]

This land reform was incomplete. Other large Philippine haciendas saw even less reform. Outside Manila, land politics is still the main form of local politics. Regional *trapos* control it more than the central state can.

Action possibilities against undemocratic landowning

The central government in Manila might extend its influence in rural Philippine places if it started programs to assure farmers would own more of the fields they till. A serious land reform would gradually balance the power of *trapo* clans in most parts of the archipelago, perhaps encouraging them to start businesses. Congress and anti-leftist soldiers have resisted such a reform, and Marcos did not achieve one. *Kudeta* to preclude land reforms threatened later presidents, notably Cory Aquino. Reformers on other issues, such as her son PNoy, have avoided raising this most sensitive matter. Most presidents have also been landholders. Marcos launched a centralist land reform, but its main result was to strengthen the local control of landholders and creditors over tillers.

Much-heralded land reforms in other countries have likewise often been ineffective for empowering farmers.[58] They bring results for growth and democracy only when state elites see political benefits from implementing them. In Taiwan during the early 1950s, for example, the mainlander-run government faced a majority of people (and landowners) who were Taiwanese; so serious land reform helped legitimate a minority-led regime there. In China after the communists' victory, or in Japan during the American occupation, dominant governments could impose land reforms. Such conditions have seldom applied in other countries, including the Philippines, where no major redistributive land reform has occurred since the Americans gave friar estates to *trapo* families that helped U.S. colonial rule.

Presuming that Filipinos want to avoid having a violent revolution, the chance of more thoroughgoing land reform and of balancing local with central power in rural areas depends on gradual economic modernization. This is already providing social and financial bases for non-landholding political elites. As congressional passage of the anemic CARP and CARPER laws suggests, many Philippine politicians realize that land is crucial to the livelihoods of most of their compatriots. Progress of a slow kind is most likely to come from the effects of industrialization and commercialization on modal types of leaders, rather than from land reforms of a more direct kind.

Notes

1 Jonathan Fox, "Editor's Introduction," in *The Challenge of Rural Democratization: Perspectives from Latin America and the Philippines*, Fox, ed. (London: Frank Cass, 1990), 6.
2 Francisco Lara, Jr. and Horacio Morales, Jr., "The Peasant Movement and the Challenge of Democratization," in *The Challenge of Rural Democratization: Perspectives from Latin America and the Philippines*, Jonathan Fox, ed. (London: Frank Cass, 1990), 144.
3 Patricio N. Abinales and Donna J. Amoroso, *State and Society in the Philippines* (Lanham, MD: Rowman & Littlefield, 2005), 81.
4 Gary Hawes, "Marcos, His Cronies, and the Philippines' Failure to Develop," in *Southeast Asian Capitalists*, Ruth McVey, ed. (Ithaca, NY: Southeast Asia Program, Cornell University, 1992), 145.
5 Edited Wikipedia entries for Ferdinand Marcos, seen variously on May 15, 2007, and November 24, 2013.
6 Rasil Mojares, *The Man Who Would Be President: Serging Osmeña and Philippine Politics* (Cebu: Maria Cacao, 1986), 124.
7 In the American colonial "Commonwealth" period, Manuel L. Quezon was elected to the presidency twice, in 1935 and 1941 (just before the Japanese invasion, which sent him into exile). After Marcos, the 1987 Constitution forbids a president's re-election.
8 Rasil Mojares, *The Man Who Would Be President*, 148.
9 See Clifford Geertz, "Deep Play: Notes on the Balinese Cockfight," *The Interpretation of Cultures* (New York: Basic Books, 1973), 412–53. The cockfight and ordination ceremony are substantially opposite—"functionally" so, reflecting the logic in Geertz's earlier writing, notably *Agricultural Involution* (Berkeley, CA: University of California Press, 1971), whose logic his later works tried to reject.
10 Imagine those two in China. Ferdinand Marcos would hardly have qualified as a *wu*-type military hero, and Imelda was by no account a literata. In Geertz's Balinese terms (which are Malay, closer to the Philippines), Ferdinand was rather like the fighting cock, although his wife was no brahmana priest. Paradigms in which people and actions are perceived can vary greatly among cultures.

11 Antonio J. Tujan, Jr., ed., *Contract Growing: Intensifying TNC [Transnational Corporation] Control in Philippine Agriculture* (Manila: IBON Foundation, 1998), 17, gives the figures 75 percent and 21 percent for these two years, considering all kinds of crops.
12 Relying partly on work by David Wurfel, see Brian Fegan, "The Philippines: Agrarian Stagnation Under a Decaying Regime," *Agrarian Transformations: Local Processes and the State in Southeast Asia*, in Gillian Hart, Andrew Turton, Benjamin White, Brian Fegan, and Lim Teck Ghee, eds. (Berkeley, CA: University of California Press, 1989)," 133, and Fegan, "Accumulation on the Basis of an Unprofitable Crop," in *Agrarian Transformations*, 160–2.
13 Umehara Hiromitsu, "Green Revolution for Whom?" in *Second View from the Paddy*, Antonio J. Ledesma, Perla Q. Makil, and Virginia A. Miralao, eds. (Manila: Institute of Philippine Culture, Ateneo de Manila University, 1983), 38–9.
14 Evidence that high-yield grains raised production but lowered farmers' incomes has been found in the Philippines by many researchers: by Hirohitsu Umehara, by an IRRI team involving Violeta Cardova and Robert Herdt, and by the ACES Foundation of Manila, and others. See Rolando B. Modina and A.R. Ridao, *IRRI Rice: The Miracle that Never Was* (Quezon City: ACES Foundation, 1987), 35.
15 Umehara Hiromitsu, "Green Revolution for Whom?" 39.
16 Brian Fegan, "Accumulation on the Basis of an Unprofitable Crop," 160–2.
17 Brian Fegan, "Between the Lord and the Law: Tenants' Dilemmas," in *View from the Paddy: Empirical Studies of Philippine Rice Farming and Tenancy*, Frank Lynch, S.J., ed., *Philippine Sociological Review*, 20:1–2 (January/April 1972), 114.
18 James K. Boyce, *The Political Economy of Growth and Impoverishment in the Marcos Era* (Quezon City: Ateneo de Manila University Press, 1993), 115–19, also 87.
19 Brian Fegan, "Between the Lord and the Law," 115.
20 This is an estimate by Belgian scientists who may not have properly included Bangladesh in their survey. Bangladesh like the Philippines has more than its share of natural disasters. Events such as the tragic Typhoon Haiyan in 2013 showed that some factors of development cannot be affected by either national or local politics. But wealth and development allow countries to face such disasters somewhat better. See Greg Bankoff, "Profiting from Disasters: Corruption, Hazard, and Society in the Philippines," in *Corruption and Good Governance in Asia*, Nicholas Tarling, ed. (London: Routledge, 2005), 165.
21 Ronald Hill, *Southeast Asia: People, Land, and Economy* (Crows Nest, NSW: Allen & Unwin, 2002), 285.
22 Benedict J. Tria Kerkvliet, *Everyday Politics in the Philippines: Class and Status Relations in a Central Luzon Village* (Berkeley, CA: University of California Press, 1990; also Quezon City: New Day, 1991), 4–6.
23 An example is Rasmus Heltberg, "Rural Market Imperfections and the Farm Size–Productivity Relationship: Evidence from Pakistan," *World Development* 26:10 (1998), 1807–26.
24 Sophie C. Jin, *The Peasant in the Produce Section: Agricultural Adjustment for China's Small Farmers* (Woodrow Wilson School Senior Thesis, Princeton University, 2011).
25 Marshall and his critics are mooted in Ashutosh Varshney, *Democracy, Development, and the Countryside: Urban–Rural Struggles in India* (New York: Cambridge University Press, 1998), 12.
26 Frank Lynch, S.J., *Philippine Society and the Individual* (Ann Arbor, MI: University of Michigan Center for South and Southeast Asian Studies, 1984), 351.
27 James K. Boyce, *The Political Economy of Growth and Impoverishment in the Marcos Era*, 150.
28 Brian Fegan, "The Philippines: Agrarian Stagnation," 176.

29 Compare Ernest Feder, *The Rape of the Peasantry: Latin America's Landholding System* (New York: Doubleday, 1971).
30 Deborah J. Yashar, *Demanding Democracy: Reform and Reaction in Costa Rica and Guatemala, 1870s-1950s* (Stanford, CA: Stanford University Press, 1997), *passim*.
31 Ernest Feder, *The Rape of the Peasantry*, vii–ix. See also Feder's book on the Philippines, *Perverse Development* (Quezon City: Foundation for Nationalist Studies, 1983).
32 Dan Slater, *Ordering Power: Contentious Politics and Authoritarian Leviathans in Southeast Asia* (New York: Cambridge University Press, 2010), 6.
33 Alfred W. McCoy, "Rent-Seeking Families and the Philippine State: A History of the Lopez Family," in *An Anarchy of Families: State and Family in the Philippines*, McCoy, ed. (Madison, WI: University of Wisconsin Center for Southeast Asian Studies, 1993), 429–536.
34 Michael Cullinane, "Patron as Client: Warlord Politics and the Duranos of Danao," in *An Anarchy of Families: State and Family in the Philippines*, Alfred W. McCoy, ed. (Madison, WI: University of Wisconsin Center for Southeast Asian Studies, 1993), 185.
35 Amando Doronila, *The State, Economic Transformation, and Political Change in the Philippines, 1946–1972* (Singapore: Oxford University Press, 1992), 6–7.
36 Quoted, from one of Marcos's advisors during a retrospective interview, in Alasdair Bowie and Danny Unger, *The Politics of Open Economies: Indonesia, Malaysia, the Philippines, and Thailand* (New York: Cambridge University Press, 1997), 128. It should be noted, however, that the government's Sandiganbayan anti-graft court, investigating the reported $10 billion that Marcos may have misappropriated to himself and his family, failed to find much money after two decades of searching. Either the fiscal looting was less than earlier imagined, or the paper trail was hidden by experts. See Carlos H. Conde, "Marcos Family Returning to the Limelight in the Philippines," *International Herald Tribune*, July 7–8, 2007, 1.
37 Jason Brownlee, *Authoritarianism in an Age of Democratization* (New York: Cambridge University Press, 2007), 186–7.
38 Ibid., 193–4.
39 Vincent Boudreau, citing Ricardo Trota Jose, *Resisting Dictatorship: Repression and Protest in Southeast Asia* (New York: Cambridge University Press, 2004), 15, 62, 185, 239.
40 Barry Gills, Joel Rocamora, and Richard Wilson, eds., *Low-intensity Democracy: Political Power in the New World Order* (London: Pluto, 1993).
41 Jason Brownlee, *Authoritarianism in an Age of Democratization*, 182.
42 Kimura Masataka, *Elections and Politics, Philippine Style: A Case in Lipa* (Manila: De La Salle University Press, 1997), 164–5, and further pages to 168.
43 Francisco Lara, Jr. and Horacio Morales, Jr., "The Peasant Movement and the Challenge of Democratization in the Philippines," 143.
44 Joel Rocamora, "Lost Opportunities, Deepening Crisis: The Philippines under Cory Aquino," in *Low Intensity Democracy: Political Power in the New World Order*, Barry Gills, Joel Rocamora, and Richard Wilson, eds. (Boulder, CO: Pluto Press, 1993), 198–201.
45 Quoted in James Fallows, "A Damaged Culture: A New Philippines," *Atlantic Monthly*, November 1, 1987, and www.theatlantic.com.
46 Deborah J. Yashar, *Demanding Democracy*, e.g., 168, 179–91.
47 Jennifer C. Franco and Turnino M. Burras, "Paradigm Shift: The 'September Thesis' and the Rebirth of the 'Open' Mass Movement in the Era of Neoliberal Globalization in the Philippines," in *Agrarian Angst and Rural Resistance in Contemporary Southeast Asia*, Dominique Caouette and Sarah Turner, eds. (New York: Routledge, 2009), 215–16.
48 Alan Berlow, *Dead Season: A Story of Murder and Revenge on the Philippine Island of Negros* (New York: Pantheon, 1996), 161.

49 Jennifer C. Franco and Turnino M. Burras, "Paradigm Shift," 209 (italics added).
50 *Philippine Daily Inquirer*, August 16, 2010, 1.
51 Marites Danguilan-Vitug, *Shadow of Doubt: Probing the Supreme Court* (Manila: Public Trust Media Group, 2010), 124–30.
52 Ibid., 130–8.
53 Ibid., 142.
54 Benedict J. Tria Kerkvliet, "Political Expectations and Democracy in the Philippines and Vietnam," *Philippine Political Science Journal* 26:49 (2005), 9.
55 Michel Punongbayan, "Team Formed to Probe 200M CARP Fund Mess," *Philippine Star*, August 7, 2013, www.philstar.com/headlines/2013/08/07/1060951.
56 Ding Cervantes, "CBCP [the Bishops' Conference] Asked to Reconsider Stand on CARP," *Philippine Star*, July 7, 2013, www.philstar.com/headlines/2013/07/07/962515.
57 Ric Sapnu, "Luisita Beneficiaries Plan to Sell Farm Lots," *Philippine Star*, July 20, 2013, www.philstar.com/headlines/2013/07/20/991121 and Ding Cervantes, "Luisita Farmers to Seek Suspension of Farmland Raffle," *Philippine Star*, July 13, 2013, www.philstar.com/headlines/2013/07/19/987541.
58 Tai Hung-chao, "The Political Process of Land Reform," in *The Political Economy of Development*, Norman T. Uphoff and Warren F. Ilchman, eds. (Berkeley, CA: University of California Press, 1972), 295–303, and related chapters in that anthology.

6 Law of rule, power of separations

Centralization is mistrusted by many Philippine elites, as Marcos unintentionally showed. Authority in that large country is divided both functionally and geographically. Such a situation may be natural in an archipelago of separate islands, most of which are further split by high volcanic ranges. American rule gave the Philippine landscape a fastidious new principle: the constitutional theory of separation of powers. To geographical facts of division, this added functional ideals of division. Just as checks among parts of the U.S. government tend to slow democratic evolution there, the American legacy on these islands produces similar effects.[1]

Federalism has sometimes been mooted as a possibility for the Philippines, but geographically defined rights are the main constitutional aspect of the American pattern that was not exported to America's colony. Filipinos sometimes make a quasi-joke that the whole archipelago should become a U.S. state (in which case it would contain almost three times as many people as does the current most populous state, California). The Spanish colonial regime in theory ran a unitary government. Neither the Malolos Republic nor the American colony—or the post-1946 independent Philippines—changed this unitary ideal (except recently to a limited extent in the Muslim-majority twelfth of Mindanao). A liberal academic, Jose Abueva, has mooted more extensive localization and autonomy.[2] But it is difficult to see how more federalism would help to pull together a nation whose central government, in the view of many analysts, remains weak.

As a Senate source said,

> we still have basically an Asian culture, but we love the West so we adopted mostly the American system. But the problem is, we tinkered with it to favor the executive. So we liked the separation of powers, but we don't like the check and balance.[3]

The Philippine Constitution follows some U.S. models, although it has acquired very important distinctive features. For example, the Supreme Court of 15 justices is supposed to be independent of the executive—but the president appoints all the justices and other judges (who can serve until age 70) without any need for legislative consent.[4] Also, the House of Representatives contains geographically elected members from 206 districts; but it also now has about 20 party-list members, and the president may appoint additional representatives up a total of 250 (i.e., 24 more). These provisions usually strengthen the chief executive.

They are countervailed by the hold of localist families on many congressional seats. The methods by which senators and the vice-president are chosen also weaken the presidency. All senators are elected, like the president, from the constituency of the whole nation. By another separate ballot, so is the vice-president. Senators win with pluralities (seldom with majorities) until the number of available Senate seats is filled—12 of them every three years. But since all senators have run and "won" in the full archipelago-wide constituency, they may imagine later victory as a potential president. Rivalry at the top of the system is intensified by these rules.

The Senate therefore tends to be independent of the president. Representatives in the House tend join the ruling presidential party, if they were not already in it when elected, because a decision to join affects the budgetary resources they receive. They need this money to attract constituents and clients.

The Philippine president appoints over 5,000 civil servants in politically sensitive posts. This number has increased over time. They include ministry chiefs, administrative heads of departments in provinces (usually chosen in consultation with the elected governors), and all military personnel with the ranks of colonel or higher (after consultations with top officers). There has been quick expansion, especially under President Arroyo, of the number of secretaries, assistant secretaries, advisors, and consultants. The president also approves appointments of over 2,000 executives in state-owned or -associated businesses. This creates a "bloated bureaucracy."[5] But as the former chair of the Civil Service Commission said, "There are 4,000 eligible people within the government waiting to be appointed. But who gets the job? So-and-so's child, relative, or minion."[6] Locally elected officials such as mayors appoint another 18,000 officials.[7]

Presidential authority remains great within the Philippine national government, even after several post-Marcos limits that restrict it. The president may still declare martial law—albeit not for more than 60 days without congressional approval, or for more than a month without a Supreme Court finding that "the factual basis of the proclamation of martial law" had been accurate.[8]

Control of money is absolutely crucial to presidential power. The chief executive proposes appropriations that Congress can approve but cannot increase— and the Philippine president has a line-item veto on expenditures. Presidential authority in foreign affairs is almost total, except that two-thirds of senators are needed to ratify treaties. Appointments of officers to most formally powerful state posts are presidential, although the Commission on Appointments (12 senators, 12 representatives, plus the Speaker) confirms many of them. This applies to high judgeships, for which the constitutionally established Judicial and Bar Council proposes three nominees among whom the president chooses.

Money can corrupt power in any country. Consideration of ways to control this danger is usually and unrealistically limited to state functionaries. The

Ombudsman's office, a.k.a. the Tanodbayan, prosecutes officials for corruption; it too is written into the constitution, and its head is appointed for terms that have usually outlasted a presidency. The Sandigbanbayan ("People's Advocate") appellate court also deals with corruption cases of officials and is likewise written into the constitution. The Civil Service Commission and the Commission on Elections are both equally constitutional. Such well-legitimated agencies do not always cooperate. The Ombudsman, for example, has not followed all directives from the Supreme Court, which nonetheless has demurred from holding that office in contempt. Monitoring procedures are punctilious and byzantine in the Philippine bureaucracy. Concerns about corruption are so grave that turf battles are often fought between agencies, with each justifying its bureaucratic independence on the basis of its clients' privacy rights.[9]

Philippine presidents' or parties' alternation in electoral success partly derive from the fiscal "pork" power of the executive office and the difficulties of using it. To stand any chance of cooperation with Congress members, whose loyalties are mostly local, a Philippine president recommends a budget of "development funds" that in the past have often been deemed by reformist intellectuals to be like corrupt bribes. "With a stranglehold on public patronage, the Philippine president exercised an extraordinary amount of influence. It is therefore not surprising that several defeated incumbents considered retaining power."[10] Departure from the presidency means a drastic reduction of political power, especially if it also leaves the former chief executive vulnerable to legal suits. (Immediate victory winning a congressional seat can continue less certain legal immunity, such as Gloria Arroyo sought in 2010 when she reluctantly left the presidency but was elected to succeed her son Mikey Arroyo to represent Pampanga's second district.) Alternation of the chief executive has been usual, except in Marcos's time. The presidential office is personal. Even when alternations involved nominal changes of political parties (such as overly impress statistical scientists of democratization), the real changes in this government have been of incumbents.

Courts' integrity and public trust in justice

Marcos publicly asked "What Went Wrong?" in the Philippines. An apologist for the dictator found the answer in politics: "Not only has the legislative arm routinely blocked the executive, but the judiciary also has often exercised a 'passion for pure law' at the expense of desperately needed government progress."[11] So Marcos suspended Congress and brought courts to heel by appointing his own cadre of judges.

Victims of Marcos's human rights abuses won rights to two billion dollars of compensation in a suit against his estate, decided in 1995 by a judge in Hawai'i. But a Makati judge as late as 2013 decreed that the victims could claim nothing from Marcos's assets in the Philippines, because of "non-exhaustion of remedies." The judge claimed that,

It is very apparent that they [the victims of abuses many decades earlier] are in deep haste to conclude the case, because their counsels ... always hammered on their constitutional right to a speedy disposition of their case.... This court cannot be compelled, let alone commanded, by a foreign court of equal jurisdiction to take directions apart from the processes available locally.[12]

The law in this case was slow and national, while justice is neither—and the former trumped the latter.

PNoy signed a "Reparations and Recognitions of Human Rights Violations Victims' Act of 2013," aiming to help people who had suffered wrongs in the Marcos era three or four decades earlier. But the Claims Board, supposed to process applications for such aid, had still not been established half a year after the act was passed.[13] Many cases involving prominent figures, not just in the Marcos family, have remained inconclusive. Imelda Marcos was found guilty of previous corruptions in the early 1990s, but she appealed the convictions serially and has always been free on bail. Thirty-two of the 901 cases brought against the Marcoses were dismissed in 2008 by a Manila regional court judge.[14] Many others are in legal limbo.

Other examples include the multiple accusations against Panfilo "Ping" Lacson, who after 2001 was Director-General of the Philippine National Police and then was elected a senator. Lacson has strong *malakas* credentials. He reportedly had been implicated in a 1995 killing of 11 fighters of a vigilante group in Quezon City, although the case against Lacson was eventually dismissed for lack of probable cause. He was later indicted in January 2010 on charges of masterminding the murder of Salvador "Bubby" Dacer, the publicist of Roberto Lastimoso, a rival who later became Philippine National Police chief. Just before charges were filed in court, Lacson was able to flee to Hong Kong. He was reported in Romania, Malaysia, and elsewhere. His website contains exculpatory claims, along with patriotic fiery speeches.[15] PNoy said that the senator would receive no special favors if he decided to reappear in the country again—but in February 2011, the Court of Appeals dismissed the murder charges. There was no sure evidence against him, but Lacson had certainly established a reputation for being fearsome. He returned to the country in 2011. By 2014, he was a presidential advisor and homecoming speaker at the alumni reunion of the Philippine Military Academy.

An experienced attorney in Manila, Alfonso Felix, Jr., who had practiced before the country's highest courts for 50 years, confided shortly before his death he had never once worked on a case where he failed to bribe the judge.... "Ninety percent of the cases are decided on the basis of money."[16] Grasing Guzman was "the Godfather" of his family's estates in Nueva Ecija. He controlled mayoralties in four towns and delivered bloc votes for the local congressman, the mayor of Cabanatuan City, and the province governor. He apparently controlled the local Philippine Constabulary. Advance information from the police warned him to be absent from his suburban Manila house when it was

122 *Law of rule, power of separations*

attacked by 300 men, some of whom had automatic weapons. Although Grasing was charged with multiple homicides, no court ever found him guilty. He mused that he might have been a good lawyer. But then he reconsidered:

> No. I could never have survived as a lawyer. I am a man of honor.... I would have to bribe judges, out of responsibility to my client. But judges are venal and may sell the case to the other side if it intervenes with a higher bid. Then I would have to kill the judge.... It is well that I used my talents otherwise.[17]

Grasing ran gambling games "out of civic duty," and he claimed that the profits went to supplement the low salaries of hardworking public officials, such as the local police chief, who appointed him a "special agent."

Further south, on the island of Negros after Marcos's fall, Alan Berlow says there was:

> no functioning system of law or justice, where government was either absent or irrelevant, and the rules regulating everyday life were dictated by a revolving cast of vigilantes, fanatical cultists, Communist revolutionaries, private armies, and the military. The Philippines may have proclaimed itself a democracy, but on Negros almost everyone vying for power was equally committed to the subversion of democratic institutions.[18]

This was less an ideal commitment than an institution or habit.

Corazon Aquino, a few days after assuming the presidency, announced the removal of all Philippine judges, including the Supreme Court justices. Many of these were justly called Marcos's "cronies." But the Anti-Graft League of the Philippines, an NGO, soon called for impeachments of some of the replacement appointees. Whatever the merit of these many cases, intellectuals who wanted orderly procedures in law increased their contempt for the independence of the judiciary.[19]

The best-known murder for which nobody was ever convicted was that of Benigno S. Aquino, Jr. Courts and prosecutors have been unable to enforce many Philippine laws. They are criticized for that failure from diverse directions. Philippine judges have often been corruptible, and no less an authority than movie-star President Joseph Erap Estrada (who himself has often been accused of corruption) called them "hoodlums in robes." Estrada's archbishop enemy, Jaime Cardinal Sin, preferred gospel referents and called them "judicial Judases."[20] Estrada and Sin were not known to agree on anything else.

A nationally famous "trial of the century," involving accusations of rape and murder against multiple defendants (including a Filipino-Spaniard named "Paco" Larrañaga, who was witnessed by some to have been hundreds of miles from the scene of the crime when it was committed) provided inconclusive evidence on what the verdict should have been.[21] But it provides extensive evidence on severe difficulties in the Philippine penal justice system. Summary conclusions from this complex case can be reached. First, the Philippine public tends to expect imposition of death penalties in high-profile capital cases, and this expectation relates to claims that the spirits of victims haunt family members until that penalty is executed. (In this case the victims' relatives were filmed acting like shamans in the courtroom, loudly making such claims while explicitly speaking for spirits of the dead.) Second, windfalls of profit for media, publishing news of such tragedies, can slow the speed and apparently affect the content of Philippine verdicts—and they place judges under public pressure that is unrelated to forensic evidence. (In this case, the judge eventually committed suicide after satisfying neither main party, since one side demanded capital punishment while the other demanded a verdict of innocence.) Third, Philippine courts—in this case, the Supreme Court—can specifically reject legal advice from foreign entities (here, EU human rights NGOs and the Spanish government) on the patriotic ground that such advice is foreign and must not affect national affairs. Fourth, a judge can in practice deny the accused the opportunity to testify in his own defense (an explicit constitutional "right to be heard by himself and counsel"[22] not withstanding). Fifth, Philippine presidents can affect local verdicts in high-profile cases. (In this instance, the accused were related to the Osmeña *trapo* clan, and at the trial's beginning nominally pro-poor Erap Estrada was president; but the result for the accused improved when Arroyo succeeded to the top office.) The effects of executive appointment powers over police, judges, and prosecutors are especially important in the Philippines, which does not use lay juries. Sixth, verdicts tend to be slow (a constitutional right to "speedy" processes notwithstanding). Many years are often required to finish deciding cases, even when the defendants do not become as famous as Larrañaga did.

The Philippine judiciary is underfinanced. The 1987 Constitution specifically prohibits the president from using the ordinary line-item veto on money for courts. Unadjusted nominal appropriations for the judiciary must in each year be no lower than in the previous year, no matter what budget Congress votes. But the judicial share of the state budget declined, from 1.17 percent of government spending in 1998 to 0.88 percent in 2004. Courthouses are often dingy, and "lower courts sometimes have difficulty paying their telephone and electric bills."[23] PNoy wanted to double the judiciary's budget, but it was doubtful that Congress would make the appropriation.[24] Judges' salaries were raised in the middle of the millennium's first decade, but afterward they were still estimated to be one-sixth of salaries for comparable private-sector work.

Philippine courts are therefore also understaffed. Vacancies have been usual in many judgeships. Large backlogs of cases slow the administration of justice. Few courts have a computerized database of cases pending. In 2008, the Philippines had just 27 judges for every million citizens. Each judge faced an average of 30,000 active cases.[25] There is supposed to be a two-year limit for resolving cases (not including appeals), but this is pure theory. Nonchalant justice is justice delayed and denied.

The Supreme Court in 2013 finally confirmed, on the basis of cases that had begun decades earlier, that the government owned shares of stock in the Coconut

Planters' Bank. Marcos's friend Eduardo "Dangding" Cojuangco, Jr., in 1975 had obtained these shares by spending public money. Thirty-eight years were used to decide this case. The court ruled that, "No further pleading shall be entertained."[26] Such finality has been unusual in high-profile cases that involved powerful people, especially when they were found guilty. The Philippine courts have been relatively politicized—but so is the Philippine military, whose effects on policy have been quicker.

A summary list of *kudeta* and coups since 1972

Philippine presidents, against several of whom there has been substantial evidence of blatant corruption, have been removed from office by term limits or by a combination of "people power" street demonstrations and soldiers' disgust. Protests with the help of generals deposed presidents Marcos in 1986 and Estrada in 2001; and they weakened Arroyo before 2010. Only two Philippine presidents have ever been re-elected: Quezon (first in 1935, then in 1941 shortly before the Japanese arrived) and Marcos (first in 1965, then 1969 and 1981). The 1987 Constitution reduced the role of elections in punishing miscreant presidents, because it limited the executive's term to six years but provided that each president could be elected just once.

Kudeta is Tagalog for *coup d'état*—but with an additional connotation: rebellious soldiers move government policies to the right (often against land reform plans) without actually overthrowing the president. A partial list of *kudeta* and similar extra-constitutional events in recent decades includes these actions:

- Marcos's 1972 martial law decree followed the 1971 Miranda Plaza assassinations of anti-Marcos politicians, the 1970 "First Quarter Storms" by students against corruption, and other violence. This was Marcos's coup, though it was longer-lived and more violent than most ordinary *kudeta*.
- February 1986 saw the "EDSA I," "People Power" demos, during which Army Chief Ramos and Defense Secretary Enrile switched support from Marcos to Cory Aquino but delayed an outright coup until the presidential election in Aquino's favor made an explicit coup unnecessary.
- July 1986 saw Arturo Tolentino, Marcos's vice-presidential running mate, fail in an attempt to claim the presidency after Marcos's resignation. Tolentino had support from about 100 soldiers; he never stood a chance of being president, but (as with many later *kudeta* hopefuls) his obvious political determination helped his re-election to the Senate in 1992.
- November 1986 saw a "God Save the Queen" *kudeta* plot against post-Marcos reformers that was discovered before it could be fully implemented. Pre-*kudeta* plans were likewise ended in July 1987 and at other times; the present list omits some *kudeta* attempts that are less well documented.
- August 1987 saw Gregorio Honasan, commandant of the Army's Special Operations School, attempting to overthrow President Corazon Aquino, in

- violence that killed 53 people. Honasan was later captured, but he managed to escape by convincing his guards of the patriotic correctness of his cause.
- December 1989 saw Honasan's second coup attempt against Aquino. The presidential Malacañang Palace was bombed and strafed, until rebel airplanes were chased off by "persuasion flights" of U.S. Phantom jets coming from Clark Air Base.[27] About 100 people died. (Honasan was again captured, again escaped, and was eventually amnestied by President Ramos in 1992.) By 1996, Honasan campaigned for a Philippine Senate seat, which he won in this democratic election with a 35 percent plurality, later in 2007 being re-elected with a 39 percent plurality, and yet again in 2013, with a 33 percent plurality.
- January 2001, "EDSA II" (pronounced in Spanish, "EDSA Dos") saw Estrada expelled from the presidency extraconstitutionally. He knew that if he had not departed from Malacañang Palace, he would have been evicted by a coup. Top Army and police officers had joined the EDSA demonstration. The Senate had voted, 11–10 (with three senators absent), not to look at evidence relevant to a motion for Estrada's impeachment.
- April 2001 brought a large crowd of Estrada supporters, mostly low-income Catholic and Iglesia ng Cristo members, for an "EDSA Tres." "Hundreds of thousands" reportedly participated, and on May 1 they attacked Arroyo's Malacañang, but police and soldiers quashed them. Arroyo briefly had former Defense Minister Enrile arrested for "rebellion."
- July 2003, in the Oakwood Mutiny, saw about 300 soldiers and sailors protesting President Arroyo, corruption, and (they claimed) social inequalities. They seized an office block in Makati. Arroyo in 2004 freed 133 of the 321 mutineers after their leaders apologized to her.
- February 2006 saw Arroyo declaring an emergency and claiming that a coup had been launched against her by 14 junior officers led by Brig. Gen. Danilo Lim of the Scout Rangers. Sen./Gen. Honasan again went into hiding. A subsequent "Manila Peninsula Rebellion" prolonged this *kudeta*. By November 2007, Gen. Danilo Lim and Navy Lieutenant Antonio F. "Sonny" Trillanes IV were able simply to walk out of their trial to the Manila Peninsula (the most swank hotel in downtown Makati), to hold a press conference insisting that Arroyo be ousted. Trillanes, leader of this mutiny, used the rebellion's striking flag and patriotic rhetoric in his 2007 (successful) campaign for a Senate seat, to which he was elected while in jail. After PNoy won the presidency in 2010, Trillanes was favored and freed because he had been so stalwart against Arroyo. He was re-elected to the Senate in 2013.

It is not clear to what extent the anti-Arroyo *kudeta* episodes seriously aimed for success as coups—or instead, mainly created convenient justifications for Arroyo to make temporary arrests. The distinctive Philippine habit of semi-coups, claimed or rumored *kudeta*, may become addictive for governments, not just militaries.

Actually, it is against Philippine law to try to overthrow the democratically elected government. Article II, Section 3, of the constitution provides that, "Civilian authority is, at all times, supreme over the military. The Armed Forces of the Philippines is the protector of the people and the State." Some soldiers have interpreted the "protector of the people" phrase to justify coups, even though the previous sentence of the basic law says civilians should rule. Revisions of the Philippine penal code in 1989 made attempted coups a crime that was supposed to carry a penalty of 40 years in jail. Laws against coups were seldom enforced, however, either because of elite resentments against sitting presidents or because of the electoral popularity of the *kudeta*-makers' strong *malakas* decisiveness. *Kudeta*, as distinguished from coups, may actually accommodate a kind of pluralism. They do not bode civil war. The Philippines has never suffered the costs—or enjoyed any eventual benefits—of a violent centralizing revolution such as has occurred in most higher-income countries after elites of either right or left have seized all coercive power.

Basic causes of *kudeta*

Military officers' particular grievances combine with popular sentiments to produce *kudeta*. Marcos's approach to the military was to promote fellow Ilocanos such as Ramos and Ver; soldiers of other ethnic groups resented this tendency. Marcos strongly encouraged the growth of paramilitary groups, "Civilian Home Defense Forces," that would obey him or local clans associated with him.[28] These were part-time vigilantes, sometimes connected to the army and Philippine Constabulary in areas dominated by Marcos's allies.

Marcos tried to keep officers loyal to himself by extending their retirement dates. But this policy discomfited younger soldiers, who established a reform movement within the military. They were informally called the "RAMboys," and their plots against the dictator grew in secrecy among mid-level soldiers. When Marcos dismissed Defense Minister Juan Ponce Enrile in 1983, Enrile became an advisor to this group (which included his protégé Gregorio Honasan and other participants in later coup attempts).[29] The RAMboys provided military units to which Enrile and Ramos defected in 1986. But the same soldiers launched nine *kudeta* attempts against Corazon Aquino, of which two (led by Col. Honasan even after she had given him military awards) nearly toppled her.[30] Aquino was lucky to keep her office, but her policies moved to the right after each such event.

Her Defense Secretary, Gen. Fidel Ramos, usually remained true to his first name, telling his fellow soldiers to stand down. He was aided in such efforts by Gen. Rodolfo Biazon, later elected to the Senate. Honasan, the main plotter of the *kudeta*, was seen by many as a patriotic hero. He had been wounded in earlier fights with communists and Muslim separatists. Ramos, after being elected president, amnestied him, and his voters liked his apparent strength. They gave no evidence of worry about his disregard for the constitution.

President Ramos, a former general, was able to head off sporadic pressure from the army against reformist policies. The Philippine military as a whole by the mid-1990s seemed to be subject to civilian democratic controls.[31] Renato de Castro hopefully wrote at that time, "The AFP is willing to pay the price of democratic decision-making," which involves incrementalism and inefficiencies. But this guess proved to be wrong. *Kudeta* resumed after Ramos left the presidency. Joseph Erap Estrada lost his office in 2001 after Defense Minister Orlando Mercado and Chief of Staff Gen. Angelo Reyes joined the "EDSA 2" rally.[32] Estrada had been elected with a higher plurality of votes than any president since Marcos. He never offered to resign. His ouster was a coup, even though it also involved "people power" on the streets. Some have quipped that Estrada was felled by a "coup d'text."

The usual democratic principle that military officers follow their elected civilian commander-in-chief is stable when the soldiers and the president-commander stick to uniform laws, using the state's coercive powers in nonpartisan ways. But Philippine presidents such as Marcos, Estrada, or Arroyo have ordered military and police units to serve their own partisan causes. Except for Gen. Ramos, such presidents inspired *kudeta*. President Arroyo's corruptions (described in Chapter 9) gave patriotic soldiers reasons to threaten her. An arguably indigenous Philippine sense of individual dignity tenses against hierarchies such as are enshrined in a constitution or in an army's chain-of-command. Graduates of the Philippine Military Academy famously address each other, regardless of rank, as "Mistah"—a word that signifies "comraderie and cooperation ... a sense of oneness that draws the ties that bind, like a mother to her children, for Filipinos amongst Filipinos."[33]

The *Magdalo* group, which launched a *kudeta* against Arroyo, comprises Philippine military men who accept no members higher than the level of lieutenant colonel—because every officer who is a colonel or higher must be approved by the presidential Commission on Appointments. They regard this system as irretrievably corrupt, whenever they see the president as corrupt. Soldier-dissidents, revolting in the Oakwood Mutiny against President Arroyo and her senior officers, took the *Magdalo* name from that of a nineteenth century radical faction of the Katipunan who were leaders of the first Philippine Republic. Their 2003 mutiny did not overthrow the president, but the rebels (and their sympathizers in a civilian group called the *Samahang Magdalo*) felt no need to eschew unconstitutional violence.

They especially feared that Arroyo would find some equally illegal way of extending her term in power. Arroyo had succeeded to the presidency in 1981 because she enjoyed the luck of being vice-president when Estrada was expelled from the top office; she inherited the presidency without an election.[34] Article VII, Section 4, of the constitution specifies that, "The President shall not be eligible for any re-election." Efforts of Philippine presidents to extend their terms were nothing new. In 1940, Manuel Quezon tried to have the Commonwealth's constitution amended to extend his presidency without an election. The U.S. High Commissioner at the time claimed this was "a precedent ... for any strong president who desires to become a dictator to prolong his tenure indefinitely."[35] The amendment passed a national plebiscite—and Quezon won a re-election that was made moot by the Japanese invasion, which sent him to exile in the U.S. where he died in 1944.

In 1970, Marcos likewise hoped to extend his presidency by holding elections for a Constitutional Convention, but he failed to control the voting. Many of the elected delegates expected to reduce his executive authority by creating a parliamentary system, in which the government would be headed by a premier alongside the president. On July 7, 1972, Marcos agreed to establish such a system—but, by September, he declared martial law, citing dangers of chaos and communism. He used his own decree to extend his own term unconstitutionally by fiat.[36]

Arroyo's aversion to leave the presidency had precedents. But the Oakwood Mutiny did not depose her, and Gen./Sen. Honasan and other "Philippine Guardian Brotherhood" plotters went into hiding. Arroyo's spokesman, when asked by reporters whether Honasan would be arrested if he came into the open, practically gave assurances that the rebel would be forgiven. "The Macapagal-Arroyo administration had reached an understanding with the Senate that there should first be a preliminary investigation of the case."[37]

The Oakwood soldiers' and sailors' sense of Arroyo's illegitimacy was shared by many others. Chief Justice Reynato Puno, despite his oath to uphold the constitution and his long history of opportunism in the Marcos years and later, was thought by some to be an alternative president because he held the top Supreme Court post. Puno was a Methodist preacher and Mason Grandmaster, but an anti-Arroyo group of Catholic bishops (Yniguez, Labayen, and Tobias) urged Puno to lead a transitional government to replace Arroyo. Puno, before giving the keynote speech at a national convention of Masons, was introduced as follows: "If the Chief Justice were to be President of the Philippines, he would be a gift to the country." Puno's response was not definitive: "My message is not SONA [State of the Nation Address]. Instead it is *sana* [Tagalog for 'perhaps']."[38] The assembled Masons in their aprons applauded. This was scarcely a coup, but it suggested that the chief judge of the country had interests that went beyond constitutional procedure.

Threats of coups in some nations (e.g., in Guatemala during the 1951–54 presidency of Arbenz Guzman) have united liberals with leftists.[39] This has only occasionally happened in the Philippines, however, because leftists demand land reform and local liberals in most Philippine regions are landowners who can veto such reform. The February 2006 plot to topple Arroyo created a brief "unthinkable alliance between the AFP [the army] and Communists." Both groups were intensely nationalist—and they both detested the president. They could agree on certain reforms in constitutional change, foreign affairs, industrial policy, and elections. Anti-Arroyo officers resented her regime's perceived leniency to communist rebels, in comparison with her perceived harshness toward dissident army officers. On the communist side, the New People's Army announced in March 2006, "we do not attack enemy [government] units that show proof of being against the regime."[40] The political pattern of that time was unusual. A future president might be as corrupt as Arroyo was seen to be—but might co-opt soldiers and civilians through patriotic and populist policies.

Kudeta plotters are usually recidivist and anti-leftist. In north Luzon, Philippine Constabulary commander and Northern Cagayan Governor, Col. Rudolfo Aguinaldo, had openly supported a *kudeta* against President Cory Aquino as part of an anti-Communist crusade. He was later killed by the New People's Army—but a politician of the same name, after having been suspended as Cagayan Governor, led a siege of the Hotel Delfino in the province capital—later escaping into the hills and becoming involved in a rebellion of December 2009.[41] Parts of north Luzon, especially Cagayan and the Cordillera provinces, have for decades suffered high rates of local violence, rivalling those in Negros and Muslim Mindanao. Such areas see considerable local violence, and in comparison the *kudeta* events of Manila may seem almost peaceful.

Semi-coups seldom result in serious setbacks for the plotters, but they regularly result in appointments of commissions to study why such events occur. The Davide Commission, whose mandate was to explore the origins of *kudeta*,

> found a mix of causes, including unaddressed military grievances, objections to the inclusion of "left-wing"/anti-military officials in the [Corazon] Aquino administration, opposition to peace negotiations with the Communists and the Moro secessionist groups, the perceived loss of power that the coup plotters suffered as a result of the outcome of people power, career dead-ends for senior coup plotters, and a "messianic complex" to save Philippine society.[42]

The Feliciano Commission, looking into the 2003 Oakwood Mutiny, endorsed the conclusions its predecessor Davide Commission and said that the Oakwood coup attempt arose from

> allegations of anomalies within the AFP [Armed Forces of the Philippines] involving the RSBS [Retirement Service and Benefits System], the military procurement system, particularly the practice of "conversion," the transfer of arms and ammunition to unauthorized parties, and the construction and repair of various facilities at the Marine Base in Cavite.

Another simple reason for these coups lies in the informal custom that plotters afterwards are safe. They can change government policy toward their and political allies' preferences—toward the right—and prove their patriotic *malakas* strength without usually serving much or any jail time. Until there is a reduction of local violence by and against Communist and Moro guerrillas, it will be difficult to lower the profile of state and nonstate coercive forces in rightist politics.

Forceful leadership, electoral democracy, and rule of law

The East Asian Barometer survey in 2003 asked Filipinos, "What do you think of having a strong leader who does not have to bother with parliament and elections?" Fully 64 percent replied they thought such a leader was "very good" or "fairly good." When the respondents were asked, "What does 'democracy' mean?" about one-third in the Philippines at first gave the open response "don't know/no response." When pressed, they secondarily mentioned freedoms, but not procedures.[43]

"What do you think about having military rule?" was a question to which more than half of Philippine respondents (53 percent) replied it would be "good" or "fairly good." Perhaps concerns about Arroyo-era corruptions made the desire for strong leadership especially high in 2003, when this survey was taken and when prominent military officers were ardently opposed to the president. The results nonetheless suggest that a century of Philippine elections had not completely legitimated liberal processes over strong *malakas* patrons.

Parliamentary government was the ostensible aim of proposals in 2005 by Arroyo's allies, Speaker Jose de Venecia and a majority of his colleagues in the House. Under this unicameral plan, Congress term limits would have been abolished—along with the whole Senate. A prime minister would have become the chief executive, and at least three-quarters of the ministers would be MPs (with Congress also electing a ceremonial president).[44] It is easy to see why a majority of the House members favored such a plan.

The parliamentary model is European, but major Philippine parties (unlike those on the continent or in Britain) have scant policy coherence. The House proposal was not passed, in part because the Philippine Constitution requires a three-fourths vote of all the representatives for basic law amendment (or else a two-thirds vote to call a constitutional convention).[45] These hurdles were too high for the Speaker and his fellow *trapos* to jump. More important was the distaste of many, especially military officers, for the threat that President Arroyo might prolong her rule. For both sides, personalities trumped constitutional considerations.

Filipinos who have a greater-than-average sense that they can influence politics tended in a survey to support *extra*-constitutional change.[46] This "civic culture" is not monotonically democratic.[47] The constitution, despite its liberal aspects, has not ended illiberal behavior in many of the country's local polities.

Action possibilities for better governance and justice

Filipinos know that the presidency can become predatory. Some advocate writing a new constitution against the "perils of presidentialism" that affect this and many other countries.[48] The Philippine Institute for Popular Democracy wants a constitutional convention to create a parliamentary and federal government for the archipelago, while retaining the nationalistic bans on economic or educational activities by foreigners (including non-citizen resident Chinese).[49]

With vintage Filipino humor, such "charter change" is popularly called "cha-cha," copying the name of the fast though hardly risqué Latin dance.

Having a federal regime would further empower localists. Having a parliamentary system could conceivably do the same unless the prime minister were a centralizing demagogue. The current charter provides rules for electing a constitutional convention ("con-con") that could make such changes. But many reformers were wary to press for them, especially by Arroyo's time, because they feared that the sitting president might continue in power by becoming prime minister.[50] Alternative to a "con-con" would be another amendment method that the 1987 constitution allows: a constituent assembly of all the current members of Congress ("con-ass" continues the standard humor). But with either a president or a prime minister heading the government in Manila, local lords would still dominate most parts of the archipelago. Experiences in other countries such as Italy or Greece suggest that parliamentary structure is no sure guarantee of good government.

Must "rule of law" and stable institutions for elite competition precede democracy? Thomas Carothers thinks not. He sees this "sequencing fallacy" as too skeptical, claiming that it delays democratization and may rationalize repression. Carothers suggests that "gradualism," building democracy slowly, is a better gambit.[51] But other comparativists, including the current author, think long-term stable electoral democracy requires prior rule of law, especially judges who do their jobs with integrity. Closer engagement of the state with "professional and civil society networks" might help, as many claim. Anti-democratic professionals or civil societies can, however, be as powerful as liberal ones.[52] In the Philippines, gradualism in rule-of-law development has been a fact; it need scarcely be recommended.

Courts are not yet firm bastions against possible or actual abuse by central, regional, or local dictators. The archipelago has seen (and might in the future see) retreats from democracy and reversals of movement toward more substantive fairness for more people. The judiciary's job is to prevent such abuse. But judges are underpaid and often bribed. No norm requires that most legal cases be concluded within a legally determined span of years, and such a law is needed to undergird the constitutional right to timely justice.[53] Because juries are not used, individual judges are crucial—and they sometimes prevent parties from presenting evidence.[54] The norm that police detectives should abandon any case on which an ombudsman has commenced investigation prevents the discovery of information about violations of laws.

"Zero tolerance" for offering or accepting judicial bribes, enforced by multiple kinds of detectives and prosecutors who can bring stiff criminal sentences, has now become necessary to establish the integrity of courts. Rule of law can replace law of rule in the Philippines. The same "zero tolerance" norm might apply to the group that has most obviously threatened Philippine elected officials, i.e., military plotters of coups. Past *kudeta* attempts, involving soldiers in central politics, were precedents for Arroyo's use of army units to help rig an election. But if any officers in the military want to stop such shenanigans, they in the future will accept constitutional constraints and obey their commander in chief. This is not to say that all past *kudeta* and amnesties of plotters were totally unjustified. But if the armed forces continue to take sides in central and local politics, they will undermine Philippine democracy further. Soldiers who violate this norm, no matter how patriotic they claim to be, could be sent to jail unless they exile themselves.

Perhaps the most important quasi-constitutional change that might reduce the "power of separations" in Philippine politics would put presidential and vice-presidential candidates on the same ticket. This would not require a constitutional amendment.[55] At present, any vice-president of the Philippines has an obvious interest in ending the term of the sitting president. That is a separation that could be bridged, if Philippine legislators wished to bridge it.

Notes

1 See Daniel Lazare, *The Frozen Republic: How the* [American] *Constitution is Paralyzing Democracy* (New York: Harcourt Brace, 1996).
2 The current constitution provides for autonomous regions in Muslim Mindanao and the Cordillera, Art. X, Sec. 1. See also José V. Abueva, "Proposed Constitutional Reforms for Good Governance and Nation Building," in *Whither the Philippines in the 21st Century*, Rodolfo C. Severino and Lorraine Carlos Salazar, eds. (Singapore: ISEAS, 2007), 54–9.
3 Rupert Hodder, *Emotional Bureaucracy* (New Brunswick, NJ: Transaction Publishers, 2011), 152.
4 The Philippine Constitution, Art. VIII, Sec. 9, provides that for any judgeship the Judicial and Bar Council presents the names of three qualified candidates (members of the Philippine bar) to the president, who chooses the one to appoint. Sec. 11 specifies that judges "hold office during good behavior until they reach the age of seventy years or become incapacitated to discharge the duties of their office." So any reformist president, wanting judges to attack corruption, has to rely on courts appointed by predecessors.
5 Sheila Coronel, quoted in Nathan Gilbert Quimpo, "The Presidency, Political Parties, and Predatory Politics in the Philippines," in *The Politics of Change in the Philippines*, Yuko Kasuya and Nathan Gilbert Quimpo, eds. (Pasig City: Anvil, 2010), 60–1.
6 Quoted in Nathan Gilbert Quimpo, "The Presidency, Political Parties, and Predatory Politics in the Philippines," 61.
7 Rupert Hodder, *Emotional Bureaucracy*, 55.
8 Article VII, Sec. 18 of the 1987 *Constitution of the Philippines*.
9 See Rupert Hodder, *Emotional Bureaucracy*, 133.
10 Mark R. Thompson, *The Anti-Marcos Struggle: Personalistic Rule and Democratic Transition in the Philippines* (New Haven, CT: Yale University Press, 1995; also Quezon City: New Day, 1996), 24.
11 Beth Day, *The Philippines: Shattered Showcase of Democracy in Asia* (intro. by Carlos Romulo, Sec. of Foreign Affairs) (New York: M. Evans, 1974), 29, in a chapter entitled "What Went Wrong."
12 Marvin Sy, "Marcoses Laud Ruling on Human Rights Case," *Philippine Star*, July 14, 2013, www.philstar.com/headlines/2013/07/14/967221. Art. III, Sec. 16, of the 1987 Constitution provides: "All persons shall have the right to a speedy disposition of their cases before all judicial, quasi-judicial, or administrative bodies." That does not happen. The alleged infractions, before this judge in 2013, pre-dated 1987—but the previous constitution contains the same wording.

13 Rhodina Villanueva, "Rights Group Seeks Immediate Formation of Claims Board," *Philippine Star*, August 8, 2013, www.philstar.com/headlines/2013/03/13/1064871.
14 See Mark R. Thompson and Philipp Kuntz, "After Defeat: When Do Rulers Steal Elections," in *Electoral Authoritarianism: The Dynamics of Unfree Competition*, Andreas Schedler, ed. (Boulder, CO: Rienner, 2006), 118, and many other sources.
15 See www.pinglacson.net.
16 Alan Berlow, *Dead Season: A Story of Murder and Revenge on the Philippine Island of Negros* (New York: Pantheon, 1996), 96.
17 Ibid., 39.
18 Ibid., xiv.
19 Cecilio T. Arillo, *Greed & Betrayal: The Sequel to the 1985 EDSA Revolution* (Makati: CTA Research, 2000), 30–2.
20 Paul D. Hutchcroft, "Sustaining Economic and Political Reform: The Challenges Ahead," in *The Philippines: New Directions in Domestic Policy and Foreign Relations*, David G. Timberman, ed. (Singapore: Institute for Southeast Asian Studies and New York: Asia Society, 1998), 33.
21 Readers of this book would follow this author's analysis of the case better after seeing an award-winning documentary, *Give Up Tomorrow*, www.firstrunfeatures.com (New York: First Run Features, 2012), directed by Michael Collins and produced by a man who is a relative of the main accused person, Francisco "Paco" Larrañaga, a Basque-Filipino who has both Philippine and Spanish citizenship. The conclusions above concerning Philippine justice are not about Larrañaga's guilt or (probable) innocence, but they are strongly substantiated by other information in the documentary.
22 Constitution, Art. III, Sec. 14 (2).
23 Paul D. Hutchcroft, "Philippines," in *Countries at the Crossroads: A Survey of Democratic Governance*, in Sanja Kelly, Christopher Walker, and Jake Dizard, eds. (Lanham, MD: Rowman & Littlefield, 1978), 532.
24 Interview with a Philippine cabinet member, 2010.
25 Marites Danguilan-Vitug, *Shadow of Doubt: Probing the Supreme Court* (Manila: Public Trust Media Group, 2010), 224–5.
26 Edu Punay, "It's Final! SC Says Gov't Owns Cojuangco UCPB Shares," *Philippine Star*, July 11, 2013, www.philstar.com/headlines/2013/07/11/964095.
27 Eva-Lotta E. Hedman, "The Philippines: Not so Military, Not so Civil," in *Coercion and Governance: The Declining Political Role of the Military in Asia*, Muthiah Alagappa, ed. (Stanford, CA: Stanford University Press, 2001), 182.
28 Richard J. Kessler, *Rebellion and Repression in the Philippines* (New Haven, CT: Yale University Press, 1989), 120.
29 Eva-Lotta E. Hedman, "The Philippines: Not so Military, Not so Civil," 172–80.
30 See Note 106 in Chapter 5, and also Alfred W. McCoy, *Closer than Brothers: Manhood at the Philippine Military Academy* (New Haven, CT: Yale University Press, 1999), 259.
31 Renato de Castro, "The Military and Philippine Democratization: A Case Study of the Government's 1995 Decision to Modernize the Armed Forces of the Philippines," in *Democratization: Philippine Perspectives*, Felipe B. Miranda, ed. (Quezon City: University of the Philippines Press, 1995), 268.
32 Eva-Lotta E. Hedman, "The Philippines: Not so Military, Not so Civil," 183.
33 Quoted from www.mistahffoundation.org/about-2/.
34 When Estrada's later 2010 candidacy for president was challenged, the Committee on Elections allowed it after an appeal—although its constitutional grounds for doing so are dubious. But his chance of winning was slim, and the Supreme Court never ruled (or needed to rule, since he lost) on his eligibility to stand for a second election. Philippine constitutional issues easily become political.
35 Jason Brownlee, *Authoritarianism in an Age of Democratization* (New York: Cambridge University Press, 2007), 78.

134 *Law of rule, power of separations*

36 Ibid., 113.
37 Inquirer.net (*Philippine Daily Inquirer*, Makati), www.inq7.net/nat/2003/aug/05/nat_1-1.htm.
38 Marites Danguilan-Vitug, *Shadow of Doubt*, 184–9.
39 Deborah J. Yashar, *Demanding Democracy: Reform and Reaction in Costa Rica and Guatemala, 1870s-1950s* (Stanford, CA: Stanford University Press, 1997), 98–9.
40 Soliman M. Santos, Jr. and Paz Verdades M. Santos, *Primed and Purposeful: Armed Groups and Human Security Efforts in the Philippines* (Geneva: Small Arms Survey, Graduate Institute of International and Development Studies, 2010), 25.
41 Ronald James May, *Vigilantes in the Philippines: From Fanatical Cults to Citizens' Organizations* (Honolulu, HI: Center for Philippine Studies, University of Hawaii, 1992), 34.
42 Carolina G. Hernandez, "The Military in Philippine Politics: Retrospect and Prospect," in *Whither the Philippines in the 21st Century*, Rodolfo C. Severino and Lorraine Carlos Salazar, eds. (Singapore: ISEAS, 2007), 84.
43 In South Korea and Japan, the liking for a strong leader was half as great, 32 percent; in Taiwan, 41 percent. Kasuya Yoko, "Democratic Consolidation in the Philippines: Who Supports Extra-Constitutional Change?" in *The Politics of Change in the Philippines*, Yuko Kasuya and Nathan Gilbert Quimpo, eds. (Pasig City: Anvil, 2010), 99.
44 José V. Abueva, "Proposed Constitutional Reforms for Good Governance and Nation Building," 46–8.
45 Philippine Constitution (1987), Art. XVII.
46 Kasuya Yoko, "Democratic Consolidation in the Philippines," 90–113.
47 See Gabriel A. Almond and Sidney Verba, *The Civic Culture* (Princeton, NJ: Princeton University Press, 1963).
48 Juan Linz, "The Perils of Presidentialism," *Journal of Democracy* (Winter 1990), 51–69.
49 The Institute's website is www.ipd.org.
50 Nathan Gilbert Quimpo, "The Presidency, Political Parties, and Predatory Politics in the Philippines," 68.
51 Thomas Carothers, "How Democracies Emerge: The Sequencing Fallacy," *Journal of Democracy* 18:1 (2007), 12–27.
52 Jeremy Kinsman and Kurt Bassuener, *A Diplomat's Handbook for Democracy Development Support* (Waterloo, ON: Centre for International Governance Innovation, 2013) may overgeneralize the virtues of "civil society" and even the legal profession.
53 The Philippine Constitution, Art. III, Sec. 16, is quoted above concerning "speedy" processes. There could be legal sanctions against judges or administrators who violate it.
54 The Philippine Constitution, Art. III, Sec. 14 (2), gives "the right to be heard by himself and counsel" to any criminal accused—but evidence (e.g., from the notorious Paco Larrañaga trial) shows that judges sometimes ignore this provision.
55 The constitution's Art. VII contains many sections saying Congress can pass laws about the election of the president and vice-president. It speaks of these two together. Sec. 3 provides that the vice-president is "elected with [?], and in the same manner, as the President." Sec. 4 says, "The Congress shall promulgate its rules for the canvassing of the certificates [sent by local authorities to the President of the Senate to certify winners of these top posts before a joint session of Congress]." No words in the constitution would preclude a law requiring that presidential and vice-presidential candidates run together on the same ticket.

7 Populist rituals and elite reformism

Studies of Philippine politics have often centered on patronism. That is justified because *trapo* patrons have in the past been powerful, first in their localities and then in Manila. But dominant modes of constructing politics can change because of policy reforms or altered contexts. What political procedures or reforms could make Philippine democracy help more of the people? That is a major question for the future.[1]

Many Filipino mass movements have been nostalgic, looking "backward toward revolution."[2] Their leaders have resented the depredations of foreigners—Spanish, Americans, Chinese—as having taken away an original paradise that they imagine to have existed previously. This idea is in the passion play that Philippine peasants acted to depict Eden prior to the sin of its human denizens. The garden is restored for believers by Christ's sacrifice and resurrection. Independence (*kalayaan*) is a political paradise awaiting the faithful of the Katipunan. The *pasyón*, which was rehearsed during Holy Week by rural Filipinos on the basis of early nineteenth century texts, traces the suffering, death, and rising of Christ. Jesus was an anti-establishment leader of poor people at a time of ferment among both Hebrews and Romans. Reynaldo Ileto shows that peasant radicals in central Luzon saw similarities between that situation and their own. The *pasyón*

> provides powerful images of transition from one state or era to another, e.g., darkness to light, despair to hope, misery to salvation, death to life, ignorance to knowledge, dishonor to purity, and so forth. During the Spanish and American colonial eras, these images nurtured an undercurrent of millennial beliefs which, in times of economic and political crisis, enabled the peasantry to take action under the leadership of individuals or groups promising deliverance from oppression.[3]

The pasyón describes the creation of brotherhoods (like the Katipunan) based on rejection of family ties for the sake of a cause and its charismatic leader. Jesus in the recited drama tells Mary that the two must part, despite his debt to repay her motherly care for him. He tells his disciples to leave their kin in order to serve God. Wealth or education count for nothing in this story. Devotion is all. Ever

136 Populist rituals and elite reformism

since the temporary successes of the Katipunan, hopes for popular uprising as a source of Philippine change have been periodic.

Ileto explains peasant enthusiasm for the Katipunan and other intended revolutionary mass movements as follows:

> When behavioral scientists today speak of social values like *utang na loób* (lifelong debt to another for some favor bestowed), *hiya* (shame), SIR (smooth interpersonal relations) and *pakikisama* (mutual cooperation), they give the impression that these values make Philippine society naturally tend toward stasis and equilibrium.... Social change, when it unavoidably occurs, is attributed less to some inner dynamism of Philippine society than to external stresses and ideological influences.[4]

Ileto argues that Philippine traditions can make people into docile sheep—but also, under other conditions, into angry lions. Rural "masses" (*tao*) have "folk religious traditions," but "cultural values such as *utang na loób* and *hiya*, which usually promote passivity and reconciliation rather than conflict have latent meanings that can be revolutionary." Ileto claims that, "Appropriated from the friars, religion gave form to peasant hopes for brotherhood and more equitable economic relationships." His argument that Filipinos have collective ideals can organize some data—although his suggestion in further publications that modern progress and democracy are not among these collective ideals is dubious.[5] Other evidence shows that the importance of families in Philippine politics did not disappear after the turn of the twentieth century. Elite clans retained their identities and prospered together with foreign imperialists.

José Rizal remains the most convincing Philippine political hero. He had intellectually revolutionary intentions, although he was usually a careful reformist in practical politics. Rizal was educated and well-off, the most important *ilustrado*, a Philippine patriot despite critical affection for Spain (and for the Spanish language), and a complex writer of subtle sardonic genius. Most Filipinos scarcely remember these traits. What they best know about Rizal is that, like Christ, he was martyred.[6] And the *pasyón* or Rizal are not the only Philippine lodestones of intended political paradise. Bernardo Carpio is a Philippine hero of the masses who (like Conradin in the imaginations of some early-modern European peasants) will reappear someday to lead them out of oppression. This legendary King Bernardo, a figure of strength rather like Hercules, is supposed to be imprisoned by his enemies in a cave at Mt. Tapusi, awaiting the day when he will break away and free his people.[7]

There is no guarantee that either reforms or revolutions will develop when states fail to solve people's problems. Political action, by the state or any other entity (e.g., in localities), usually requires leaders. When relatively central political networks are fragmented and cannot control resources, insurgents claim these factors without necessarily doing so for any large collective cause. In such cases, as a comparativist writes, local political entrepreneurs continue to dominate local markets, including clandestine ones, and use this social domination to buy off members of mass movements. As their new patrons give them access to weapons and protection against rivals, the organizational position of members who pursue individual economic interests is enhanced, while the people with more overt [public] ideological agendas are marginalized.[8]

Most politics requires both material and ideal resources. As Cesar Cala writes, "the traditional [Philippine] elite maintains their hegemony not only through their much-touted powers of guns, goons, and gold but by ruling through what Gramsci would call the people's common sense."[9] The strong trump the weak, not just in open conflict that can be documented by public behavior. Ideologies are actively supported to deflect most citizens from attempting any serious influence.[10]

Revolts as mirrors of repressions

Particular forms of state repression shape the particular responses of those who oppose the government. If a regime tolerates some level of intellectual dissent but oppresses trade unionists or ethnic separatists, then dissidents catch on, doing what they can. Intellectuals protest, avoiding or using whatever modes challenge state symbols and power effectively. Oppositions use established institutions. If a dictatorship tries to rule a country where churches are important (as Marcos did in the mid-1980s), then nuns appear in the front lines against it. If an army is not surely unified, a dictator finds that troops are more reluctant to use weapons on his behalf. If religious friars run local regimes for a foreign government that is seen as repressive, then religious passion plays may shape the discourse about independence from it.

Philippine politics embodies two types of democracy that compete with each other: "elite democracy, and democracy from below."[11] Elections, free speech, a broadly egalitarian spread of means of violence, and enthusiastic mass participation in politics are all evident in this country—but these factors have not quickly made the government more effective. Oligarchy, "cacique democracy," and lack of enterprise outside the Manila area stand in the way. Many Western observers join most Philippine intellectuals in tending to find angels and devils.[12] Reformers are usually put into the angelic category, and conservative landed families into the hellish set.

A few treatments of Philippine politics by Filipinos, however, take a more distant and critical attitude toward practically all personalities. Rizal's lampoons of his countrymen's practices may have inspired this habit of mind. It was revived in the 1920s among Congress members such as Vicente Sotto, who was a trenchant critic of Osmeña and Quezon "Nacionalistas." They proclaimed their devotion to Philippine independence—while bargaining with Washington on how to run a colony. Examples from much later decades range from Senator Miriam Defensor-Santiago to Congressman Walden Bello, whose different personal styles are adaptive without impeding their critical capacities.

Perhaps this mixed habit of admitting political weakness while sounding political trumpets meshes with the sense of identity that anthropologist Frank Lynch described among Bicol peasants, who eschewed violence for change but demanded more equity. Some writers such as Mina Roces have described a popularly perceived Philippine right to rule in terms of Western norms. Others such as Ileto have suggested this discourse about legitimacy comes from indigenous roots (as these developed under Catholic monks). These researchers despite their differences all argue that legitimacy—not just pesos and physical threats—shapes Philippine power. Roces writes that,

> two sets of values existing side by side are responsible for the ambivalent behavior exhibited by Filipinos. While patronage is a factor (patronage is an offshoot of kinship politics), it appears that in major turning points in postwar Philippine history, Western values have made the difference. In the republican period, no administration [except Marcos's?] could get re-elected. Had patronage politics been the sole determining factor, then we would find the incumbent administration being re-elected almost consistently, since it has more patronage sources in its power.[13]

That interpretation may overestimate the sway of the president, who even within the central government is not omnipotent. It may underestimate the extent of local or senatorial re-elections. Roces likes an "hypothesis of contesting discourses [that] leaves room for ideology as a contending factor in political culture." She contrasts this with "the patron–client model which proposes that ideology is not a factor at all." Yet the recurrent behavior of Philippine voters suggests that most of them are content to see local patronism as ideologically legitimate. Roces studies the Lopez family of Cebu and argues that, "the Lopezes represent the ambivalent Filipino—torn between kinship values and Western discourses."[14]

Such an analysis may protest too much against admitting the political role not just of occasional open violence but also of its psychological effects. Murders make more than just news stories. Decisions may be influenced by fear—even if violence is not actualized—although this causation is difficult to document. It nonetheless is evidence of power.[15] Many data suggest it has been important in local Philippine politics.

Yet another approach focuses on various kinds of greed for money. Rich oligarchs include some Philippine reformers, just as other rich oligarchs are conservatives. Jeffrey Winters presents a materialistic paradigm of four types of oligarchy that seeks to deal with violence as well as money. These four are generated by needs for "wealth defense" that vary "by the threats they confront." Either "warring" or "sultanistic" oligarchies appear when factions are fragmented. They are "warring" when coercion is in many hands, or "sultanistic" when force is controlled by a dictator. "Ruling" or "civil" oligarchies emerge when collective institutions control coercion, again depending on whether force is segmented or centralized. This paradigm at first tends to deny that norms are important. But norms can stabilize the "ruling" or "sultanistic" types, and indeed the segmented types too. Winters writes that, "The existential motive of all oligarchs is the defense of wealth," without stressing other commitments (e.g., to make money rather than just defend it, or to gain local prestige for being powerful).[16] These in practice can become habitual even if they originate in material interests.

Farmer rebels and educated rebels

The Philippine left has had two different kinds of leaders: intellectuals and peasants. In late Spanish times, *ilustrados* such as Rizal became members of the Propaganda Movement, advocating major political reforms without secession from Spain—and they contrasted with "*filibusteros*," who demanded independence and came from varied backgrounds. The liberal Malolos Republic of 1898–1901, which lasted until its president Emilio Aguinaldo was captured by the U.S. Army, passed laws that restricted voting to wealthy men only. The more populist Katipunan, led by Andres Bonifacio, vied with Aguinaldo's group until the latter had the former killed in 1897. Bonifacio was originally a proletarian (albeit also a demagogue), and he emerged as a threat to upper-class totalist reformers led by Aguinaldo. Lack of trust between lower- and higher-wealth Filipinos impedes efforts by reformists.[17]

Such hindrances to reform have persisted through many eras of Philippine politics. The title of a 1930s newspaper, *Sakdal* (*To Accuse*) sounds like Zola. This name was adopted by a political party, and then by a short-lived uprising near Manila. But such reformism led by intellectuals often lacked punch. It was critical politics against egregious corruption, without pressing the cause to full victory by more forceful politics, engaging material support from large portions of the population.

An alternative method developed in local contexts. In Pampanga in 1937 and 1940 and in central Luzon in 1946, the Popular Front and Democratic Alliance recruited peasants' votes and support on progressive platforms. These populists had some minor successes against Nacionalista and Liberal candidates. In the 1940 campaigns for Pampanga governor and mayoralties, for example, the Popular Front "demanded that landlords allow their tenants to decide for themselves whom to vote for and stop threatening tenants with eviction if they did not vote as the landlords instructed."[18] They organized parades for clean elections and against vote-buying.

Spanish, American, and Japanese imperialists were able to muster at least some support from elite families that held land. For example, José Laurel (1891–1959) was president of the Japanese version of the Republic of the Philippines. Benigno S. Aquino, Sr., was Speaker of the House under the Japanese. (This "Igno" lived from 1894 to 1947 and was the father of "Ninoy," assassinated in the late Marcos era, and grandfather of "Noynoy," a.k.a. "PNoy," who was elected president in 2010.) The Japanese militarists followed previous foreign occupiers in garnering help from local old-family *caciques* in their attempt to govern these islands.[19]

The Japanese occupation, and then the growth of Hukbalahaps and landlord armies to oppose them, led to violence and temporarily reduced the importance of electoral legitimation. (The word *Hukbalahap* is a shortening of the Tagalog for "People's Anti-Japanese Army.") This guerilla movement was led by elites of both landed and poor family backgrounds. It expanded in post-war years. After the Japanese departed, and especially after 1952, the Huk movement diminished—nonetheless recurring in poor areas, especially in central Luzon, whenever would-be tillers could not make the livelihoods they expected. Most elites eschewed such violence, preferring elections as a way to get power.

Trapo families occasionally bred leftist revolutionaries. Bulacan, in the Tagalog area north of Manila, had been among the most important seedbeds of the uprising against Spain. This province provided leaders for the Katipunan, as well as reformists and Hukbalahaps in the following half century. The Philippine Communist Party and the Hukbalahaps became allied in the 1940s and 1950s. Many revolutionary Bulacan leaders in various eras came from the Lava lineage. The *Partido Komunista ng Pilipinas* was led by the well-educated, landowning Lava brothers. As "Buddy" Lava admitted,

> The Huk movement in the Bulacan-Guiguinto-Malolos triangle was organized around the extended family system and the semi-feudal tenancy system. Thus Lavas, Paraisos, Bulaongs, Maclangs, and perhaps Borlongans found their way into the Huk and CPC [Communist Party of the Philippines] structure.[20]

Clientelism was wholly compatible with revolutionary rhetoric. *Trapo* factions with leftist policies could sometimes succeed against their rivals. When patrons are the local organizers of peasants for any cause, they personally will not be overthrown.[21]

The head of the Huks, Luis Taruc, was by contrast a Pampanga peasant.[22] Later, the Communist Party of the Philippines was led by university lecturer Jose Maria Sison, whereas Commander Dante (Bernabe Buscayno) of the New People's Army had been a peasant. After 1948, the Democratic Alliance of Huks and Communists was violently repressed by President Elpidio Quirino, the Philippine Constabulary, and rightist vigilantes with help from the United States.

Populist calls for democracy and patriotism have long been a potent weapon in *cacique* rivalries. Sergio "Serging" Osmeña, Jr., was by 1950 a Manila millionaire. He had been born in his clan's main base on Cebu (whence his father had succeeded to the presidency, as recognized by the U.S., from 1944 to 1946). Serging had been convicted—but later was acquitted—of collaboration with the Japanese "independent" Republic of the Philippines.

Osmeña–Cuenco electoral struggles in Cebu went back for many decades, and in 1951 Manuel Cuenco ran for Governor. Serging Osmeña rose to this challenge, declared his candidacy, and vowed, like a democrat, "to wipe out blood-stained tyranny and systematic persecution." He was referring to the rival clan.

I am running to redeem all that we treasure but have lost—to redeem our God-given civil liberties, freedom of thought, freedom of expression, freedom of the press, freedom to assemble peacefully without being harnessed [sic], freedom from fear, and freedom to earn a decent living.[23]

Serging Osmeña projected himself "like a latter-day Cincinnatius, the fifth-century B.C. patriot who was called from his small farm to be dictator of Rome and save the city from its enemies." Notwithstanding the large size of Osmeña farms, Serging was likened to David, fighting the Goliath of the Cuencos. After "pouring his own money into the campaign and arming his followers," he defeated Manuel Cuenco and became governor. This was a suitable post from which to hope for the presidency.

Ramon Magsaysay, as Defense Secretary after 1950, became a populist to wage his relatively successful campaign against the Hukbalahaps. Then in 1953 he was elected president by a landslide—with a 30 percent turnout increase over the previous presidential election. He had begun as a mechanic, the first non-lawyer to become president.[24] Reform rhetoric of the demagogic *malakas* kind did not produce reform policies so much as it produced electoral excitement.

Paradigms for popular progress

Quimpo, following Kerkvliet, criticizes three models of Philippine politics—"clientelist," "colonialist," and "elitist"—for presenting "static, one-sided, and top-down" views.[25] Philippine politics have not been static, even though they may seem defective when viewed from the political left or the social bottom. Some dynamism in the Philippine system comes from peasant movements such as the Huks and New People's Army, and perhaps even Muslim secessionists. These are locally organized in opposition to other local leaders, some of whom participate in the state. Dynamic disputes among elites produce local political equilibria that may look static in macroscopic view but are lively and changing in local polities.

Quimpo says that Hutchcroft is "somewhat dismissive" to write that, "Non-oligarchic social forces never seem to achieve the 'critical mass' necessary to force major overhaul of the system."[26] For both these writers, though, the question becomes: What would give such forces greater mass, greater weight? One answer could be: more money in the hands of regional leaders who were either reformist or revolutionary, but not in the long term oligarchic. Local entrepreneurs could be like this, if enough of them started successful businesses. But the growth of their numbers (except in Metro Manila) is not just slow; it also in many places is politically restrained.

Democratic leftist Joel Rocamora describes reasons why progressive reform remains weaker than land-based conservatism. One reason is that most voters are rural:[27]

> The Makati Business Club represents what might be called the "modernizing bourgeoisie," a segment of the business class most against

rent-seeking.... Civil society cross-overs provide bridges to civil society, the Association of Major Religious Superiors of the Philippines (AMRSP), and progressive sections of the Catholic Church. These groups and individuals are the political expressions of an upper- and middle-class political project for a strong, efficient state.... However, they are not powerful enough to bring the regime down or pry loose the politicians in local governments and the House.

Democracy at the national level can scarcely serve local people, when most local polities are hidebound traditional. Yet national reformers lack enough mass voters to change the modal structure of politics in most Philippine places. So electoral democracy legitimates local oligarchs.

Why does the minority of the Philippine educated elite that wants radical change abjure the Communists and the New People's Army? Most revolutionary dissidents join the electoral process in leftist nonviolent parties (such as the Citizens' Action Party, *Akbayan*). Or they write biting satires, as Rizal did. Or they found hopeful NGOs. One explanation for their careful reticence may be that the Philippine state has seldom repressed them effectively. Even under Ferdinand Marcos, many of his radical or liberal enemies could express themselves politically at least to some extent—no matter whether they came from the left or from the right. Vigilantes of various kinds have killed many people, but only some of the victims were elites. The most obvious exception to this norm was the major reason for Marcos's downfall: the assassination of Ninoy Aquino. Marcos's most crucial political allies defected from him because of this killing. Marcos was lucky that his opponents who were rich were separated from those who fought in the jungle. Groups of dissidents, no matter whether they are Marxist, Islamic, liberal, or rightist, have usually survived over time in the Philippine polity.

The armed left and the Muslim rebels have received far more violence from the state than have armed rightists. The specter of communist revolution haunts Philippine elites, including bishops and intellectuals who groan about the political weakness of most Filipinos. Even when such elites detest leftist and rightist vigilantes, coups, and *kudeta*, they are content enough to tolerate these.

Elections as spurs of politics

The spectacle of electoral struggle is a major support for democracy. E.E. Schattschneider described this process, and he hoped mobilization through electoral wrestling would gradually give "the people" more control of government.[28] What determines the quick or slow speed of democratization? The answer lies in links between local, medial, and central power networks. If any of these sizes of polity becomes so dominant that the others cannot constrain it, information and resources in the weak nodes are reduced. The system then misses opportunities for mutual benefit among different sizes of political network.

The crucial hinges of the Philippine balloting system, connecting grassroots clients with elected politicians, are low-level canvassers called *lider*. Wooing votes, in any electoral democracy, is a local process. A Filipino politician is cued by canvassers to attend "KBL": *Kasal* (weddings), *Binyag* (baptisms), and *Libing* (burials).[29] Such events involve much drama that is symbolic, but

> the political field through the electoral ritual suddenly hails [each person] as a political competent: a voter.... Elections are just one moment in people's lives.... They engage in an electoral exercise because they see it as one occasion for asserting their claims (security, jobs, additional government support).[30]

"Elections prompt politicians to make alliances to fight the contests. After the elections, a new political wind starts to blow and changes the alliance system."[31] The kaleidoscope of shifting local (and national) coalitions turns often. Mayor Umali of Lipa City was re-elected twice, albeit on each occasion under a different party banner. "In both cases, a new factional configuration emerged, and the relations among the factions and their relations with the national parties had totally changed."[32]

The reasons why Filipinos switch parties can depend on existential trusts or rivalries, or in other cases on expected material benefits. Landé claimed,[33]

> In many localities, these rivalries are so deeply felt and so embedded in long-standing social alignments and personal feuds that their abandonment is almost inconceivable. Not a few local leaders may swallow their pride and join the opposition for substantial material advantages, but a great many others refuse to do so. Some even switch from the stronger to the weaker party. Thus, should the party in power nationally allow some local leader of the opposition to switch over and join its ranks, it may happen that another local leader, previously committed to the majority party but a personal rival of the newcomer, will switch to the opposite party in protest and take most his sub-leaders with him.

In this view, local politics present patterns that are constantly interesting to voters because conflicts are frequently changing, albeit they bring no coherent social policy.

Electoral struggle is supposed gradually to benefit ordinary people in most democracies.[34] This logic has operated with particular slowness in the Philippines. Contests for votes attract attention. The people participate, but they do not soon become more "sovereign." That should present a greater theoretical conundrum for democrats than has yet been sufficiently explored.

Non-governmental societies

Civil societies in the Philippines are many. The number of NGOs is so extraordinary that some analysts claim there is a higher density of them in this country than anywhere else on earth. Civil societies may be categorized in two types. First, researchers from Tocqueville to Putnam or Berman have famously described an "associational" kind, which generates "social capital" and is sometimes supposed to promote democracy. Second, a more radical kind of non-governmental polity provides "counterweights," in full opposition to a regime.[35] This second sort is often ephemeral, but it has appeared in Philippine "people power" movements against Marcos in 1986, Estrada in 2001, or (less obvious on streets) Arroyo in 2010. Some such events caused changes of incumbents. Each came at a time when crucial elements of the military agreed with "the people." Civil societies are very active in the Philippines, but their effect on modal structures that could link national democratic institutions to popular interests has been slow. Many local institutions in the rural areas where most Filipinos live are not democratic; they are authoritarian and collectively predominant.

Several important non-governmental organizations are religious. Some priests in the Philippines, from Spanish times onward, have preached in favor of socio-political reform or liberation theology, especially in the era influenced by John XXIII and the Second Vatican Council. Later, however, all but the most recent successor of that pope appointed bishops and cardinals who were increasingly conservative. The Catholic Church has occasionally, in other countries, supported coalitions of liberals with communists (e.g., in Costa Rica).[36] The hierarchy in Manila generally sided with anti-leftists—even though after the egregious assassination of Ninoy Aquino the church turned against Marcos. The hierarchy's politics, albeit not that of all priests, is usually conservative. Following Iberian traditions, the Philippine bishops do not shy away from politics when they think they are right.

Civil societies of other kinds are also evident in this country, but they employ less than 2 percent of the economically active population. Just 6 percent of adults do volunteer work. These rates are "average" among 19 developing countries in a 2004 study.[37] Some professional leaders move between governmental and NGO posts. "Under presidents [Cory] Aquino, Ramos, and Estrada," according to Pinches, "leading NGO figures, many of them identified with the left, took on high-level government appointments with responsibility in areas in which they sought reform."[38] But these reformers did not generally have much long-term success in progressive terms. They took their posts and then could do little.

Clarke finds evidence that,

> civil society in the Philippines is both *captured* by elite interests (as suggested by Hedman 2006) and *anti-developmental* in effect (representing an institutional complement to the anti-development state portrayed in Bello 2004) ... elite control elicits a reaction in the form of mass movements based on syncretic and indigenous forms of Christianity supported by up to 12 million Filipinos, the vast majority of them poor or on low incomes.[39]

Civil society of this kind is ineffective for either modern development or egalitarian purposes. The creation of participatory and pro-poor truly "civil" societies in the Philippines is incomplete.

Ostensible trust among elites, distrust among non-elites

A striking aspect of Philippine elite politics is the extent to which national leaders and their families are able to come together in a semblance of friendship, even after they have been in violent conflict. The top political figures in this country know each other well. Against each other, they usually must shy away from heavy-handed forcefulness such as some of them use in patronist local polities. When Ferdinand Marcos's children, Imee and "Bongbong" Marcos, attended the funeral of Corazon Aquino (in whose husband's assassination the elder Marcos is thought by many to have been involved), this was newsworthy but not shocking. Formal courtesy is a Philippine elite tradition. Modern *principalia* families usually appear to get along, even when they have histories of violent strife against each other.

Educated, high-income, or urban Filipinos have been polled to have some mutual trust, while low-income, less-educated, or rural citizens have less (or perhaps are less able to hide their feelings of wariness). A Social Weather Stations survey used a stratified sample of Philippine adults, showing that measures of trust are relatively higher among Filipinos with high educational attainment, high family income, and large-city residence. Along many dimensions (frequency of contact, occasions of help with jobs or sickness or debt, and others) this relationship between trust and status is statistically strong. But low-status Filipinos (as defined by income, education, or residence) have measurable low levels of trust in each other.[40] This situation may also obtain in other societies too, and it deserves further research.

Electoral campaigns, either national or local, tend to pit similar elite candidates against each other. They seldom mobilize support along class or status lines. Ben Kerkvliet points out the reasons:

> Confrontational politics can be engaged by the rich, but not by the poor. Then there is the fact that family linkages and vertical ties to people in higher status or class positions inhibit unity among most of the poor or most peasants during election campaigns. Peasants have run for village office ... as candidates of the two alliances [in a village of central Luzon, Gregorio and Castro families vs. Cruz and Trinidad clans], not as "peasant" candidates.[41]

Blood is thicker than policy. Family or familistic bonds trump links within classes or status groups. This does not mean that local Filipinos are unable to mount political, even armed, resistance when their living is deeply threatened; but the most permanent institution is still kinship. "Everyday resistance" remains weak; it is ephemeral and has not changed large institutions. Livelihood and dignity are the two basic demands of peasants.[42] As for livelihood, incomes remain unequal and few people receive much material help. As for dignity, Philippine elites grant that to many in symbolic terms.

A norm for "pleasing the group," *pakikisama*, stresses the importance of smooth personal relations. Timberman says this gives Philippine politics "its 'show biz' quality, its reliance on political rituals, and the indulgence of politicians in *palabas* (hyperbole and ostentatious show)." "Imelda Marcos once commented to an interviewer that 'Ninoy [Benigno Aquino, Jr.] was all sauce and no substance.' In response to his wife's observation, Ferdinand Marcos replied: 'Sweetheart, that is the essence of Filipino politics.'"[43]

Most Philippine elections are like political fiestas, although they are not necessarily fated to be so forever. Candidates are expected to make their political speeches communal and happy, emphasizing personalities rather than policies. A rally (*miting de avance*) in San Isidro, Bataan, was "a political campaign and musical show rolled into one … [although the] candidates all come here and talk with us, they know that we are a big clan and that we vote as a bloc."[44]

In legislative halls, the audiences are less likely to be as accommodating as in campaign rallies. Many Philippine lawmakers, whom journalists sarcastically call the "Comité de Silencio," seldom or never say anything in Congress.[45] They deliver the local speeches, roads, and contracts. Their local allies and canvassers deliver the voters in elections. That still exhausts for them the business of politics.

The local government code

Many Philippine intellectuals and reformers have wanted more critical politics. In the early 1990s, after several quasi-coups that threatened Corazon Aquino's presidency and then after the election of Fidel Ramos, there was a period of reforms that echoed types of thinking that went back at least to Rizal—and also bears some similarity to the time of some reforms after PNoy's election in 2010. Two major changes were made.

After the 1987 "people power" Constitution was passed, it was followed by a Local Government Code of 1991 (Republic Act 7160), which established "development councils" all over the archipelago. Money is allocated to these councils for use according to multi-year plans. But, in practice, an "annual investment plan is formulated by the [provincial] governor, the mayors, and the whole provincial legislature along with heads of provincial offices and representatives of national offices." This large group divides up the money, often giving each political "stakeholder" a project to which his or her name can be attached.[46] This reform strengthened local elites on the pretense of strengthening development.

More than 50,000 barangay governments cover the whole archipelago. Forty percent of the national budget is allotted by the 1991 law to provinces, municipalities, and barangays. The localities decide how to use most of these funds. Political incumbents are legitimated by handing out this money. All these units, including the barangays, also have the power to impose local taxes.

The 1991 Code mandates this local use of central tax revenues. Seven-tenths of the devolved money goes into administrative salaries.[47] At least until 2010, most of it financed existing patron–client networks: canvassers, clients, and relatives. When a very knowledgeable interviewee was asked what percentage of the devolved money has capitalized industries or financed infrastructure, he wanted anonymity and answered, "Roughly zero."

The Code ostensibly aimed at more local democratization. As Steven Rood has written, concerning efforts to judge the code's results, "this is an attempt to pin down local governance, not necessarily local *democratic* governance."[48] As Ledivina Cariño says, "Devolution has not always produced local governments attuned to democratic governance."[49] The 1991 Local Government Code nonetheless inspired NGOs to hope for support from barangay and provincial elected politicians toward ends such as environmental protection, expanded schooling, and corruption control. The progressives were disheartened, when they found that local democracy instead often financed local politicians who stymied their plans.

Latin American countries share Iberian political legacies with the Philippines. A major study of Mexico found that there, too, decentralization became a "double-edged sword," sending more resources "down" to local elites without making those officials more accountable to any substantively democratic process.[50] In some countries, such as Brazil, democratic values may recently have flourished at municipal more than at national levels; deliberation about local budgets there has become more widespread.[51] Manila's constituent cities occasionally show some comparability with this evolution, but effective political participation in most parts of the archipelago is a potential for the future more than a current reality.

Party-list representatives

The Local Government Code of 1991 has encouraged the creation of a group of NGOs called the Barangay-Bayan Governance Consortium. This network aims to try "multiple lanes for engagement" to connect NGOs with political parties and local government officials. The *Akbayan* Party later became the consortium's national expression.[52] So the decentralization code related to a second reform: the Party-List System Act of February 1995, which was signed into law by President Ramos after the Congress surprisingly passed it. This change could be conceived as a symbolic move to "let off steam" in a democracy where power is dramatically unequal among citizens. But the change also put critical new voices into bully pulpits.

The allowance of party-list Congressmen might have been counter-predicted, on the premise that *trapos* would have been unwilling to reform the structure of their political system. Yet President Ramos apparently pushed hard for the establishment of this system. It gave an opportunity for previously unrepresented civil society NGOs to have benefits of information and expression that are inherent in the role of a Congress member. Legislators of this new type, party-list members, were "noses under the tent" of the previous system. The current author believes that *trapos* in Congress who refrained from voting against this reform did not foresee its effects. They did not know what they were doing. They allowed some minor harm to their immediate interests—and in the long term served their country.

Party-list representation is available only for parties that do not run candidates in districts. The law that qualifies them mandates that these groups should represent "marginalized and underrepresented sectors, organizations, and parties ... who lack well-defined political constituencies but who could contribute to the formulation and enactment of appropriate legislation that will benefit the nation as a whole."[53] They are supposed to speak on behalf of workers, senior citizens, women, farmers, fisherfolk, teachers, or minority language regions (such as the Bicol or Waray areas). Party-list groups nominate up to three candidates in each congressional election. The Committee on Elections receives in advance a list of the order in which the candidates would be seated, depending on the votes the parties receive. Each voter may cast ballots both for a geographical representative and for a party that has such a list. If any such "sectoral" party receives 2 percent of the nationwide ballots, its first nominee is seated. After that, a complex mathematical formula determines whether the party receives a second or third seat—up to a maximum of one-fifth of the House.[54]

The party-list reform resulted from pressures by intellectual elites, not the Philippine poor. Filipinos have been polled whether they prefer a party-slate system to their usual system of choosing each candidate separately in geographic districts for each office. Over 80 percent replied in 1992 that they liked their normal practice.[55] This "plurality voting" rule is still used for the vast majority of Philippine offices, including most seats in the House.

The Philippines has three main leftist parties, with different action programs: the socialist *Akbayan* or "Citizens' Action Party," the Marxist *Sanlakas* or "One Strength," and the Maoist *Bayan Muna* or "People First" that is the legal branch of the New People's Army. All three have fielded candidates for local elections, winning municipal posts. All have been represented in Congress (and this is especially notable because of Bayan Muna's link to the NPA). The Philippine state recognizes nonviolent elected representatives who are implicitly connected to nonstate organizations that use violence. This is not unique in democracies, as Northern Irish experience shows; but it is unusual. In effect the Philippine state admits it does not have a monopoly of violence, and this is no more than a situation.

To some extent these three parties compete with each other. As Quimpo writes, "Bayan Muna's leftist rivals encountered more problems with NPA guerrillas than with the *trapos*' goons."[56] Rightist groups also launch party-list candidates. *Anakpawis*, which describes itself as the radical wing of the trade union movement, is another sectoral party-list group that has won seats. *Alagad* represents the Iglesia ni Cristo church, although it is not legally supposed to do so "for religious purposes." Most of the party-list seats go to local and occupational groups, and by no means are all of these leftist. The constitutional test is that a party-list group should be underrepresented in Congress among the geographically elected members. The Supreme Court disqualified a party that the second-richest man in the country, Lucio Tan, tried to establish.

The *Akbayan* was founded as a nonviolent worker and peasant party to oppose *trapos*. Led by intellectuals, *Akbayan* would have scant hope of winning in geographical districts, but it can garner enough votes nationwide to contest the three House memberships allowed to it. In 1998, *Akbayan* won a just a single seat in the House; but in 2001, it won two; and by 2004, three seats. It had less luck winning congressional places than in convincing municipal mayors to join *Akbayan* after their elections. Its emphasis has been on barangay organization.[57]

Akbayan is above all local. The party's declared aim is to build its base in municipalities, moving into the central state gradually. As a statement from its 2003 national conference announced, "*Akbayan* employs the strategy of combining a determined struggle for ideological and cultural hegemony, establishing building blocks through radical reforms and sustained organizing and constituency building in local communities, sub-classes, and sectors and institutions."[58]

Akbayan members have worked harder than most of their peers in parliament. Congresswoman Eta Rosales was so dutiful in her first term, the House leadership made her chair of the Committee on Civil, Political, and Human Rights after she was re-elected. Twenty bills that she authored or co-authored passed the House (whose other members remained mostly *trapo*).[59] New ideas that could garner majorities had clearly been needed, and the party-list representatives helped to break this logjam. Hutchcroft and Rocamora identify a "democratic deficit" in the Philippines.[60] Part of the deficit was that members of the *trapo*-dominated legislature had failed to present proposals that could, after debate, achieve consensus. Some party-list members addressed this lack.

Akbayan Congressman Walden Bello, similarly, has had much greater influence than his party's miniscule representation in the House would predict, e.g., because of details that he publicized in a scathing mid-2010 "privilege speech" against the corruptions of President Gloria Macapagal Arroyo. Bello is a well-known academic, a former professor at the University of the Philippines (and a sociology Ph.D. from Princeton). Because of parliamentary immunity, Congress members may not be sued for remarks they make in speeches on the floor of Congress. A major power of party-list representatives (also used by a few senators such as Miriam Defensor Santiago) stems from their "bully pulpits" that are immune to libel suits. They can try to detail chains of corruption without being tied up for many future years in courts—and, of course, Philippine reporters and TV carry such news more broadly. These Congress members were emphatically not in the "Comité de Silencio." It is a sign of mutual acknowledgement among Philippine elites that they set up the party-list system, which makes a quasi-constitutional dent in older patterns of politics. It goes beyond the slower reform that socioeconomic modernization brings to the Philippine polity.

Trapos naturally disliked the party-list system, which was explicitly designed to give House representation to new kinds of leaders. Traditional politicians have been able only partially to hijack it. After the first relevant election, the Supreme Court disqualified 60 would-be party-list parties for being "mainstream" rather than "marginal," as by law they are required to be. By 2000, however, conservative groups succeeded in nominating members of *trapo* families to compete as party-list candidates anyway. Of the party-list candidates in the following election, one analysis estimated that one-fifth were "members of political clans, and almost half can be classified as millionaires or multi-millionaires"—even when they claimed to represent more typical Filipinos.

Organizations supporting *trapo* candidates in regular district elections also bankrolled party-list candidates. A survey concluded that four-fifths of the party-list groups in the 2010 Congress "can be classified as 'traditional,' those having links with traditional political forces, administration, political clans, big business, and emerging religious dynasties."[61] The portion of non-*trapos* among party-list congressmen decreased. Yet the party-list system still allowed new voices in Congress, albeit not in the national executive. It also spurred coordination of groups that were able to increase their power in some (not all) municipal executives, to which the 1991 fiscal reform had transferred more money.

Populism and reformism

The Philippines remains an "elite democracy." Electoral democracies can create problems for "the people" they are supposed to serve. Many states that use voting have been variously categorized as "defective democracies," "hybrid regimes," "new authoritarianisms," "electoral authoritarianisms," and other kinds of semidemocratic regimes-with-adjectives. Most such categorizations are meant to typify national governments, rather than local polities. One of the best expositions of these types shows that, in electoral authoritarianisms, votes "cannot be taken as reliable expressions of 'the will of the people,'" because balloting is easy for incumbent elites to manipulate. Money, coercion, fear, and brainwashing all affect election results. Schedler, attempting political science, writes an equation for this: $V=pi$, where V are votes, p represents "citizen preferences," and i is "electoral integrity" (ranging from zero to one).[62] Such analyses, and the eagerness with which political scientists can use election statistics that seem comparable from national jurisdictions, underplay that national polities are not most important for most citizens. Local regimes can have different types from state regimes on the same turfs. The problem is not that previous classifications of states are wrongheaded; instead, it is that "sovereign" governments are often not the most powerful political networks in their areas.

In the Philippines, where local polities trump the state polity, national coalitions are rare or fairly weak. Outside Metro Manila, the most relevant arenas for political drama are regional turfs. A problem of Philippine democracy is that both the redistribution and the creation of new resources that might reorganize politics are stunted. Formally democratic institutions have been entrenched for most of a century, but new elites (even potentially populist leaders who favor redistribution) cannot easily change the long-legitimated political structure while also making social allocations that would sustain their power. They may do so eventually, and in the new millennium they seem to have begun. The road ahead will still be long.

Action possibilities for sustainable reforms

If more local leaders were reformist "angels" rather than "devilish" *trapos*, polities of several sizes in the Philippines would serve more of the people. In Metro

Populist rituals and elite reformism 151

Manila, this has to some extent happened already, because of politicians from groups that Rocamora calls the "modernizing bourgeoisie." The founding of more enterprises (not just the passage of time) in poorer parts of the country could bring analogous results there. Development that hires people depends on investments for infrastructure, ranging from rural education to better transportation. This would raise the variety of regional leaders who contest Philippine elections, and it would allow more democratic choices for citizens.

The surprising 1990s reform that allowed party-list Congress members shows that many Philippine political elites know their own variety should be greater. The Local Government Code of the same era has almost surely had opposite effects, strengthening traditional patronage by giving regional power networks more money. Philippine politics including its fiscal aspects is still largely clientelist, especially in localities outside Metro Manila. But two social discourses have for decades overlaid clientelist institutions. One, which can be called "populist" and can be very corrupt, include politicians such as Erap Estrada and others who mainly tell Filipinos, "I am like you." The main alternative, which can be called "reformist," is anti-corruption; its proponents include elites such as PNoy, most bishops, some progressive businesspeople, and many intellectuals. Recent elections suggest continuing long-term strengths of both these rival discourses.[63]

A difficulty of Philippine substantive democratization is that its institutions are already ostensibly democratic. Governments in many countries use their powers, including their coercion, to change the distribution of resources in society. To predict future regime-type change, an analyst must look at the current distribution of resources available to crucial groups. Leaders form coalitions to control or increase their access to these goods.[64] When elites are divided, their ability to mobilize or repress mass protests often determines the result: either distributional change, or else merely a change of incumbents, or continuation of the status quo. When an elite that can sustain redistribution because other elites which might subvert it must nonetheless go along with it, then people from various classes participate in politics. The outcome becomes more substantially democratic.

Notes

1 This follows Benedict J. Tria Kerkvliet, "Political Expectations and Democracy in the Philippines and Vietnam," *Philippine Political Science Journal* 26:49 (2005), 16–21. Some nationalist academics, however, have resented any use of patron–client concepts in describing modal Philippine politics, even as situations alter, and have assumed that Filipinos' own notions of "progress" must be remnants of colonialism. Any convincing conceptualization needs to match evidence—and changes of evidence over time—more than it needs to match the researcher's identity.
2 This phrase is the title of a book by Edward Friedman about the Chinese revolution.
3 Reynaldo Ileto, *Pasyón and Revolution: Popular Movements in the Philippines, 1840–1910* (Quezon City: Ateneo de Manila University Press, 1979), 18–19.
4 Reynaldo Ileto, *Pasyón and Revolution*, 12; next quotations from 13 and 318.
5 Chapter 10, below, criticizes Reynaldo Ileto, *Knowing America's Colony: A Hundred*

152 *Populist rituals and elite reformism*

    Years from the Philippine War, esp. Lecture 3, "Orientalism and the Study of Philippine Politics" (Honolulu, HI: Center for Philippine Studies, 1999).
6 Reynaldo Ileto, *Pasyón and Revolution*, 132–4.
7 Ibid., 122–7.
8 William Reno, "The Politics of Insurgency in Collapsing States," *Development and Change* 33:5 (December 2002), 837–58; quote from abstract, concerning cases in Nigeria—but this applies equally to the Philippines.
9 Cesar Cala, "Publisher's Foreword," in *[De]scribing Elections: A Study of Elections in the Lifeworld of San Isidro*, Myrna J. Alejo, Maria Elena Rivera, and Noel Inocencio Valencia, eds. (Quezon City: Institute for Popular Democracy, 1996), xii.
10 See John Gaventa, *Power and Powerlessness: Quiescence and Rebellion in an Appalachian Valley* (Urbana, IL: University of Illinois Press, 1980), Steven Lukes, *Power: A Radical View* (London: Macmillan, 1974), and E.E. Schattschneider, *The Semi-Sovereign People: A Realist's View of Democracy in America*, intro. by David Adamany (Hinsdale, IL: Dreyden Press, 1975).
11 Nathan Gilbert Quimpo, *Contested Democracy and the Left in the Philippines* (New Haven, CT: Southeast Asia Council, Yale University, 2008), 45.
12 This has been standard discourse in Thai politics for decades. See David Murray, *Angels and Devils: Thai Politics from February 1991 to September 1992—A Struggle for Democracy?* (Bangkok: White Orchid Press, 1996).
13 Mina Roces, *The Lopez Family, 1946–2000: Kinship Politics in Postwar Philippines* (Manila: De La Salle University Press, 2001), 14.
14 Ibid., 15.
15 For an analysis of kinds of power, see John Gaventa, *Power and Powerlessness*, and Gaventa, "Three Faces of Power: A Framework for Advocacy," www.careinternational.org.uk/download.php?id=44.
16 Jeffrey A. Winters, *Oligarchy* (New York: Cambridge University Press, 2011), 34.
17 Recent statistical findings that may be relevant are in Ricardo G. Abad, *Aspects of Social Capital in the Philippines: Findings from a National Survey* (Quezon City: Social Weather Stations, 2006). It is unclear how long this tendency will last, however.
18 Benedict J. Tria Kerkvliet, "Contested Meanings of Elections in the Philippines," in *The Politics of Elections in Southeast Asia*, R.H. Taylor, ed. (New York: Cambridge University Press; and Washington, DC: Woodrow Wilson Center, 1996), 150–1.
19 A treatment of the Japanese period is Augusto V. De Viana, *Kulaboretor! The Issue of Political Collaboration During World War II* (Manila: University of Santo Tomas Publishing House, 2003).
20 Jose Y. Dalisay, Jr., *The Lavas: A Filipino Family* (Pasig City: Anvil, 1999), 64.
21 Compare Vivienne Shue, *Peasant China in Transition: The Dynamics of Development Toward Socialism, 1949–1956* (Berkeley, CA: University of California Press, 1980), which offers evidence about rich rural or industrial Chinese who supported the communist revolution and were sometimes treated less harshly during land reforms.
22 Richard J. Kessler, *Rebellion and Repression in the Philippines* (New Haven, CT: Yale University Press, 1989), 29.
23 Rasil Mojares, *The Man Who Would Be President: Serging Osmeña and Philippine Politics* (Cebu: Maria Cacao, 1986), 52–3.
24 Amando Doronila, *The State, Economic Transformation, and Political Change in the Philippines, 1946–1972* (Singapore: Oxford University Press, 1992), 94–7.
25 Nathan Gilbert Quimpo, *Contested Democracy and the Left in the Philippines*, 41.
26 Quoted in Nathan Gilbert Quimpo, *Contested Democracy and the Left in the Philippines*, 44.
27 Joel Rocamora, "From Regime Crisis to System Change," in *Whither the Philippines in the 21st Century*, Rodolfo C. Severino and Lorraine Carlos Salazar, eds. (Singapore: ISEAS, 2007), 21.

28 E.E. Schattschneider, *The Semi-Sovereign People*.
29 KBL was also the acronym for Marcos's political party, the *Kilusang Babong Lipunan* (New Society Movement). See John T. Sidel, "The Philippines: The Languages of Legitimation," in *Political Legitimacy in Southeast Asia: The Quest for Moral Authority*, Muthiah Alagappa, ed. (Stanford, CA: Stanford University Press, 1995), 146.
30 Myrna J. Alejo, Maria Elena Rivera, and Noel Inocencio Valencia, *[De]scribing Elections*, 70 and 92.
31 Kimura Masataka, *Elections and Politics, Philippine Style: A Case in Lipa* (Manila: De La Salle University Press, 1997), 204.
32 Ibid., 247.
33 Carl H. Landé, "Party Politics in the Philippines," in *Six Perspectives on the Philippines*, George M. Guthrie, ed. (Manila: Bookmark, 1968), 99.
34 E.E. Schattschneider, *The Semi-Sovereign People*.
35 Nathan Gilbert Quimpo, *Contested Democracy and the Left in the Philippines*, 95–6. Also, Sheri Berman, "Civil Society and the Collapse of the Weimar Republic," *World Politics* 49 (April 1997), 401–29, points out that some civil societies support dictators.
36 A case in which the Church decisively supported rightists was 1954 Guatemala. Deborah J. Yashar, *Demanding Democracy: Reform and Reaction in Costa Rica and Guatemala, 1870s–1950s* (Stanford, CA: Stanford University Press, 1997), contrast 109–10 with 198.
37 Kasuya Yoko, "Democratic Consolidation in the Philippines: Who Supports Extra-Constitutional Change?" in *The Politics of Change in the Philippines*, Yuko Kasuya and Nathan Gilbert Quimpo, eds. (Pasig City: Anvil, 2010), 111.
38 Michael Pinches, "The Making of Middle Class Civil Society in the Philippines," in *The Politics of Change in the Philippines*, Yuko Kasuya and Nathan Gilbert Quimpo, eds. (Pasig City: Anvil, 2010), 295.
39 Gerard Clarke, *Civil Society in the Philippines: Theoretical, Methodological, and Policy Debates* (London: Routledge, 2013), 194.
40 Ricardo G. Abad, *Aspects of Social Capital in the Philippines: Findings from a National Survey* (Quezon City: Social Weather Stations, 2006).
41 Benedict J. Tria Kerkvliet, *Everyday Politics in the Philippines: Class and Status Relations in a Central Luzon Village* (Berkeley, CA: University of California Press, 1990; also Quezon City: New Day, 1991), 227.
42 See ibid., 255–65, and references there to political theorist Henry Shue and political anthropologist James Scott.
43 The Tagalog *palabas* is a cognate of Spanish *palabras*, "words," with the connotation "empty words, promises from which nothing comes." For more, see David G. Timberman, *A Changeless Land: Continuity and Change in Philippine Politics* (Armonk, NY: M.E. Sharpe, 1991), 20.
44 Myrna J. Alejo, Maria Elena Rivera, and Noel Inocencio Valencia, *[De]scribing Elections*, 36–8 and 40, see also 123.
45 Renato S. Velasco, "Does the Philippine Congress Promote Democracy?" in *Democratization: Philippine Perspectives*, Felipe B. Miranda, ed. (Quezon City: University of the Philippines Press, 1995), 288.
46 Ledivina V. Cariño, "Devolution toward Democracy: Lessons for Theory and Practice from the Philippines," in *Decentralizing Governance*, Shabbir Cheema, ed. (Washington, DC: Brookings, 2007), 102.
47 Interviews with longstanding experts on the Philippines, August 30 and 31, 2004.
48 Steven Rood, "Researching Decentralized Governance," in *Democratization: Philippine Perspectives*, Felipe B. Miranda, ed. (Quezon City: University of the Philippines Press, 1995), 314, italics in original.
49 This relies on Ledivina V. Cariño, "Devolution and Democracy: A Fragile Connection," in *East Asia's New Democracies: Deepening, Reversal, Non-Liberal Alternatives*, Yin-wah Chu and Siu-lun Wong, eds. (London: Routledge, 2010), 186.

50 Marilee S. Grindle, *Going Local: Decentralization, Democratization, and the Promise of Good Governance* (Princeton, NJ: Princeton University Press, 2007).
51 Archon Fung, "Reinventing Democracy in Latin America," *Perspectives on Politics* 9:4 (December 2011), 857–71.
52 John Gaventa, *Triumph, Deficit, or Contestation: Deepening the 'Deepening Democracy' Debate*, IDS Working Paper 264 (Brighton: Institute of Development Studies, 2006), 17.
53 Republic Act No. 7941, www.chanrobles.com/republicactno7941.htm.
54 This system was established by the Republic Act 7941 of 1995, providing that one-fifth of the House may be filled by party-list representatives. The total membership of the House was set to be no more than 250 by a later law. The president may appoint additional Congress members up to the 250 maximum after geographical and party-list members are seated. The formula for determining second- and third-seat representation of party-list parties is a complex multi-step protocol decided by the Supreme Court. It would interest formalists in political science, and internet sites describe it. The Supreme Court has also issued an eight-point guideline for determining the criteria that qualify a "sectoral" party.
55 From a 1992 poll conducted by the Social Weather Stations, Inc.; thanks are due to Jeanette M. Ureta for telling the author about this result.
56 Nathan Gilbert Quimpo, *Contested Democracy and the Left in the Philippines*, 151, and quotation on 155.
57 Joel Rocamora, "Impossible is Not So Easy: Party Building and Local Governance in the Philippines" (essay provided by courtesy of the author), *passim*.
58 Quoted in Nathan Gilbert Quimpo, *Contested Democracy and the Left in the Philippines*, 125.
59 Ibid., 167.
60 Paul D. Hutchcroft and Joel Rocamora, "Patronage-based Parties and the Democratic Deficit in the Philippines: Origins, Evolution, and the Imperatives of Reform," in *Routledge Handbook of Southeast Asian Politics*, Richard Robison, ed. (Abingdon: Routledge, 2013), 97–119.
61 Bobby Tuazon, "Clans Use the Party-List System to Remain Dominant in 15th Congress," sent by Prof. Tuazon to the author by e-attachment.
62 Andreas Schedler, "The Logic of Electoral Authoritarianism," in *Electoral Authoritarianism: The Dynamics of Unfree Competition*, Andreas Schedler, ed. (Boulder, CO: Rienner, 2006), 8.
63 Mark R. Thompson, "Reformism vs. Populism in the Philippines," *Journal of Democracy* 21:4 (2010), 154–68.
64 This stress on leadership coalitions allows political scientists to combine two types of observations: about agents who found regime types, and about social structures that help or hinder democratization. Compare Deborah J. Yashar, *Demanding Democracy*, 14–21.

8 Voting, pork, policy, and media

The Philippine president and vice-president are now chosen for six-year terms. These elections coincide with voting for half of the Senate (12 members with six-year terms). The whole House is chosen at the same time (212 geographical delegates plus party-list representatives, with three-year terms). Provincial, city, and barangay officials are all elected on the same three-year cycle. So the House and administratively lower officials stand for elections at the start and in the middle year of any presidential term.

Voter turnout is exceptionally high in the Philippine democracy, often between 80 and 85 percent. In the 1998 election, 86 percent of all eligible Philippine voters actually cast ballots.[1] Turnout in 2010 remained high, at 74 percent.[2]

Three-fifths of all the nation's voters live on Luzon, an island that includes several linguistically distinctive regions. About a quarter of Luzon voters live in Metro Manila, and the population of the surrounding Tagalog areas is also considerable. Urban and peri-urban rural voters do not cast ballots at a higher rate than do citizens in the rural rest of the country. Wurfel found, "evidence of a higher election turnout in rural than in urban areas, and in local rather than national elections, [and this] pointed to the importance of the patron–client relationship in voting."[3] Local patrons have been able to commandeer large blocs of votes with dependable regularity.

Surveyors divide Philippine society into five socioeconomic classes: A for "super rich," B for "normal rich," C for small managers and officials, D for the "lower class," and E for the indigent. The "ABC classes" together account for only a tenth of the population.[4] Successful politicians must therefore win votes from the poor "D" and penniless "E" classes. But communal solidarity under a leading family usually trumps class or left–right policy preferences in voting anyway.

It is useful though not essential for a presidential or senatorial candidate, who runs throughout the archipelago, to be able to make speeches in a Visayan language as well as in Tagalog/"Pilipino," the language of Manila that is taught in schools and is with English the language of media and government. The Philippines' diversity of local tongues, even though they are all in the same broad Malay language family, strengthens political regionalism.[5] President Quezon in the 1930s complained, when he visited Pampanga just 100 miles north of the capital, that he could not make himself understood in public speeches until he got a translator to repeat his words in Capampangan.[6]

Compared to the number of Filipinos who speak Tagalog in their homes (as distinguished from the number who can speak it because of schooling), more than twice as many speak mutually intelligible Visayan languages such as Cebuano.[7] These come from the central islands and now also dominate Mindanao. Compared to native Tagalog speakers, roughly half as many speak Bicol or Ilocano tongues in their families, and fewer speak the languages of Pangasinan or Pampanga.

The most usual way for a candidate to win the presidency is to do exceptionally well on Luzon. Many national majorities for president or vice-president (elected separately) have been founded on victory in the heavily populated corridor from the Southern Tagalog provinces up through Manila to Pangasinan. This "Lucena-Pangasinan" swath, from the isthmus south of the capital to the Lingayan Gulf, contains 40 percent of the national electorate.

The winning strategy for a Philippine presidential (or vice-presidential) candidate is to have a plurality in two of the three main parts of the country, which are: Luzon, the Visayas, and Mindanao. These three very large regions are represented on the Philippine flag by three stars. For all pre-1961 elections, the winning president took all three (Garcia in 1957, Magsaysay in 1953, Quirino in 1949, Roxas in 1946, and Quezon in 1941 and 1935). All three were won by PNoy in 2010, and by Marcos in 1981 and 1969. The most interesting cases are those in which the winner takes pluralities in two of the regions, but not the third. Arroyo did this in 2004 (with the Visayas and Mindanao but not Luzon). Ramos in 1992 and Cory Aquino in 1986 carried Luzon and Mindanao, but not the Visayas. Marcos and Macapagal in 1965 and 1961 had pluralities in Luzon and the Visayas, but not Mindanao. This is a complete list of Philippine presidential elections since 1935.[8]

Regional affiliations do not determine all results, and voters in Philippine elections may be further classified into two kinds. Some cast their ballots freely on the basis of issues, or more often, of public images; these can be called "market voters." Others, called "command voters," come from the ethno-linguistic bailiwicks (*baluartes*) and especially from political machines that depend on money and local patronist organizations.[9]

These two types affect all elections, not just presidential balloting. In 1992, Ramos's plurality relied partly on ethnic factors (10 percent of this Protestant Ilocano's ballots came from a solid turnout in his native Pangasinan, although the population there is not very great). These were bailiwick ballots, but Ramos also had an "image" reputation for being uncorrupt and for having helped the people power revolution of 1986. "Erap" Estrada and "Noynoy" Aquino, despite their many differences, can both also be classed as "image" candidates. Their main election opponents (respectively, De Venecia and Villar) relied heavily on "command votes" generated by their political machines, which did not carry the day nationally.

Image votes have been increasingly important in presidential balloting, except in the 2004 election of Arroyo (the only occasion on which a Philippine president won by taking pluralities in the Visayas and Mindanao while losing

Luzon). Image politics of various sorts might continue to trump machine politics in future elections. It is much less clear whether the images favored by voters will tend toward the reformist or the demagogic forms of populism.

Comelec, voting fraud, money, and force

The Commission on Elections registers candidates and supervises civilian oversight of vote counts. Comelec deputizes teachers, police, and soldiers to watch polls. The Commission tallies the ballots and declares the winners.[10] It does this not just for national elections; it also administers barangay balloting, as well as elections of Youth Councils (*Sangguniang Kabataan*) that govern local chapters of the Youth Federation (*Kapitunan ng Kabataan*).[11] These groups were reformed during the 1991 localization movement, and they receive money to sponsor sports and other activities centering on late-teen youths. They are not powerful, but they breed new politicians even though young members of old families are often active in them.

Comelec declaration of a victor is an important and sometimes chancy event. Candidates try to secure the official proclamation of victory as soon as possible after an elecion, because pre-declaration protests by rivals about voting irregularities can delay certification and lead to long suits in court. Noel Cariño should have won his 2001 race to represent Pasig City in Congress, for example, but because of electoral fraud he was declared the loser. He appealed to Comelec and then to the relevant congressional committee, which took two-and-a-half years finally to declare him the winner—and he was sworn into his seat on the very last day of his term.[12]

Election frauds were temporarily modernized in the Philippines during Marcos's time and in some later years, when bribes to individual voters were replaced by bribes to those who reported the results of balloting. "Certificates of Canvas" are the official summaries of votes at provincial and municipal levels. Such reports have sometimes been faked and sold. Vote-buying is more efficient wholesale than retail.

One way in which candidates attempt to cheat is to invent whole "ghost precincts" that have entirely fictitious lists of voters. This is difficult for candidates to manage on a large scale, but some have tried. Vote fraud also occurred in other forms: the deletion of neighborhoods from registration lists, altering the marks on ballots, stuffing or destroying ballot boxes, and "flying voters."[13] A flying voter (*hakot*), is one who moves

> stealthily from one precinct to another in order to cast multiple ballots. Through "chains" of voters known as *lanzadera*, members deposit a ballot that has been prepared for them in advance and then leave the booth with the fresh ballot they have been given, in order that it too might be prepared and passed on to the next link. And at the end of the process, *dagdag-bawas* (add-subtract) may take place, with election officials blatantly padding and shaving the totals to produce the desired outcomes.[14]

Lider sometimes require that voters use carbon paper when filling in their ballots. Then these canvassers collect the copies, to make sure votes were coerced or bought effectively. According to one report from Danao City, "even the dead vote." Registration rolls there in some years grew faster than the adult population.[15]

Independent election monitors aim to reduce vote-count fraud, and the Philippines has increasing battalions of election monitors. The National Citizens' Movement for Free Elections (Namfrel) is an NGO that was first established in 1951. It was revived in 1983 after Ninoy Aquino's assassination during the Marcos period. Namfrel's moment of greatest fame was "Operation Quick Count" in 1986, claiming evidence that Corazon Aquino defeated Ferdinand Marcos—before the latter could rig the results sufficiently to let a corrupted Comelec claim otherwise.

Both monitoring organizations, however, now have somewhat checkered histories. In the 2004 election of incumbent Arroyo, her taped "Hello Garci" telephone call to Comelec commissioner Garcillano, planning to rig that election, discredited Comelec even though it is the constitutional monitor of elections. Namfrel's problem has been largely in Mindanao, where in 2004 it ignored its own local agents' evidence of similar rigging.[16] The Roman Catholic Church has established yet a third major election-monitoring institution: the Parish Councils for Responsible Voting. The Catholic Church, the most powerful religious institution in the country, now joins others in an important role that could also be performed honestly by the state or secular groups, in fact, by any group that can be impartial, as they have not always been.

Votes can be counted fairly—after they may have been predetermined by force or bribes. By no means does all the dubious money in Philippine elections go toward buying votes. Many pesos are spent to prevent voters from supporting candidates' rivals. Direct vote-buying is a sign of weak patrons who cannot depend on reflexive support from their clients. When subalterns are so presumptively enmeshed in a patron's network that voting for anybody else would be unthinkable (or might lead to physical danger), no bribe is needed.

This clientelist way of controlling votes may now be waning. Seekers of high offices have large constituencies, with too many voters to know personally. So they recruit and pay canvassers whose local prestige is crucial. Building a network of competent middlemen is the key to electoral success. Most money is spent between elections, to create canvassing organizations and make friends. If a candidate waits until election day, he/she may be seen as insincere. Money may then no longer be enough to buy ballots.

Force can also influence votes. Habitual violence can confirm power in local networks, for example by giving a reputation for decisive leadership to its organizer. Alternatively, it may make voters cast their ballots against candidates they perceive as violent. A hundred people died, and another 141 were injured during the 2001 campaigns. In the next bout of voting, when merely 76 people were killed, the chair of the monitoring commission said this figure, which he considered low, showed that the elections were "generally peaceful."[17] As Chapter 3 noted, the elections of 2010 involved about 100 deaths (not counting the unusual massacre by Ampatuan clan supporters in Mindanao that year). Statistics must be uncertain on exact murder rates that surround elections, because voting is just one of the occasions of factional violence.

Most voting by 2010 was computerized. This reform definitely raised the integrity of the official reported results. The ballots of voters remained secret. As the head of a major election-watching NGO said, "The parties have not yet [sic] figured out how to cheat on the vote count, when the counting is done by machines."[18] The automated vote-counting equipment was quick.[19] Candidates had less time to bribe officials who tally the totals of ballots.

The new machines raised public trust in reports of voting; and after the 2013 elections, Comelec spent 43 days on a "random manual audit" of results that came from precinct-count optical scanners (PCOS). This large sample survey determined that they were 99.97 percent accurate.[20] The survey covered votes for senators, Congress members, and mayors. This result greatly pleased Comelec officials, and it showed a major improvement of Philippine electoral democracy.

Exit polls have also served as a rough check on vote-count fraud. Exit polling is detested by some politicians, perhaps because any unexpected pre-election popularity of candidates may affect ballots, or because it inhibits rigging the final results. Pollsters at the Social Weather Stations and Pulse Asia have been subject to legal suits against their very professional exit polls. When these cases came to courts, the SWS and Pulse Asia have won. In a 2010 case, in which SWS sought damages of one million pesos in a "counterclaim" against Senator Richard "Dick" J. Gordon, a regional trial court in Quezon City denied the senator's application for a restraining order against the pollsters.[21] The Comelec head whom PNoy appointed, Sixto Brillantes, Jr., nonetheless came under some suspicion because of earlier links to Erap Estrada and the infamously violent Ampatuan clan of Mindanao.[22] Brillantes threatened suit against the Social Weather Stations and Pulse Asia, saying the law required them to publicize a list of their subscribers, since their pre-election polls might affect voters. Brillantes was controversial, but surveys showed that the public increasingly perceived Philippine election results to be reported fairly.

New voting machines and new transparency reduced electoral fraud. They did not end post-election legal suits by apparent losers. In 2013, Comelec established standard procedures for obtaining data if "losing" candidates filed suits in trial courts. Guidelines advised the courts to access specific electronic information from optical scan machines, laptops, and storage devices. Comelec's own election officers, however, were instructed "to retain custody of the book of voters" and copies of all the electronic data.[23] Apparently there was an understanding that the courts might be corruptible. Judges could hear election cases, but they were not in sole possession of the relevant data; the election monitors had these too.

Free and fair elections are undoubtedly a democratic ideal, but they do not guarantee substantive policies for equal treatment of citizens. A survey has shown that local election performances by politicians in the Philippines do not correlate well with perceptual measurements of their "governance quality."[24] The information that is available to voters, and the strength of their incentives to act on it in their own interests, are important along with non-procedural bases of government.

A free and expensive press

The Philippines has a free press in the sense that media are outside state control. But the main information sources, like those in other democracies such as Italy, are run by nonstate power networks. ABS-CBN TV, perhaps the most influential single news supplier in the archipelago, is owned by the Lopez clan of Cebu (as the *Manila Chronicle* has been since 1947). The GMA Network is also headquartered in Quezon City under private ownership. Free media tend to publish information that sells well. So they stress violent struggles, sex scandals, lewd evidence presented at trials, and government mistakes. Corruption is often a lead story in the Philippines. When media can infer that the rivals of their owners are corrupt, such news is published with gusto.

There is nonetheless also professionalism in the print and electronic press, especially in Manila. A 1997–98 survey of 100 top Philippine reporters found that plain offers of money, to publicize news coming from electoral candidates or their rivals, were not very frequent at the national level. Two-thirds of the correspondents in a survey said they had refused such offers (after having received them). These professionals deemed free lunches and dinners more acceptable than money bribes. Less prestigious local reporters were far less fastidious.[25]

Columnist Ellen Tordesillas, covering Ramos's 1992 presidential campaign, was given an envelope full of pesos. Refusing to slant her reportage because of a bribe, she returned the money to a Ramos staff member—who told her that many similar envelopes were supposed to have been delivered to her during previous months. She never found out who ended up with the accumulated money.[26]

In the hard-fought 1998 presidential race, Speaker De Venecia (who himself had briefly been a reporter) paid a TV anchor "millions of pesos" to be a "consultant" on his campaign. This did not win the election for de Venecia, because a different medium (movies) had created Estrada's populist image as a tough "Pinoy," and this attracted even more voters. Estrada won the presidency with a larger plurality (40 percent) than is usual in such elections that have more than two candidates. As Estrada's press secretary vouched, "Definitely, the media are a battleground as far as the campaign is concerned."[27]

Choosing "Miss Philippines" receives somewhat less news attention than choosing the republic's president—and nearly as much as electing anybody else. Media financed by corporate advertising has normalized this context. One of the easiest critiques of democracy in any country is that companies usually control information and can brainwash electorates.[28] Advertising sways cultures, including norms of politics. Ads may influence people to buy from specific companies, but their more general effect is to advocate types of personal identity: shoppers, conformists to ever-changing styles, women who are young or white or slim rather than intelligent or independent, men who are strong and decisive rather than thoughtful.

Important newspapers include the *Philippine Daily Inquirer* and the *Philippine Star*, as well as the *Manila Times* and *Manila Bulletin*. These are all in English. Partly for that reason, electronic media such as television—which is in Tagalog as well as English—are increasingly important. "Taglish" code-switching mixes these two languages, which often alternate within a single sentence during TV or radio programs. The most influential television channel is ABS-CBN, although there are others too. As in many countries, whether democratic or not, electronic media now tend to displace print media as means of information for most citizens.

Local candidates could seldom afford to buy coverage in the national press or television. But in one campaign, a rich candidate paid the whole newsstand price of three local tabloids that ran his own press releases—in 30,000 to 50,000 copies each. These papers, looking like normal daily editions, were then delivered through regular distribution networks. The newspaper retailers, who did not have to buy what they hawked, received money when they sold the papers—which they thus distributed happily in the candidate's district.[29]

The Philippine Press Institute, following principles that are also usual in other democracies, has lobbied against Philippine laws that restrict paid election propaganda. Such rules do not prevent the practice, which is based in principles of free speech that includes paid speech. Philippine papers often informally put news page space up for sale. Their charges for political advertisements disguised as news depend on placement—higher on the first page than inside, higher yet if above the fold on p. 1, and highest if the story carries a banner headline and includes a photo of the candidate. Publication of a candidate's press release (not labeled as such) may be less expensive on an inside page.

Some television stations had similar practices. A marketing company called "Roaring Thunder" sent a letter, intended as confidential, to Senator Miriam Defensor-Santiago during her election campaign. The letter proposed that:

> At a time when [publicity] is crucially needed [by candidates such as Santiago], it is rendered inutile by Republic Act 6646, banning all paid political advertisements.... [But] there are a thousand and one ways of skinning the cat ... one of which is a three-minute interview portion ... solely dedicated to you, to be aired at prime time on Channel 5, March 28.[30]

The Roaring Thunder marketer made a mistake, however. Sen. Santiago is usually a reformer—and she published the letter. If the price were low enough, many Philippine candidates would have bought the air time, instead. This was an effective way to reach voters, because by 2001 fully 85 percent of Philippine households had TV sets. In twenty-first century elections, Philippine presidential candidates as a group spent more than half of their reported campaign budgets on advertising.[31]

Policy parties?

Schattschneider, a scholar of the U.S., showed that, "Political parties created democracy ... democracy is unthinkable save in terms of the parties."[32] Writing in the mid-1960s about the Philippines, Landé claimed that, "There have been but two major parties at any specific time. Third parties have been either small, or short-lived, or both."[33] But later developments show how radically this pattern could change. The word "party," as used in the Philippines, denotes a more loose organization even than in the U.S.—or especially in Europe, where parties are more disciplined. Major Philippine parties were, and are, coalitions surrounding personalities. They are seldom unified by policy preferences.

Joel Rocamora calls Philippine parties "temporary campaign organizations, malleable, unstable, with no organizational reality other than what their leaders choose to give them at each specific point in time."[34] Economic modernization, giving rise to leftist parties of labor and rightist parties of capital, has not occurred in the Philippines sufficiently to produce that pattern. Ethnic or religious divisions of the kind that give stable party structures to a few smaller democracies such as Belgium or Ireland do not create policy parties in Manila, because ethnic divisions in the Philippines (outside Muslim Mindanao and the minorities of the north Luzon mountains) are not severe.

Research on political parties is mostly Western. This weakens the applicability in many countries of concepts about parties that have been developed by political scientists, especially those from the U.S. Philippine parties vary, but even relatively "strong" ones are loose coalitions. That trait is also somewhat present in the West, but democratic ideology and the prevalent hunch that all politics must be social interest aggregation have made most political scientists neglect it everywhere.[35] The "mythic model" of a policy party applies only partially in the West—and hardly at all among major Philippine "parties."

It is possible to attempt to design charts of "the spectrum of political forces in the Philippines" along a right–left dimension. Karaos has tried this for one time period, but the policy stability of parties has been so shaky, the project is very difficult.[36] Party platforms are required by the Commission on Elections, but practically nobody reads them. The *Philippine Daily Inquirer* called them "the usual motherhood statements."[37]

Parties in this archipelago have historically been temporary alliances among personalistic networks of clients. Under the American colonial regime, the Nacionalistas dominated elections, despite alternations between the Osmeña and Quezon factions after 1922.[38] Neither was a policy group. A renewed two-party structure between Nacionalistas and Liberals continued this pattern after the Japanese period, although even presidential candidates lacked loyalty to their nominal parties. Magsaysay in 1963 doffed his Liberal label to run as a Nacionalista and win. In presidential races, the Liberals won in 1946 and 1948 (Roxas and Quirino), and 1961 (Macapagal). The Nacionalistas won in 1953 and 1957 (Magsaysay and Garcia), and 1965. That mid-1960s case is the most famous instance of a top leader switching parties: Liberal President Macapagal announced he would run for re-election. So Liberal senator Marcos, impatient to hold the presidency, declared himself a Nacionalista, won that party's nomination—and then the office.

Party disloyalty is encouraged by the constitution. Presidential and vice-presidential candidates are elected on separate ballots. The winners are often in different parties. The vice-president, who assumes the top office if the president is deposed for any reason, has no partisan or policy motive for loyalty to the chief. These two highest officials have more incentives for rivalry than cooperation. The method of electing senators also weakens parties, since the senatorial candidates run against each other in the same national constituency. The constitution gives them personal reasons to distrust each other, regardless of any potential agreements on policy.

"Crossing the floor" in the House of Representatives is particularly common, because legislators tend to move into a newly elected president's party for purely financial reasons. The chief executive controls the release of state money. He/she proposes a budget to Congress, which may change it only in ways that reduce rather than increase total spending. The president also has a line-item veto. Even if this power is not used at the budget authorization stage, a presidential audit board must certify that money is available, before it can be appropriated and spent. So the president's party is functionally different from any other because of presidential influence on pork. But this distinction is irrespective of specific policies.

Parties pretend to coalesce, especially in the House, while their members' actual loyalties remain uncertain and flighty. The *Kampi*-Liberal party in 2004 claimed 116 representatives, but their rivals said they had only 79.[39] Perhaps the legislators had no solid net reasons to be clear where they stood in partisan terms, when (as at that time) the president was unpopular. Except among some party-list representatives, legislators seldom form parties for policy reasons. This low aggregation of parties is sometimes explained in terms of the post-Marcos constitutional rule that each president may be elected just once. Without discussing the fiscal attraction to Congress members of presidential favor, Hicken points out that early prediction of winners became more difficult after presidential incumbents could not run.[40]

Just as blocs of representatives reshuffle themselves after each major election, these groupings are also internally diverse. The 2010 ruling majority in the House, all supposedly in President Benigno Aquino's coalition, included figures as different as Walden Bello (a former communist and proudly socialist *Akbayan* party-list representative), Imelda Marcos (former first lady and wife of a dictator whom Bello had opposed and who some observers implicate in the murder of PNoy's father), Manny Pacquiao (boxing champion from Mindanao, populist but not nearly so left as Bello or yet so elite as Marcos—but a possible future president), along with assorted actresses, *trapos*, TV anchors, and others.[41]

The Philippine Senate presents a different picture, because it is much smaller and its members are all elected nationally. From 1945 to 1971, no party except the two main ones held more than two senatorial seats; so practically all senators claimed to be either Liberals or Nacionalistas. But from 1986 to 2012, after Marcos, in only a couple of years has any party claimed more than nine of the 24 seats.

A "block voting" method is used to elect the Philippine Senate: each voter nationwide may cast as many ballots as there are vacancies (12 in any election). Most students of voting would predict that, under this system, one well-organized party that could induce each of its supporters use all 12 votes for the candidates of that party should be able to win a landslide of seats. Yet the Philippine parties are unwilling or uninterested in persuading their voters to cast all the available ballots for a single slate of senatorial nominees. Filipinos voted for an average of just seven senators in the 2013 election, although they were entitled to vote for 12. Those in Metro Manila voted for about ten; electors in poor or Muslim regions voted for about five.[42] The Philippine senatorial ballot is a long one, and party-slate voting has been unusual.

The party affiliations of senators are therefore quixotic; many of those legislators are in practice independents, even if they have party labels. As many as six competing parties, identified with relatively small groups of senators, have recently been represented. Pluralities sufficient for election to the Senate have been won by a great variety of famous Filipinos: traditional politician Juan Ponce Enrile, reformist Miriam Santiago, self-made businessman Manny Villar, basketball star Robert Jaworski, news anchors Loren Legarda and Noli de Castro, presidential sons Jinggoy Estrada and "Bongbong" Marcos, sibling senators named Cayetano (whose father was also a senator), even leaders of failed coups Gregorio Honasan and Antonio Trillanes IV (elected while still in jail). Such people can attract voters nationally. House seats, by contrast, very often go to the scions—either sons or daughters—of families that have previously also bred office holders in the same regional constituency.

The small size of the Senate gives each senator considerable clout when the chamber is almost evenly divided. Temporary personal relations between senators can determine political outcomes. This occurred in 2010, for example, when Senate President Juan Ponce Enrile was canvassing to assure his coalition would have a majority. Reformist Senator Miriam Defensor Santiago finally, in that year, received a committee chairmanship in the potentially important panel on Constitutional Amendments, Revision, Codes, and Laws. But a sharply diverse set of rival senators had to coalesce, at least temporarily, to approve her as head of the committee. They included Manuel Villar (recently defeated for the national presidency), Vicente Sotto III (majority leader in the Senate), and Gregorio Honasan (recidivist *kudeta* leader). These solons together arranged a meeting of Santiago with Enrile. Because of severe spats in the past between the outspoken Santiago and the modernized *trapo* Enrile, the latter ruminated, within hearing of a reporter, "What was her reason for having a little irritation against me?" But they were vaguely reconciled: "Well, she explained, I never said that, I've never done that. And she understood.... She kissed me on the cheeks." With that, Enrile declared Santiago his goddaughter, "And I am the *ninong* (godfather)."

It was hoped that Santiago would join the Nacionalista majority that had elected Enrile as head of the Senate. But the content of any constitutional reforms would continue to be influenced by compromises of the kind that had been required for Santiago's appointment. Enrile said he would be "very cooperative" with the Aquino administration, but he and Sotto also planned to head an "independent Senate."[43]

In 2013, the 24 Philippine senators included five women. They did very well in elections, perhaps because only pluralities are needed for a senatorial seat and half the eligible voters are women. They provide a sample. All came from well-known families and often from fame in media. Pia Cayetano had been a TV host; Loren Legarda had likewise been a TV anchor, while Nancy Binay, Cynthia Villar, and Grace Poe all had very famous politicians as a father, adoptive father, or brother.[44] None of these lacked other family members in prominent political posts.

As Salvador Miranda writes,

> Parties play a minor role, if at all any, in the recruitment of candidates, in financing their campaigns, and in shaping the political careers of their members. In general, the reverse is usually the case: the party's fate rests in the hands of the candidate.[45]

Most Philippine parties do not hold primary elections. So there is no sure need to compile formal lists of party members. Candidates and office-holders declare or change their party affiliations blithely, and "independent" legislators are many. Party labels cannot be used reliably to predict voting patterns in Congress, especially among senators. Crucial ballots on personnel, such as the election of the Senate president, show that senators from the same party often vote for different candidates. Philippine politicians have been, from a spatial analysis of politics standpoint, like suspended particles in random Brownian motion.

The personal style of any candidate for election nonetheless affects votes. If a nominee is seen as a policy wonk, perhaps bright but diffident, his/her chance of winning a geographical seat in Congress is slim. Extroverts do well in campaigns, as do candidates with recognizable names. Most Filipinos tend to vote for candidates of families—not of ethnicities, religions, ideologies, or classes. When the party leader falls or dies, the party ceases to exist unless there is a clear successor. For example, Marcos's Party the Kilusang Bagong Lipunan (KBL) was patronist rather than Leninist. So it was typical of Philippine political parties, despite its atypical temporary strength. In 1986, when Marcos fell, the KBL practically ceased to exist.[46] The Philippine elite has a tradition of "party-less clientelism." Thus far, "even the periodic strongman is unable to sustain his dominance."[47] As Hicken says,[48]

> Few if any post-Marcos parties could be described as national parties. Parties have been unable to cultivate lasting nationwide support (witness the high level of electoral volatility) and most lack a national policy focus.

Even during the pre-1972 two-parties system, the Nacionalista and Liberal parties are best seen as shallow alliances of locally based and locally focussed politicians ... candidates, and their respective parties, have a focus that is more local than national.

Persons *are* the "institutions" of Philippine politics. When it became clear to leaders in the Liberal Party that Noynoy Aquino was the strongest presidential candidate, he in effect displaced the party. The parties are loose coalitions, but Philippine democracy arguably does not just need "stronger" parties. It needs a more modern kind. This different sort, with serious policy platforms, would give voters clearer choices on what they want their government to do. Such parties would require social bases and more industries. The main factor that prevents the Philippines from having a modern polity is the lack of a modern economy.

Most Nacionalistas elected to the House in 2013 joined PNoy's Liberal Party majority. Presidential strength in the 2013 House was evident when 244 members voted for Speaker Belmonte, out of 267 then present. So just 35 other members, who were split between leftists and rightists, had under House rules to choose a Minority Leader. Various "Makabayan" leftists turned out to be the swing votes in the opposition, and they made sure that Ilocos Norte Representative Imelda Romualdez Marcos did not get the title of Minority Leader. This remaining minority-of-the-minority, including her and former President (now Pampanga Representative) Gloria Arroyo, was anathema to the leftists. "We cannot work with them; we cannot be in the same group."[49] PNoy's government had very diverse supporters, and also very diverse opponents.

Senator Ferdinand Marcos, Jr., declared that his Nacionalista Party demanded to "ensure that local officials, including Congress representatives, would not be left out of the release of their pork barrel."[50] In theory, PNoy could use a line-item veto on those funds. But doing so would have wrought a quasi-constitutional change in the Philippines.

The Philippines does not lack general social legislation. During Ramos's presidency especially, from 1992 to 1998, 85 "social reform laws" were passed, including the Poverty Alleviation Law, the Indigenous People's Rights Act, the Anti-Rape Law, the Family and Child Courts Law, and repeal of the Anti-Squatting Act.[51] Other periods have seen considerable legislative reformism too. The problems are funding for national programs—and enforcement, whenever such laws contravene the interests of local power holders. Party policy is still primarily pork.[52]

Do parties aid democratization? Many in the West might imagine this question answers itself positively. All rich liberal states have parties. But as Philippine politics demonstrates in spades, "parties" come in wildly various kinds. Also, democratization is a process; its start is not its continuation. Some de facto one-"party" polities, such as Singapore or Botswana (or Japan for many decades), have had mostly technocratic and professionalized leaderships. In many democracies, as Vicky Randall writes,

> When it comes to assessing parties' contribution to democratic consolidation ... there is generally a sense of disappointment ... they are upbraided for failing to provide the electorate with meaningful choice, for failing to instill democratic values—for instance, through internal party procedures—and for offering either ineffectual, or alternatively irresponsible, opposition.[53]

Parties' contribution to development can be slim when multiple parties shift kaleidoscopically and tend to be centered on individual politicians, as in the Philippines. Policy parties of left or right (and ethnic parties in very few modern countries) are not the same as personality parties.

Term limits, "breakers," and proposals against personalism

Especially after Marcos, reformers floated various suggestions to reduce patronist and personalist politics. Term limits have been passed for the presidency and other posts—but Philippine familism undermined such measures in local elections. Mayors, when term limits forced them out of office, have run their spouses or children to succeed them as "breakers" (until they regained eligibility for the following election). Mayor Jose Ginez endorsed his wife "Pinky" for the mayoralty of Santa Maria, Bulacan. The same phenomenon appeared in the same year for mayoralties of four other cities nearby. Two of Pinky's rivals for the post also had the surname Ginez.[54] Philippine voters are sometimes thought to cast ballots for candidates with their own surnames. As a rural elector explained, "It's better to elect a relative or a person with a last name the same as yours. They might be long-lost relatives, after all."[55]

Family names have electoral value in other democracies too. Voters may prefer a Kennedy, Gandhi, Kirchner, Roosevelt, Taft, Bush, or Clinton to a less familiar name. In many Philippine places, candidates with such names run against each other, and the results are accordingly hard to predict. When a long-serving mayor of a Visayan town died, his clan ran a nephew in elections—but,[56]

> without the personal stature of his late uncle, his candidacy was effectively challenged by the family's traditional rivals. The uncertainty of the outcome of the election reportedly led both sides to hire expensive well-armed urban thugs, or "goons," to help "protect" their candidates and persuade the voters whom to elect. The pre-election period was extremely tense, shots were fired on a number of occasions, and at least one person was killed.... In effect, the semblance of moral order that had previously characterized the politics of the town was now in ruins.

Having a parliamentary system could strengthen policy-based parties. These might develop more coherent platforms and might nominate more candidates from outside the lineages that still supply many traditional politicians. So a parliamentary system has occasionally been mooted in the Philippines. But the

Spanish legacy of indirect government and the American legacy of having separate executive and legislative branches have combined with fears of any constitutional amendment (that might allow a president to prolong his or her power), preventing a move toward parliamentary government.

The most important law to encourage policy coalitions has been the provision for party-list parties, discussed above. Yet this allows for just a small minority of House members, whose power comes more from their voices than from their votes. A 2010 political party reform bill would have included public subsidies for policy-based parties. It would have allowed the state to audit the accounts of campaigns that accept public money. Contributions would have had to go through regular banks.[57] Congress at the time did not pass this law.

Proportional representation could also give parties incentives to have more distinct policies. It might concentrate Filipino voters' minds on plans rather than personalities, but PR would be difficult to pass in a constitutional convention comprised of current politicians. A popular president, shortly after election, could conceivably have some success in making such reform—if he or she had the will to push for it. PNoy did not. His spokesman Ricky Carandang said that "President Aquino has many other things to resolve than giving priority to amending the 1987 Constitution."[58] He chose to be more careful than daring.

The ostensibly patriotic ban against political candidacies by Philippine citizens who are dual nationals disqualifies from government many talented professionals. It is difficult for Overseas Filipino Workers who are solely citizens of the Philippines to cast ballots. Application of the "Overseas Absentee Voting Act" has usually meant that OFWs who want to vote must travel personally to a Philippine consulate. If they have permanent residence in the country of their jobs, they must sign affidavits that they will return to the Philippines within three years. Few bothered. Some NGOs have suggested that easing these restrictions might have good effects on the nation's political system. Such changes would almost surely help reformers in party-list elections. They would make the vote-controlling tasks of local canvassers more difficult. Most voters would still be as they presently are, but the potential number of OFW voters is considerable.

There is a more important possibility: that candidates for office might be OFW returnees. Currently, dual-citizen Filipinos who have acted to acquire foreign nationality may run for office in the Philippines only after taking an oath of supreme allegiance to the Philippines, renouncing the other citizenship. Patriots think this rule is natural and right. But it impedes talented professional Filipinos from participating in elections that they would sometimes win (as dual-citizens have done in other countries). They might well improve the quality of Philippine democracy as most people perceive it. It is unclear that patriotic intentions always lead to patriotic results.

A nominee of a party-list group called the Overseas Filipino Workers Family Club, representing voters outside the country, actually won a seat in the House. But a petition to disqualify him was immediately filed, because he had not given up his American passport.[59] Some democracies (the U.S., U.K., Armenia, and many others) allow dual-citizens to compete for public office, and occasionally these candidates are elected or appointed to important posts without any evident harm to the nations they are trying to help govern. The Philippines forswears this possibility.[60]

Pork as policy

The main policy of Philippine politicians in the past has been to deliver money to their clients. Members of Congress and members of local councils all receive "community development funds" (CDFs). The word "development" can be interpreted in localist and short-term ways. In Quezon City, for example, Mayor Herbert Bautista urged his council members to use their CDFs "for worthy programs that provide direct services to their constituents, instead of earmarking them for projects like waiting sheds [at bus stops], road humps, and markers."[61] The councilmen tended to line up with their mayor politically, but they were not required to follow his advice concerning these funds, which are always called "pork."

Most citizens still expect politicians to attach their names even to small public works projects such as bus-stop shelters, footbridges, barangay halls, or basketball courts. An electoral candidate's CDF or campaign budget could include money for immediate goods that constituents might need, such as a medicine with the candidate's name written prominently on the bottle.[62] Some Congress members issued "political ID" cards or personally signed letters of recommendation, on the basis of which state hospitals could use pork money to pay the medical expenses for approved constituents.[63] This was socialized medicine of a cozy personal sort, not available to all citizens.

Tillers or recently urbanized peasants tend to judge election candidates according to concrete benefits that officials deliver in short time periods. A bus stand, an expression of condolence, a handout of money, a village visit (perhaps in the company of a beauty queen or other celebrity)—such benefits are more important to most voters than reformist or conservative policies, parties, governance, or dubious promises about long-term prosperity. Peasants may not mind vote-buying when they are the sellers. They may not be disgusted by corruption money, so long as some of it trickles down to themselves. They may not resent being clients, if the patrons give them fatherly respect, protection, and provision.[64]

Many of these patrons are urban and educated, gaining power from having clients. Because some of them have been socialized in liberal notions, they also have periodic impulses to change structures away from "feudal" forms. They are of two minds. Many think that patronism weakens their country in comparison with higher-income nations. They are divided, however, on what to do about this problem. So long as local leaders deliver goods, other activities are deemed by many voters to be irrelevant. This causes "the electorate in many places repeatedly to elect convicted criminals, underworld characters, and known grafters."[65]

On an immediate basis, patronism gives clients access to some resources. Comparative political scientists have documented clients' liking for patronism.

It is a diferent fact that strong patron–client networks also encourage rent-seeking and corruption (as detailed in the next chapter), slowing the empowerment of poor people who receive these immediate benefits. As Fox shows, Mexico had *caciques* like those in the Philippines; patrons there were for many years mostly organized in the Institutional Revolutionary Party, and they followed Roman emperors in offering bread and circuses to subalterns.[66] In Senegal, *marabout* patrons performed somewhat similar functions, as did *mafia* dons in Sicily.[67] Many impoverished people support such organizations because of the short-term benefits.

As a member of the Philippine House said, "Congress is largely a private-based sphere, where you outsmart the system of laws. Gift giving validates the fact that *nakisama ka* [you tried to be with the group]." A legislative staffer said constituents "look at congressmen as if they were banks on wheels, ATM machines." Local fiestas, e.g., on saints' days, are times for canvassing and generosity. "If you have 300 barangays, you give 5000 pesos per fiesta. That's 1.5 million pesos a year. And even then, they curse you and call you a skinflint."[68]

Carlos P. Romulo wrote that:

> The length of a politician's life is measured in terms of the favors, such as jobs or loans of money, he is able to give his supporters. In turn, the latter are obligated according to the code of *utang na loób* to keep the politician in office.... The landlord who has once saved the child of a tenant from illness feels free to exploit the services of the tenant with perfect impunity, since he is protected by a code freely accepted by all within his society. Indeed, he would not even realize that he is exploitative.[69]

In legal terms, the use of funds by electoral candidates has often been criminal. "They don't just buy votes. They pay the antis so they will not vote." But the law has differed from many practices.

The most effective money is given at the last minute, not for long-term development.

> You know, it's useless to have projects. Let's just save the money and then use it at the eleventh hour.... Don't count on *utang na loób* [debts of gratitude] from those you've helped. They'll sell you out, because it's the present that's important.... During the final hour, the one who is going to give them fifty pesos, which they can use for their needs, is the one they're going to vote for.[70]

At least ten million pesos were necessary by the mid-1990s for "mounting a credible campaign for a senatorial candidate." For House posts, between three and 12 million were budgeted and spent. Some of the money was paid for "Operation Bawas-Dagdag," to bribe Comelec canvassers for vote fraud.[71] The precinct count optical scanners have lessened the opportunities for such fraud; so money goes into other aspects of electoral campaigns.

Action possibilities for more democratic representation

In most large electoral democracies where parties offer voters policy choices, there are extensive industries. The main political cleavage in these polities is between "left" and "right" (Labour or Conservative in Britain, Democratic vs. Republican in the U.S., relatively socialist vs. relatively capitalist in European countries or Japan). International comparisons suggest that the lack of a pro-poor vs. pro-capital cleavage, in a few democracies that have major ethnic divisions, can create a functionally equivalent situation in which rival parties appeal to voters. Just to the Philippines' north, Taiwan has developed a vibrant democracy that for some years has been based on quasi-ethnic divisions between Chinese mainlanders (who once ran an authoritarian government there) and self-identifying Taiwanese. Just a few other democracies have also maintained democratic systems that are not mainly based on the left–right, labor–capital division. But, in the Philippines, linguistic cleavages are not deep and do sustain coherent national parties. Economic inequalities certainly exist in the Philippines, but for better or for worse they do not create the usual split between labor- and capital-based parties.

Democratic choice for citizens might be enhanced by elite compacts that were nationally comprehensive. Experiences of some smaller Iberian-influenced nations show this possibility. One analyst suggests a possible alternative to the worker–owner cleavage in the political history of Costa Rica, where at least "a class compromise was established between the rising middle class and the divided oligarchy."[72] Bourgeois professionals can coalesce with at least some landowning oligarchs, and the result lets the electorate choose governors when such a coalition can dominate the polity.

If liberal urbanites and elite landowners were to join together in the future of Philippine national politics, the central government structure in Manila would, until it is strengthened, still be a less important site for such cooperation than local polities. Constitutional changes to link the president with the potential successor vice-president more closely, and to give senators more incentives to cooperate with the president, might help such a project because they would make the Philippine government more coherent.

The "standard method of assisting third-world countries to develop more effective political parties for substantive democracy," according to Thomas Carothers is "typified by the two- or three-day workshop, seminar, or conference led by a few experts flown in from the sponsoring country." This method is fundable—and ineffective.[73] Strengthening parties is standard (and generally good) advice for democratizers. But few Filipinos yet want to commit themselves to parties; their jobs and contexts give them scant incentive to do this. Surveyors have asked them, "With what political party do you identify?" Between 80 and 90 percent responded: "None." They did so in each major part of the country and in each major income group. Just once, among 14 separate surveys, could any party claim the loyalty of more than 10 percent of Philippine household heads.[74]

172 *Voting, pork, policy, and media*

Building effective political institutions takes time. Even more, this process takes economic evolution. "Political party development is related to, and is probably conditioned by, broader and deeper societal change that usually takes place over one, two, or three decades if not more," as Erdmann writes.[75] Intellectuals want to understand things at the speed of light, but societies and economies take longer. Quick fixes for Philippine sociopolitical problems may be inadequate. Analysts can look for intermediate democratic improvements, while retaining confidence that further socioeconomic change will continue to favor more fairness and opportunities for citizens.

Notes

1 Steven Rood, "Elections as Complicated and Important Events in the Philippines," in *How Asia Votes*, John Fu-sheng Hsieh and David Newman, eds. (New York: Chatham House, 2002), 148–50.
2 Internet sources differed slightly but are easy to find.
3 David Wurfel, *Filipino Politics: Development and Decay* (Ithaca, NY: Cornell University Press, 1988), 40.
4 Frederic Charles Schaffer, "Disciplinary Reactions: Alienation and the Reform of Vote Buying in the Philippines," paper for the American Political Science Association Annual Meeting, 2002, and interviews by this author.
5 A language "diversity index" is high for the Philippines, at 0.85. All major Philippine tongues are "Malayo-Polynesian." For the three-fourths of Filipinos who do not normally speak Tagalog in their households, this makes study of Tagalog easier than study of non-Malay tongues such as English. See www.ethnologue.com/show_map. asp?name=Philippines.
6 Now Tagalog has spread widely because of schools. But see Benedict Anderson, "Elections and Participation," in *The Politics of Elections in Southeast Asia*, R.H. Taylor, ed. (Washington, DC: Woodrow Wilson Center, 1996), 21–2.
7 Similar situations affect other countries too, notably in Southeast Asia. In Thailand, the most-spoken tongue is not Bangkok Thai, but instead is the related language Lao (which has many more speakers in populous Isan, northeast Thailand, than in Laos—with considerable effects on Thai politics). In Indonesia, the official language, Malay, has been dubbed "bahasa Indonesia." This is taught in schools but is native mainly to the small Riau islands not far from Singapore. Far more populous groups of Javanese, Sundanese, Balinese, and others on Sumatra, Kalimantan, Sulawesi, etc., speak other Malayo-Polynesian languages. These are, like Malay, also related to the indigenous Philippine languages—although they are not mutually comprehensible with them or with each other.
8 Maps and details are at http://en.wikipedia/wiki/list_of_philippine_presidential_ election_results.
9 Julio C. Teehankee, "Image, Issues, and Machinery: Presidential Campaigns in post-1986 Philippines," in *The Politics of Change in the Philippines*, Yuko Kasuya and Nathan Gilbert Quimpo, eds. (Pasig City: Anvil, 2010), 118–19.
10 David G. Timberman, *The 1992 Philippine Elections* (New York: Asia Society, 1992), 10.
11 These organizations started as youth arms of Marcos's party and were headed from 1975 to 1984 by his daughter Imee.
12 Anon., "Democracy as Showbiz," *The Economist*, July 1, 2004, www.economist.com/ research/backgrounders/displaystory.cfm?story_ID=2876966.
13 David G. Timberman, *The 1992 Philippine Elections*, 13.

14 William Case, "Manipulative Skills: How Do Rulers Control the Electoral Arena," in *Electoral Authoritarianism: The Dynamics of Unfree Competition*, Andreas Schedler, ed. (Boulder, CO: Rienner, 2006), 104–5.
15 Michael Cullinane, "Patron as Client: Warlord Politics and the Duranos of Danao," in *An Anarchy of Families: State and Family in the Philippines*, Alfred W. McCoy, ed. (Madison, WI: University of Wisconsin Center for Southeast Asian Studies, 1993), 187.
16 Cleo Calimbahin, "Capacity and Compromise: COMELEC, NAMFREL, and Election Fraud," in *The Politics of Change in the Philippines*, Yuko Kasuya and Nathan Gilbert Quimpo, eds. (Pasig City: Anvil, 2010), 182–5.
17 Frederic Charles Schaffer, "Disciplinary Reactions," 42.
18 Interview with an NGO head.
19 Interview with well-informed political analyst in Manila who requested anonymity, August 2010.
20 Sheila Crisostomo, "Manual Audit Shows May Poll 99.97% Accurate: Comelec," *Philippine Star*, June 29, 2013, www.philstar.com/headlines/2013/06/29/959549.
21 Social Weather Stations, *Silver! 25 Years of Statistics for Advocacy* (Quezon City: SWS, 2010), 11.
22 "Brillantes: Give Me a Chance," www.abs-cbnnews.com/nation/01/17/11/.
23 Sheila Crisostomo, "Guidelines in Court Compliance on Poll Protests Set," *Philippine Star*, July 4, 2013, www.philstar.com/headlines/2013/07/04/961431.
24 Joseph J. Capuno, "Local Governance and Development," in *Dynamics of Regional Development, the Philippines in East Asia*, Arsenio Balisacan and Hal Hill, eds. (Cheltenham: Elgar, 2007).
25 Chay Florintino-Hofileña, *News for Sale: The Corruption of the Philippine Media* (Quezon City: Philippine Center for Investigative Journalism and Center for Media Freedom and Responsibility, 1998), 97–8.
26 Ibid., 27.
27 Ibid., 5, also 41.
28 An angry book, concerning the United States, is Gregory Shafer, *Reassessing Democracy: A Rebel's Guide* (Boca Raton, FL: BrownWalker, 2004).
29 Chay Florintino-Hofileña, *News for Sale*, 30.
30 Ibid., 51.
31 Julio C. Teehankee, "Image, Issues, and Machinery: Presidential Campaigns in Post-1986 Philippines," in *The Politics of Change in the Philippines*, Yuko Kasuya and Nathan Gilbert Quimpo, eds. (Pasig City: Anvil, 2010), 121.
32 E.E. Schattschneider, *Party Government* (New York: Farrar & Rinehart, 1942), quoted in Allen Hicken, *Building Party Systems in Developing Democracies* (New York: Cambridge University Press, 2009), 1.
33 Carl H. Landé, "Party Politics in the Philippines," in *Six Perspectives on the Philippines*, George M. Guthrie, ed. (Manila: Bookmark, 1968), 102.
34 Joel Rocamora, "Introduction," in *[De]scribing Elections: A Study of Elections in the Lifeworld of San Isidro*, Myrna J. Alejo, Maria Elena Rivera, and Noel Inocencio Valencia, eds. (Quezon City: Institute for Popular Democracy, 1996), xxvii.
35 Gero Erdmann, "Lessons to be Learned: Political Party Research and Political Party Assistance," www.scribd.com/doc/42881636, 10/10/2010.
36 Anna Marie A. Karaos, "The Current Political Spectrum," in *The Aquino Government and the Question of Ideology*, Raul J. Bonoan, Agnes Colette Condon, and Soledad S. Reyes, eds. (Quezon City: Phoenix Publishing House, 1987), 51.
37 Quoted in Nathan Gilbert Quimpo and Yuko Kasuya, "The Politics of Change in a Changeless Land," in *The Politics of Change in the Philippines*, Yuko Kasuya and Nathan Gilbert Quimpo, eds. (Pasig City: Anvil, 2010), 6.
38 The best treatment is Julio C. Teehankee, "Electoral Politics in the Philippines," in *Electoral Politics in Southeast and East Asia*, Aurel Crossant and Marei John, eds. (Bonn: Friedrich-Ebert-Stiftung, 2002), 149–202.

39 Philippine Center for Investigative Journalism, "De Venecia's Reign is Challenged," July 26–27, 2004, www.pcij.org/stories/2004/house.html.
40 Allen Hicken, *Building Party Systems in Developing Democracies* (New York: Cambridge University Press, 2009), 149–79.
41 Robin Broad and John Cavanagh, "Protest to Power in the Philippines," *The Nation* (December 6, 2010), 24.
42 Sheila Crisostomo, "Majority of Pinoy's did not Vote for 12 Senators: Audit," *Philippine Star*, June 20, 2013, www.philstar.com/headlines/2013/06/30/959839.
43 "Miriam Gets Senate Committee, Extends Leave," *Philippine Star*, August 6, 2010, 10.
44 See www.senate.gov.ph/photo_release/2013/0722_03.asp.
45 Salvador Miranda, "The Politics of Pork, or Why the CDF, the CIA, and PWA are Here to Stay," *Politik* 3:2 (November 1996), 37, quoted in Kent Eaton, *Politicians the Economic Reform in New Democracies: Argentina and the Philippines in the 1990s* (University Park, PA: Pennsylvania State University Press, 2002), 97.
46 See Mark R. Thompson and Philipp Kuntz, "After Defeat: When do Rulers Steal Elections," in *Electoral Authoritarianism: The Dynamics of Unfree Competition*, Andreas Schedler, ed. (Boulder, CO: Rienner, 2006), 122.
47 Jason Brownlee, *Authoritarianism in an Age of Democratization* (New York: Cambridge University Press, 2007), 198.
48 Allen Hicken, *Building Party Systems in Developing Democracies* (New York: Cambridge University Press, 2009), 155.
49 Anon., "House Minority Group Headed for a Split," *Philippine Star*, July 25, 2013, www.philstar.com/headlines/2013/07/25/1009781.
50 Christina Mendez, "Nacionalista Party Members Join House Majority: Villar," *Philippine Star*, June 27, 2013, www.philstar.com/headlines/2013/06/27/958863.
51 Gabriella R. Montinola, "Parties and Accountability in the Philippines," *Journal of Democracy* 10:1 (1999), 132.
52 Kawanaka Takeshi, *Power in a Philippine City* (Chiba: Institute of Developing Economies, 2002), 17.
53 Vicky Randall, "Political Parties and Democratic Developmental States," *Development Policy Review* 25:5 (2007), 638.
54 *South China Morning Post*, May 8, 1998, 19.
55 This San Isidro woman voted for a senatorial candidate solely because his surname was the same as her mother's. Myrna J. Alejo, Maria Elena Rivera, and Noel Inocencio Valencia, *[De]scribing Elections*, 42.
56 David L. Szanton, *Estancia in Transition: Economic Growth in a Rural Philippine Community* (Quezon City: Ateneo de Manila University, 1971), 124.
57 Interview with Ramon Casiple, head of the Philippine Institute for Political and Electoral Reform, August, 2010.
58 See www.mb.com.ph, of August 17, 2010.
59 Sheila Crisostomo, "Disqualification of Party-List Group's 2nd Nominee Sought," *Philippine Star*, July 16, 2013, www.philstar.com/headlines/2013/07/16/975441.
60 The author has had several Filipino students at Princeton. Some, including Imee Marcos who is Governor of Ilocos Norte where her last name surely helps her, have been elected to major offices. Trina Firmalo, Chief of Staff for her father Governor Eduardo C. Firmalo of Romblon, certainly could win future elections too. Others, such as Carlos Lazatín (who has a well-known Pampanga name and might have done likewise) instead began a very professional career outside the Philippines—and once a young person starts in such a direction, the apparently patriotic law against any candidate's dual nationality guarantees that the country will waste such talents.
61 *Manila Bulletin*, August 9, 2010, 2.
62 Steven Rood, "Decentralization, Democracy, and Development," 114 and passim.
63 Yvonne Chua and Booma B. Cruz, "Pork is a Political, not a Developmental, Tool," September 6–7, 2004, www.pcij.org/stories/2004/pork.html.

64 Anek Laothamatas, "A Tale of Two Democracies: Conflicting Perceptions of Elections and Democracy in Thailand," in *The Politics of Elections in Southeast Asia*, R.H. Taylor, ed. (Washington, DC: Woodrow Wilson Center, 1996), 201–23.
65 Paul D. Hutchcroft and Joel Rocamora, "Strong Demands and Weak Institutions: Addressing the Democratic Deficit in the Philippines" (essay provided by courtesy of Dr. Rocamora), 3, also relying on work by Emmanuel deDios and Hutchcroft. Politicians convicted of corruption have been re-elected to high offices in other democracies too, e.g., Louisiana's.
66 Jonathan Fox, "The Difficult Transition from Clientelism to Citizenship," *World Politics* 46 (January 1994), 151–84.
67 Derick W. Brinkerhoff and Arthur A. Goldsmith, *Clientelism, Patrimonialism, and Democratic Governance: An Overview and Framework for Assessment and Programming* (Bethesda, MD: Abt Associates for AID, 2002), 3.
68 Yvonne Chua, "Fat Salaries, Big Allowances," March 22–24, 2004, http://pcij.org/stories/print/congress3.html. The tendency of U.S. congressmen to equate democracy with elections, overlooking egregiously undemocratic aspects of electoral systems, is compounded because they face somewhat similar challenges.
69 In Romulo's introduction to Beth Day, *The Philippines: Shattered Showcase of Democracy in Asia* (New York: M. Evans, 1974), 9.
70 Yvonne Chua and Booma B. Cruz, "Pork is a Political, not a Developmental, Tool," September 6–7, 2004, www.pcij.org/stories/2004/pork.html.
71 Renato S. Velasco, "Does the Philippine Congress Promote Democracy?" in *Democratization: Philippine Perspectives*, Felipe B. Miranda, ed. (Quezon City: University of the Philippines Press, 1995), 287.
72 Deborah J. Yashar, *Demanding Democracy: Reform and Reaction in Costa Rica and Guatemala, 1870s-1950s* (Stanford, CA: Stanford University Press, 1997), 90.
73 Thomas Carothers, "International Assistance for Political Party Development," Anti-Corruption Resource Centre, Michelson Institute, Bergen, www.cmi.no/publications/file/3015.
74 This exception was in the December 1995 survey, when the ruling Lakas/Christian Democratic coalition garnered a still-unimpressive 12 percent, and the loyalty to "none" option plummeted to a still-overwhelming 77 percent. Fully 79 percent of Manila residents at this time said they were loyal to no party—as did 79 percent of both the best-off and worst-off social classes as coded by interviewers on the basis of their types of dwelling (because reported income would be a less reliable index). This was the only poll in which a single party broke the single-digit barrier. This information, or any data with so much careful detail about Philippine elections in the 1990s, comes from the Social Weather Stations, Inc.
75 Gero Erdmann, "Lessons to be Learned: Political Party Research and Political Party Assistance," www.scribd.com/doc/42881636, 22.

9   Corruption

If the title of this chapter were "Glorious Corruption," many Filipinos would immediately recognize it as a reference to President Gloria Macapagal Arroyo. Yet corruption is not glorious, and she has certainly not been the only central or local Philippine politician widely perceived to be corrupt. Court cases against her, as against others in and out of government, grind their ways slowly through the judiciary. Laws are usually thought most effective when they sanction behavior, not mere perceptions, and behavioral evidence of Arroyo's corruptions is extensive but not more so than that of other politicians (including her fellow former presidents Marcos and Estrada). Another part of the problem is that endemic corruption emerges from modal structures of business and government, including structures of existential norms in them; it involves individuals but always has collective aspects. It is less unpopular than most intellectuals think; corrupt actors are sometimes admired as strong.

Corruption as perceived, and as requiring two groups

Corrupt acts are often hidden. The main method for attempting to measure corruption is not behavioral but is perceptual. It is possible to survey people about their sense of the extent of corruption. The *Philippine Democratic Assessment* of 2010 reported that, "Arroyo continuously rates, in many surveys and public opinion polls, as the most unpopular president the Philippines has ever had."[1] This was certainly true when the survey was taken; but Arroyo was not the Philippines' most corrupt president in terms of the amount of missing money. Marcos or Estrada almost surely exceeded her on that measure. In any case, corruption is perceptual, communal, and structural, not just personal.

The standard (and inadequate) definition of corruption would require evidence of misuse of a government office for the benefit of an individual or a few, when the office was instead supposed to serve many. This definition does not stress that such evidence must be based on the viewpoint of a group, that different people often perceive information differently, and that private corruptions usually coexist with public ones. Corruption is hard to measure behaviorally for other reasons too:

- Corruption is an idea that changes over long periods of historical time. But it *always implies two identifiable groups*: one larger, one smaller. It is evidenced by benefit to the smaller group that "should" instead have benefitted the larger—according to whoever makes the accusation of corruption.[2] Sometimes the smaller of the two groups is an individual, although this is relatively rare. From the viewpoint of norms in the benefitted group (generally the smaller one), the act is not obviously corrupt.[3]
- Corruption may be deemed minor, a mere gaffe; or instead, it may involve major resources and be seen as predatory. Its extent is in principle measurable, but in practice its extent is always charted as a perceived variable. Its varying amounts can be used to classify regime types along a new dimension.[4]
- Corruption is socially and politically anathema, perhaps in some cases causing the downfall of a person who is found to be corrupt. But alternatively, at least some degree of corruption may be taken as acceptable, understandable, familial, or natural. Examples of the latter include governmental "pork" that is legally guaranteed—and many nations including democracies such as the Philippines or the U.S. have seen this phenomenon. Officials who have been convicted of corruption can win populist re-elections. Some studies of corruption (mostly by Americanists, who would learn more about democracy if they were comparativists) limit themselves to thefts by appointed officials, as if elected politicians have so much legitimacy that the term corrupt cannot properly be applied to them.[5] This limit on the definition is arbitrary; elected officials can certainly be corrupt.
- Corruption is often seen as necessarily involving the participation of a government official. But if it is conceived more broadly, in terms of two groups, it may also include private thefts in which no representative of the state is involved. Political power networks are not all public. Private and public corruptions almost always emerge in a polity together. They grow in bunches, like asparagus.
- Corruption is usually a long-term trait sustained by the structure of a polity. Occasionally it may result from shorter-term phenomena (e.g., windfalls that Chinese or ex-Soviet cadres enjoyed when they privatized to themselves assets that formerly had been public property). Extensive corruptions that cannot increase indefinitely, because public assets available to be stolen are not infinite, may differ slightly from other structural corruptions. But various kinds of corruption tend to legitimate each other; they all increase the indifference of actors to political uncleanliness.
- Corruption is usually kept secret, for legal reasons. So despite its political importance, the main epistemological bias of social science (the notion that quantitative measurement of revealed *behavior* is the proper test of any phenomenon) is difficult to satisfy when seeking evidence of it. So the most common measure is of *perceived* corruption. Some scholars have used the time lag between prosecutions and sentencings of corrupt acts as a proxy for

behavioral corruption.[6] But no fully satisfactory measure has been found. Corrupt actors only occasionally advertise their specific corrupt acts —when they want to be open about their help to clients (which require these acts), showing their faithfulness to their small communities.

Successful politicians in many countries ballyhoo their dedication to home groups. Opportunities for corruption are sometimes presented as understandable or laudable reasons for "public servants" to run in elections. When, in 1950, President Quirino approved an inquest into alleged corruptions by Senate President Jose Avelino, the latter replied:

> Why did you have to order an investigation, honorable Mr. President?... What are we in power for? We are not hypocrites. Why should we pretend to be saints, when in reality we are not? We are not angels. And besides, when we die we all go to hell. Anyway, it is preferable to go to hell where there are no investigations, no Secretary of Justice, no Secretary of Interior to go after us.[7]

Many high leaders in the Philippines have agreed that corruption is pervasive there. Jose De Venecia, former Speaker of the House and the very model of a traditional politician, once admitted that, "Money politics distorts public policies and tilts electoral competition in favor of the 'haves' ... and we are all too familiar with the unholy alliances between high politicians and oligarchic interests to extract economic rent."[8]

Gambling profits and police support of them have been a particular issue for many decades. They were important in colonial times and after the 1935 "Commonwealth" was established under elected President Quezon.[9] *Jueteng* is a gambling game played by millions of poor Filipinos, as well as by rich people.[10] The odds of winning are tiny, but the very uncertain potential payout to the gambler is large—as is the certain long-term profit to the illegal gambling operator. *Jueteng* is addictive and creates social problems. Hope of immense fortune is the lure, even though it is practically never realized. The Catholic Church supports the retention of laws that criminalize it, and most presidents vow to enforce them. Others such as Estrada have been *jueteng* addicts. Some politicians, such as Senator Enrile, say *jueteng* should be legalized because the efforts to suppress it have proven to be ineffective. The relevant politics are often compared to those surrounding alcoholic beverage prohibition in the U.S. from 1920 to 1933. *Jueteng* has proved too profitable to prohibit, and thus difficult to regulate. Like state "pork," it is a nonstate source of financial accumulation that too seldom goes into productive capital.

Development pork

The relationship between corruption and economic growth has long been debated. Countries such as China in recent decades (or arguably America from about 1865 to 1929, or Japan in a similar period) have enjoyed rambunctious growth, lubricated by entrepreneurial risk-taking and corruption. An empirical survey found that investment from other economies internationally, which is often important in such periods, is nonetheless hindered by corruption.[11] Foreign investors do not trust locals—but trust among locals substitutes for market regulations, which are usually not enacted until later.

Low corruption, as perceived, can be linked statistically with capital inflows into many countries. This relationship is robust when controlled for per-capita income, domestic savings rates, and raw materials exports. An empirically based scatter diagram relating capital inflows to perceived corruption in many countries has been published. When perceptions of corruption are graphed against productivity (the ratio of GDP to capital stock), there is even more scatter than in a diagram relating corruption to inflows.[12] Corrupt rake-offs discourage influxes of foreign capital, lowering that factor of growth. Bribes act like a tax on foreign direct investment.

Locals trust each other better than foreigners trust them, however. So corruption may serve to boost "social capital" among domestic entrepreneurs. In the Philippines, there was (at least until the new millennium) rather slow growth and a great deal of perceived corruption.[13] The perceptual part of this is crucial, because no absolute definition of corruption stands the test of time. In Europe during the middle ages, and at present in some Muslim societies, taking interest has been seen as corrupt usury.[14] The interpersonal intimacy of giving can be seen as a social value. Pork and love are both four-letter words.

Edcel Lagman, a congressman from Albay in Bicol (a particularly conservative region) opined in 2013 that,[15]

> Without the PDAF [Priority Development Assistant Funds, "pork"], a footbridge in the hinterlands may never be constructed, a typhoon-damaged school building in an isolated barangay may never be rehabilitated, an indigent patient may die without seeing a doctor, and a talented but financially handicapped student may never get to college or to technical-vocational school.

This localist vision of good "retail" government enables leaders to help citizens directly; it is attractive to many people. "Wholesale" corruption in large "modern" government bureaucracies is more frequently perceived as immoral. But there can be corruption in Edmund Burke's local "little platoons" too.[16]

Barangays receive amounts of government money depending on their populations. Allocations for a single barangay can range above 100 million pesos, and local chiefs as well as council members claim portions of these funds. The extent to which each kind of allocation leads to fair and efficient use of public funds remains an issue of debate in the Philippines.

When Marcos dismissed Congress after declaring martial law, the legislative "pork" that had previously been delivered to representatives' constituents temporarily disappeared. Some congressmen were jailed for misuse of funds.

All the rewards and punishments of the political system were now coming from the top. In effect, Martial Law radically reduced the distribution of power among the middle and lower rungs of the traditional political system, increasing and concentrating it instead at the apex.

Local politicians were supposed to "demobilize", and an anthropologist claims that, "there were no more political advantages to be had by maintaining a large and loyal work force. Indeed, throughout the system, the saliency of patron–client relations ... was at least temporarily reduced."[17] Local military officers took charge. The rate of violent crimes committed by ordinary citizens went down. More cases came to court.[18] But this centralizing reform did not end bribery, and its effects were not structurally permanent. Marcos himself gave handouts of "2000 pesos to nearly every barrio captain in the nation, supposedly for village development but in fact for votes."[19] As a supporter of another populist leader elsewhere in Southeast Asia said, "Perhaps he is corrupt—I don't know. Everybody in power is corrupt. But at least he gave benefits to the poor."[20]

Manager-entrepreneurs as canaries in the corruption mine

Poverty reduction is logically seen in the Philippines as the best measure of progress. The pollster Mahar Mangahas has observed that, "Economic growth isn't 'development.'"[21] Personal perceptions of optimism or pessimism, food sufficiency or hunger, fairness or unfairness to the poor, adequate or inadequate health, housing, and transport are all measures of development. Economic indices such as GDP per capita relate to these, but perceptual indices propel politics. Among surveys assessing "legitimacy" in 51 countries in the 1990s, the Philippine state was seen by its citizens as relatively legitimate, ranked 16 in a set of 51. But when the respondents were asked about "justice," they ranked their state radically worse: 45th among the 51.[22] These Filipinos said their political system was legitimate but unjust.

Corruption was widely perceived, and attempts to measure it survey the private individuals most often involved in it. So Philippine urban managers were asked, in repeated polls between 2000 and 2007, what they thought of the proposition that: "Corruption is part of the way government works." In each of those years, at least 40 percent agreed. In the 2007 survey during Arroyo's presidency, 50 percent agreed.

A sample of managers and a separate sample of the general public in 2005–06 were asked, "When there is corruption involving both a businessman and a government official, who in your opinion is to blame?" More than two-thirds of each group responded that, "Both are equally to blame." When the managers were asked, "How much corruption do you think there is in the public sector?" in each year more than three-fifths replied, "A lot," and another third replied "Some." In other words, three-quarters of Filipino business people found their government corrupt.

They were in the best position to say. Despite personal and company disincentives to frankness, they revealed a great deal—and arguably served patriotic purposes by doing so. They knew of frequent specific instances of corruption; and, if guaranteed anonymity, they readily reported these: "When was the last time you had personal knowledge of a corrupt transaction with the government by a company in your sector of business?" Between one-quarter and one-third replied, "In the last month."

These managers unsurprisingly claimed that most of the problem involved the state officials. When, in seven different surveys with careful samples of business people, they were asked, "How much corruption is there in the private sector?" only 8 to 14 percent replied "A lot."[23] But many Filipinos believe that institutionalized "pork" contributes to corruption. The agencies supporting this habit are mostly empowered by democratic elections.

A chairperson of any important committee in the Philippine Congress can dispose of large funds. Positions on the House Appropriations Committee are valuable to all its members. Even a vice-chair, Rep. Augusto Syjuco (Iloilo), estimated that, "I could get about 200 million pesos a year [in 'projects'] for my district."[24] Posts on the Public Works Committee or any committee dealing with transport or communication were also useful for those who wanted to control contracts. The Committee on Games and Amusements screened applications for franchises worth millions of pesos. Seats on the Appropriations Committee, which had 45 members in the first Congress after Marcos's demise, became so coveted that by the much later 2004 Congress the number of members on that committee rose to 170 (three-quarters of the entire House).[25]

About one-fifth of the Philippine state's total procurement budget in the early 2000s went directly "to the pockets of legislators, officials, and contractors alone," according to the Chair of the House Appropriations Committee, Rep. Rolando Andaya, Jr. An earlier estimate, from the Finance and Budget Secretary, Salvador Enriquez, was that as much as 45 percent of these pork funds went to corrupt "commissions." For infrastructure projects, the portions were somewhat smaller but ran up to 30 percent.[26]

> Government auditors themselves say they are in the dark over how Congress spends most of its money, in part because there is hardly any paper trail to help them scrutinize how lawmakers use public funds.... On the average, the upkeep of legislators has risen ten percent every year since 1994 [to 2004].[27]

In addition to monetary allowances and free staff, "a committee position can also be used to shake down businesses in efforts disguised as 'inquiry in aid of legislation.'"[28] Chairing a committee can be profitable. As Speaker de Venecia said, "For every committee, there is a request from 10 to 15 [representatives for chairmanships]. There are 60 applicants for [12 House slots in the joint congressional] the Commission on Appointments."[29]

A 1997 Presidential Commission Against Graft and Corruption reported that items in the Congress budget "are not liquidated and audited in the same manner as expenses of public funds by all other government officials."[30] Congressmen

182 *Corruption*

signed receipts for money that they received, but they did not at that time need to prove how the funds were used. In particular, they needed to submit no payrolls of their district staffs. This meant that local *lider*-canvassers could be paid by the state for work that was private. An official of the Commission on Audit said, "The House is a political body. We don't want to get into trouble." Another admitted, "We're scared of congressmen. We're scared of the system. *Babalikan kami* [They'll seek revenge]. We don't want to tolerate corruption, but nothing happens to our reports. We just become subject to harassment."[31]

Each Philippine senator by 2004 cost the taxpayers about one million pesos *monthly*.[32] Each Congress member had a "Priority Development Assistance Fund" that could be used at the discretion of the representative. The Speaker of the House could legally put into his own fund any "savings" from other appropriation bills. Many such funds were then returned to Congress members who had voted for the winner during the race for the speakership. "And once the Speaker is in place,... Congressmen who do not belong to the ruling coalition, and party-list representatives, are said to receive 50,000 pesos a month, while 'favored' Congressmen reportedly get double or even triple that."[33]

The president of the republic is still supposed to govern the six-tenths of expenditures that are the national (non-local, central) part of the total state budget.[34] Because Congress members also depend extensively on this money, the Speaker of the House has strong incentives to remain loyal to the president. But in 2008, the son of Speaker Jose De Venecia, Jr., accused President Arroyo's husband of corruption involving a Chinese firm. Soon a big majority of House members voted to depose the Speaker. They would break with De Venecia but not with the president. The Speaker accused Arroyo of failing to protect him and his family from physical violence, and his melancholy verbiage confirmed that the Speaker–president link is nearly constitutional because of presidential power over spending:

> It pains me grievously to hurt the President and to hurt the First Family, because I have invested so much more than any of you in this chamber to help the President become Vice-President and then become President, [but] I will join the opposition to denounce corruption in this administration.[35]

De Venecia also reported that, four months earlier, the head of the Philippine Army, Gen. Santos, had come personally to his home with this message: "Mr. Speaker, you and your son [should] keep quiet, because they want to kill you and I know they have killed other people." Gen. Santos later denied having said this, but there were several witnesses. De Venecia's son reported the threat to Manila police, and the Speaker wrote a letter to Arroyo: "Dear Madam President, I write to you because Gen. Santos came to me and said to me ... that they wanted to kill myself and my son.... Please do something." Perhaps this threat of government violence against a very high official was real. In any case, it shows a climate as recently as 2008 in which fear affected politics at the heart of the central government.

PNoy's position on pork, as he assumed the presidency in 2010, was that PDAF allocations should be retained—and raised—but better audited. One of his early acts was to more-than-double "development assistance" funds. The aim was to support infrastructure projects, but also to tighten the monitoring of those funds' use.[36] PNoy's reformist predecessor, Fidel Ramos, in 1996 likewise had increased the "development funds" that each House member could allocate locally. Ramos had supported a Public Works Act that gave further pork to Congress delegates for "infrastructure" in their districts.[37] Whether increased auditing toward reducing corruption trumps the increased allocations, or vice versa, always remained a question. PNoy raised the total pork allocation in his 2014 budget proposal by two billion pesos over the 2013 amount.[38] PNoy has a "Presidential Social Fund" too, which is financed partly from a levy on casino profits. Although its amount was not included in an article about it, his spokeswoman gave assurances that, "The use of that particular fund is very transparent."[39]

One of PNoy's allies, Senate President Pro-Tem Ralph Recto said, "I am in favor that we have a line-item budget.... Even the pork barrel should have a performance indicator." As Senator Recto presented the president's 2014 budget to Congress, he specified general targets of deliverables by each civilian and military department, including the national police, the departments for health and education and others, the National Intelligence Coordinating Agency (which was ordered to write more reports), and other branches of government.[40] The presidential party wanted to apply Thatcherite measures of accountability to a tradition of semi-feudal prebends that had acquired local democratic legitimacy.

Progress of post-2010 corruption auditing

By 2012, a repeat of the corruption survey among businessmen showed a considerable decline in perceived corruption, especially in the public sector. More than 60 percent of Philippine executives, asked about government corruption in multiple polls from 2000 to 2009, had always reported "a lot." But in 2012, a somewhat lower portion (42 percent) claimed "a lot" of public sector corruption. Still 41 percent of executives said that "most or almost all" companies in their own sectors offered bribes for public contracts. This was hardly a brilliant report card; but there was a spike of hope that the national executive would be able to fight corruption. Some agencies that deal with extensive parts of the country (Public Works and Highways, Land Transportation, Internal Revenue, Customs, and Comelec) still received "bad" or "poor" ratings.[41]

Congress members' "Priority Development Assistance Funds" have come under increasing attack. Many official funds continue to be used without much transparency. "Ghost projects," performed by "bogus NGOs," became a flourishing corrupt business of the Janet Lim Napoles Group of Companies in 2013. A whistle-blower named five senators and 23 House members as having transferred "pork" funds to Napoles's bank accounts. The offending politicians were not immediately identified; but the reported relevant senators included Enrile, Honasan, and senator sons of former presidents Estrada and Marcos. Their colleague Miriam Santiago suggested that, "Out of *delicadeza*, the senators should go on leave, to erase any doubt that they might use their power or their money to pressure the investigators."[42]

Three senators associated with PNoy's Liberal Party (Trillanes, Pimentel, and Legarda) were accused in 2013 of having misused such funds—but PNoy's prestigious Justice Minister Leila de Lima explicitly exonerated them even before investigations on "PDAF" uses were complete. The other senators, also accused, "vehemently denied any wrongdoing." The secretary general of the Liberal Party announced that he opposed proposals to end these "pork" funds.[43]

> PDAF has brought good things to so many communities, especially those in far-flung barangays. The medical assistance it provides has likewise been a big help to [those] seeking medical service from major government hospitals. What we are seeing from the media are those [funds] that fail, but there are so many success stories on the use of the PDAF. We should not abolish this, and instead we should ensure that it is put to good use.

PNoy's spokeswoman stressed that the National Bureau of Investigation looked into allegations that funds had been misused—partly by members of the president's party. But she said the inquiry should not be rushed. Any Philippine president who is unwilling to use much violence against rivals (as Marcos did) apparently still needs the pork system in order to maintain support for his or her policies in Congress.

Speaker Belmonte, in the acceptance speech after his 2013 re-election to that top House post, vowed to fight corruption of "pork," ensuring that "every centavo of taxpayers' money is not wasted or pocketed."[44] The Makabayan bloc of House members (from five party-lists plus seven independents) went further and proposed abolishing all PDAFs. Speaker Belmonte replied that members did not have to use their money, if they wished to reject it.[45] A few days later, seven party-list representatives said they would do exactly what the Speaker suggested, foregoing their collective pork allocations of 70 million pesos in each of the following three years for which they had been elected. Four of the seven who took the vow were newly elected and had not "tasted pork."[46] These seven "radicals" in effect challenged the integrity of others who spoke against pork allocations but were willing to take the money until the law changed.

It had been hoped that the constitutionally few party-list delegates in the House would break *trapo* patterns concerning pork. But as one of them said, "We can't fight pork because it's institutionalized. *Hinahanap 'yan ng tao* [people look for it]. What we can do is just to look for projects that address the needs of our constituents."[47] They pointed out that PNoy, using his presidential line-item veto, might abolish these appropriations immediately.[48] That would have revived a policy of Marcos. But if PNoy had done this, his ability to pass laws through Congress would have dropped sharply.

No senators and only a few party-list House members took the pledge to reject future PDAF allocations. The legitimacy of localism was confirmed in 2013 when PNoy's spokeswoman announced his support for "good pork":[49]

> The President believes the theory that the PDAF can be used for the correct reasons [since it] is really the share of the constituents in the budget. Technically, the job of the legislator is to bring to the attention of the national government the concerns that are not attended to on the national level but are needed by the district or municipality that the local government is unable to fund.... The national government cannot be everywhere at once. That's where the input of local officials and legislators comes in, so they can say which matters need urgent attention in their districts.

This habit of pork has acquired nearly constitutional status. The pork tradition, supported by a reformer-president and more conservative *trapos* alike, is specifically localist.[50]

Perceptions of relatively corrupt or clean institutions

Churches scored better than other kinds of organization (among 13 types) in a 2000 survey of the extent to which Filipinos "trust" their institutions. Media, the civil service, and the armed forces and police did moderately well in this survey. Less trusted were Congress, "major companies," and labor unions. The central government and political parties were least trusted.[51]

Some agencies received good ratings from managers for "net sincerity" in fighting corruption, and these included the Department of Trade and Industry, Social Security regulators, the Supreme Court, usually the Department of Health, and (more predictably from these respondents) Filipino business associations.[52] But other agencies, including trial courts, the Department of Budget and Management, the Office of the President (then under Arroyo), the Senate, the Presidential Anti-Graft Commission, the Armed Forces—and notably the Ombudsman—received "net sincerity" scores that were "statistically indistinguishable from zero."

Below that, the Department of the Interior and Local Government, the Justice Ministry, the Philippine Commission on Good Government, the Department of the Environment, and the Philippine National Police received negative scores. Agencies that did worst on this index of perceived sincerity in combating corruption included the Land and Transportation Office, the House of Representatives, the Commission on Elections, the Internal Revenue Bureau, and the Department of Public Works and Highways. The Bureau of Customs brought up the very rear of this blacklist. In the views of many Philippine entrepreneurs, large parts of their government were rotten. After 2010, evaluations of the presidency and some (not all) official agencies improved.

PNoy in his 2013 State of the Nation Address excoriated the Bureau of Customs for inefficiency and corruption. He said that customs officers tried to "outdo each other's incompetence." So Customs Employees' Association members donned black armbands and held a rally against PNoy's "sweeping remarks." A customs labor leader claimed that,

> Everyone has a dirty laundry in the bag. But instead of trying to put down the agency, help us out.... We are part of your team, Mr. President, along with your political appointees. We have done our share in making your appointees look good. Yet the employees, the rank and file, have been for the last few months a political punching bag.

The Employees' Association issued a statement saying the president had "inaccurate and wrong information" that two billion pesos of customs revenue that should have been collected had been foregone, and that there was "rampant smuggling of illegal drugs and firearms into the country." The employees admitted that, "The target may never have been met, but like the BIR [Bureau of Internal Revenue], collections are definitely higher than the previous year."[53]

The Commissioner of Customs in mid-2013 asked all 54 top customs officials to submit "courtesy resignations," so that they might be vetted and reassigned. Of the 54, 45 complied—not including the chief inspector at Manila's main airport or the head at Iloilo port. Senate Majority Leader Peter Cayetano called on the Ombudsman to make a "lifestyle check" of all customs officials. He said that, "moving people around is nothing more than a reorganization."[54] Some bureaus of the central state hierarchy, notably including Customs, have been deemed corrupt by practically everyone who cares about such matters in the Philippines.

Filipinos are polled to be approximately as satisfied with their local governments and local politicians as they are with the national institutions and politicians. An August 2012 survey found 73 percent of household heads satisfied with their municipal governments. Fully 42 percent gave city or municipality authorities credit for solving whatever problem they deemed most pressing. But this word "local" can refer to more than one size of polity. Barangay authorities received satisfactory reports from only 23 percent of respondents, as compared to 22 percent for the national government. Such figures fluctuate in different quarterly polls. Degree of trust by individuals is not linear with respect to size of polity. Medial sizes are surveyed to satisfy Filipinos best, and such regions are often associated with prestigious clan leaders.

Household heads in 2012 who saw "a lot" of corruption at the national level were 79 percent; those who saw that much corruption in municipal institutions was somewhat lower (68 percent).[55] These statistics also vary over time. But the contrast with other East Asian countries, e.g., China where surveys rate national leaders much more highly than local ones, is notable. Very local and police authorities are resented in countries where they have the habit of using means of violence frequently.

When Transparency International published its "corruption barometer" for the Philippines in 2013, its survey showed that 69 percent of Filipinos believed the police were corrupt. This showing was closely followed by 64 percent who thought civilian officials were corrupt, 58 percent who thought that about political parties, 56 percent about the judiciary, and 52 percent about the legislature. The army, however, was deemed corrupt by only 43 percent of the respondents. Still, one-third of the surveyed Filipinos thought corruption had increased, and 37 percent thought it had gone down.[56] This was progress, although it was limited.

Memories of past corruptions and presidents

It has become a tradition that Philippine chief executives should speak against nepotism just after they ascend to the top post. President Ramon Magsaysay promised at the start of his term to abolish nepotism: "I will not hesitate to send my own father to jail!" Ferdinand Marcos opposed nepotisms in rival clans—while suspending the Constitution and making his wife Imelda Governor of Metro Manila (and holder of other posts too), his daughter Imee head of the Youth League (*Kabataang Barangay*), his sister Elizabeth Governor of Ilocos Norte, and his young son Ferdinand "Bongbong" Marcos, Jr., the Vice-Governor. Populist leaders such as Marcos (or Thaksin, or Bo Xilai, or Hitler) often launch selective anti-corruption campaigns against their rivals.

Tax compliance is one measure of public cleanliness, and it has been uneven in the Philippines for many decades. Efren Plana, after Marcos appointed him to head the Bureau of Internal Revenue, led a three-pronged attack on corruption. First, he was able to raise tax collectors' legal salaries, so that they would be less reliant on bribes; and he rotated revenue officials among jurisdictions, ostensibly promoting them by merit criteria. Second, he brought in a team of new certified public accountants, as well as intelligence officers—some military, and some civilian—as outsiders to do research on the Internal Revenue Bureau. Third, he was able to dismiss officials of whom corruption was suspected (although after some of these were indicted in criminal prosecutions, only a few were convicted). Outside the bureau, he set up a "selective quality audit" to find taxpayers whose returns suggested they were violating laws. Legislation also made the tax system more transparent. The Philippines Commission on Audit was enlisted to check on delivery of taxes that were due.[57] Marcos clan rivals were more affected by these reforms than were his political friends.

When Corazon Aquino assumed the presidency, she declared,[58]

> I believe in leadership by example. I will not change my style. I will certainly remain what I am. I said that I wouldn't give posts to anybody from my family. Now, some are complaining that it is just a shame that they happen to be my relatives. But I will keep my promise. That's a simple method of reintroducing credibility and integrity into our government.

She appointed a Presidential Commission on Good Government and insisted that the "Febrev" (February "Revolution" of 1986) would end bribery in the

188   *Corruption*

Philippines. But Cojuangco and Aquino relatives nonetheless benefitted from having their kinswoman in the Malacañang Palace—whether or not she was personally active in arranging their large loans (e.g., from Australia) or their reacquisitions of firms that had earlier been taken from their families or political allies by relatives or friends of the Marcoses. As Corazon Aquino's brother-in-law put it,

> I would like to point out that if these companies were ill-gotten, they were ill-gotten from their previous owners, who thus have a prior right to reacquire these companies.... This prior right is not diminished or impaired simply because one of the previous owners happens to be an in-law of the President.[59]

About 15 of Aquino's relatives ran during her presidency for political offices—and most of them won.

Some famous elected Philippine politicians are reputedly uncorrupt. Corazon Aquino had a "clean" reputation, despite criticism by leftists that she helped to maintain legal exploitative institutions. Politicians with relatively clean reputations may do better in national elections for that reason, even if they are seen as less decisive than populist "anti-corruption" strongmen. Neither Fidel Ramos nor Miriam Defensor-Santiago (who were the top two vote-getters in the 1992 presidential election) had been predicted to do so well. Both had less money and weaker political machines than other candidates—but many voters saw them as relatively incorruptible.[60] Together, they received two-fifths of the votes, with the other three-fifths going to *trapos*. Ramos had just a small plurality, less than 24 percent of the vote, but it was enough to make him president.[61]

Ramos's best-known relevant action was to appoint Vice-President Erap Estrada to head an anti-corruption commission. Conflicts between Ramos and Estrada soon developed. Before the next presidential election, anchorman Manuel Murato on his TV talk program showed a video in which presidential candidate Estrada was shown playing baccarat in the Heritage Hotel Casino's Super VIP Room, along with "suspected gambling and drug lord Charlie Ang." Estrada called Murato's move "black propaganda, a smear drive, and a political demolition job." He said President Ramos was behind it. Estrada claimed Murato had paid 20 million pesos for the tape. In riposte, Murato announced that if Estrada were elected (as soon happened), he would file impeachment proceedings, partly because of a law against that kind of gambling by public officials and partly on the report that Estrada had accepted 500,000 pesos in chips from a Sindhi businessman who was Ang's brother-in-law. Murato also headed a government agency promoting Lotto all over the Philippines.[62]

Erap Estrada at the start of his presidential term declared, "I am warning them.... No friend, no relative, will be allowed to take advantage of their relationship with me." Then, after his impeachment for corruption began, President Estrada denied he had any cronies—although he acknowledged being "blessed with many friends."[63]

President Estrada was ousted from Malacañang after one of his drinking and gambling partners, Gov. Jose Singson of Ilocos Sur, discovered that the president "planned to set up a bingo network to rival his [Singson's] *jueteng* [gambling] organization"—and reported that he had paid Estrada US$8 million from *jueteng* profits, plus $2.5 million "as the president's 'cut' of the tobacco excise taxes" from Ilocos Sur.[64] After some time, and after he was forced to leave the presidency, Estrada was convicted of corruption—this case was clear, and Philippine courts were abnormally swift to close it. (Later by 2007, President Arroyo needed all the support she could get; so she pardoned him.)

Arroyo's main reputation and its results

Gloria Macapagal Arroyo claimed to have an anti-corruption program and appointed a famously tough commissioner to head the Bureau of Internal Revenue. He resigned, after an anonymous threat to bomb his office. When the term of a very corrupt national ombudsman ("a crook," according to one interviewee) ended, Arroyo appointed a man named Marcelo to this important prosecutorial job. Conviction rates soon doubled, albeit just from 6 to 12 percent of all corruption cases that were tried. President Arroyo decreed permanent job tenure for all lawyers whom she had appointed to the civil service (PNoy later revoked this). Marcelo sued several politicians for corruption—but none of the court cases involved the president or figures close to her.

Arroyo announced with pride that she doubled the staff of the Ombudsman anti-corruption agency, which the Philippine Constitution enshrines. In 2001, she met with her Indonesian counterpart, Megawati Sukarnoputri, who had just promised "not to allow any opportunity for corruption, collusion, and nepotism." The women presidents of these two most populous Malay countries vowed to help each other and re-establish the close link that had existed between their populist fathers, former presidents Macapagal and Sukarno.[65] Arroyo claims she spent 3,000,000,000 pesos "to battle corruption." She set up a Procurement Transparency Group to monitor government contracts. Yet hers was by many accounts one of the most corrupt presidencies in recent Philippine history.

President Arroyo's administration in December 2002 proposed a law concerning government procurements. The law was designed to reduce corruption—and Congress passed it. An experienced interviewee said, "They didn't know what they were doing." The law required that contracts for procurement be posted on the internet. Collusion among bidders on official contracts became a legal offense. This law did not change what Arroyo herself was doing, and it may have provided cover for corruption in the short term while reducing it in the long term.

The "Procurement Transparency Group" apparently escaped Arroyo's control when it looked into her government's broadband TV contract with ZTE Corp., a Chinese company that reportedly overpriced its services (at US$330 million) in order to cover kickbacks of $130 million to First Gentleman Mike Arroyo and Comelec Chair Benjamin Abalos.[66] Reportedly a deal was agreed between

Arroyo and the company's executives as they enjoyed a crab feast at a Shenzhen golf course in late 2006. Jose De Venecia, Jr., personally witnessed some of these dealings; he was at that time in Arroyo's camp—but left it when he was voted out of the Speakership.[67]

Non-monetary abuses of power were as important among Arroyo's corruptions as were mere embezzlements. Professional military men became especially active in politics against Arroyo after the public release of the "Hello Garci" tape of her telephone conversation with a head of the Commission on Elections, Virgilio Garcillano. The tape made clear that Arroyo had secretly ordered soldiers to help rig the 2004 presidential election in her favor. Officers who were outraged by this revelation included Brig. Gen. Danilo Lim, commander of the elite Scout Rangers. A previously less political figure was Col. Ariel Querubin, second-in-command of the marines, whose previous promotions had been based on his prowess as a professional soldier against rebels (both Muslim and communist). Querubin held the Medal of Valor, the highest Philippine award for bravery in combat. (Much earlier, in December 1989, Querubin had led an assault on Camp Aguinaldo in a failed *kudeta* against President Cory Aquino. He was nearly killed during that failure, although in 1995 he was restored to his marine posting because of his outstanding military record.) Arroyo knew she could not last long in the Malacañang, if too many respected soldiers were able to act against her.

So in February 2006, the president ordered the jailings of discontented officers who might have deposed her. She had Querubin imprisoned at Camp Aguinaldo. Under some traditions, that jailing might seem the rightful act of an elected commander-in-chief. In the totally politicized Philippine context of Arroyo's presidency, however, many perceived her detention of officers whom she deemed to be potential mutineers as corrupt.

This created a further reaction among commanders who could claim to be patriotic (albeit sometimes disobedient to superior officers who threaten coercion on behalf of corrupt presidents). A prominent example was Navy Senior Lieutenant (later Senator) Antonio F. Trillanes IV. During Arroyo's term, the leaders of Scout Rangers and Marines clearly hoped for a mass protest movement to oust her; after all, similar extraconstitutional campaigns had succeeded in deposing Marcos and Estrada. The pro-*kudeta* officers reportedly tried to persuade the Chief of Staff of the Armed Forces, Gen. Generoso Senga, to join a peaceful march of soldiers against President Arroyo. But, instead, Gen. Senga reported to Arroyo's office which units were slated to participate; so a coup was aborted.[68] Some soldiers, such as Defense Secretary Norberto Gonzalez, opposed the military reformers and supported Arroyo. Lim and Trillanes were both jailed for leading the *kudeta* (and were released by PNoy soon after his election).

Many government agencies, not just the presidency, were increasingly seen as corrupt during Arroyo's last years in office. By 2006–07, the Internal Revenue Bureau was perceived by business people, in a Social Weather Stations survey, as having a negative "net sincerity" score for fighting corruption.[69] By late 2010, the Bureau of Internal Revenue head, Kim Jacinto-Hinares, quoted a predecessor claiming that the BIR had a good staff ("the best and the brightest in government service")—but this must have been faint praise, because Hinares also reported that 120 revenue district officers in scattered parts of the archipelago "failed to hit their individual collection targets."[70] Tax evasion remained common.

By late 2011, after her presidential term ended, Arroyo herself was detained on corruption charges. She wanted to leave the country (to Hong Kong, for medical treatment of a thyroid complaint). The Philippine Supreme Court granted her permission to depart; she had appointed 12 of the 15 justices. But she was stopped at the airport from boarding a flight; and on November 19, 2011, she was served a formal arrest warrant.[71] The judiciary is hearing many cases against her. If lower courts convict, those decisions will be appealed to the Supreme Court, where the judges were likely for some time to be mostly Arroyo appointees. Legal efforts to convict Arroyo of corruption have not been totally inconclusive. When the Supreme Court denied one of Arroyo's petitions in mid-2013, the legal cases against her electoral fraud and fiscal plunder both continued to plod through lower courts and the Sandiganbayan without final results. She was held in a hospital, but was also still a Pampanga representative in Congress.[72]

PNoy entered office as a new broom, hoping to clean out his predecessor's nepotisms and corruptions. It is difficult, even in a whole presidential term, for a reformer to make much progress against old habits, even though PNoy tried. Court cases against alleged corruptions drag on for so long in Philippine courts that natural deaths often overtake punishments. PNoy's first action, creating a special agency to investigate Arroyo-era rakeoffs, had precedents. Between 1950 and 2001, various Philippine presidents had established no fewer than 13 special anti-graft agencies.[73] Marcos set up the most important of these, the Tanodbayan, as well as the Sandiganbayan that is a specialized criminal court for corruption cases. After a temporary rise of anti-corruption prosecutions in the Ramos era, the number of cases and criminalizations declined.

The prosecutions rarely exceeded a sixth or eighth of the cases that were recommended for investigation. "Even worse than the low rate of prosecutions is the rare number of cases in which a penalty is imposed [only 554 occasions from 1988 to 2001], only 15 percent of all prosecutions."[74] The ratio of penalties to prosecutions rose in the new millennium, but the portion of recommended cases that were actually brought to court declined. Many plausible criminals (especially from the Estrada and Arroyo eras) got off scot free.

On a Corruption Perception Index published early in the new millennium, the Philippines was approximately as corrupt as India or Pakistan, though less so than Indonesia or Bangladesh.[75] By 2010, the Philippines was surveyed as equal to Bangladesh in corruption (or Nigeria, Zimbabwe, or Ukraine), but Indonesia and India had improved, while Pakistan had not.[76] The countries close to the Philippines on this index were dubious democracies at best.

Corruption, like any other social variable, is not spread evenly over space. The Sandiganbayan anti-graft court provided 2007 figures suggesting that, although corruption was widespread throughout the islands, by far the largest amount of corrupt money was concentrated in Manila. Corruption during 2007 was mostly perceived in two types of agents: the Office of the President (then Arroyo) and private company executives. A congressional source characterized businessmen:

> They are so used to the corruption ... they have already set aside ten percent or twenty percent of the project price for the guy who signs the paper. To them, it is no longer whether it is corrupt or not—it is part of the business ... if this thing is OK with you as you grow older, your tolerance level goes up. So I was content with one percent, now I want three percent, four percent, five percent, and so on.... Of course, there are still those who, whether you give them 1 or 2 or 20,000 pesos, they absolutely won't [take it]. I hate to say it, but they are the exceptions rather than the rule.[77]

Official anti-corruption agencies did not always act against local non-officials who were involved in private corruptions. These set social norms both within the government and outside it. When either the Ombudsman/Tanodbayan or the Sandigbayan/anti-graft appellate court act, they are only concerned with corruptions by public officials (except that the Ombudsman may indict non-officials involved in the same crimes along with government employees). This makes for very incomplete coverage of graft. Wholly private cases are seven-tenths of the work that Hong Kong's ICAC handles.[78] These cases involve behavioral power; they are no less political for being non-governmental. If anti-corruption agencies neglect non-state local power networks, they fail to do most of their natural job. State politics are inseparable from politics outside the state, e.g., where money is involved.

Types of economic corruption

Corruption cost the Philippine government US$48 billion in the last two decades of the millennium—a greater sum than the US$41 billion of foreign debt then—according to a plausible report.[79] The varieties of economic local corruption were many. Examples from the Philippines' Bureau of Internal Revenue include "speed money" (*lagay*) to hasten government legal services and "arrangements" (*arreglo*) for illegally low tax assessments. Other bribes are available when government bureaucrats convince citizens that tipping them is necessary in order to avoid hassles by officials. Within the Bureau, opportunities for corruption were numerous and lucrative. Falsified accounts made embezzlement hard to detect. Extra printing of labels and stamps for receipts increased the money that came to officials rather than to the public treasury. Tax collectors' posts could be sold. Monitoring accountants could be bribed to keep quiet. This is just a sample of the many kinds of opportunities for ordinary theft through corruption.[80]

The most common bribes have been for "getting local government permits and licenses." Other occasions for bribery involved central government permissions, taxes owed, payments due, and permits to import goods. In various years even after 2010, only 5 to 9 percent of surveyed managers reported officials' requests for bribes to anti-corruption agencies. Most of them shrugged, "nothing will be done anyway." Nearly half said they were afraid of reprisals from the officials who had asked for bribes, or "standard practice is not to report incidents," or "it's too small a thing to bother with," or "I cannot prove it."[81]

The loss of tax revenue accounts for part of the central government's weakness. Corrupt officials in the Bureau of Internal Revenue at one point stopped their work, going on strike, to protest a boss who tried to prevent them from taking bribes.[82] The Finance Secretary in 2013 reported, "We have a total of 1.8 million professionals. Of this number, only 400,000 [22 percent] are paying taxes, reporting an average income of P33,000, which is about the monthly minimum wage." He figured that if an "ongoing campaign" could make at least 1.5 million professionals pay taxes averaging P200,000 (which sample surveys had suggested was fair), then the government could increase its revenue by P300 billion annually.

The revenue performance of the Customs Bureau remained low long after PNoy excoriated that agency for its towering ineptness. Tariff collections were up just 1.2 percent in the first half of 2013, although the supervising department had made surveys and mandated a 17.3 percent increase. The Customs Commissioner, when reporters asked whether he could meet his 2013 and 2014 targets, replied that he could not. "We have been posting an increase in our collections every year. Our collections have been the highest in the history of the Bureau." When asked why the 17.3 percent goal was so high, he said, "It's beyond me"—and he suggested that "part of the blame" should go to the Development Budget Coordinating Committee, which sets such targets.[83]

Tax and tariff evasions have been massive for many years, and they combine with politicians' addition to pork, practically legitimating financial laxness. It has been estimated that during Ramos's term evasion was "between 53 percent and 63 percent for domestic sales taxes, and between 48 percent and 55 percent for import taxes." Evasion of salary taxes was guessed as "between 24 percent and 43 percent, and on professional income between 65 percent and 83 percent."[84] The Ombudsman estimated that the government was losing more than 100 million pesos per day. So corruption was draining about one-fifth of the national budget, or about 4 percent of GNP. The Department of Education, Culture, and Sports was particularly cited for kickbacks. The Department of Public Works and Highways, according to one estimate, lost 20 to 40 percent of its project costs.[85]

Pork allocations to politicians combine with this tax cheating and the habit of political rakeoffs from government appropriations to bolster norms that foster corruption. Art. VI, Sec. 14, of the Philippine Constitution says that no senator or representative may

> directly or indirectly be interested financially in any contract with, or in any franchise or special privilege granted by the government, or any subdivision, agency, or instrumentality thereof, including any government-owned or -controlled corporation or a subsidiary, during his term of office.

194   *Corruption*

Such provisions are hard to enforce in any democracy, although some Philippine reformers have tried to make them meaningful.

Substandard construction work that violates government contracts has been common. A senator said,

> There is simply no way to monitor how well these [contracts] are implemented. If they tell you they will dredge x cubic meters, who will check where the hell that number of cubic meters went? The same with asphalt overlay. Whether it is one centimeter or ten inches, nobody knows.

Auditors may be employed to check the work. Then they can be bribed.

> You have the inspector who does the after-project report and gets 0.5 percent of the pork. You have the director who gives his opinion or approves the report, and you go up the ladder. For the Commission on Audit, that must be about 10 percent or 15 percent of the pork all in all.[86]

Local officials, when their terms of office ended, often left government debts worth hundreds of millions of pesos. Their successors inherited official coffers that were empty. The Commission on Audit has found severe local-government indebtedness in Metro Manila, Cebu, and many poorer places.[87]

Corruption has only occasionally been proven in the Philippine Army. Discipline and (after the Marcos era) some reputation for rectitude has often prevailed in central units of the main military, albeit not in many rural detachments. In February 2011, former Army Chief Gen. Angelo Reyes (who had held three cabinet posts under various presidents) committed suicide. This tragedy occurred during a congressional investigation of alleged corruption by several top officers. They were supposed to have embezzled money that had been appropriated for the army, financing lavish lifestyles in Manila and property purchases in the United States. Reyes himself had been widely admired for hard work over many years. But as a memorial to him put it,

> corruption in the Philippines has become so pervasive that public officials from the very top down to the barangay *tanods* can be in on the take.... But corruption exists only because it is tolerated.... So if we are to be completely honest with ourselves, we know who really killed Angelo Reyes; we look at that person every day in the mirror.[88]

Reportedly Reyes had received a customary golden parachute upon retirement, but he felt so dishonored by the congressional investigation that he killed himself. Many at the time opined that others among soldiers and especially among civilians had been more guilty of corruption.

Corruption in the constabulary is worse. No less a figure than the Chief of the Philippine National Police, Avelino Razon, Jr., appointed by Arroyo, had led a ring that embezzled public money in 2007 for ghost repairs of police vehicles.

The new PNoy-appointed Ombudsman as late as 2013 filed charges in the Sandiganbayan court against this graft of 400 million pesos.[89]

Criminal investigators in the National Police and in the National Bureau of Investigation (under the Department of Justice) had functions that in practice overlapped and could cause intra-governmental conflict. A police detective in 2013, for example, claimed that "an NBI agent was spotted in a four-month surveillance visiting the apartment of captured shabu [methamphetamine] suppliers" named Li "Jackson Dy" Lan Yan and his wife Wang Li Na. The policeman also said that,

> even some government officials and members of the media are behind the drug den. Their focus now is to destroy and discredit the police unit and operatives. They can easily do it, as they have entrenched connections among law enforcers, prosecutors, judges, and even the media.

This charge brought a furious response from Secretary of Justice de Lima, who challenged the police detective either to "shut up" or else to reveal the names of the allegedly miscreant NBI agents.[90]

Laws for corruption

Senator Miriam Defensor Santiago has been outspoken about links between *jueteng* and criminality. In September 2010 she delivered a "privilege speech" on the floor of the Senate, where her legal immunity prevented slander suits by *jueteng* operators whom she named. She called on PNoy either to enforce the laws against gambling or else replace them with legalization and regulation. Santiago expressed scant hope that enforcement would be feasible. She asserted that, under successive previous presidents, the Chief of the Philippine National Police and the Secretary of the Interior and Local Government had on average received about 30 million pesos per month from *jueteng* profits. She said that,[91]

> The President can be manipulated to profess ignorance, because the two lords of the gambling industry [both presidential appointees] will insidiously make the president dependent on their support. For example, they can act as the praetorian guard of the president when he is under siege, such as when a *coup d'état* lurks on the horizon and the PNP has to head off the nascent uprising. Or in times of political crisis, the two racketeers [PNP chief and Interior Minister] will contribute cash in the hundreds of millions, solicited from *jueteng* operators and destined for distribution to certain members of Congress.

Regulatory laws that illegalize gambling add a premium (mainly bribes to prevent enforcement) to the financial rakeoffs for those who can break the laws. Philippine regulations have often been structured to maximize rent-seeking. Gambling is illegal—but bets on cock fights, the numbers game *jueteng*, and other games like *sakla* and hi-lo, are common. "Authorities find it more profitable to retain the law, making these networks illegal, and to connive in their continued operation."[92]

Petty corruptions follow the same pattern. Street vending in Manila is illegal, for example, but that law is enforced if it leads to bribes for police. When a strict conservative mayor in part of the city tried to eliminate street vendors, local officials (who enjoyed pay-offs from the vendors) stymied that reform. They would have lost their bribes if the vendors really had to close down. Later, when a very anti-conservative, progressive NGO tried to legalize street selling, that effort also failed. The local officials would have lost bribes if vending had become legal. Then the vendors would have needed to give no money to police.[93] Local actors can be "strategic hypocrites."[94] They can honor and abuse laws in whatever ways they benefit most.

Civil service offices often became clan prebends. Children have followed their parents into the same agencies, sometimes the same posts.[95] The Philippine bureaucracy in 2004 employed 1.33 million people. Two-thirds theoretically worked for the central executive branch. One-fifth were in local governments (provincial or below), and 7 percent were in state companies. The Department of Education was the largest bureaucracy, and seven-eighths of its employees were primary or secondary teachers. The next largest was the Department of Interior and Local Government, of which nine-tenths were uniformed officers, mostly police. Just 1.4 percent of the civil servants were supposed to be political appointees making important decisions. That portion would be much higher, however, if appointees of local political networks were fully accounted. Teachers and police dispersed throughout the islands were very aware of local potentates. Rupert Hodder recommends centralizing recruitment under a "larger and more powerful Civil Service Commission and extend probation from six months to several years." He also argues for "the positive quality of informality [that] provides the room and atmosphere for creative thought, discussions, and decisions."[96] Such informality may correlate with corruption, and many local Philippine polities tolerate it.

Muckraking

Press freedom correlates internationally with low corruption. This relationship is hardly unexpected. A free press should decrease corruption by publicly shaming the corrupt. The correlation is large and significant—and it is found internationally not just among all countries, but also within the subset of developing nations. Government censorship can protect corrupt officials, and this may be a reason media freedom correlates with low corruption (to the extent these variables can be accurately measured).[97]

The Philippines, however, has a raucously free press that often castigates officials—yet it also has high levels of perceived corruption. It is an outlier case. This country boasts rambunctious newspapers with rich reporting of many types of public theft (both measured and anecdotal). Comparing levels of corruption and freedom at a single time, however, does not surely tell whether a free press reduces corruption progressively over decades. Reporters may well have this effect, but it may take a long time. The mechanism that creates the general correlation of press freedom with low corruption works less automatically than liberals might tend to imagine, and these islands are a good place to study it.

When journalists cover corruption in the Philippines, they may put themselves in physical danger. On May 10, 2005, the publisher of a weekly in the town of Dingalan, north of Manila, was shot dead as he sat down to dinner. His newspaper had included articles on local corruption. In rural towns,

> bigwigs riled by the words of a scribbler can easily find an assassin (for about 5,000 pesos, $93 [in 2005]) to end the matter.... Another factor, though hardly a justification for murder, is that many local hacks are shysters, given to raking up (or making up) dirt on local dignitaries, and then blackmailing them to keep it under wraps ... officials have suggested that journalists should carry firearms in order to defend themselves.[98]

Corruption of Philippine media occurs in many forms. A confidential survey of 100 journalists reported that they had received envelopes of money from businesses and politicians wanting to shape the news. (In China, such *hongbao* envelopes are conventional means of giving presents.) "Envelopmental journalism," according to its Manila critics, is frequent in that profession. If reporters demurred to be paid money for publishing biased news, they might nonetheless receive invitations to visit nightclubs, or other perks, "in lieu thereof" (called ILTs). Correspondents received free gifts of many sorts from organizations that sought to influence their news reports.[99]

Journalistic corruption comes in forms for which Filipinos have coined concise acronyms: "AC-DC" refers to "attack, collect, defend, collect" sequences, in which a reporter does a hatchet job on a politician, collecting from a rival—but then defends the politician who was earlier bruised, and tries to collect yet again for that remedial service. "ATM journalism" involves periodic payments to reporters for good stories. "Smiling money" establishes more general trust with media, even outside electoral seasons.[100] During campaigns, politicians pay their own cameramen to film them, conveying favorable footage to TV studios—along with incentives to broadcast it.

A "Freedom of Information" bill in 2012 had support from both Senate President Enrile and House Speaker Belmonte on grounds that it would aid investigations of government corruption. Some in Congress also pushed to include a provision that would give aggrieved parties (including politicians) rights of reply to accusations in media. Some expressed disappointment that PNoy, in his unprecedentedly long State of the Nation speech, did not mention this issue at all.[101]

Agencies against corruption and informal network modernizations

The evolution of institutions to fight corruption began with the constitutional Ombudsman and Corruption Court. The Ombudsman/Tanodbayan is a prosecutorial office, but it also conducts general research. The roles of Ombudsman and Corruption Court are sometimes difficult to differentiate clearly. The Ombudsman is supposed to rely on "persuasive power, plus the ability to require that proper legal steps be taken to compel [officials accused of corruption] to comply."[102] The Sandigbayan is an appellate court, but because its speciality is graft cases there are practical overlaps with the expertise and role of the Ombudsman/Tanodbayan. Both bodies have tended to favor the political friends of whichever president appointed most of their members. Often that has been the previous rather than the current president. Both agencies are written into the constitution no less surely than are the presidency or legislature. They are, as regards each other and further branches, stronger as checks than as balancers.

After a charge of corruption is filed with the Ombudsman, neither other prosecutors nor the Civil Service Commission will investigate it.[103] Complaints of corruption against government cadres are "essentially the prerogative of management"—and the manager is usually the elected appointer of the official. So if an elected politician stands behind an agent who engages in corruption, and if the charges can soon be referred to an ombudsman (who may be a political ally), the complaint goes nowhere. This norm, together with slow court appeals if the judiciary becomes engaged, makes corruption convictions rare.

The Transparency and Accountability Network (TAN), headed by Vincent Lazatín, seeks to reduce corruption, changing "low-risk high-reward" corruption into a "high-risk low-reward" behavior. The TAN lobbied PNoy to appoint a Minister of Justice who would go "hammer and tongs against the social cancer of corruption."[104] Comparativist Robert Klitgaard's main recommendation for reformers against corruption is to "find Mr. Clean and support him."[105] PNoy found "Ms. Clean" instead. The appointment of Leila de Lima presumably pleased the TAN NGO—but it is easier to switch officials than to reform multilayer governmental structures.

As a reformist Congressman put it, de Lima "blossomed" in the job despite having a less impressive earlier career. She expanded her department's role, demanding universal application of human rights.[106] Later, when Philippine police and others badly botched a swat operation against a deranged gunman who killed tourists from Hong Kong, de Lima chaired the committee to recommend legal and administrative sanctions. She is widely credited with having been fair in her sensitive tasks. But there is a lot of cleaning for this broom to do, and structures not just personalities are likely to be needed.

After Arroyo politicized the Ombudsman-prosecutor and the Sandigbayan Corruption Court, PNoy could not remove those constitutionally legitimated agencies' members quickly. So his Executive Order No. 1 created the Philippine Truth Commission of 2010, which was empowered to find "the truth regarding the reported cases of graft and corruption during the previous administration," in order "to recommend the prosecution of the offenders and secure justice for all."[107] This Truth Commission was not charged to investigate current acts of corruption, but past ones only. It overlapped the functions of the Ombudsman—but this was seen as necessary, because the incumbent Ombudsman (Gutierrez) had been appointed by the main person subject to investigation (Arroyo). PNoy's new Justice Secretary announced that Arroyo had lost her immunity from corruption suits upon leaving the presidency, despite having been elected a congresswoman.[108] Then, in November 2010, PNoy abolished his Presidential Anti-Graft Commission because it "duplicated the functions of other agencies, especially the Office of Ombudsman." Several offices in the executive branch were still empowered to investigate alleged wrongdoings by appointed officials.

Malacañang lawyers also mooted a "draft executive order" creating a new Presidential Commission Against Corruption, to be headed by former senator Panfilo Lacson, who planned to have a staff of 100 investigators.[109] "Heavyweight" politicians are often eager to head anti-corruption police. It was still unclear whether this new agency might look into corruptions by private as well as public agents. It is difficult but not impossible to have an anti-corruption agency that is independent and fair, reporting only to the chief executive in hopes that the president wants to enforce all the laws.

Former Senator Lacson's hope of heading a new corruption agency was still unfulfilled in 2013, when he continued to urge PNoy to create this additional anti-graft agency. Reformist Senator Miriam Santiago, citing previous court decisions, said Lacson's suggestion was "unconstitutional, illegal, immoral, and egoistic," as well as "unintelligent." Congress, she said, creates public agencies—and the Office of the Ombudsman should do its job.[110]

This task, if well done, is important but dangerous because it would inhibit people who can make a great deal of money from corrupt practices. An M-26 hand grenade was found in 2012 beside the house of Ombudsman Conchita Carpio-Morales. So the government bought an 8.5 million-peso car, in which she could "be riding in the comfort and security of a brand new bullet-proof vehicle." Ombudsman Morales showed a kind of *malakas* virtue by saying, "I'm a fatalist; if it's your time, it's your time."[111] But her colleagues had reason to think their Ombudsman deserved more solid protection.

When patrons become very predatory, they may cease to be perceived as patrons. Greed on a grand scale emerged as a modern aspect of Philippine politics especially in the Marcos period but also in other times. That change has extended the slow decay of traditional politics along patron–client lines. Dyadic clientelism becomes less feasible when networks become large. They depend on face-to-face contact between patrons and clients. When the former are respected as dominant by followers, rebellion is unthinkable and serving a faction is not perceived as corrupt by people who are inside the family-like group. But patronage in larger organizations can become non-personalistic. Networks of a modern type may command more resources simply because of their size, but

Action possibilities against corruption

Corruption in Philippine government contracting has been severe—reportedly up to half the cost of some projects during the Arroyo era. So President Arroyo invited Tony Kwok Man-wai, Head of Operations in the ICAC, Hong Kong's internationally admired Independent Commission Against Corruption, to visit the Philippines. Kwok made recommendations about ways for cutting corruption. Arroyo did not follow them.[112]

In May 2011, after PNoy's election, Kwok was invited back to the Philippines. He made a speech at the Ateneo de Manila, complaining that the Office of the Ombudsman "has no ammunition" because it cannot arrest suspects; the police do that if they wish. "Here it is a haven for corrupt officials. They know their bank accounts cannot be checked. They know their homes cannot be searched. Nobody will listen to their phone calls, except if they are President." He insisted that corruption is not cultural—or at least that Chinese culture in Hong Kong is as antithetical to controlling corruption as any Philippine tradition: "We love money and wealth creation, and the family to us is everything—but the secret is zero tolerance for corruption."[113]

Kwok suggested the appointment of a new post-Arroyo Ombudsman, as well as empowering responsible "integrity managers" in many agencies, a commitment by courts to conclude nine-tenths of corruption cases within 12 months, and better coordination between the Ombudsman, the Commission on Audit, and the Civil Service Commission. He said that this improved institutional framework could sharply reduce Philippine corruption within three years—as during the 1970s Hong Kong's ICAC had actually done.

The problem is that many elected politicians in a democracy do not mind corruption when they benefit from it. "Zero tolerance" may be easier for a small, high-income-per-person place such as Hong Kong, where mass elections do not generate the executive, than in the Philippines. Creation of the ICAC in 1974 was a British colonial regime's response to corruption (especially that of Englishman Peter Godber, HK Police Chief Superintendent, later convicted of bribery) that was especially embarrassing to foreigners who were trying to rule a Chinese city. ICAC officer Kwok's recommendations to reduce Philippine corruption came from a credible source, and his specific ideas could still be highly useful for Philippine reformers. In addition to reforms such as Kwok suggested and other institutional reforms such as tight auditing or reduction of politicians' "pork" funds, the long-term goal of lessening corruption almost surely will progress if the Philippines develops a more diversified and richer market economy.

Notes

1 Edna Co, Nepomuceno Malaluan, Artur Neame, Marlon Manuel, and Miguel Rafael V. Musngi, *Philippine Democracy Assessment: Rule of Law and Access to Justice* (Quezon City: Action for Economic Reforms, 2010), 13.
2 See Lynn White, "Changing Concepts of Corruption in Communist China: Early 1950s vs. Early 1980s," in *Changes and Continuities in Chinese Communism*, Yuming Shaw, ed. (Boulder, CO: Westview Press, 1988), 316–53, reprinted in *The Politics of Modern China*, Zheng Yongnian, Lu Yiyi, and Lynn White, eds. (London: Routledge, 2009).
3 Sometimes the groups' sizes are less important than their ethnicities. Occasionally, states that claim to represent large national groups may be accused of corruption because they seize resources that are perceived to have better uses in smaller groups. Neither of these two conditions is usual in the Philippines, where practically all perceptions of corruption attribute it to smaller groups and where the state is relatively weak and local leaders are powerful.
4 See Peter B. Evans, "Predatory, Developmental, and Other Apparatuses: A Comparative Political Economy Perspective on the Third World State," *Sociological Forum* 4:4 (1989), 561–87.
5 The current author recalls a job talk at Princeton, by an Americanist, in which the speaker assumed that only appointed (not elected) officials could properly be conceived as corrupt. That analysis was inadequate.
6 See Andrew Wedeman, "China's War on Corruption," in *Preventing Corruption in Asia*, Ting Gong and Stephen K. Ma, eds. (New York: Routledge, 2009), 15–29.
7 Quoted in Patricio N. Abinales and Donna J. Amoroso, *State and Society in the Philippines* (Lanham, MD: Rowman & Littlefield, 2005), 177.
8 Quoted in Nathan Gilbert Quimpo, "The Presidency, Political Parties, and Predatory Politics in the Philippines," in *The Politics of Change in the Philippines*, Yuko Kasuya and Nathan Gilbert Quimpo, eds. (Pasig City: Anvil, 2010), 65.
9 Alfred W. McCoy, *Policing America's Empire: The United States, the Philippines, and the Rise of the Surveillance State* (Madison, WI: University of Wisconsin Press, 2009), 349–71.
10 *Jueteng*, pronounced rather like its *pinyin* spelling *Huateng*, is derived from Chinese for "flower bet."
11 Susan Rose-Ackerman, *Corruption in Government: Causes, Consequences, and Reform* (Cambridge: Cambridge University Press, 1999).
12 J.G. Lambsdorff, "Corruption in Comparative Perception [sic]," in *Economics of Corruption*, A.K. Jain, ed. (Boston, MA: Kluwer, 1998) 80–93.
13 Filipino-Chinese and their rich associates elsewhere in the diaspora may be more distrusted than other Filipino investors are. A corollary is that part of China's own high growth in recent decades probably results from the ethnic Chinese origin the "foreign" capital inflow, most of which has been from Hong Kong or Taiwan.
14 Benjamin Nelson, *The Idea of Usury: From Tribal Brotherhood to Universal Otherhood*, No. 3, "History of Ideas" Series (Princeton, NJ: Princeton University Press, 1953).
15 Albay's capital is named after the Spanish *conquistador* Legazpi, and it is dominated by the (active and very beautiful) stratovolcano, Mt. Mayon. For once, see http://en.wikipedia.org/wiki/Mayon_Volcano. Jess Diaz, "Lagman: 'Pork' Not Graft-Ridden," *Philippine Star*, June 29, 2013, www.philstar.com/headlines/2013/06/29/959556.
16 See quotation in Chapter 3, above, from Edmund Burke, *Reflections on the Revolution in France* (seen at Bartleby.com).
17 David L. Szanton, *Estancia in Transition: Economic Growth in a Rural Philippine Community* (Quezon City: Ateneo de Manila University, 1971), 125–6.

18. David L. Szanton, *Estancia in Transition: Economic Growth in a Rural Philippine Community* (Quezon City: Ateneo de Manila University, 1971), 125–26.
19. Benedict J. Tria Kerkvliet, "Contested Meanings of Elections in the Philippines," in *The Politics of Elections in Southeast Asia*, R.H. Taylor, ed. (New York: Cambridge University Press; and Washington, DC: Woodrow Wilson Center, 1996), 142.
20. This refers to Thaksin Shinawatra. Lucy Ash, "Seeing Red in Rural Thailand," *Crossing Continents: Thailand*, BBC Radio 4 (BBC News), heard April 23, 2009. Comparators to Marcos arguably include politicians as varied as Thaksin, Hitler, Bo Xilai, perhaps Andrew Jackson, and others. They expand polities to include new groups, their platforms are very patriotic, they strenuously attack corruption among their rivals only, they discriminate (or worse) against minorities, they show scant restraint against using state violence, and their human rights records are abysmal.
21. This is the title of his article for the *Philippine Daily Inquirer*, September 3, 2011.
22. Bruce Gilley, *States and Legitimacy: The Politics of Moral Authority* (Ph.D. dissertation, Politics Department, Princeton University, January 2007), 69.
23. Linda Luz Guerrero, ed., *The 2006–2007 SWS Surveys of Enterprises on Corruption* (Quezon City: Social Weather Stations, 2007), 5–8. It is possible that if the respondents had been civil servants rather than managers, more than 14 percent might have reported "a lot" of corruption in the private sector—but probably not many more.
24. Ibid.
25. Philippine Center for Investigative Journalism, "Representatives Scramble for Power, Peso, and Privileges," July 26–27, 2004, www.pcij.org/stories/2004/house2.html.
26. Yvonne Chua and Booma B. Cruz, "Legislators Feed on Pork," Philippine Center for Investigative Journalism website, September 6–7, 2004, www.pcij.org/stories/2004/pork2.html.
27. Yvonne Chua, "An Expensive—and Unaccountable—Legislature," Philippine Center for Investigative Journalism website, March 22–24, 2004, www.pcij.org/stories/2004/congress2.html. See also Philippine Center for Investigative Journalism and Institute for Popular Democracy, *Pork and Other Perks: Corruption and Governance in the Philippines* (Quezon City: Philippine Center for Investigative Journalism, 1998).
28. Philippine Center for Investigative Journalism website, "Representatives Scramble for Power, Peso, and Privileges," July 26–27, 2004.
29. Philippine Center for Investigative Journalism website, "De Venecia's Reign is Challenged," July 26–27, 2004.
30. Yvonne Chua, "An Expensive—and Unaccountable—Legislature."
31. Ibid. In various quotations of this book, when short Tagalog sentences or phrases are translated in brackets among English sentences, the speakers originally used English for most of their expression but switched temporarily into Pilipino/Tagalog. (This easy alternation is a frequent linguistic phenomenon in many parts of the world, including the Philippines.)
32. At that time, when about 50 pesos (more than usual) bought a dollar, this amounted to about US$20,000 per senator or $10,000 per representative monthly.
33. Yvonne Chua, "Fat Salaries, Big Allowances, and Other Perks of Lawmaking," Philippine Center for Investigative Journalism website, March 22–24, 2004, www.pcij.org/stories/2004/congress3.html.
34. Philippine Constitution (1987), Art. VI, Sec. 28.
35. See http://en.wikipedia.org/wiki/Jose_de_Venecia,jr.
36. *Manila Bulletin*, August 11, 2010, 1 and 4.
37. Kent Eaton, *Politicians the Economic Reform in New Democracies: Argentina and the Philippines in the 1990s* (University Park, PA: Pennsylvania State University Press, 2002), 113.
38. Jess Diaz, "PNoy Hikes Congressional Pork to P27 B," *Philippine Star*, July 25, 2013, www.philstar.com/headlines/2013/07/25/1009451.

39 Camille Diola, "Palace Defends PNoy's 'Pork,'" *Philippine Star*, July 16, 2013, www.philstar.com/headlines/2013/07/16/977411.
40 Marvin Sy, "Recto Lauds Innovation in 2014 Budget," *Philippine Star*, July 28, 2013, www.philstar.com/headlines/2013/08/28/1022121.
41 *SWS 2012 Survey of Enterprises on Corruption*, www.sws.org.ph/pr20120918.html.
42 Edu Punay, "Witness to Get Protection; Probe vs Fake NGOs Sought," *Philippine Star*, July 16, 2013, www.philstar.com/headlines/2013/07/16/975401.
43 Leonard D. Postrado, "De Lima Clears Three Solons, DA [Department of Agriculture] Chief in Pork Scam," August 2, 2013, *Manila Bulletin* http://mb.com.ph/News/Main_News/25148/.
44 Paolo Romero, "Belmonte Vows Tighter Regulation of 'Pork,'" *Philippine Star*, July 23, 2013, www.philstar.com/headlines/2013/07/23/1002291.
45 The pork money that the refuseniks rejected had still been appropriated for "development," so that it may have reverted to the Speaker Belmonte's own control. Anon., "SB, Lawmakers don't use PDAF if you Oppose It," *Philippine Star*, August 2, 2013, www.philstar.com/headlines/2013/08/02/1041651.
46 Jess Diaz, "Militant Lawmakers Give Up P1.5 B," *Philippine Star*, August 6, 2013, www.philstar.com/headlines/2013/08/06/1057011.
47 Yvonne Chua and Booma B. Cruz, "Pork is a Political, not a Developmental, Tool," Philippine Center for Investigative Journalism website, September 6–7, 2004, www.pcij.org/stories/2004/pork.html.
48 The president's line-item veto is in the Constitution (Art. VI, Sec. 27[2]), which must supersede the 1991 law, even though local elected officials are now used to receiving two-fifths of the national revenues.
49 Genalyn D. Kabiling, "'Pork' is Good—Aquino," *Manila Bulletin*, August 3, 2013, http://mb.com.ph/News/Main_News/25302.
50 Other constitutions, such as that of the U.S. in amendments 9 and 10, also have localist aspects. Federations are all somewhat regionalist. Few if any other systems, however, give district representatives as much individual statutory power over public money as Philippine members of Congress and local officials have.
51 Ricardo G. Abad, *Aspects of Social Capital in the Philippines: Findings from a National Survey* (Quezon City: Social Weather Stations, 2006), 65.
52 "Net sincerity" in fighting corruption was measured by the percentage of managers assessing these agencies as being "very/somewhat sincere" minus the percentage calling them "very/somewhat insincere." Linda Luz Guerrero, ed., *The 2006–2007 SWS Surveys of Enterprises on Corruption*, 12–13.
53 Raymund F. Antonio, "Customs Men Protest PNoy's 'Sweeping' Corruption Raps," *Manila Bulletin*, August 2, 2013, http://mb.com.ph/News/Main_News/25149/.
54 Evelyn Macairan, "45 of 54 Customs Officials Relinquish Posts," *Philippine Star*, July 30, 2013, www.philstar.com/headlines/2013/07/30/1029001.
55 See www.sws.org.ph/index_pr20121029.htm.
56 Alexis Romero, "PNP Most Corrupt Agency—Survey," *Philippine Star*, July 11, 2013, www.philstar.com/headlines/2013/07/11/964084.
57 Robert Klitgaard, *Controlling Corruption* (Berkeley, CA: University of California Press, 1988), 52–62.
58 Quoted in Mina Roces, *The Lopez Family, 1946–2000: Kinship Politics in Postwar Philippines* (Manila: De La Salle University Press, 2001), 240.
59 Ibid., 244.
60 Benedict J. Tria Kerkvliet, "Contested Meanings of Elections in the Philippines," 161.
61 The runner-up was Santiago, with less than 20 percent of the vote. No fewer than five presidential candidates (Santiago, Eduardo Cojuangco, Jr., Ramon Mitra, Jr., Imelda Marcos, and Jovito Salonga) each got between 10 and 20 percent in the 1992 election. This was a fragmented political elite—but the voter turnout, 76 percent, was high.

204   *Corruption*

62   From www.electionline98.com.ph; but later the website was apparently closed. Bibliographical purism sometimes mixes badly with money politics, because the latter is more serious.
63   Mina Roces, *The Lopez Family*, 252–3.
64   Patricio N. Abinales and Donna J. Amoroso, *State and Society in the Philippines*, 275.
65   Thomas Fuller, "Megawati and Arroyo Pledge Mutual Assistance," www.nytimes.com/2001/08/22/news/22iht-mega_ed3_.html.
66   "Transparency Group to Check vs. Corruption—Arroyo," *Nation*, www.gmanews.tv, February 19, 2008.
67   "Pinaswatcher6," "China Used ETZ to Buy Arroyo Influence," www.youtube.com/watch?v=re964P4a32k and Jess Diaz, "Jose De Venecia to Reveal Inside Dealings of Gloria Arroyo," *Philippine Star*, May 20, 2013, www.philstar.com/headlines/2012/05/20 and www.youtube.com/watch?v=whNFGnia6Bo for video.
68   Interview with Francisco Nemenzo, a senior and exceptionally cogent political scientist—and former President of the University of the Philippines.
69   Linda Luz Guerrero, ed., *The 2006–2007 SWS Surveys of Enterprises on Corruption*, 12–13.
70   Anon., "BIR Sets Revamp," *Manila Bulletin*, December 8, 2010, www.mb.com.ph.
71   "Corruption Arrest for Philippine Ex-President," *Sydney Morning Herald*, November 19, 2011, www.smh.com.au.
72   Edu Punay, "SC Dismisses GMA Appeal," *Philippine Star*, July 24, 2013, www.philstar.com/headlines/2013/07/24/1006041.
73   Greg Bankoff, "Profiting from Disasters: Corruption, Hazard, and Society in the Philippines," in *Corruption and Good Governance in Asia*, Nicholas Tarling, ed. (London: Routledge, 2005), 176.
74   Ibid., 177.
75   China was reportedly perceived as less corrupt, although it is especially unclear whether perception reports can be used for comparisons between tightly and loosely monitored polities. Greg Bankoff, "Profiting from Disasters," 170.
76   The Corruption Perceptions Index attempts to measure public sector "abuse of entrusted power for private gain." Perceptions of businesses and individuals are surveyed, because direct observation of many hidden corruptions is impossible. See www.transparency.org/policy_research/surveys_indices/cpi/2010/results.
77   Rupert Hodder, *Emotional Bureaucracy* (New Brunswick: Transaction Publishers, 2011), 123 and 118, interview with a Senate source who preserved anonymity.
78   The Hong Kong Civil Service's reputation for punctiliousness, especially in finance, makes comparisons with the Philippine situation difficult. This is just to say, however, that the ICAC has been generally effective.
79   This Ombudsman estimate, accepted by the World Bank, is quoted from Nathan Gilbert Quimpo, *Contested Democracy and the Left in the Philippines* (New Haven, CT: Southeast Asia Council, Yale University, 2008), 49; the specific numbers refer to the 1977–97 period.
80   Robert Klitgaard, *Controlling Corruption*, 19–20.
81   Linda Luz Guerrero, ed., *The 2006–2007 SWS Surveys of Enterprises on Corruption*, 11 (and for earlier quotation, 10).
82   Anon., "Democracy as Showbiz," *Economist*, July 1, 2004, www.economist.com/printerfriendly.cfm?story_ID=2876966.
83   Jess Diaz, "BIR's Income Tax Drive Targets 1.5M Professionals," *Philippine Star*, August 8, 2013, www.philstar.com/headlines/2013/08/13/1064641.
84   Quoted in Patricio N. Abinales and Donna J. Amoroso, *State and Society in the Philippines*, 251, from estimates by Sicat and Abdula.
85   Quoted in Greg Bankoff, "Profiting from Disasters: Corruption, Hazard, and Society in the Philippines," in *Corruption and Good Governance in Asia*, Nicholas Tarling,

Corruption 205

ed. (London: Routledge, 2005), 168–9. These losses, estimated at the turn of the millennium, applied to the previous dozen years.
86 Yvonne Chua and Booma B. Cruz, "Legislators Feed on Pork."
87 Michael Punongbayan, "Local Execs Face Empty Coffers," *Philippine Star*, August 5, 2013, www.philstar.com/headlines/2013/08/05/1053461.
88 "Who Really Killed General Angelo Reyes?" unsigned editorial, www.philnews.com/2011/04a.htm.
89 Camille Diola, "Ex-PNP Chief Razon, 32 Others Face Graft for Armored Vehicles Scam," *Philippine Star*, July 12, 2013, www.philstar.com/headlines/2013/07/12/964655.
90 Camille Viola, "Enraged De Lima to Cop: Name NBI Agent Involved with Drug Lords," *Philippine Star*, July 25, 2013, www.philstar.com/headlines/2013/07/25/1011861.
91 Miriam Santiago, "DILG plus PNP equals Jueteng," http://antipinoy.com. Miriam Defensor was born into a *trapo* family from Iloilo, but she trained as a lawyer and serves concurrently as a judge of the International Criminal Court and a senator. Corazon Aquino appointed her to clean up corruption as Commissioner of Immigration and Deportation (a department whose cadres had profited from making fake passports), and she has done other prosecutorial jobs. She has said, "I eat death threats for breakfast."
92 James Clad, *Behind the Myth: Business, Money, and Power in Southeast Asia* (London: Hyman, 1989), 33.
93 Kusaka Wataru, "Governing Informalities of the Urban Poor: Street Vendors and Social Order Making in Metro Manila," in *The Politics of Change in the Philippines*, Yuko Kasuya and Nathan Gilbert Quimpo, eds. (Pasig City: Anvil, 2010), 362–90.
94 Compare Justin V. Hastings, "Strategic Hypocrisy: Sovereignty, Commerce, and Security in Archipelagic Southeast Asia," in *Democratization in China, Korea, and Southeast Asia? Local and National Perspectives*, Kate Zhou, Shelley Rigger, and Lynn White, eds. (Abingdon: Routledge, 2014), ch. 4.
95 See Rupert Hodder, *Emotional Bureaucracy*, 146.
96 Ibid., 214, also 2.
97 Aymo Brunetti and Beatrice Wede, "A Free Press is Bad News for Corruption," *Journal of Public Economics* 87:7–8 (2003), 1801–24.
98 "Watch What You Write: One Way to Deal with Irritating Reporters," *Economist*, June 18, 2005, 39.
99 Chay Florintino-Hofileña, *News for Sale: The Corruption of the Philippine Media* (Quezon City: Philippine Center for Investigative Journalism and Center for Media Freedom and Responsibility, 1998), xiv.
100 Ibid., 15–16.
101 Cynthia D. Balana, "Despite Aquino Snub, FOI will be Pushed, Lawmaker Vows," *Philippine Daily Inquirer*, July 25, 2012.
102 Cecilio T. Arillo, *Greed & Betrayal: The Sequel to the 1985 EDSA Revolution* (Makati: CTA Research, 2000), 32–3.
103 Rupert Hodder, *Emotional Bureaucracy*, 56.
104 Caroline J. Howard, "Noynoy Urged: Appoint Good People, Form Independent Anti-Graft Body," *ABS-CBN News*, June 12, 2010.
105 Robert Klitgaard, *Controlling Corruption*, 188.
106 Interview with a member of the Philippine Congress.
107 See www.gov.ph/2010/07/30/Executive-Order-No-1.
108 Christian V. Esguerra and Gil C. Cabacungan, Jr., "Arroyo Loses Immunity from Suit," *Philippine Inquirer*, June 30, 2010, http://newsinfo.inquirer.net/inquirerheadlines/nation/view/20100701-278526/Arroyo-loses-immunity-from-suit.
109 Delon Porcalla, "Palace Fine-Tunes EO on Anti-Corruption Body," *Philippine Star*, July 1, 2013, www.philstar.com/headlines/2013/07/01/960213.

110 Delon Porcalla, "Palace keeps Distance from Miriam, Ping Word War," *Philippine Star*, July 18, 2013, www.philstar.com/headlines/2013/07/18/983281. The United States has made donations to the Philippines, through its Millennium Challenge Fund, for three purposes: improving tax collection, paving roads, and strengthening the Ombudsman's office.
111 Michael Punongbayan, "Morales to Ride a P2.5-M Bullet-Proof Vehicle," *Philippine Star*, June 27, 2013, www.philstar.com/headlines/2013/06/27/958727.
112 Interview in Manila, August 2010.
113 See www.jimwes.com/integrity/id58.html.

10 PNoy, "Pacquiaos," and Philippine progress

Most national policies, to the extent the Philippine central government produces them, have been based on the personal preferences of the president. This is especially true during the honeymoon of popularity that normally follows presidential elections. After that, unless the president remains popularly legitimate for an extended period (as PNoy did and Arroyo did not, as attested by surveys), the Philippine political system creates scant coherent policy on any subject. Congress has more difficulty passing bills, and lame-duck presidents become most concerned to avoid losing their political allies. From the viewpoints of most Filipinos, the personal policies of local leaders toward them are more important than the policies of the president.

Once a national chief executive becomes vulnerable, especially if coups or corruptions weaken the Malacañang resident, politics shifts from policymaking to quarrels among rivals preparing for the next elections. At this stage, rumors abound that the incumbent president wants to amend the constitution to allow a longer term. This late period of policy stasis has, under many presidents, lasted longer than the earlier period of policymaking. Similar dynamics have also been evident in other democracies; they apply strongly in the Philippines.

This pattern is not just recent; it has pertained for decades. Presidents' programs have not been surely predictable on partisan bases. Top politicians' policies have varied even when they were nominally in the same party. Nacionalista President Garcia, for example, had programs quite unlike those of his predecessor Magsaysay. Liberals Quirino and Macapagal had different policies in many areas.[1] Often there was variance within a single presidential term; Cory Aquino followed a "honeymoon" of reformism with policy retrenchments under threats of *kudeta*. Ramos was a partial exception; he was able to extend his policymaking period longer than most (in part because military officers refrained from attempting *kudeta* against a former general). Arroyo inherited the office from Estrada, but neither of these managed to have notable honeymoons after their elections. PNoy's strength lasted longer than that of most, even though old structures of power still constrained him greatly. As in other presidential democracies, some Philippine chief executives simply have had few public plans. In such cases, even less happened.

Presidents Corazon Aquino, Fidel Ramos, and Joseph Estrada all began their terms with roughly 60 percent "net satisfaction ratings" (i.e., portions of surveyed respondents satisfied, minus portions dissatisfied). All three saw precipitous declines in popular net satisfaction during their terms. Cory Aquino and Erap Estrada ended with net ratings barely above 0 percent, although Ramos ended with 20 percent. President Arroyo began her period at that low net level, when she succeeded Estrada constitutionally upon the latter's (unconstitutional) ouster. Her net rating was never more than 35 percent, was about 0 percent at the time of her close election, and was negative in her post-election term.[2] PNoy was extremely popular at the time of his election, and his net rating remained high for a relatively lengthy time thereafter. But political honeymoons in the Philippines have seldom lasted so long. National surveys also do not capture geographical variation in satisfaction ratings—although former presidents' regional successes in elections (e.g., Estrada's 2013 Manila mayoralty, or Arroyo's 2010 Pampanga seat in the House) are yet another indication that the national polity is not homogeneous.

Hopes for policy

Eaton contrasts "a candidate-centered electoral system (the Philippines) and a party-centered electoral system (Argentina)." "Legislators in the lower Philippine house face some of the most particularistic incentives anywhere in the world."[3] Government-led reforms have had limited success, except to some extent under Marcos, Ramos, and PNoy. Some chief executives such as Ramos were able to make reforms because the Philippine Constitution gives the presidency so much control over central government money. A president can in practice shift money between different authorized uses and can withhold funds from some uses. Yet even Ramos could not persuade his Congress to have tax reforms for simpler rates, a broader tax base, fewer deductions, and a more efficient value-added tax.

The reputation of a president's lineage may help raise his or her general credibility. For example, PNoy had a distinguished *trapo* background. His great-grandfather Servillano Aquino participated in the 1898 Malolos Congress that declared the first independent Philippine republic. His grandfather Benigno, Sr. ("Igno"), was Speaker of the House in 1943–44, albeit under the Japanese. After the assassination of his father Benigno, Jr. ("Ninoy"), his mother Corazon was elected president in 1986. This is a suitable ancestry, to say the least. But a few months before the 2010 elections, a national survey of Philippine voters still showed that Noynoy Aquino was not among the three most likely winners.[4] Then his mother died; yellow campaign banners flew, and the sympathy vote was enormous. Other forms of fame, including professional prowess in fields that range from broadcasting to boxing, may well later displace some of the trust that Filipino voters show to politicians with familiar last names.

PNoy won the 2010 presidential election convincingly with 42 percent of the vote in a nine-candidate field. However, the vice-presidential candidate of PNoy's Liberal Party was defeated. Only three of the 12 elected senators were

Liberals. The other senators elected then were actually independent of any "party" control; they included sons of deposed presidents Marcos and Estrada. Only a quarter of winners for House seats were Liberals. Half were, at the time of the election, still formally in the party of PNoy's archenemy, Gloria M. Arroyo—although House representatives' need for funds under presidential control made many soon switch, "crossing the aisle" and declaring new allegiance, becoming Liberals.[5]

PNoy's presidency may be classified as reformist, and it was more effective for actual reforms than his mother's had been, although some of the reasons may lie in recent socioeconomic progress rather than in PNoy's policies. Both Aquinos came into office with indistinct positive goals but with a clear negative aim: to destroy the political legacy of their predecessors, Marcos and Arroyo. Corazon Aquino had an agenda

> characterized by a case-to-case brinkmanship game of walking the tightrope to please competing interests within the coalition. This eventually became 'standard procedure' through her term and exposed the tragedy of being caught at, or trying to hold on to, the dead center of the political spectrum.[6]

But both presidents Aquino had "easy acts to follow." PNoy benefitted from economic growth in the 2000s and from decreased threats of *kudeta* on his policies, which nonetheless were never radical. He avoided the most crucial local issue, a potential land reform that might change the ownership of fields.

PNoy campaigned as an egalitarian. For example, it had been common for high politicians, trying to get through Manila's traffic jams, to ride in official cars with revolving lights and sirens (called "*wangwang*"). PNoy announced that he would not use *wangwang*, proclaiming that, "None is above others." No state president could with ease trump the local policies that decreasingly dominate the Philippines, but gradual socioeconomic change made mildly reformist policies more viable in PNoy's time than they had earlier been.

Economic stagnancy, such as the Philippines suffered for the last four decades of the previous millennium, was often associated either with insufficient investment or else with insufficient consumption. The Philippines until recently had both problems. The difficulty was not an inappropriate balance between them; it was a dearth of both consumers buying and investors saving. To raise consumption, and also to raise his new administration's popularity, PNoy wanted to increase the portion of the state budget (from five billion to 30 billion pesos annually) that was allocated for the poorest Filipinos. This effort was to be coordinated by the Department of Social Welfare, with help from the departments of Health and Education. Building classrooms, clinics, and hospitals was prioritized. These public contracts were corruptible, even though they also were designed to help millions of citizen voters.

The new president vowed to fight tax fraud and corruption. The largest tax evader in the country was reportedly Lucio Tan, who had enterprises in many fields ranging from cigarettes to the Philippine Airlines. Tan had offered a contribution to PNoy's presidential campaign, but this was turned down. Largely to weaken Tan, PNoy advocated an "open skies" policy, allowing more competition among airlines. He also proposed "rationalization" of cigarette taxes that were expected to net 20 to 30 billion pesos yearly for the public treasury. PNoy and his friends clearly hoped that Tan would become a more publicized example of excessive greed, and that punishing him would discourage others like him.[7]

Dedication to popular causes does not necessarily mean dedication to all kinds of law. PNoy amnestied Antonio "Sonny" Trillanes IV, who had been arrested after the Oakwood Mutiny for breaking the law against coups, because of their mutual disgust with former president Arroyo. Trillanes had been elected to the Senate in 2007 while in jail, and he could not legally be freed from prison until that legislative body ratified PNoy's amnesty decision.[8] This eventually was agreed, and "Sonny" Trillanes returned to make passionate patriotic speeches, filing many bills and conducting active constituency work that ranged from his election as president of the national Table Tennis Association to praise of fellow Bicolanos who won beauty queen contests. Trillanes is a formidable *malakas* politician, both within and without the bounds of the Philippine Constitution. His liberalism is less obvious than his patriotism or electability. Such figures could become more important than less zesty reformers in future Philippine politics.

PNoy's most crucial ministerial appointments were tough-minded. His choice of Leila de Lima as Justice Minister was an example. To the Department of Interior and Local Government, PNoy appointed Jesse Robredo, an advocate of increasing the independent centralized capacity of the Philippine National Police. That might have reduced local barons' control of local violence; but this issue was sensitive to many members of Congress, and PNoy had to prioritize his policy agenda. If he pressed too quickly for too much police centralization, he would face more congressional resistance on the rest of his legislative agenda.[9]

PNoy came into office as head of a structurally weak government. He appointed reformists to several important ministries, including Finance as well as Justice and Interior. But his need to deal with Congress made his own predilections harder to discern. As journalist Maria Ressa wrote, PNoy's "early political compromises are exacerbating problems in the weak institutions he has promised to reform." He could not easily reduce his ties to the relatively traditionalist "Samar faction," named after the street where his campaign headquarters was located, and including figures such as Defense Secretary Gazmin who had also served during Cory Aquino's presidency. But PNoy also appointed younger and more reformist professionals from the "Balay faction," who were particularly intent on punishing corruptions that had occurred during the Arroyo presidency.[10] These two different types of Liberals, Samar or Balay, both constrained the president; he tried to balance them, while also balancing broader groups of reformers and *trapos* in Congress.

Shortly after PNoy's election, 85 percent of Filipinos were reliably surveyed to trust him. Only 2 percent did not.[11] Later surveys showed that high percentages of adult Filipinos remained satisfied with PNoy's government (68 percent in September 2011, 62 percent in June 2011, 72 percent in December 2012).

Rates of dissatisfaction ranged in his first year between 12 and 17 percent only. So rates of "net satisfaction" (i.e., percentages approving minus those disapproving) were high—albeit slightly less in Metro Manila than in other parts of the archipelago. The independent Social Weather Stations, which conducts such surveys regularly, also asked Filipinos whether it is "too early to judge the success or failure of PNoy"—and in mid-2011, more than two-thirds sensibly responded that it was indeed too early.[12]

When the 2011 polls asked for ratings on various specific policy issues, the government was perceived to be doing well (though no better than its general performance) on "improving the quality of children's education" and "helping the poor." Its reputation was lower for "telling the truth" and "fighting terrorism," lower yet (at a net satisfaction of 27 percent) for "eradicating graft and corruption"—and just 9 percent for "fighting inflation." Differences of income level or geographic region created no big differences in these ratings.[13]

Net satisfaction with very local governments as a group was generally low. (This was like the situation in many other countries such as China, where top leaders in the capital are surveyed to be more legitimate than local leaders, especially those who run the police.) The lowest net scores were given for Philippine local officials' tepid efforts to "eradicate graft and corruption." Respondents in 2011 perceived some reduction of graft in Luzon outside Manila, a lesser reduction in the Visayas, but an increase in Mindanao.[14]

PNoy was popular, and late-2012 surveys showed positive net satisfaction ratings also for Vice-President Binay, Senate President Enrile, Speaker Belmonte, and Chief Justice Sereno. All of these (except the Chief Justice) had received even higher average kudos in previous quarterly surveys, but popular confidence in central government institutions remained positive.[15] It is likely that the improving economy was a major reason.

What was causing this growth, and what was holding it back?

Wages and births, economy and theology

Poverty in the Philippines documentably correlates with family size. Social Weather Stations head Mahar Mangahas found on the basis of extensive polls that,

> Families suffering from economic deprivation are generally larger than other families.... To the complaisant stance that 'with every mouth, God also creates a pair of hands,' the counter-argument continues to be that it takes many years before those hands are able to feed that mouth.[16]

Frank Lynch, S.J., one of the sharpest social scientists of the Philippines, as early as 1972 expressed his hope that,

> the Church may soon speak more directly to her members, telling them in clear and certain terms, in pulpit and publications, on TV and radio, that the

folk or folk-Catholic belief that one should place no control on family size or child spacing is opposed to the Church's official position on the responsibility parents have toward their children.

This Jesuit spoke against "the false morality of those who extol large families and abandonment to Divine Providence as prima facie evidence of supreme virtue. We priests and our bishops have barely begun to fight."[17] More concretely, Lynch's statistical research showed that the plenteous supply of labor was a crucial factor that kept Philippine workers' pay low.[18] He subjected many such factors to empirical tests, and the only other (among eight variables) that he found to be important was incompetence among enterprise managers. He found that landholders' greed and five other factors were less important in preserving Philippine poverty than was oversupplied labor.

Surveys of women have long shown that many Filipinas would like to stop having children.[19] But men and women have an "elective affinity," they get married, and children may be born. The Catholic Church (unlike the Iglesia ng Christo and some Protestant sects) has resisted family planning, despite the documentable wage-lowering effects of high birth rates. The bishops say "sanctity of life" first principles (as they define these) should prevail over principles derived from empirically proven results.[20] Some Catholics and others, however, see tensions between that choice and the Catholic social doctrine that the poor (about whom Jesus had good words) must be helped.[21] The Bishops Conference of the Philippines has actively opposed linkage of favoritism for the disadvantaged with birth planning, regardless of Christ's clear teachings about "the least of these" who need help.[22] The current Philippine population is over 100 million, and the growth rate, if it remains high, suggests that the country will have about twice as many people by the early 2030s. The bishops have thus far declined to worry about the impoverishing effects of a phenomenon that economists at the Asian Development Bank report in simple terms: "Labor supply is outstripping labor demand."[23]

The Philippines, like most other nations that emerged from former Iberian empires, has had a few clerics interested in liberation theology. One of them, Romeo J. Intengan, S.J., wrote that, "Christian faith is a person's free and wholehearted acceptance of God's self-revelation as mankind's liberator in Jesus Christ."[24] So a believer who wants to imitate Christ will try to free others. This idea is powerful in its simplicity. It has not always meshed as well with the views of most church hierarchs as it does with the widely perceived need to raise Philippine incomes. It is still unclear whether Pope Francis is able or willing to change this situation. Like a reformist Philippine president, his office may be weaker than it seems because of inertia in the structure he is supposed to lead.

Filipinos are 83 percent Roman Catholic, 8 percent Protestant (including the Philippine Independent Church),[25] 2 percent Iglesia ng Kristo,[26] and reportedly 2 percent animist. "Folk Catholicism," mixing pre-Spanish with Christian symbols, is widespread among the Catholic majority. A rosary or sacred book may be deemed an amulet (*anting-anting*), effective for protecting the believer from dangers. Politicians tend to be more successful if they are seen to attend church and to respect prelates.[27] But most Filipinos, when surveyed, deem family planning a personal choice in which the state should not interfere.[28]

A Reproductive Health Bill was mooted regularly in the Philippine Congress for many years, but the Catholic Bishops' Conference always opposed it.[29] Art. II, Sec. 12 of the 1987 Constitution (drafted by a committee that included a bishop) provides that, "The State ... shall equally protect the life of the mother and the life of the unborn from conception." The Department of Health estimated that in one year, 400,000 illegal abortions were performed in the Philippines—and that 12 percent of maternal deaths were caused by unsafe abortions.[30]

The Reproductive Health Bill staggered through House committees in 2011. PNoy at first avoided controversy. He said, "I'm a Catholic; I'm not promoting it. My position is more aptly called 'responsible parenthood' rather than 'reproductive health.'"[31] But by 2012, the renamed "Responsible Parenthood and Reproductive Health Bill" passed Congress—despite a "Prayer Power Rally" on EDSA organized by the Bishops' Conference, whose head had suggested that PNoy might be excommunicated if he signed the bill—as he did (and as the bishops did not, despite their warning).

Catholic bishops gave PNoy a "failing mark" in 2013 "on matters of justice which deeply touch the lives of the poor," although they did not present evidence to disprove Father Lynch's showing that the high birth rate creates poverty by keeping wages low. The incoming president of the Catholic Bishops' Conference, whose organization had lobbied against the health and parenthood bill, claimed that,

> The Church is not a lobby group, the Church is not an NGO ... the Church is not a political group.... We are not against any political party. We are against anyone who would destroy the stability, the solidity, the integrity, the sanctity of the family.[32]

The bishop was pleased that the Supreme Court had suspended implementation of the law to explore its constitutionality. But he warned that no matter how the justices might decide, the bishops would not change. Soon, however, the new Pope Francis was telling his flock to pay more attention to women's dignity and the problem of poverty. Perhaps even the Philippine bishops may in the future expand their social vision. However this turns out, the new health-and-economics law was a case in which many individuals (especially women) asserted themselves enough to govern, acting from both global and local sizes of polity.

Local confidence vs. national confidence

Some scholars suggest that a state must be enmeshed in "society" in order to be strong. In the Philippines, however, a very political "society" has embedded the state, and the national top elites have often been divided locally. Doubts about identity inspire frenzy that can be anti-foreign or can occasionally even seem anti-national. This country's most credible hero, Rizal, was also its most trenchant critic.[33] Rupert Hodder psychologizes about a "chronic self-doubt" among Filipino thinkers,

> rooted in part with the lack of closure on so many questions surrounding political leaders from Rizal to Bonifacio and Aguinaldo at the birth of the country, to the [U.S. collaborator] Roxas and [Japanese collaborator] Laurel families during World War II, and to Marcos, Ninoy Aquino, Cory Aquino, Ramos and Estrada.[34]

One of every five Filipinos has wanted to emigrate, according to surveys.[35]

> Jokes about the long lines for visas at the U.S. Embassy, about hiring former Singapore prime minister Lee Kwan Yew to run the Philippines, and about the likely overwhelming victory of a referendum making the Philippines the fifty-first state are legion.[36]

Marcos railed against the islands' "old oligarchy," wanting to replace it with a "new society" (which began to resemble a new monopoly instead). He tried to justify his dictatorship by claiming to fix "What went wrong?" in the Philippines.[37]

PNoy, who had grown up partly in the U.S. during his father's forced exile, asked frank questions in his 2010 presidential inauguration speech:

> In moments when I thought only of my own welfare, I also wondered: is it possible that I can find the peace and quiet that I crave in another country? Is our governnment beyond redemption? Has it been written that the Filipino's lot is to suffer?[38]

The new president's answer to the question was naturally and appropriately negative—but he raised the question.

When respondents in Manila were asked to associate a Tagalog word with the cognate *demokrasya*, the overwhelming response was *kalayaan*, meaning "independence" or "freedom." Filipino poor people want a "class politics of dignity," in which rulers may be rich but should also be respectful.[39] Philippine democracy delivers the dignity of voting, but not much else.

As PNoy's term progressed, the Philippine public still trusted him despite continuing perceptions of elite corruption and mass poverty. The economic uptick was good news, but it did not soon help the poor. The basic problem was not PNoy's. A less progressive and more demagogic president (such as Philippine voters are likely to elect in at least some future terms) might have helped most Filipinos less. The structure of informal politics is crucial, and the strength of local polities still limits what any leader of this national administration can do.

The Philippine state is generally seen by citizens to be legitimate in normative terms, but ineffective for security or development. These two views are in practical tension with each other. Democratic institutions raise expectations of what the government should deliver, but they do not ensure fulfillment of these hopes.[40] Democracy after PNoy's election was nonetheless seen by more Filipinos as working in their interest, and a March 2103 survey found a record-high 74 percent of the people saying they were satisfied with the current performance of the country's democracy. This portion was up from 65 percent one year earlier. It exceeded the previous records of 70 percent in September 1992 and July 1998. Six-tenths of the people claimed that "democracy is always preferable to any other kind of government," although two-tenths said, "under some circumstances, an authoritarian government can be preferable to a democratic one."[41]

The demagogue danger

What determines the likelihood of a new elected dictator (e.g., a "new" Marcos)? Democracies have sometimes gone out of style for either domestic or international reasons.[42] The overthrow of liberal regimes has been frequent in developing countries, including those with previous periods of democratic politics; so this possibility for the Philippines cannot be dismissed. It has happened before, in 1972–86, although the Marcos experience may provide some limited immunity to recurrence. Brazil, Chile, Argentina, Peru, Uruguay, and many smaller Latin American and African countries have seen their democratic regimes end at least for a time. Asian countries are not immune (e.g., Japan after the Taishō era, Thailand after Thaksin, Burma in the late 1950s and early 1990s). Liberals naturally hope that democracies are durable, but in low- and medium-income countries they have not always been so.

Analysts ranging from Aristotle to Barrington Moore or Samuel Huntington suggest that farmers in developing countries (a majority) can be organized by demagogues. Such populist leaders (especially if they are generals) may overthrow liberals in a coup. Or demagogues may win electorally if they can organize large blocs of illiberals (often peasants) to win democratic legitimacy. But the chance of self-sustaining democracy is raised where reformist coalitions have been able to combine participation by scattered industrial or commercial elites with redistributive policies. New local actors, especially entrepreneurs controlling economic nonstate power networks, may have sufficient incentives to support national liberals and revenues while constraining potential dictators.

In some Asian countries (Taiwan, parts of Japan, China, or South Korea), the state governments are strongly influenced by manufacturers and retailers, of whom at least some are in small networks. In these places, representatives of landowners are relatively less powerful than they are in the Philippines. Liberals and professionals may yet be able to stabilize Philippine democracy sooner than a new patriotic demagogue, another Marcos, can undermine it. Or they may miss doing this. Comparative and Philippine data suggest that both possibilities are open.

Any Filipino with a famous name and an ample wallet can have success as a politician. Welterweight champion Emmanuel "Manny" Pacquiao grew up poor. But he made a great deal of money in the boxing ring, founded his own political party (the People's Champ Movement), bought a bulletproof Hummer, and was elected in 2010 to Congress, representing Sarangani in Mindanao. Being busy as a boxer, he hired vote-canvassers to organize his election. As he told a reporter, "I've already established my machinery. It's like a car. It's fixed already. You just have to get in and drive it."[43]

Manny Pacquiao had prizefight money to buy his political machine, and a boxer's *malakas* credentials are obvious. They will remain so, especially if he continues to win in the ring until he may decide to retire to full-time politics and his work in Manila. His patriotic credentials are enhanced in the eyes of many Filipinos whenever he wins international matches. Pacquiao has also been famed throughout the archipelago as a devout Catholic. His campaign slogan was in English: "For God and Country." The motto of his adversary in the 2010 Sarangani election, Roy Chiongbian, was more situational: "Sarangani is Not for Sale." Chiongbian came from the political family that long dominated Sarangani Province (where his mother had been governor), but his name and looks both betray his Chinese background.

Pacquiao was advised by a politician friend "to appoint a leader at every voting station and give him 15,000 pesos to bribe voters with. The leader would 'distribute 100 each, that way you'll be certain to win.'" Pacquiao at one of his campaign rallies treated the crowd to 20,000 hamburgers. At another rally, he gave everyone a lunchbox of adobo chicken with rice. His campaign cost over 300 million pesos. Another of his advisors said, "Don't forget to rent out all the public buses or jeepneys. In villages there are really only two or three of these; so only your supporters can vote." Rumors circulated in both the Pacquiao and Chiongbian camps that the other side had paid voters in neighborhoods that were likely to support the opponent to have their fingers inked in advance, so that they could not vote. As Pacquiao vaguely told a reporter, "We dropped an atomic bomb. That's why I'm confident." As another journalist said, "Pacquiao ran on an anti-poverty platform, yet he spent millions of dollars."[44] Of course, he won. He was re-elected in 2013, while continuing his lucrative day job as a boxer.

Populist democrats are nothing new. Democrat Fredinand Marcos had no problem with elections so long as he could control them. Even after he declared martial law, he held a presidential election in 1981, two elections for the national legislature, two elections for local governments throughout the archipelago, and five nationwide referenda.[45] After his death, Imelda Marcos won elections to Congress from Leyte in 1995 and from Ilocos Norte in 2010. As of 2013, she was re-elected to the House, winning 77 percent of the vote at age 84. Son "Bongbong" was in the Senate. Daughter Imee was Governor or Ilocos Norte. Imelda Marcos was the second-richest Philippine politician (after boxer Manny Pacquiao).

Erap Estrada also exemplifies the type of politician who is illiberal but populist. Estrada was not from a *trapo* family; his father was a medical doctor. "Erap" is an inversion of *pare* (*kumpare*, "pal," "buddy," ritual kin). He combined a pro-poor image with *malakas* "big man" strength, and he has been very successful in elections on that basis. In movies, "Estrada had played policemen, farmers, priests, bus drivers, and an ice cream vendor, though nearly all of his characters ended up in a triumphant bloodbath by the final reel." He was said to have four families (one of them legal). He gambled illegally—as many Filipinos do—and did not hide that fact.

Estrada was elected in 1969 Mayor of San Juan, a city within Metro Manila, as a political ally of Marcos. That loyalty never wavered, and in 1987 even after the "people power revolution" Estrada won a Senate seat, still nominally running as the candidate of Marcos's party, which was then defunct in most localities. One of Estrada's 2009 feature films, *Sa Kuko ng Agila* (In the [American] Eagle's Claws), hinted at his patriotic opposition to the Subic Bay naval base. As a senator, he advertised his nationalist credentials by voting against continuation of all U.S. bases. He won the vice-presidency in 1992, even as his political rival Fidel Ramos was elected president. Estrada was proudly anti-intellectual. In 1993, he authorized a book of his own mutilations of the English language, *ERAPtions: How to Speak English Without Really Trial*. President Ramos retorted, saying he would launch a book entitled, *Erap Estrada for President and Other Jokes*.[46]

Despite tensions with President Ramos, and despite—or perhaps because of—his tough-guy reputation, Ramos appointed Vice-President Estrada to chair the Presidential Anti-Crime Commission. In this new post, he insisted he would resign this job unless he could use *malakas* methods: "If the need arises, I will arrest [criminals] personally or shoot them personally."[47] Estrada's colorful reputation as a bad boy certainly did not disturb supporters, who continued to vote for him. It attracted them, and the actor played brilliantly to these interests. Estrada said he wanted to be president "so that I can get rid of the 'vice' in front of my name."[48]

In 1998, he won the presidency with a 40 percent plurality, the largest since Marcos and more than twice as large as that of the runner-up, Jose de Venecia, Jr. Estrada donned his formal *barong tagalog* shirt and decided to be inaugurated at Malolos, where the first Philippine Constitution had been enacted in 1898 (until the U.S. Army suppressed it two years later). As president, Estrada claimed to continue anti-corruption efforts—but he went too far for his own good when in 2000 he sponsored investigations against misuse of public funds by his former friend Luis "Chavit" Singson, governor of Ilocos Sur. In revenge, Singson claimed that he had personally given Estrada 400 million pesos to protect *jueteng* illegal gambling. Manuel Villar, Speaker of the House but by then no friend of Estrada, made sure that the representatives voted to impeach President Estrada. The case duly went for trial in the Senate, where attention focused on a sealed envelope that allegedly contained evidence about Estrada's crimes. On the basis of a legal technicality, the Senate voted 11–10 not to open the envelope. So the president was impeached but not convicted.

He was unable to stay in office long after that. Crowds gathered at the EDSA Shrine where Marcos's presidency had met its end 15 years earlier. Armed

Forces Chief of Staff Angelo Reyes announced his change of allegiance to Vice-President Arroyo, whom the Supreme Court Chief Justice swore in as President on January 20, 2001.[49] Estrada issued a statement that he would move out of Malacañang Palace despite the illegitimacy of Arroyo's presidency. An EDSA rally of his supporters from impoverished districts was dispersed by the army using tear gas.

Criminal cases against Estrada languished in courts and in the Sandiganbayan appellate court for many years (as is typical for corruption cases against Philippine politicians). He was sent to a hospital, then to a military camp, then to house arrest. Eventually he was found "beyond reasonable doubt" to be guilty of plunder, and he had to forfeit 730 million pesos in two bank accounts, as well as the villa where he had installed one of his mistresses. (That house was called Boracay Mansion, named after the famous holiday isle whence sand had been brought to Manila to surround the villa's swimming pool.) Estrada was quoted by former Chief Justice Artemio Panganiban as having asked:[50]

> Chief Justice, why was I convicted of plunder and sentenced to a life in jail when I was charged merely with receiving (1) the broker's commissions in the sale of listed shares owned by the Social Security System, and (2) *jueteng* money [from illegal gambling]? Assuming [these charges are] true, how can I be guilty of any crime when I did not steal public funds?

Estrada's concept of corruption was explicitly narrower than the legal definition, although it was identical to the one that many political scientists use. Corruption within private networks undergirds corruption in the misuse of public office. Both are illegal—and the two kinds abet each other.[51]

The 2004 Global Transparency Report puts Estrada tenth on the list of "the world's all-time most corrupt leaders." It reports his illicit earnings of 80 million dollars.[52] (Marcos was second on that list, allegedly netting between five and ten billion dollars.) Estrada's corruption did not hurt him permanently. By late 2007, President Arroyo—who at that time needed all the allies she could muster—granted him "executive clemency." He ran again for president in 2010, achieving more than a quarter of the total vote and coming in second after PNoy. If Estrada had won, his second election to the presidency might have violated the constitution (which can be read to have ambiguous wording on this point; so he might in future try again).[53] His many voters are disinclined to worry about legal niceties. In mid-2013, Estrada ran for Mayor of Manila and won handily with 53 percent of the vote, beating the incumbent Alfredo Lim.

Mark Thompson speculates that Philippine elite politics cycles among populism, patronism, and reformism.[54] These can be interpreted in terms of their different bases. Populists appeal to most of the electorate as pure or poor (even if these politicians themselves are rich). Since the gap between low- and high-income Filipinos is large, candidates who can identify with impoverished "Pinoys" attract many votes, as Estrada did, and candidates such as Pacquiao in the future may do.[55] Patrons, the second kind of elite, appeal to their clients on more local grounds. That magnet for votes is slowly giving way to the third, more modern image- or issue-based reformist way of attracting support, even though patron–clientelism remains dominant in rural areas. Reformists mostly appeal to a small and largely urban electorate, including those who vote for anti-traditional party-list candidates to the House, based on ideals of fairness or progress.

Elections in the Philippines, as in other countries such as Thailand, favor populists who can wield money and violence along with "regular guy" images and may support serious pro-poor policies for health, schools, housing, and welfare. They can defeat traditional politicians with smaller networks as well as liberal reformists. Such candidates may be corrupt demagogues, but their images in the Philippines can simultaneously be nationalistic, democratic, and true-Filipino "Pinoy."

Authoritarian populism can mix patronist styles with electoral legitimacy. As Karaos has argued,[56]

> Populist leaders create and maintain their populist appeal by challenging—at least in rhetoric if not in their actions—the existing power structure and typically portray themselves as the enemy of the elite.... Populism and clientelism ... share an important characteristic: their abhorrence for institutions and institutionalized channels of interest representation.

Rocamora calls this kind of populism "demobilizing." The Philippines could nonetheless see more of it in the future. Politicians who adopt it are less restricted by geography than *trapos* have been. They may start in localities or regions, but their appeal is not localist.

"Manny" Pacquiao by mid-2013 admitted he had "thoughts on the Presidency," although he claimed they were "merely aspirations" for the future.[57] Many Filipinos, when asked whether he might be a future president, reply in the affirmative but say he should first have longer experience in political offices. Since the constitution requires a president to be age 40 or more, Pacquiao cannot run in the 2016 election for the top office (or for the vice-presidency). Both Speaker Belmonte and Comelec Chair Brillantes offered him advice to run for a Senate seat (which he could win with at least a plurality). A few years later, Pacquiao might become a democratically legitimated populist president. His name is in the title of this chapter, in quotation marks, only to represent a general kind of future chief executive who would probably round up many votes on the basis of welfare policies, while making scant progress against corruptions of his political friends as distinct from his enemies. The chance that his policies would be reformist or moderately so, like PNoy's, is slight.

Income inequality or economic recession could conceivably, if a populist demagogue were elected to a recentralized presidency, threaten the continuance of Philippine liberalism. Fortunately, however, the Philippine economy has picked up steam in recent years. A comparative study argues that inequality is of ambiguous help to further moves toward a more democratic regime.[58] Local liberalism requires elite decisions. Popular discontent may shape these, but so may other factors. In the Philippines, elections and liberalism may be already sufficiently established that, even with a continuation of high Gini inequality (48 in 2000, slightly improved to 46 in 2006), grinding poverty could persist for a long time without much change of the currently low quality of democratic governance in most localities.

Academic argument 1: orientalism, evidence, and hopes for the people

Is it wrong to dwell on dark facts because they may seem to humiliate a valid patriotism? An occupational hazard of publishing about any country is that some of its intellectuals may feel insulted not just by an author's factual mistakes or futuristic hopes, but also by evidenced descriptions of the nation's problems. This happens particularly when the writer's nationality is that of the previous colonial power, e.g., when an American like the present author writes about the Philippines. Partly because many have deemed that nation slow among East Asian countries in developing wealth and power, or partly also because this process has recently accelerated, the musings of a foreign researcher may be scrutinized by patriotic Philippine academics for possible scents of "orientalism." The current author, who has mainly studied China, is comfortable with the option of discounting all nationalisms, including that of the USA, in academic work.[59] Existential patriotisms need not get in the way of trying to figure out what will help people. Any student of democracy will naturally be interested in the Philippines, if only because that polity holds competitive elections. Successes or problems with the regime type there may throw light on any other democracy too.

Reynaldo Ileto's work on origins of Philippine would-be revolutionary sentiments in nineteenth century Catholic dramas of Christ's passion has inspired other historians.[60] It is possible to wonder whether Ileto's observation that Filipinos have collective ideals justifies his claim that American researchers who are interested in progress there are "orientalists." He chastises Alfred McCoy, John Sidel, Paul Hutchcroft, David Steinberg, Carl Landé, Glenn May, Oliver Wolters, Edgar Wickberg, Norman Owen, Harry Benda, Michael Cullinane, Benedict Anderson, and others who actually do not all present identical ideas.[61] A problem with Ileto's critique of these researchers from the former colonial power is extensive evidence that many Filipinos include economic modernization and political democracy among their own collective ideals. Arguably they do so not just because of colonial and post-colonial brainwashing.

Greed and force are more important in democracies than most liberals imagine. John Sidel, for example, has provided well-documented descriptions of violent bossism in Cavite and Cebu.[62] The evidence that Sidel exposes often points to unattractive aspects of the Philippine politics, but it is informative and is surely within bounds of conceptualization and language. (Ludwig Wittgenstein's critique of grammar as a practical activity explains this, and this philosopher is relevant because of his importance to the post-modern epistemology on which Ileto explicitly relies.)[63] Patriotism in social thinking is nothing new, and it is not unique to the Philippines.[64] "German history" was a fad in nineteenth century Germany. "American political science" tends to insist on "methodological individualism," tending to presume that people act freely without having been socialized; this is a blindered understanding of action that methodological collectivism could amend. Recent Chinese writers have been keen to find "international relations theory with Chinese characteristics." North Korea has *juche*—which might be translated "independent self-reliance," but the notion is mystical and in principle untranslatable. Dubious precedents of this kind do not justify substituting the patriotic ideology of any country in the project of trying to find situational bases for making democracy serve more people.

One of Ileto's targets is criticized for wanting "'good government,' 'rational administration,' and the practices of nation-building ... the [modal past Philippine] system is seen to revolve around personal ties (dyads) rather than collective organization."[65] Yet most collective organization is local. And many Filipinos, not just foreigners, hope for more inclusive democratic and economic progress in the Philippine future. Hopes for beneficial development in the Philippines can survive these facts: not all the problems which revolutionary consciousness might solve are foreign, most are already well-perceived by Filipinos, and many are material rather than ideal.

Knowledge often travels with a national passport, but truth does not. It is important to make sure that discussions, by anybody, of political problems and possibilities remain open. Fortunately, most people in the Philippines and elsewhere are less interested in epistemological debates of any kind than in questions of substantive democracy.

Academic argument 2: priority among regimes of different sizes and kinds

This book studies state formation, but it does not presume that a national regime type wholly determines the shape of local institutions, or vice versa. Evidence shows causation in many directions. National, regional, and local styles of governance differ, and the local-to-national vectors sometimes dominate. Hutchcroft carefully describes the Philippine state as patrimonial but feeble, controlled by "a powerful oligarchic class that enjoys an independent economic base outside the state, yet depends on particularistic access to the [state] political machinery as the major avenue to private accumulation."[66] The government may not be autonomous, no matter who tries to run it. Private networks are "embedded" in parts of officialdom. The Philippine government, to be effective, has to get into bed with oligarchs and local *trapos*, no less than they with it.

This country has often turned the "state" part of the "developmental state model" upside down. The islands show connections between large and small networks, but much planning is local rather than national. Few central or regional agencies are developmental. Profits and capital, when they are large, usually go to private groups that tend to value prestige more than growth. Hutchcroft writes that,

> a false dichotomy is often drawn between the character of national and local politics. In fact, the different territorial layers of government within the Philippine polity are deeply interwoven via a patronage system that has its apex in Manila and extends outward to provinces, cities, towns, and barangays throughout the archipelago.

He sees a process of "patronage-based state formation" that creates elite national cohesion—but also makes for bad governance. He argues that it is therefore

> essential to move beyond excessive reliance upon localist strategies of change to carefully considered strategies of political reform that can address the pathologies of the patronage system as they exist and interact at both the national and local levels of the Philippine polity.[67]

Because of this interaction, changing styles in Manila may alter those of local politics, which have long made the model of Philippine politics. If so, the process is at least slow.

Does this large polity's extent improve or hinder governance? Links between effective rule and state size have been theorized since the days of ancient Greek city-states, in some of which the citizens met to decide public affairs directly. So an early idea was that the size of a state should be small enough for the citizens to know each other. James Madison famously turned this Greek ideal on its head, advising a government to "expand the sphere," to become large and more diverse. Then no democratic majority would emerge permanently on all issues considered together. The chance of a minority being ostracized would decline.[68] A comparative book on *Size and Democracy* nonetheless argues that, "No single type or size of unit is optimal for achieving the twin goals of citizen effectiveness and system capacity."[69] The variant ways in which state and nonstate power networks interact with each other are more important for determining governance quality.

Using ideas from Albert Hirschman, Mark Warren notes that, "the more nonvoluntary an association,... the greater the likelihood there will be pressure within the association for voice [political complaint].... So associations subject to nonvoluntary forces may be more likely to provide democratic experiences." Exit is easy from most NGOs, but difficult from clan-type organizations. Families are the least voluntary and most pervasive of all political associations. When they hone the rhetorical skills of members and legitimize cooperation, they probably help train democrats. But they are not public polities. NGOs tend to be more egalitarian and transparent, although they usually make less effective claims to resources than families can. Voluntary NGOs provide fewer Tocquevillian experiences of effective voice. Sizeable patronist clans may raise the costs of complaint for insiders, and but that form of local politics inspires voice from rival clans.[70] Warren attempts an analysis of associational traits that help or hinder democracy. Because these can be combined freely along various dimensions, he finds no fewer than 162 types of association; yet two types that he does not

> carry over into my analysis ... are [those that are] politically organized, non-vested, and have low possibilities for exit. These groups include organized crime, gangs, and secret revolutionary cells. Such groups challenge the state's monopoly over the means of legitimate violence and must therefore organize themselves through coercion—even if members initially make the voluntary choice to join. Both are easy to assess in terms of their potential democratic effects: they have few, if any.[71]

The difficulty of excluding them from analysis of many countries' politics is that they are often locally powerful. Any theory that stresses "developed liberal democracies," as Warren's does, makes it inapplicable in much of the world. This is also a common failing of many liberal political philosophers.[72]

Charles Tilly, E.E. Schattschneider, and others have proffered definitions of democracy that they admit no state has ever fully met. Then they explore the paths or processes in which states move toward (or away from) those characteristics. For Tilly, "a regime is democratic insofar as it maintains broad citizenship, equal citizenship, binding consultation of citizens at large with respect to governmental activities and personnel, as well as protection of citizens from arbitrary action by governmental agents."[73] Two of these criteria are normative: the ideal political equality of citizens, and enough widely perceived inclusion in the polity to establish sufficient trust in it. The other two concern political situations rather than political norms: whether the state protects citizens (especially from its own agents), and whether it is bound by any procedures (e.g., elections) to consult them in a way that binds the state leaders.[74]

These criteria exhaust a logical field.[75] Tilly summarizes his view neatly by saying that, "When *protected consultation* reaches high levels,... we begin to speak of democracy."[76] The protection presumes the equality of individuals whether they are officials or not. The consultation presumes some level of trust between the state as a collective and the smaller power networks that may help to legitimate it. As Tilly writes,

> Without significant transformations in the arenas of inequality and networks of trust, strictly governmental changes toward democracy remain either unstable or nonexistent.... We are looking for change mechanisms that directly promote creation of citizenship ... broaden citizenship ... equalize citizenship ... expand binding claims by citizens over a government's agents ... and finally strengthen citizens' protections against arbitrary action by governmental agents.[77]

Democratization is that kind of change.

When various countries have democratized, they have done so through processes impelled by fundamentally different kinds of factors.[78] No adequate list of necessary or sufficient conditions for democratization, except arguably over long periods, has been found.[79] Whenever a scholar proposes such a list, another is liable to counter by pointing to a democracy that emerged differently (or a non-democracy that meets most or all of the conditions). Democracies usually fail if there are no effective constraints on executives who use the state's means of violence against the forces of some local leaders in favor of others.[80]

Diamond and Morlino, evaluating "democratic quality," posit that "the three main goals of an ideal democracy" are "civil freedom, popular sovereignty (control over public policies and the officials who make them), and political equality (in these rights and powers)."[81] If so, the quality of democracy in the Philippines is very partial, although it may recently have been improving. Freedoms on the archipelago are many, but popular control of policies and officials is even more haphazard than in most other countries that hold competitive elections. Political equality is mainly among oligarchs. Democracy is more an aspiration than a reality in any country, but the Philippines has developed "quality democracy" more slowly than most political scientists of all-country national regimes would have predicted.

An important 2009 book on *Democracies in Danger*, coordinated by Alfred Stepan, criticized previous works in democratization for having paid inadequate attention to three issues: ethnic and religious conflicts, new democracies' policies for their security apparatuses, and the variant democratic types of presidentialism and parliamentarism.[82] That book does not mention the Philippines, and a fourth unlisted issue that creates dangers for democracy (as for other regime types) is conflict among national, regional, and local regimes. Political scientists of democratization have usually written about power networks as if they were only national. Academic work on democratization will be further improved when other polities inside "sovereign" states are also considered.[83]

Action possibilities for future progress

Ferdinand Marcos's legacy cast doubt on presidentialism among some writers and politicians. The "long 1970s" under an elected dictator tended to delegitimize democracy in the Philippines.[84] It created "disillusion with the state" in general, especially as the economy faltered. U.S. government support for Marcos, at least until he and his officials terminally discredited his regime, spurred anti-Americanism among many Philippine intellectuals. The U.S. involved the Philippines in a Vietnam War that served the interests of few if any Filipinos. Patriotic intellectuals very self-consciously sought political forms for their nation that would differ from those of America. In Resil Mojares's words, even "one's use of English had become a sign of complicity and guilt."[85] Marxism and more circumspect forms of "Marxianism" underlay Filipinos' and others' new analyses of classes in the Philippines.[86] Realist analyses of violence in the nation's politics, however, were distrusted by some as late-colonialist or insulting, especially if they were written by Americans. Any discussion of patrons or clients, or even of existential traditions by which Filipinos often get along with each other, fell under a similar shadow of doubt. More important, and more positively in intellectual terms, this "turn" of thinking about the Philippines also led to more study of localities.

A few places in the Philippines have created institutions that relieve the destructions that come from local greed and the greed of globalized markets for raw materials.[87] These locations are exceptional, however. A broader pattern is that the weakness of government regulators, relative to the greater strength of both regional and supranational political networks, has brought deforestation, quick runoff of rains, erosion, desertification, unemployment, poverty, and problems for citizens who try to influence the state.[88] Will the political system in the future do more to solve these problems?

Philippine electoral democracy can produce leaders who are liberals, working toward more transparency in politics, a more benign environment, and higher wages for citizens. It may also legitimate leaders who cite patriotic grounds for trying to centralize the state, as Marcos did, but might still do so mainly in ways that benefit small rather than large groups and would thus be perceived as corrupt. It is likely that this democracy, like others, will see both reformism and kleptocracy in future presidents and local elected officials. Liberal and especially electoral traditions promote honesty among only some of the politicians.

The Philippines needs more than just "state-building." Some of its citizens see that their country needs local and central power networks that are coordinated to serve Filipinos better. Families and traditional politicians have been able to stabilize Philippine politics in their own interests for decades. Political "society" has been strong—and the state has been weak in comparison.[89] The democratic need is not just to build new institutions, but to transform old ones that impede many Filipinos' hopes for more fairness and wealth.

What array of what kinds of institutions (both national and local) can increase benefits that go to more of the people? It is by no means clear that centralization under a dictator can achieve that, as the Marcos era made clear. What the Philippines needs may not just be a stronger central government, but a Manila and more local regimes that interact more beneficially with each other. To foster more liberty and economic happiness, the institutions of local, regional, and national power would need to coordinate their natural sovereignties.

Modernity, more than revolution, is a collective ideal of many Filipinos. Unintended effects of economic growth can promote that. Intended, educated, critical reform efforts can also be effective. This requires less fear, more independence, more knowledge, and more business enterprise among individuals. As Rizal said, "Without education and liberty, that soil and that sun of mankind, no reform is possible, no measure can give the result desired."[90]

Notes

1. Carl H. Landé, "Party Politics in the Philippines," in *Six Perspectives on the Philippines*, George M. Guthrie, ed. (Manila: Bookmark, 1968), 128.
2. Social Weather Stations, graph of "Net Satisfaction Ratings of Presidents of the Philippines, May 1986 to November 2006," *Fourth Quarter 2006 Social Weather Report.*
3. Kent Eaton, *Politicians and Economic Reform in New Democracies: Argentina and the Philippines in the 1990s* (University Park, PA: Pennsylvania State University Press, 2002), 15, 20–1, 25.
4. Interview with a political analyst in Manila, August 2010.
5. Mark R. Thompson, "Reformism vs. Populism in the Philippines," *Journal of Democracy* 21:4 (2010), 154–6.
6. Eric U. Gutierrez, Ildefonso Torrente, and Noli G. Narca, *All in the Family: A Study of Elites and Power Relations in the Philippines* (Quezon City: Institute for Popular Democracy, 1992), 158.
7. Interview with a high-placed member of PNoy's administration.
8. See www.mb.com.ph/content/news of October 15, 2010.
9. Interview with a Philippine cabinet member, 2010.
10. Maria A. Ressa, "Noynoy Flunks His First Test," *ABS-CBN News*, October 9, 2010.
11. Pulse Asia, "Presidential Trust Ratings, Presidential Appointments, and Expectations for the First Six Months of the Aquino Administration," *Ulat ng Bayan* press release, July 2010.
12. Social Weather Stations survey, "'Too Early to Tell' if Aquino will Succeed or Fail," *Business World*, June 26, 2011, www.bwonline.com.
13. A graph on "net satisfaction" with the C. Aquino, Ramos, Estrada, Arroyo, and B. Aquino administrations is available at www.sws.org.ph. See also Mahar Mangahas, "Still Smooth Sailing," *Philippine Daily Inquirer*, October 22, 2011; the B. Aquino rating of early 2010 was higher than any other. The Arroyo rating at the end of the previous year was lower than any other. The averages in both the Ramos and Estrada periods were generally high.
14. Mahar Mangahas, "The 2011 Survey on Local Governance," *Philippine Daily Inquirer*, October 15, 2011.
15. See www.bworlonline.com/app.content.php?section, "Top Gov't Officials, State Institutions Post Lower Ratings," February 3, 2013.
16. Mahar Mangahas, "Economic Deprivation and Family Size," *Philippine Daily Inquirer*, February 10, 2012, http://opinion.inquirer.net/22811/.
17. Frank Lynch, S.J., *Philippine Society and the Individual* (Ann Arbor, MI: University of Michigan Center for South and Southeast Asian Studies, 1984), 413.
18. Ibid., esp. a chapter on "Sugarlandia" in Negros, 281 ff.
19. Robin Broad and John Cavanaugh, *Plundering Paradise: The Struggle for the Environment in the Philippines* (Berkeley, CA: University of California Press, 1993), 143.
20. For a critique of this preference as "irresponsible," see Max Weber, "Politics as a Vocation," in *From Max Weber: Essays in Sociology*, trans. H.H. Gerth and C.W. Mill (New York: Oxford University Press, 1946), 77–128. The term "elective affinities" was Bendix's translation of Weber's probabilistic treatment of causation, which was like quasi-chemical interactions as between men and women in a love story by Goethe (*Die Wahlverwandschaften*).
21. One text is the encyclical *Rerum Novarum* (1891). Another is *Gaudium et Spes* (1965) (translation at home.comcast.net/~chtongyu/liberation/chronology.html):

> While an immense number of people still lack the absolute necessities of life, some even in less advanced areas live in luxury and squander wealth. Extravagance and wretchedness exist side by side. While a few enjoy very great power

of choice, the majority are deprived of almost all possibility of acting on their own initiative and responsibility, and often subsist in living and working conditions unworthy of the human person...

22 For example, "Inasmuch as ye have done it unto one of the least of these my brethren, ye have done it to me" (Matthew 25:40). Also in the Old Testament, e.g., "He that oppresseth the poor reproacheth his Maker: but he that honoureth Him hath mercy on the poor" (Proverbs 14:31). The translations were made by King James's brilliant committee.
23 Patricio N. Abinales and Donna J. Amoroso, *State and Society in the Philippines* (Lanham, MD: Rowman & Littlefield, 2005), 295.
24 Romeo J. Intengan, S.J., "Christian Faith, Ideologies, and Social Change," in *The Aquino Government and the Question of Ideology*, Raul J. Bonoan, Agnes Colette Condon, and Soledad S. Reyes, eds. (Quezon City: Phoenix Publishing House, 1987), 68.
25 The Philippine Independent Church (Iglesia Filipina Independiente, IFI—interestingly, the Spanish name is official) split from Catholicism in 1902, after Rizal's assassination and partly because of strong resentment against Spanish priests' role in having run the country as a colony. The first Philippine president (Aguinaldo) and the first prime minister (Mabini) were both members. The Independent Church's theology is mainstream Protestant, and now the IFI is in full communion with a smaller local church that is Anglican.
26 The Iglesia ng Cristo, founded in 1914, is charismatic-evangelical, strongly unified, increasingly international, usually anti-Catholic, and regularly involved in supporting candidates for Philippine elections. High portions of the membership turn out and vote as the ministry directs. The theology emphasizes eschatology as in Revelations, and the distinctive architecture of Iglesia ng Cristo temples uses many strikingly sharp steeples.
27 Patricio N. Abinales and Donna J. Amoroso, *State and Society in the Philippines*, 11–12.
28 "Family Planning Gains Favor," based on a Social Weather Stations survey, *Business World*, August 8, 2011, www.bwonline.com.
29 "Church to Lobby Against RH Bill," *Manila Times*, August 5, 2010, 1.
30 Fatima Juarez, Josefina Cabigon, Susheela Singh, and Rubina Hussain, "The Incidence of Induced Abortion in the Philippines," *International Family Planning Perspectives* 31:3 (2005), www.thefullwiki.org/Abortion_in_the_Philippines#cite_note-guttmacherr1-2.
31 Philip Tubeza, "Aquino Eases Up on Reproductive Health Bill," *Philippine Daily Inquirer*, March 15, 2010, newsinfo.inquirer.net.
32 Camille Diola, "Catholic Bishops give Noy 'Failing Mark,'" *Philippine Star*, July 8, 2013, www.philstar.com/headlines/2013/07/08/981161.
33 José Rizal, *The Indolence of the Filipino*, tr. Charles Derbyshire (Manila: Hard Press, 1913).
34 Rupert Hodder, *Emotional Bureaucracy* (New Brunswick: Transaction Publishers, 2011), 25.
35 A reliable survey, reported in Walden Bello, *The Anti-Development State: The Political Economy of Permanent Crisis in the Philippines* (Manila: Anvil, 2009), 3.
36 John T. Sidel, "The Philippines: The Languages of Legitimation," in *Political Legitimacy in Southeast Asia: The Quest for Moral Authority*, Muthiah Alagappa, ed. (Stanford, CA: Stanford University Press, 1995),143.
37 Beth Day, *The Philippines: Shattered Showcase of Democracy in Asia* (intro. by Carlos Romulo, Sec. of Foreign Affairs) (New York: M. Evans, 1974), 29.
38 See www.philstar.com/subcategory.aspx of June 30, 2010.
39 Frederic Charles Schaffer, "Disciplinary Reactions: Alienation and the Reform of

Vote Buying in the Philippines," paper for the American Political Science Association Annual Meeting, 2002, 22 and 15–16.
40 For comparative perspective, see Robin Luckham, Anne Marie Goetz, and Mary Kaldor, "Democratic Institutions and Democratic Politics," in *Can Democracy be Designed? The Politics of Institutional Choice in Conflict-Torn Societies*, R. Luckham and S. Bastian, eds. (London: Zed Books, 2003), ch. 1.
41 Social Weather Stations, www.sws.org.ph/pr20130715.htm.
42 Samuel P. Huntington, *The Third Wave: Democratization in the Late Twentieth Century* (Norman, OK: University of Oklahoma Press, 1991).
43 Andrew Marshall, "Packing a Punch: Manny Pacquiao," *Post Magazine*, August 1, 2010, 14.
44 Ibid., 15–16.
45 William Case, "Manipulative Skills: How Do Rulers Control the Electoral Arena," in *Electoral Authoritarianism: The Dynamics of Unfree Competition*, Andreas Schedler, ed. (Boulder, CO: Rienner, 2006), 109.
46 Joel Rocamora, "Estrada and the Populist Temptation in the Philippines," in *Populism in Asia*, Mizuno Kosuke and Pasuk Phongpaichit, eds. (Kyoto: Kyoto University Press, 2009), 41–65.
47 Alfred W. McCoy, *Policing America's Empire: The United States, the Philippines, and the Rise of the Surveillance State* (Madison, WI: University of Wisconsin Press, 2009), 455. For much more documentation on "Estrada's Racketeering," see McCoy's chapter 15, 471–97.
48 *Time*, December 22, 1997, 22.
49 Concerning General Reyes's 2011 suicide, see the previous chapter about corruption. But this was a later event, apparently unrelated to his 2001 switch of loyalty from Estrada to Arroyo.
50 Raissa Robles, "Joseph Estrada: A Changed Man?" *Post Magazine*, July 28, 2013, 18–21.
51 Many political scientists use a public-only definition of corruption, and some do research imagining that the concept can only apply to appointed officials, since elected officials are democratically legitimated. Democratic faith can lead scholars astray. For more, see Lynn White, "Political Mechanisms and Corruption," in *Routledge Handbook of the Chinese Economy*, Gregory Chow and Dwight Perkins, eds. (Abingdon: Routledge, 2014 [forthcoming]).
52 For this and some material above, see http://en.wikipedia.org/wiki/joseph_estrada.
53 The Constitution's Art. VII, Sec. 4, says,

> The President [only the sitting one?] shall not be eligible for any [?] re-election. No person who has succeeded as President and has served as such for more than four years [Arroyo was in this category, but not Estrada who "served" for just three and a half years] shall be qualified for election to the same office at any time.

However, the Sandigbanbayan in 2007 sentenced Estrada to *reclusión perpetua*, a verdict from old Spanish that legally might have made him "perpetually" ineligible to hold public offices—but this did not stop him becoming Mayor of Manila. If he should ever want to be president again, he would need a good lawyer. He is a proven vote-getter, even though many educated Filipinos detest him.
54 Mark R. Thompson, "After Populism: [Arroyo] Winning the 'War' for Bourgeois Democracy in the Philippines," in *The Politics of Change in the Philippines*, Yuko Kasuya and Nathan Gilbert Quimpo, eds. (Pasig City: Anvil, 2010), 21–46.
55 Pacquiao's youthful "autobiography" does nothing to hide his ambition, although he may understand (as many Filipino voters do) that he should become at least a senator before trying for the presidency. That is, for him, an easily attainable step. See Manny Pacquiao, with Timothy James, *Pacman: My Story of Hope, Resilience, and*

Never-Say-Never Determination (orig. Nashville,TN: Dunham, 2010; also Manila: Anvil, 2010).

56 Quoted in Joel Rocamora, "From Regime Crisis to System Change," in *Whither the Philippines in the 21st Century*, Rodolfo C. Severino and Lorraine Carlos Salazar, eds. (Singapore: ISEAS, 2007), 28–9.

57 Llanesca T. Panti, "Pacquiao Backs Off, Drops Palace Dream," *Manila Times*, July 30, 2013, or www.manilatimes.net/pacquiao-backs-off-drops-palace-dream.24886/.

58 This is based on an interpretation of evidence in Christian Houle, "Inequality and Democracy: Why Inequality Harms Consolidation but Does Not Affect Democratization," *World Politics* 61:4 (2009), 589–622.

59 See George Kateb, *Patriotism and Other Mistakes* (New Haven, CT: Yale University Press, 2006).

60 See Chapter 7, above, concerning Reynaldo C. Ileto, *Pasyón and Revolution: Popular Movements in the Philippines, 1840–1910* (Quezon City: Ateneo de Manila University Press, 1979). There were several peasant revolts in the late nineteenth century Philippines, although none of them created a social revolution then. Elites ran the Katipunan.

61 Reynaldo C. Ileto, "Orientalism in the Study of Philippine Politics," *Knowing America's Colony: A Hundred Years from the Philippine War* (Honolulu, HI: Center for Philippine Studies, 1999), and John T. Sidel, "Response to Ileto: Or, I am Not an Orientalist," *Philippine Political Science Journal* 23:46 (2002), 129–38.

62 John T. Sidel, *Capital, Coercion, and Crime: Bossism in the Philippines* (Honolulu, HI: University of Hawaii Press, 1999), Reynaldo C. Ileto, "Orientalism in the Study of Philippine Politics," and Sidel, "Response to Ileto: Or, I am Not an Orientalist." The scholars whom Ileto calls "orientalists" relate their concepts to the U.S. colonial project in different ways; not all are guilty as charged. (He interestingly on p. 49 recognizes that "power flows from the bottom up"; the terms "bottom" and "up" may be problematic, but of course this current book is "localist" too.) Ileto suspects colonialism in any writer who uses clientelist concepts or is influenced by rationalistic enlightenment ideas such as "progress." The scholars he mentions are Americans; Philippine or Japanese writers with similar ideas are oddly exempt. Perhaps Ileto's verve against the former imperium relates to his father Rafael "Rocky" Ileto's long and extensive cooperation with it; Reynaldo Ileto has written briefly about this in "Philippine Wars and the Politics of Memory" (*positions: asia critique* 13:1, spring 2005, 215–34), which convincingly argues that dark aspects of the American empire's past and present are ignored by some U.S. writers. It is most ironic that Ileto's "orientalists" include Alfred McCoy, who has revealed more about these topics than has any other scholar.

63 Ludwig Wittgenstein, *Philosophical Investigations* (New York: Macmillan, 1953) shows how haphazardly language develops, so that terms without completely clear referents are the best we can expect of any writing. Strongly posited arguments, such as Ileto's, can never in this view be absolute truths but are aggregations of perceived evidence presented for mutual and social discussion. A book that inspired Ileto (Edward Said's *Orientalism*, New York: Vintage, 1978) was influenced positively by Wittgenstein (and negatively by U.S. support for Israeli violence against Said's fellow Palestinians). Post-modern followers of Wittgenstein sometimes see that his understanding of conversational discovery can justify existential statements. But it also recommends to each participant in the conversation a sense that the "last word" on a subject is never possible, especially if it is separate from circumspect attempts to perceive evidence.

64 For other Southeast Asian examples, see Norman G. Owen, "Introduction: In Search of Southeast Asian History," in Owen, ed., *Routledge Handbook of Southeast Asian History* (London: Routledge, 2013).

65 Ileto, "Orientalism in the Study of Philippine Politics," 52, concerns Carl Landé who

links changes in patronism to modernization. That linkage is an empirical question; see James C. Scott, "The Erosion of Patron–Client Bonds and Social Change in Rural Southeast Asia," *Journal of Asian Studies* 32:1 (November 1972), 6–37, and many other writings about modernization. Ileto's more lasting issue concerns "bottom-up" aspects of Philippine local political structures and the sometime claims of clients on patrons.

66 Paul D. Hutchcroft, *Booty Capitalism: The Politics of Banking in the Philippines* (Quezon City: Ateneo de Manila University Press, 1998), 12.
67 Paul D. Hutchcroft, "Dreams of Redemption: Localist Strategies and Political Reform in the Philippines," in *The Politics of Change in the Philippines*, Yuko Kasuya and Nathan Gilbert Quimpo, eds. (Pasig City: Anvil, 2010), 418–19.
68 Madison, *Federalist No. 10* (in Bobbs-Merrill or other reprints).
69 Robert A. Dahl and Edward R. Tufte, *Size and Democracy* (Stanford, CA: Stanford University Press, 1973), 138.
70 See Mark E. Warren, *Democracy and Association* (Princeton, NJ: Princeton University Press, 2001), 106.
71 Ibid., 134–7, 139.
72 For example, John Rawls, *A Theory of Justice* (Cambridge, MA: Harvard University Press, 1971), is based on ideal premises that apply even less among polities outside "the West" than they do in the places from which Rawls drew them.
73 Charles Tilly, "Processes and Mechanisms of Democratization," *Sociological Theory* 18:1 (March 2000), 4.
74 The categories "norm" and "situation" are old-style functionalist, and Tilly might abjure that connection. The similarity between his categories and those of Parsons nonetheless is perceivable; see Talcott Parsons, *The Social System* (Glencoe, IL: Free Press, 1951).
75 Such a field is generated along just two dimensions in Lynn White, "Functional Stories: Uses for Communist, Developmental, Military, and Individualist Ideologies," in *The Challenge of Change: East Asia in the New Millennium* (a *Festschrift* in honor of Chalmers Johnson), David Arase, ed. (Berkeley, CA: University of California Institute of East Asian Studies, 2003), 341–71.
76 Charles Tilly, "Processes and Mechanisms of Democratization," 5, emphasis added.
77 Ibid., 9.
78 Kate Zhou, Shelley Rigger, and Lynn White, eds., *Democratization in China, Korea, and Southeast Asia? Local and National Perspectives* (Abingdon: Routledge, 2014).
79 Charles Tilly, "Processes and Mechanisms of Democratization," does not emphasize democratization over long time periods—but many researchers following Seymour Martin Lipset (e.g., Carles Boix or Susan Stokes recently) have looked at long spans and show conditional links between modern economic development and democratization.
80 This is the main argument in Ethan B. Kapstein and Nathan Converse, "Why Democracies Fail," *Journal of Democracy* 19:4 (October 2008), 57–68. This article does not mention either Marcos or democratic problems in the Philippines.
81 Larry Diamond and Leonardo Morlino, "Introduction," in *Assessing the Quality of Democracy*, Larry Diamond and Leonardo Morlino, eds. (Baltimore, MD: Johns Hopkins University Press, 2005), xi.
82 Alfred Stepan, ed., *Democracies in Danger* (Baltimore, MD: Johns Hopkins University Press, 2009).
83 The classic on this is E.E. Schattschneider, *The Semi-Sovereign People: A Realist's View of Democracy in America*, intro. by David Adamany (Hinsdale, IL: Dreyden Press, 1975).
84 Vicente L. Rafael, "Contracting Colonialism and the Long 1970s," *Philippine Studies* 61:4 (2013), 477–94.

85 Resil B. Mojares, "Making a Turn: Thoughts on a Generation of Philippine Scholarship," Keynote Address at the Philippine Studies Conference, Kyoto, Japan, February 28 to March 2, 2014 (kindly supplied to the author by Norman G. Owen, originally distributed on Facebook by Vicente L. Rafael).
86 Especially Temario C. Rivera, *Landlords and Capitalists: Class, Family, and State in Philippine Manufacturing* (Quezon City: University of the Philippines Center for Integrative and Development Studies, 1994), Benedict J. Tria Kerkvliet, *Everyday Politics in the Philippines: Class and Status Relations in a Central Luzon Village* (Berkeley, CA: University of California Press, 1990; also Quezon City: New Day, 1991), and many of the best Southeast Asianists in Australia.
87 Agnes C. Rola, *An Upland Community in Transition: Institutional Innovations for Sustainable Development in Rural Philippines* (Laguna: Southeast Asian Regional Center for Graduate Study and Research in Agriculture, 2011).
88 Philippine Center for Investigative Journalism and Institute for Popular Democracy, *Patrimony: 6 Cases on Local Politics and the Environment in the Philippines* (Pasig City: Philippine Center for Investigative Journalism, 1996).
89 See Joel S. Migdal, *Strong Societies and Weak States: State–Society Relations and State Capabilities in the Third World* (Princeton, NJ: Princeton University Press, 1988).
90 José Rizal, *The Indolence of the Filipino*, trans. Charles Derbyshire (Manila: Hard Press, 1913), 23.

References

The author is deeply indebted to past scholars of the Philippines, many of whom are listed as authors below. He has also learned from interviewees, especially in Manila; the most important of these are acknowledged earlier in the book. The list below is of books and journal articles; newspapers quoted in the footnotes have been especially helpful for their coverage of events during PNoy's presidency.

Abad, Ricardo G., *Aspects of Social Capital in the Philippines: Findings from a National Survey* (Quezon City: Social Weather Stations, 2006).
Abao, Carmela, "Dynamics among Political Blocs in the Formation of a Political Party," in *Philippine Democracy Agenda*: vol. 3, *Civil Society Making Civil Society*, Miriam Coronel Ferrer, ed. (Quezon City: Third World Studies Center, University of the Philippines, 1997), 271–88.
Abenir, Luis E., and Pedro R. Laylo, Jr., "The 1995 Senatorial Election Surveys" (Diliman: Social Weather Stations Bulletin, 1996).
Abenir, Luis E., and Pedro Laylo, Jr., "Monitoring Recent National Elections in the Philippines: The SWS 1992 and 1995 Surveys" (Diliman: Social Weather Stations Occasional Paper, 1997).
Abinales, Patricio, ed., *The Revolution Falters: The Left in Philippine Politics after 1986* (Ithaca, NY: Cornell Southeast Asia Program, No. 15, 1996).
Abinales, Patricio N., *Images of State Power: Essays on Philippine Politics from the Margins* (Diliman: University of the Philippines Press, 1998).
Abinales, Patricio N., and Donna J. Amoroso, *State and Society in the Philippines* (Lanham, MD: Rowman & Littlefield, 2005).
Abrenica, Ma. Joy, *Building the Capital Goods Sector: An Agenda for Development* (Quezon City: Philippine Center for Policy Studies, n.d., c.1993).
Abueva, José, "Dissatisfaction with the Way Our Democracy Works," in *Towards a Federal Republic of the Philippines: A Reader*, José Abueva, ed. (Manila: Center for Social Policy and Governance, 2002), 1–15.
Abueva, José V. [former UP president], *Towards a Nonkilling Filipino Society: Developing an Agenda for Research, Policy, and Action* (Riverbanks, Marikina: Aurora Aragon Quezon Peace Foundation and Kalayaan College, 2004).
Abueva, José V., "Proposed Constitutional Reforms for Good Governance and Nation Building," in *Whither the Philippines in the 21st Century*, Rodolfo C. Severino and Lorraine Carlos Salazar, eds. (Singapore: ISEAS, 2007), 43–77.

Acemoglu, Daron, and James A. Robinson, *Why Nations Fail: The Origins of Power, Prosperity, and Poverty* (New York: Crown Business, 2012).
Adams, Dale W., H.Y. Chen, and M.B. Lamberte, "Differences in Uses of Rural Financial Markets in Taiwan and the Philippines," *World Development* 21:4 (April 1993), 555–63.
Aganon, Marie E., Melisa R. Serrano, Rosalinda C. Mercado, and Ramon A. Certeza, *Revitalizing Philippine Unions: Potentials and Constraints to Social Movement Unionism* (Manila: Friedrich Ebert Stiftung and UP School of Labor and Industrial Relations, 2008).
Agpalo, Remigio E., *Adventures in Political Science* (Quezon City: University of the Philippines Press, 1992).
Aguilar, Filomeno V., "Of Cocks and Bets: Gambling, Class Structuring and State Formation in the Philippines," in *Patterns of Power and Politics in the Philippines*, James F. Eder and Robert L. Youngblood, eds. (Tempe, AZ: Arizona State University Program for Southeast Asian Studies, 1994), 147–96.
Aguilar, Filomeno V., *Landlessness and Hired Labour in Philippine Rice Farms* (Swansea: Centre for Development Studies, 1981).
Aguilar, Filomeno V., *Clash of Spirits: The History of Power and Sugar Planter Hegemony on a Visayan Island* (Honolulu, HI: University Press of Hawaii, 1998).
Alagappa, Muthiah, ed., *Military Professionalism in Asia: Conceptual and Empirical Perspectives* (Honolulu, HI: East-West Center, 2001).
Alejo, Myrna J., Maria Elena P. Rivera, and Noel Inocencio P. Valencia, *[De]scribing Elections: A Study of Elections in the Lifeworld of San Isidro* (Quezon City: Institute for Popular Democracy, 1996).
Almond, Gabriel A., and Sidney Verba, *The Civic Culture* (Princeton, NJ: Princeton University Press, 1963).
Anderson, Benedict, "Elections and Participation in Three Southeast Asian Countries," in *The Politics of Elections in Southeast Asia*, R.H. Taylor, ed. (Washington, DC: Woodrow Wilson Center, 1996), 12–33.
Anderson, Benedict, *The Spectre of Comparisons: Nationalism, Southeast Asia and the World* (London: Verso, 1998).
Anderson, Benedict, "Cacique Democracy in the Philippines: Origins and Dreams," *New Left Review* 169 (May/June 1988), 3–31; reprinted in Anderson, *The Spectre of Comparisons* (London: Verso, 1998), 192–226.
Anderson, Benedict, "Murder and Progress in Modern Siam," *New Left Review* 181 (1990), 33–48.
Anderson, James N., "Buy-and-Sell and Economic Personalism: Foundations for Philippine Entrepreneurship," *Asian Survey* 9:9 (September 1969), 641–68.
Ang See, Teresita, "People of the Philippines vs. Crimes," in *Philippine Democracy Agenda*, vol. 2, *State–Civil Society Relations in Policy-Making*, Marlon A. Wui and Ma. Glenda S. Lopez, eds. (Quezon City: Third World Studies Center, University of the Philippines, 1997), 125–39.
Ang See, Teresita, "The Ethnic Chinese as Filipinos," in *Ethnic Chinese as Southeast Asians*, Leo Suryadinata, ed. (Singapore: Institute for Southeast Asian Studies, 1997), 158–210.
Ang See, Teresita, *Chinese in the Philippines: Problems and Perspectives*, vol. 3 (Manila: Kaisa Para sa Kaunlaran, 2004).
Ang See, Teresita, and Go Bon Juan, *The Ethnic Chinese in the Philippine Revolution* (Manila: Kaisa Para sa Kaunlaran, 1996).
Angeles, Jocelyn Vicente, "The Naga City Urban Poor Federation and Pro-Poor

Ordinances and Policies," in *Philippine Democracy Agenda*: vol. 2, *State–Civil Society Relations in Policy-Making*, Marlon A. Wui and Ma. Glenda S. Lopez, eds. (Quezon City: Third World Studies Center, University of the Philippines, 1997), 97–112.

Angeles, Leonora C., "The Political Dimension in the Agrarian Question: Strategies of Resilience and Political Entrepreneurship of Agrarian Elite Families in a Philippine Province," *Rural Sociology* 64:4 (December 1999), 667–92.

Angeles, Leonora C., "Grassroots Democracy and Community Empowerment: The Political Requirements of Sustainable Poverty Reduction in Asia," paper for the conference on "Democracy and Civil Society: Challenges and Opportunities in Asia," Queen's University, Montreal, August 2000.

Angeles, Leonora C., and Francisco A. Magno, "The Philippines: Decentralization, Local Governments, and Citizen Action," in *Decentralization, Democratic Governance, and Civil Society in Comparative Perspective: Africa, Asia, and Latin America*, Philip Oxhorn, Joseph S. Tulchin, and Andrew D. Selee, eds. (Washington, DC: Woodrow Wilson Center, 2004).

Antlöv, Hans, and Joel Rocamora, *Citizen Participation in Local Governance: Experiences for Thailand, Indonesia, and the Philippines* (Manila: Institute for Popular Democracy, 2004).

Aquino, Benigno S., Jr., "What's Wrong with the Philippines?" *Foreign Affairs* 46:4 (July 1968).

Arillo, Cecilio T., *Greed & Betrayal: The Sequel to the 1985 EDSA Revolution* (Makati: CTA Research, 2000).

Armas, Armando, Jr., *Dual Presidential Dynasties: Betrayal of Cory Aquino?* (Manaoag, Pangasinan: Manaoag House, 2010).

Arroyo, Dennis M., "Selected Personal Characteristics which May Affect the Chances of National Candidates in 1992" (Diliman: Social Weather Stations Bulletin, 1991).

Arroyo, Dennis M., "Emerging Cracks in the Political Machine" (Diliman: Social Weather Stations Bulletin, 1992).

Arroyo, Dennis M., "Surveys of Satisfaction with Democracy, 1991–95" (Diliman: Social Weather Stations Bulletin, 1995).

Arroyo, Dennis M., "Midway in the Race for the Presidency" (Diliman: Social Weather Stations Bulletin, 1997).

Arugay, Aries A., J. Carizo, and Djorina Velasco, "The Party-List System of Representation: Trojan Horse for a New Politics?" *Political Brief* (IPD), 12:4 (2004), 1–29.

Azurin, René B., *Power Without Virtue: A Critical Perspective on Philippine Government* (Manila: Anvil, 2008).

Balisacan, Arsenio, "Poverty and Inequality," in *The Philippine Economy: Development, Policies, and Challenges*, Arsenio Balisacan and Hal Hill, eds. (Manila: Ateneo De Manila University Press, 2003), 311–41.

Balisacan, Arsenio, and Hal Hill, eds., *The Philippine Economy: Development, Policies, and Challenges* (Manila: Ateneo De Manila University Press, 2003).

Balisacan, Arsenio M., "Rural Growth Linkages, Poverty, and Income Distribution," *Philippine Review of Economics and Business* 29:1 (June 1992), 62–85.

Balisacan, Arsenio M., "Getting the Story Right: Growth, Redistribution, and Poverty Alleviation in the Philippines," *Philippine Review of Economics and Business* 34:1 (June 1997), 1–37.

Basilican, Arsenio M., "Why Does Poverty Persist in the Philippines?" in *Whither the Philippines in the 21st Century*, Rodolfo C. Severino and Lorraine Carlos Salazar, eds. (Singapore: ISEAS, 2007), 201–21.

Balisacan, Arsenio M., and Shigeaki Fujisaki, ed., *Causes of Poverty: Myths, Facts, and Policies* (Quezon City: University of the Philippines Press, 1999).
Balisacan, Arsenio M., Fuwa Nobuhiko, and Margarita H. Debuque, "The Political Economy of Philippine Rural Development Since the 1960s," at www.h.chiba-u.ac.jp/mkt/philippines.pdf.
Banfield, Edward, with Laura Fasano Banfield, *The Moral Basis of a Backward Society* (New York: Free Press, 1958).
Bankoff, Greg, "Profiting from Disasters: Corruption, Hazard, and Society in the Philippines," in *Corruption and Good Governance in Asia*, Nicholas Tarling, ed. (Abingdon: Routledge, 2005), 165–85.
Banlaoai, Rommel C., "Globalization and Nation-Building in the Philippines: State Predicaments in Managing Society in the Midst of Diversity," in *Growth and Governance in Asia*, Yoichiro Sato, ed. (Honolulu, HI: Asia-Pacific Center for Security Studies, 2004), 203–14.
Barreveld, Dirk J., *Erap Ousted: People Power versus Chinese Conspiracy?... How the Philippine Nation Almost Became a Victim of a Chinese Conspiracy to Turn the Country into a Gambling and Entertainment Paradise, With a Blueprint for Survival* (Mandaue City, Cebu: Arcilla Travel Guides, 2001).
Batalla, Eric Vincent, "Entrepreneurship and Philippine Development," *Canadian Journal of Development Studies* 31:3–4 (2010), 341–65.
Batara, John, *The Comprehensive Agrarian Reform Program: More Misery for the Philippine Peasantry* (Manila: Ibon Philippines Databank and Research Center, 1996).
Bautista, Luz A., Joy L. Casuga, and Gerardo A. Sandoval, "Public Opinion Surveys and Local Governance: The Quezon City 1993–96 Surveys" (Diliman: Social Weather Stations Occasional Paper, 1997).
Bello, Walden, *The Anti-Development State: The Political Economy of Permanent Crisis in the Philippines* (Manila: Anvil, 2004).
Bello, Walden, and John Gershman, "Democratization and Stabilization in the Philippines," *Critical Sociology* 17:1 (1990), 35–56.
Belmonte, Patricia A., "Opinion Surveys about Term Limits" (Diliman: Social Weather Stations Bulletin, 1997).
Bendix, Reinhard, *Max Weber: An Intellectual Portrait* (New York: Doubleday, 1960).
Berlow, Alan, *Dead Season: A Story of Murder and Revenge on the Philippine Island of Negros* (New York: Pantheon, 1996).
Berman, Sheri, "Civil Society and the Collapse of the Weimar Republic," *World Politics* 49 (April 1997), 401–29.
Berner, Erhard, and Rüdiger Korff, *Dynamik der Bürokratie und Konservatismus der Unternehmer: Strategische Gruppen in Thailand und den Philippinen* (The Dynamics of Bureaucracy and the Conservatism of Entrepreneurs: Strategic Groups in Thailand and the Philippines), *Internationales Asienforum* 22:3–4 (November 1991), 287–305.
Bhargava, Vinay K., and Emil Bolongaita, *Challenging Corruption in Asia: Case Studies and a Framework for Action* (Washington, DC: World Bank, 2004).
Bionat, Marvin P., *How to Win (or Lose) in Philippine Elections* (Pasig City: Anvil Publishing, 1998).
Blaker, James, *The Philippine Chinese: A Study of Power and Change* (Ph.D. dissertation, Ohio State University, 1970).
Blitz, Amy, *The Contested State: American Foreign Policy and Regime Change in the Philippines* (Lanham, MD: Rowman & Littlefield, 2000).

236   References

Bonoan, Raul J., Agnes Colette Condon, and Soledad S. Reyes, eds., *The Aquino Government and the Question of Ideology* (Quezon City: Phoenix Publishing House, 1987).

Boudis, Howarth E., and Lawrence J. Haddad, *Agricultural Commercialization, Nutrition, and the Rural Poor: A Study of Philippine Farm Households* (Boulder, CO: Lynne Rienner, 1990).

Boudreau, Vincent, *Grassroots and Cadre in the Protest Movement* (Quezon City: Ateneo de Manila University Press, 2001).

Boudreau, Vincent, *Resisting Dictatorship: Repression and Protest in Southeast Asia* (New York: Cambridge University Press, 2004).

Bowie, Alasdair, and Danny Unger, *The Politics of Open Economies: Indonesia, Malaysia, the Philippines, and Thailand* (Cambridge: Cambridge University Press, 1997).

Boyce, James K., *The Political Economy of Growth and Impoverishment in the Marcos Era* (Quezon City: Ateneo de Manila University Press, 1993).

Bray, Francesca, *The Rice Economies: Technology and Development in Asian Societies* (Berkeley, CA: University of California Press, 1986).

Brinkerhoff, Derick W., and Arthur A. Goldsmith, *Clientelism, Patrimonialism, and Democratic Governance: An Overview and Framework for Assessment and Programming* (Bethesda, MD: Abt Associates, report for the U.S. Agency for International Development, 2002).

Briones, Roehlano M., "Asia's Underachiever: Deep Constraints in Philippine Economic Growth" (Los Baños: UP College of Economics and Management, CEM Working Paper, 2009).

Broad, Robin, *Unequal Alliance: The IMF, the World Bank, and the Philippines* (Berkeley, CA: University of California Press, 1988 [and in original form, a Princeton University Woodrow Wilson School Ph.D. thesis]).

Broad, Robin, and John Cavanaugh, *Plundering Paradise: The Struggle for the Environment in the Philippines* (Berkeley, CA: University of California Press, 1993).

Broad, Robin, and John Cavanagh, "Protest to Power in the Philippines," *The Nation* (December 6, 2010), 22–4.

Brownlee, Jason, *Authoritarianism in an Age of Democratization* (New York: Cambridge University Press, 2007).

Brunetti, Aymo, and Beatrice Weder, "A Free Press is Bad News for Corruption," *Journal of Public Economics* 87:7–8 (2003), 1801–24.

Calimbahin, Cleo, "Capacity and Compromise: COMELEC, NAMFREL, and Election Fraud," in *The Politics of Change in the Philippines*, Yuko Kasuya and Nathan Gilbert Quimpo, eds. (Pasig City: Anvil, 2010), 162–89.

Canlas, Dante B., and Shigeaki Fujisaki, eds., *The Philippine Economy: Alternatives for the 21st Century* (Diliman: University of the Philippines Press, 2001).

Canlas, Dante B., Muhammad Ehsan Khan, and Juzhong Zhuang, eds., *Diagnosing the Philippine Economy: Toward Inclusive Growth* (Quezon City: Anthem Press, 2011).

Canlas, Mamerto, Mariano Miranda, and James Putzel, *Land, Poverty, and Politics in the Philippines* (Quezon City: Claretian Publications, 1988).

Caouette, Dominique, and Sarah Turner, *Agrarian Angst and Rural Resistance in Contemporary Southeast Asia* (New York: Routledge, 2009).

Carandang, Ricky, "Shrinking Middle Class," *Newsbreak*, April 12, 2004.

Cariño, Ledivina V., "Devolution toward Democracy: Lessons for Theory and Practice from the Philippines," *Decentralizing Governance*, Shabbir Cheema, ed. (Washington, DC: Brookings, 2007), 92–107.

Cariño, Ledivina V., "Devolution and Democracy: A Fragile Connection," in *East Asia's*

New Democracies: Deepening, Reversal, Non-Liberal Alternatives, Yin-wah Chu and Siu-lun Wong, eds. (Abingdon: Routledge, 2010), 185–205.

Cariño, Theresa Chong, *Chinese Big Business in the Philippines: Political Leadership and Change* (Singapore: Times Academic Press, 1998).

Cariño, Theresa Chong, "Chinese Chambers of Commerce in the Philippines: Communal, National, and International Influence," in *Chinese Populations in Contemporary Southeast Asian Societies*, M. Jocelyn Armstrong, R. Warwick Armstrong, and Kent Mulliner, eds. (Richmond: Curzon, 2001), 97–122.

Carothers, Thomas, "How Democracies Emerge: The Sequencing Fallacy," *Journal of Democracy* 18:1 (2007), 12–27.

Carothers, Thomas, "International Assistance for Political Party Development," Anti-Corruption Resource Centre, Michelson Institute, Bergen, www.cmi.no/publications/file/3015.

Carroll, John J., S.J., *The Filipino Manufacturing Entrepreneur, Agent and Product of Change* (Ithaca, NY: Cornell University Press, 1965).

Carroll, John J., S.J., "Growth, Agrarian Reform, and Equity: Two Studies [in Bulacan and Bikol]," in *Second View from the Paddy*, Antonio J. Ledesma, Perla Q. Makil, and Virginia A. Miralao, eds. (Manila: Institute of Philippine Culture, Ateneo de Manila University, 1983), 15–23.

Carroll, John J., S.J., *Engaging Society: The Sociologist in a War Zone* (Quezon City: Ateneo de Manila University Press, 2006).

Case, William, "Manipulative Skills: How Do Rulers Control the Electoral Arena," in *Electoral Authoritarianism: The Dynamics of Unfree Competition*, Andreas Schedler, ed. (Boulder, CO: Rienner, 2006), 95–112.

Casper, Gretchen, *Fragile Democracies* [esp. the Philippines]: *Legacies of Authoritarian Rule* (Pittsburgh, PA: University of Pittsburgh Press, 1995).

Castillo, Gelia T., *All in a Grain of Rice* (Laguna: Southeast Asian Regional Center for Research in Agriculture, 1975).

Castillo, Gelia T., *How Participatory is Participatory Development? A Review of the Philippine Experience* (Manila: Philippine Institute for Development Studies, 1983).

Casuga, Joy L., "Perceived Honesty and Ethical Standards of People from Various Occupations" (Diliman: Social Weather Stations Bulletin, 1995).

Chan, Cheris Shun-ching, "Creating a Market in the Presence of Cultural Resistance: The Case of Life Insurance in China," *Theory and Society* 38 (2009), 271–305.

Chavez, Frank, *Blighted!* [fiction based on "verified and verifiable corruptions"] (Mandaluyong: Primex Printers, Fairnews Media, 2009).

Cheema, Shabbir, and Dennis Rondinelli, "From Government Decentralization to Decentralized Governance," *Decentralizing Governance*, Cheema, ed. (Washington, DC: Brookings, 2007).

Chikiamco, Calixto V., *Reforming the System: Essays on Political Economy* (Manila: Orange Publications and Kalikasan Press, 1992).

Chu, Hung M., Evan Leach, and Russell Manuel, "Cultural Effect and Strategic Decision among Filipino Entrepreneurs," www.icsb.org/pbs/98icsb/j010.htm.

Chu, Richard T., *Chinese Merchants of Binondo in the Nineteenth Century* (Manila: University of Santo Tomas Publishing House, 2010).

Chua, Yvonne T., *Robbed: An Investigation of Corruption in Philippine Education* (Quezon City: Philippine Center for Investigative Journalism, 1999).

Clad, James, *Behind the Myth: Business, Money, and Power in Southeast Asia* (London: Hyman, 1989).

238   References

Clarke, Gerard, *Civil Society in the Philippines: Theoretical, Methodological, and Policy Debates* (Abingdon: Routledge, 2013).

Co, Edna, Nepomuceno Malaluan, Artur Neame, Marlon Manuel, and Miguel Rafael V. Musngi, *Philippine Democracy Assessment: Rule of Law and Access to Justice* (Quezon City: Action for Economic Reforms, 2010).

Cornwall, Andrea, Jorge Romano, and Alex Shankland, "Brazilian Experiences of Participation and Citizenship: A Critical Look" (Brighton: Institute for Development Studies, IDS Discussion Paper 389, 2008).

Coronel, Sheila S., "How Representative is Congress?" Philippine Center for Investigative Journalism website, November 12, 2006, www.pcij.org/stories/2004/congress.html.

Coronel, Sheila S., ed., *Betrayals of the Public Trust: Investigative Reports on Corruption* (Quezon City: Philippine Center for Investigative Journalism, 2000).

Coronel, Sheila S., Yvonne Chua, Luz Rimban, and Booma Cruz, *The Rulemakers: How the Wealthy and Well-Born Dominate Congress* (Quezon City: Philippine Center for Investigative Journalism, 2004), with accompanying data disk, *The Ties that Bind: A Guide to Family, Business, and Other Interests in Congress* (provided to the author by courtesy of Dr. Steven Rood, The Asia Foundation, Makati).

Corpus, Victor N., Lt. Gen., *Silent War* (Quezon City: VNC Enterprises, 1989) (the author was in the Armed Forces of the Philippines, then defected to the communist New People's Army, then was restored to the AFP).

Crozier, Michel, Samuel P. Huntington, and Joji Watanuki, *The Crisis of Democracy* (New York: New York University Press, 1975).

Cullinane, Michael, "Burgis Projects in the Post-Marcos Era," *Pilipinas* 21 (1993), 74–6.

Cullinane, Michael, "Patron as Client: Warlord Politics and the Duranos of Danao," in *An Anarchy of Families: State and Family in the Philippines*, Alfred W. McCoy, ed. (Madison, WI: University of Wisconsin Center for Southeast Asian Studies, 1993), 163–242.

Cullinane, Michael, *Ilustrado Politics: Filipino Elite Responses to American Rule, 1898–1908* (Manila: Ateneo de Manila Press, 2004).

Dahl, Robert A. and Edward R. Tufte, *Size and Democracy* (Stanford, CA: Stanford University Press, 1973).

Dahl, Robert A., Ian Shapiro, and José Antonio Cheibub, eds., *Democracy Sourcebook* (Cambridge, MA: MIT Press, 2003).

Dalisay, José Y., Jr., *The Lavas: A Filipino Family* (Pasig City: Anvil, 1999).

Danguilan-Vitug, Marites, *Kudeta: The Challenge to Philippine Democracy*, Rigoberto Tiglao, ed. (Quezon City: Philippine Center for Investigative Journalism, 1990).

Danguilan-Vitug, Marites, *Shadow of Doubt: Probing the Supreme Court* (Manila: Public Trust Media Group, 2010).

Day, Beth, *The Philippines: Shattered Showcase of Democracy in Asia* (intro. by Carlos P. Romulo, Sec. of Foreign Affairs) (New York: M. Evans, 1974).

Dayag-Laylo, Carijane C., "Filipino Perceptions on the Social Reform Agenda" (Diliman: Social Weather Stations Bulletin, 1997).

De Castro, Renato, "The Military and Philippine Democratization: A Case Study of the Government's 1995 Decision to Modernize the Armed Forces of the Philippines," in *Democratization: Philippine Perspectives*, Felipe B. Miranda, ed. (Quezon City: University of the Philippines Press, 1995), 241–79.

de Dios, Emmanuel S., and Raul V. Fabella, eds., *Choice, Growth, and Development: Emerging and Enduring Issues* (Quezon City: University of the Philippines Press, 1996).

de Guzman, Raul P., and Mila A. Reforma, eds., *Decentralization Towards Democratization and Development* (Manila: Eastern Regional Organization for Public Administration, 1993).

de la Cruz, Edwin S., "Litigants' Perceptions of Court Decisions: A Case Study of a Workers' Community in Malabon," in *Philippine Democracy Agenda*: vol. 1, *Democracy and Citizenship in Filipino Political Culture*, Maria Serena I. Diokno, ed. (Quezon City: Third World Studies Center, University of the Philippines, 1997), 239–54.

De Viana, Augusto V., *Kulaboretor! The Issue of Political Collaboration During World War II* (Manila: University of Santo Tomas Publishing House, 2003).

Diamond, Larry, and Leonardo Morlino, "Introduction," in *Assessing the Quality of Democracy*, Larry Diamond and Leonardo Morlino, eds. (Baltimore, MD: Johns Hopkins University Press, 2005), i–xliii.

Diamond, Larry, and Marc F. Plattner, eds., *Democracy: A Reader* (Baltimore, MD: Johns Hopkins University Press, 2009).

Diamond, Larry, Marc Plattner, and Philip Costopoulos, eds., *Debates on Democratization* (Baltimore, MD: Johns Hopkins University Press, 2010).

Doner, Richard, "Politics and the Growth of Local Capital in Southeast Asia: Auto Industries in the Philippines and Thailand," in *Southeast Asian Capitalists*, Ruth McVey, ed. (Ithaca, NY: Southeast Asia Program, Cornell University, 1992), 191–218.

Doronila, Amando, *The State, Economic Transformation, and Political Change in the Philippines, 1946–1972* (Singapore: Oxford University Press, 1992).

Dunning, Thad, *Crude Democracy: Natural Resource Wealth and Political Regimes* (New York: Cambridge University Press, 2008).

Eaton, Kent, *Politicians the Economic Reform in New Democracies: Argentina and the Philippines in the 1990s* (University Park, PA: Pennsylvania State University Press, 2002).

Eaton, Kent, "Restoration or Transformation: *Trapos* vs. NGOs in the Democratization of the Philippines," *Journal of Asian Studies* 62:2 (May 2003), 469–96.

Eberhard, Wolfram, "Chinese Regional Stereotypes," *Asian Survey* 5:12 (December 1965), 596–608.

Eder, James F., *A Generation Later: Household Strategies and Economic Change in the Rural Philippines* (Quezon City: Ateneo de Manila University Press, 2000).

Eder, James F., and Robert L. Youngblood, eds., *Patterns of Power and Politics in the Philippines: Implications for Development* (Tempe, AZ: Arizona State University Program for Southeast Asian Studies, 1994).

Eggan, Fred, "Philippine Social Structure," in *Six Perspectives on the Philippines*, George M. Guthrie, ed. (Manila: Bookmark, 1968), 1–48.

Elkins, David, and Richard Simeon, "A Cause in Search of its Effect, or What Does Political Culture Explain?" *Comparative Politics* 11 (January 1979), 127–46.

Emmerson, Donald K., "Southeast Asia in Political Science: Terms of Enlistment," in *Southeast Asia in Political Science: Theory, Region, and Qualitative Political Science*, Erik Martínez Kuhonta, Dan Slater, and Tuong Vu, eds. (Stanford, CA: Stanford University Press, 2000), 302–24.

Endriga, José N., "The National Civil Service System of the Philippines," in *Civil Service Systems in Asia*, John P. Burns and Bidhya Bowornwathana, eds. (Cheltenham: Elgar, 2001), 212–48.

Erdmann, Gero, "Lessons to be Learned: Political Party Research and Political Party Assistance," www.scribd.com/doc/42881636/.

Esguerra, Emmanuel F., and Richard F. Meyer, "Collateral Substitutes in Informal Financial Markets in the Philippines," in *Informal Finance in Low-Income Countries*, Dale W. Adams and Richard Meyer, eds. (Boulder, CO: Westview, 1992), 149–64.

Fabella, Raul V., "Strategic Household Behavior in Labor Surplus Economies," *Philippine Review of Economics and Business* 28:2 (December 1991), 119–26.

Fallows, James, "A Damaged Culture: A New Philippines," *Atlantic Monthly*, November 1, 1987, and www.theatlantic.com.

Feder, Ernest, *The Rape of the Peasantry: Latin America's Landholding System* (New York: Doubleday, 1971).

Feder, Ernest, *Perverse Development* (Quezon City: Foundation for Nationalist Studies, 1983).

Fegan, Brian, "Between the Lord and the Law: Tenants' Dilemmas," in *View from the Paddy: Empirical Studies of Philippine Rice Farming and Tenancy*, Frank Lynch, S.J., ed., *Philippine Sociological Review*, 20:1–2 (January/April 1972), 113–28.

Fegan, Brian, "Accumulation on the Basis of an Unprofitable Crop," in *Agrarian Transformations: Local Processes and the State in Southeast Asia*, Gillian Hart, Andrew Turton, and Benjamin White, eds. (Berkeley, CA: University of California Press, 1989), 159–78.

Fegan, Brian, "The Philippines: Agrarian Stagnation Under a Decaying Regime," in *Agrarian Transformations: Local Processes and the State in Southeast Asia*, Gillian Hart, Andrew Turton, and Benjamin White, eds. (Berkeley, CA: University of California Press, 1989), 125–43.

Fegan, Brian, "Entrepreneurs in Votes and Violence: Three Generations of a Peasant Political Family" in *An Anarchy of Families: State and Family in the Philippines*, Alfred W. McCoy, ed. (Madison, WI: University of Wisconsin Center for Southeast Asian Studies, 1993), 33–108.

Fisman, Raymond, and Edward Miguel, "Cultures of Corruption: Evidence from Diplomatic Parking Tickets," NBER Working Paper 12312 (June 2006).

Florintino-Hofileña, Chay, *News for Sale: The Corruption of the Philippine Media* (Quezon City: Philippine Center for Investigative Journalism and Center for Media Freedom and Responsibility, 1998).

Formilleza, Liezl S., "Comparing Enterprise Development in the Philippines and China," *Currents: Newsletter of the Philippine–China Development Resource Center* 11:1 (January/June 2000), 24–7.

Fox, Jonathan, ed., *The Challenge of Rural Democratization: Perspectives from Latin America and the Philippines* (London: Frank Cass, 1990).

Fox, Jonathan, "Editor's Introduction," in *The Challenge of Rural Democratization: Perspectives from Latin America and the Philippines*, Fox, ed. (London: Frank Cass, 1990), 1–13.

Fox, Jonathan, "The Difficult Transition from Clientelism to Citizenship," *World Politics* 46 (January 1994), 151–84.

Franco, Jennifer C., *Elections and Democratization in the Philippines* (Ph.D. dissertation, Political Science, Brown University, 1997).

Franco, Jennifer C., *Campaigning for Democracy: Grassroots Citizenship Movements, Less-than-Democratic Elections, and Regime Transition in the Philippines* (Quezon City: Institute for Popular Democracy, 2000).

Franco, Jennifer C., "The Philippines: Fractious Civil Society and Competing Visions of Democracy," in *Civil Society and Political Change in Asia: Expanding and Contracting Democratic Space*, Muthiah Alagappa, ed. (Stanford, CA: Stanford University Press, 2004), 97–137.

Franco, Jennifer C., and Turnino M. Burras, "Paradigm Shift: The 'September Thesis' and the Rebirth of the 'Open' Mass Movement in the Era of Neoliberal Globalization in the Philippines," in *Agrarian Angst and Rural Resistance in Contemporary Southeast Asia*, Dominique Caouette and Sarah Turner, eds. (New York: Routledge, 2009), 203–20.

Fung, Archon, "Reinventing Democracy in Latin America," *Perspectives on Politics* 9:4 (December 2011), 857–71.

Gaventa, John, *Power and Powerlessness: Quiescence and Rebellion in an Appalachian Valley* (Urbana, IL: University of Illinois Press, 1980).

Gaventa, John, "Finding the Spaces for Change: A Power Analysis," *IDS Bulletin* 37:6 (November 2006), 23–34.

Gaventa, John, "Triumph, Deficit, or Contestation: Deepening the 'Deepening Democracy' Debate" (Brighton: Institute of Development Studies, IDS Working Paper 264, 2006).

Geertz, Clifford, "Deep Play: Notes on the Balinese Cockfight," in *The Interpretation of Cultures* (New York: Basic Books, 1973), 412–53.

Geertz, Clifford, *Agricultural Involution* (Berkeley, CA: University of California Press, 1971).

Ghate, Prabhu B., "Lending to Micro Enterprises through NGOs in the Philippines," *Financial Landscapes Reconstructed: The Fine Art of Mapping Development*, F.J.A. Bouman and O. Hospes, eds. (Boulder, CO: Westview, 1994), 125–41.

Gills, Barry, Joel Rocamora, and Richard Wilson, eds., *Low-intensity Democracy: Political Power in the New World Order* (London: Pluto, 1993).

Gills, Barry, Joel Rocamora, and Richard Wilson, "Low Intensity Democracy," in *Low Intensity Democracy: Political Power in the New World Order*, Barry Gills, Joel Rocamora, and Richard Wilson, eds. (Boulder, CO: Pluto Press, 1993), 3–34.

Gonzalez, Eduardo T., and Magdalena L. Mendoza, *Governance in Southeast Asia: Issues and Options* (Makati: Philippine Institute for Development Studies, 2003).

Gonzalez, Eduardo T., ed., *Reconsidering the East Asian Economic Model: What's Ahead for the Philippines?* (Pasig City: Development Authority of the Philippines, 1999).

Greenhalgh, Susan, "De-Orientalizing the Chinese Family Firm," *American Ethnologist* 21 (1994), 746–75.

Grindle, Marilee S., *Going Local: Decentralization, Democratization, and the Promise of Good Governance* (Princeton, NJ: Princeton University Press, 2007).

Gruta, Eileen M., "Review of Government Performance in 1994: Grades from the People's Perspective" (Diliman: Social Weather Stations Bulletin, 1995).

Guerrero, Linda Luz B., and Rumelia Mañgalindan, "The Chineseness of Filipinos: The SWS December 1996 National Survey" (Diliman: Social Weather Stations Bulletin, 1997).

Guerrero, Linda Luz, ed., *The 2006–2007 SWS Surveys of Enterprises on Corruption* (Quezon City: Social Weather Stations, 2007).

Guerrero, Linda Luz, ed., *The 2009 SWS Surveys of Enterprises on Corruption* (Quezon City: Social Weather Stations, 2010).

Guidote, Tony, "1998 Presidentiables, Part II: Socio-Demographic Profile of Public Opinion" (Diliman: Social Weather Stations Bulletin, 1996).

Guthrie, George M., "The Philippine Temperament," in *Six Perspectives on the Philippines*, Guthrie, ed. (Manila: Bookmark, 1968), 49–84.

Gutierrez, Eric U., *The Ties that Bind: A Guide on Family, Business, and Other Interests in the 9th House of Representatives* (Pasig City: Philippine Center for Investigative Journalism, 1994).

Gutierrez, Eric U., Ildefonso Torrente, and Noli G. Narca, *All in the Family: A Study of Elites and Power Relations in the Philippines* (Quezon City: Institute for Popular Democracy, 1992).

Harrison, Lawrence, and Samuel P. Huntington, eds., *Culture Matters: How Values Shape Human Progress* (New York: Basic Books, 2000).

Hastings, Justin V., "Strategic Hypocrisy: Sovereignty, Commerce, and Security in Archipelagic Southeast Asia," in *Democratization in China, Korea, and Southeast Asia? Local and National Perspectives*, Kate Zhou, Shelley Rigger, and Lynn White, eds. (Abingdon: Routledge, 2014), ch. 4.

Hawes, Gary, *The Philippine State and the Marcos Regime* (Ithaca, NY: Cornell University Press, 1987).

Hawes, Gary, "Theories of Peasant Revolution: A Critique and Contribution from the Philippines," *World Politics* 42:2 (1990), 261–98.

Hawes, Gary, "Marcos, His Cronies, and the Philippines' Failure to Develop," in *Southeast Asian Capitalists*, Ruth McVey, ed. (Ithaca, NY: Southeast Asia Program, Cornell University, 1992), 145–60.

Hawes, Gary, and Liu Hong, "Explaining the Dynamics of the Southeast Asian Political Economy: State, Society, and the Search for Economic Growth," *World Politics* 45:4 (July 1993), 629–60.

Hedman, Eva-Lotta, "The Philippines: Not So Military, Not So Civil," in *Coercion and Governance: The Declining Political Role of the Military in Asia*, Muthiah Alagappa, ed. (Stanford, CA: Stanford University Press, 2001), 165–86.

Hedman, Eva-Lotta, *In the Name of Civil Society: From Free Election Movements to People Power Movements in the Philippines* (Quezon City: Ateneo de Manila University Press, 2006).

Heltberg, Rasmus, "Rural Market Imperfections and the Farm Size–Productivity Relationship: Evidence from Pakistan," *World Development* 96–10 (1998), 1807–26.

Hernandez, Carolina G., "The Military in Philippine Politics: Retrospect and Prospect," in *Whither the Philippines in the 21st Century*, Rodolfo C. Severino and Lorraine Carlos Salazar, eds. (Singapore: ISEAS, 2007), 78–99.

Hicken, Allen, *Building Party Systems in Developing Democracies* (New York: Cambridge University Press, 2009), esp. chapter 6, "Term Limits, Aggregation Incentives, and the Number of Parties in the Philippines."

Hicks, George L., and Geoffrey McNicoll, *Trade and Growth in the Philippines: An Open Dual Economy* (Ithaca, NY: Cornell University Press, 1971).

Hicks, George L., and S. Gordon Redding, "Culture and Corporate Performance in the Philippines: The Chinese Puzzle," *Philippine Review of Economics and Business* 19 (1982), 199–215.

Hill, Ronald, *Southeast Asia: People, Land, and Economy* (Crows Nest, NSW: Allen & Unwin, 2002).

Hodder, Rupert, *Between Two Worlds: Society, Politics, and Business in the Philippines* (London: Routledge-Curzon, 2002).

Hodder, Rupert, *Emotional Bureaucracy* (New Brunswick: Transaction Publishers, 2011).

Hollnsteiner, Mary Racelis, *The Dynamics of Power in a Philippine Municipality* (Quezon City: Community Development Research Council, University of the Philippines, 1963).

Hossain, Mahabub, "Economic Development in the Philippines: A Frustrated Take-Off?" *Philippine Review of Economics and Business* 33:1 (June 1996), 88–118.

Houle, Christian, "Inequality and Democracy: Why Inequality Harms Consolidation but Does Not Affect Democratization," *World Politics* 61:4 (2009), 589–622.

Hubo, Colin, Dionisio Papelleras, Jr., Rolando Dy, Winston Conrad Padojinog, and Gilbert Llanto, *The Road Less Travelled: Project Development by LGUs* [Local Government Units] *for LGUs* (Pasig City: University of Asia and the Pacific, 2010).

Huntington, Samuel P., *Political Order in Changing Societies* (New Haven, CT: Yale University Press, 1968).

Huntington, Samuel P., *The Third Wave: Democratization in the Late Twentieth Century* (Norman, OK: University of Oklahoma Press, 1991).

Huntington, Samuel P., "The West: Unique, not Universal," *Foreign Affairs* 75:6 (November/December 1996), 28–46.

Hutchcroft, Paul D., "Philippines," in *Countries at the Crossroads: A Survey of Democratic Governance*, in Sanja Kelly, Christopher Walker, and Jake Dizard, eds. (Lanham, MD: Rowman & Littlefield, 1978), 515–48.

Hutchcroft, Paul D., "Oligarch and Cronies in the Philippine State: The Politics of Patrimonial Plunder," *World Politics* 43 (April 1991), 414–50.

Hutchcroft, Paul D., "Booty Capitalism: Business–Government Relations in the Philippines," in *Business and Government in Industrializing Asia*, Andrew MacIntyre, ed. (Ithaca, NY: Cornell University Press, 1994), 216–43.

Hutchcroft, Paul D., "Sustaining Economic and Political Reform: The Challenges Ahead," in *The Philippines: New Directions in Domestic Policy and Foreign Relations*, David G. Timberman, ed. (Singapore: Institute for Southeast Asian Studies and New York: Asia Society, 1998), 23–48.

Hutchcroft, Paul D., *Booty Capitalism: The Politics of Banking in the Philippines* (Quezon City: Ateneo de Manila University Press, 1998) (orig. "Predatory Oligarchy, Patrimonial State: The Politics of Domestic Commercial Banking in the Philippines," Ph.D. dissertation, Political Science Department, Yale University, 1993).

Hutchcroft, Paul D., "Colonial Masters, National Politicos, and Provincial Lords: Central Authority and Local Autonomy in the American Philippines, 1900–1913," *Journal of Asian Studies* 59:2 (2000), 277–306.

Hutchcroft, Paul D., "Obstructive Corruption: The Politics of Privilege in the Philippines," in *Rents, Rent-seeking, and Economic Development: Theory and Evidence in Asia*, Mushtaq H. Kahn and K.S. Jomo, eds. (New York, Cambridge University Press, 2000), 207–47.

Hutchcroft, Paul D., "Dictatorship, Development, and Plunder: The Regimes of Park Chung Hee and Ferdinand Marcos Compared," paper for the American Political Science Association Annual Meeting, 2002.

Hutchcroft, Paul D., "Dreams of Redemption: Localist Strategies and Political Reform in the Philippines," in *The Politics of Change in the Philippines*, Yuko Kasuya and Nathan Gilbert Quimpo, eds. (Pasig City: Anvil, 2010), 418–54.

Hutchcroft, Paul D., and Joel Rocamora, "Strong Demands and Weak Institutions: Addressing the Democratic Deficit in the Philippines" (essay provided by courtesy of Dr. Rocamora); also *Journal of East Asian Studies* 3 (2003), 259–92.

Hutchcroft, Paul D., and Joel Rocamora, "Patronage-Based Parties and the Democratic Deficit in the Philippines: Origins, Evolution, and the Imperatives of Reform," in *Routledge Handbook of Southeast Asian Politics*, Richard Robison, ed. (Abingdon: Routledge, 2013), 97–119.

Hutchcroft, Paul D., *Deciphering Decentralization: Central Authority and Local Bosses in the Philippines and Beyond* (New York: Cambridge University Press, forthcoming).

Hutcheon, Pat Duffy, "Power in the Philippines: How Democratic is Asia's 'First Democracy'?" *Journal of Asian and African Studies* 6:3–4 (1971), 205–16.

Hutchison, Jane, "Class and State Power in the Philippines," in *Southeast Asia in the 1990s: Authoritarianism, Democracy, and Capitalism*, Kevin Hewison, Richard Robison, and Garry Rodan, eds. (St. Leonards, NSW: Allen & Unwin, 1993), 191–212.

Hutchison, Jane, "Labour Politics in Southeast Asia: The Philippines in Comparative Perspective," *Routledge Handbook of Southeast Asian Politics*, Richard Robison, ed. (Abingdon: Routledge, 2013), 40–52.

Ibon Workers Desk, *The Philippine Garment and Textile Industries* (Manila: Ibon Foundation, 2001).

Ileto, Reynaldo Clemeña, *Pasyón and Revolution: Popular Movements in the Philippines, 1840–1910* (Quezon City: Ateneo de Manila University Press, 1979).

Ileto, Reynaldo Clemeña, *Knowing America's Colony: A Hundred Years from the Philippine War*, esp. Lecture 3, "Orientalism and the Study of Philippine Politics" (Honolulu, HI: Center for Philippine Studies, 1999), 41–65.

Institute for Popular Democracy, *Face to Face, All Politics is Local: Interviews with Candidates* (Quezon City: Institute for Popular Democracy, March 2010).

Intengan, Romeo J., S.J., "Christian Faith, Ideologies, and Social Change," in *The Aquino Government and the Question of Ideology*, Raul J. Bonoan, Agnes Colette Condon, and Soledad S. Reyes, eds. (Quezon City: Phoenix Publishing House, 1987), 67–79.

Itao, Arnulfo F., and Myrna R. Co, eds., *Entrepreneurship and Small Enterprises Development: The Philippine Experience* (Quezon City: University of the Philippines Institute for Small Scale Industries, 1979).

Jin, Sophie C., *The Peasant in the Produce Section: Agricultural Adjustment for China's Small Farmers* (Woodrow Wilson School Senior Thesis, Princeton University, 2011).

Jones, Gregg R., *Red Revolution: Inside the Philippine Guerrilla Movement* (Boulder, CO: Westview, 1989).

Kaplan, Paul F., and Cynthia Hsien Huang, "Achievement Orientation of Small Industrial Entrepreneurs in the Philippines," *Human Organization* 33:2 (Summer 1974), 173–82.

Kapstein, Ethan B., and Nathan Converse, "Why Democracies Fail," *Journal of Democracy* 19:4 (October 2008), 57–68.

Karaos, Anna Marie A., "The Current Political Spectrum," in *The Aquino Government and the Question of Ideology*, Raul J. Bonoan, Agnes Colette Condon, and Soledad S. Reyes, eds. (Quezon City: Phoenix Publishing House, 1987), 47–54.

Karaos, Anna Marie A., "Democracy and Citizenship among Urban Middle Class Families," in *Philippine Democracy Agenda*: vol. 1, *Democracy and Citizenship in Filipino Political Culture*, Maria Serena I. Diokno, ed. (Quezon City: Third World Studies Center, University of the Philippines, 1997), 113–32.

Kasuya, Yuko, and Nathan Gilbert Quimpo, eds., *The Politics of Change in the Philippines* (Pasig City: Anvil, 2010).

Kasuya, Yoko, "Democratic Consolidation in the Philippines: Who Supports Extra-Constitutional Change?" in *The Politics of Change in the Philippines*, Yuko Kasuya and Nathan Gilbert Quimpo, eds. (Pasig City: Anvil, 2010), 90–113.

Kateb, George, *Patriotism and Other Mistakes* (New Haven, CT: Yale University Press, 2006).

Kawanaka Takeshi, *Power in a Philippine City* [Naga City, Bikol] (Chiba: Institute of Developing Economies, 2002).

Kerkvliet, Benedict J. Tria, *The Huk Rebellion: A Study of Peasant Revolt in the Philippines* (Berkeley, CA: University of California Press, 1977).

References 245

Kerkvliet, Benedict J. Tria, *Everyday Politics in the Philippines: Class and Status Relations in a Central Luzon Village* (Berkeley, CA: University of California Press, 1990; also Quezon City: New Day, 1991).

Kerkvliet, Benedict J. Tria, "Toward a More Comprehensive Analysis of Philippine Politics: Beyond the Patron–Client, Factional Framework," *Journal of Southeast Asian Studies* 26 (September 1995), 401–19.

Kerkvliet, Benedict J. Tria, "Contested Meanings of Elections in the Philippines," in *The Politics of Elections in Southeast Asia*, R.H. Taylor, ed. (New York: Cambridge University Press; and Washington, DC: Woodrow Wilson Center, 1996), 136–63.

Kerkvliet, Benedict J. Tria, "Political Expectations and Democracy in the Philippines and Vietnam," *Philippine Political Science Journal* 26:49 (2005), 1–26.

Kerkvliet, Benedict J. Tria, and Rasil Mojares, eds., *From Marcos to Aquino: Local Perspectives on Political Transition in the Philippines* (Quezon City: Ateneo de Manila University Press, 1992).

Kessler, Richard J., *Rebellion and Repression in the Philippines* (New Haven, CT: Yale University Press, 1989).

Khandker, Shahid, ed., *Impact of the East Asian Financial Crisis Revisited* (Makati: Philippine Institute for Development Studies, 2002).

Kikuchi Yasushi, *Uncrystallized Philippine Society: A Social Anthropological Analysis* (Quezon City: New Day Publishers, 1991).

Kimura Masataka, *Elections and Politics, Philippine Style: A Case in Lipa* (Manila: De La Salle University Press, 1997).

Kinsman, Jeremy, and Kurt Bassuener, *A Diplomat's Handbook for Democracy Development Support* (Waterloo, ON: Centre for International Governance Innovation, 2013).

Klitgaard, Robert, *Controlling Corruption* (Berkeley, CA: University of California Press, 1988).

Koike Kenji, "Group Management of Business Groups in the Philippines," in *Philippine Business Leaders*, in Perla Q. Makil, Leonora A. Reyes, and Koike Kenji, eds. (Tokyo: Institute of Developing Economies, 1983), 30–49.

Koike Kenji, "The Reorganization of *Zaibatsu* Groups under the Marcos and Aquino Regimes," *East Asian Cultural Studies* 28:1–4 (1989), 127–43.

Kosuke, Mizuno, and Pasuk Phongpaichit, eds., *Populism in Asia* (Singapore: NUS Press, 2009).

Kuhonta, Erik Martinez, *The Institutional Imperative: The Politics of Equitable Development in Southeast Asia* (Stanford, CA: Stanford University Press, 2011).

Kusaka, Wataru, "Governing Informalities of the Urban Poor: Street Vendors and Social Order Making in Metro Manila," in *The Politics of Change in the Philippines*, Yuko Kasuya and Nathan Gilbert Quimpo, eds. (Pasig City: Anvil, 2010), 362–90.

Lambsdorff, J.G., "Corruption in Comparative Perception [*sic*]," in *Economics of Corruption*, A.K. Jain, ed. (Boston, MA: Kluwer, 1998), 80–93.

Landé, Carl H., "Party Politics in the Philippines," in *Six Perspectives on the Philippines*, George M. Guthrie, ed. (Manila: Bookmark, 1968), 85–132.

Landé, Carl H., *Leaders, Factions, and Parties: The Structure of Philippine Politics* (New Haven, CT: Yale University Southeast Asia Monograph Series, 1965).

Landé, Carl H., *Southern Tagalog Voting, 1946–63: Political Behavior in a Philippine Region* (DeKalb, IL: Northern Illinois University Center for Southeast Asian Studies, 1973).

Landé, Carl H., *Post-Marcos Politics: A Geographical and Statistical Analysis of the 1992 Presidential Elections* (Singapore: Institute of Southeast Asian Studies, 1996).

Landé, Carl H., and Allan Cigler, "Social Cleavages and Political Parties in the Post-Marcos Philippines," final report for the U.S. Department of State by the External Research Program of the University of Kansas (1990).
Laothamatas, Anek, "A Tale of Two Democracies: Conflicting Perceptions of Elections and Democracy in Thailand," in *The Politics of Elections in Southeast Asia*, R.H. Taylor, ed. (Washington, DC: Woodrow Wilson Center, 1996), 201–23.
Laquian, Aprodicio, and Eleanor R. Laquian, *Joseph Ejercito "Erap" Estrada: The Centennial President* (Diliman: College of Public Administration, University of the Philippines, 1998).
Lara, Francisco, Jr., and Horacio Morales, Jr., "The Peasant Movement and the Challenge of Democratization in the Philippines," in *The Challenge of Rural Democratization: Perspectives from Latin America and the Philippines*, Jonathan Fox, ed. (London: Frank Cass, 1990), 143–57.
Larkin, John A., *The Pampangans: Colonial Society in a Philippine Province* (Berkeley, CA: University of California Press, 1972).
Larkin, John A., "Philippine History Reconsidered: A Socioeconomic Perspective," *American Historical Review* 87:3 (1982), 595–628, www.jstor.org/stable/1864158.
Larkin, John A., *Sugar and the Origins of Modern Philippine Society* (Berkeley, CA: University of California Press, 1993).
Lawyers' Committee for Human Rights, *"Salvaging" Democracy: Human Rights in the Philippines* (New York: Lawyers' Committee, 1985).
Lazare, Daniel, *The Frozen Republic: How the [American] Constitution is Paralyzing Democracy* (New York: Harcourt Brace, 1996).
Lazatín, Carlos Manuel, *The Challenge of Economic Reform in a Democracy: The Philippines and Thailand in the 1990s* (Princeton University Senior Thesis, Woodrow Wilson School, 1999).
Le Bon, Gustave, *The Crowd: A Study of the Popular Mind* (Mineola, NY: Dover, 2002).
Lee-Chua, Queena N., *Successful Family Businesses: Dynamics of Five Filipino Business Families* (Quezon City: Ateneo de Manila University Press, 1997).
Levi, Carlo, *Christ Stopped at Eboli* (Cristo si è fermato a Eboli), tr. Frances Frenaye (London: Penguin, 1982).
Lewis, Henry T., *Ilocano Rice Farmers: A Comparative Study of two Philippine Barrios* (Honolulu, HI: University of Hawaii Press, 1971).
Lewis, W. Arthur, "Economic Development with Unlimited Supplies of Labour," *Manchester School of Economic and Social Studies* (1954), 139–91.
Lim-Mangada, Ladylyn, "Grooming the Wards: Dynamics Between a Political Party and Community Groups," in *Philippine Democracy Agenda*: vol. 3, *Civil Society Making Civil Society*, Miriam Coronel Ferrer, ed. (Quezon City: Third World Studies Center, University of the Philippines, 1997), 259–70.
Linz, Juan, "The Perils of Presidentialism," *Journal of Democracy* (winter 1990), 51–69.
Lipset, Seymour Martin, *Political Man: The Social Bases of Politics* (Baltimore, MD: Johns Hopkins University Press, orig. 1961, expanded edn. 1981).
Luckham, Robin, Anne Marie Goetz, and Mary Kaldor, "Democratic Institutions and Democratic Politics," in *Can Democracy be Designed? The Politics of Institutional Choice in Conflict-Torn Societies*, R. Luckham and S. Bastian, eds. (London: Zed Books, 2003), ch. 1.
Lund, Susan-Marie, "Informal Credit and Risk-Sharing Networks: Empirical Evidence from the Philippines" (Ph.D. dissertation, Stanford University, 1996).

Lynch, Frank, S.J., *Social Class in a Bikol Town* (Chicago: Philippine Studies Program, Anthropology Department, University of Chicago, 1959).

Lynch, Frank, S.J., *Social Class in a Bikol Town* (Chicago, IL: Philippine Studies Program, Anthropology Department, University of Chicago, 1959).

Lynch, Frank, S.J., ed., *View from the Paddy: Empirical Studies of Philippine Rice Farming and Tenancy, Philippine Sociological Review* 20:1–2 (January/April 1972), 3–274.

Lynch, Frank, S.J., *Philippine Society and Culture* [selected essays], rev. edn., Aram Yengoyan and Perla Q. Makil, ed. (Quezon City: Ateneo de Manila Institute of Philippine Culture, 1984); orig. published as *Philippine Society and the Individual* (Ann Arbor, MI: University of Michigan Center for South and Southeast Asian Studies, 1984).

McBeath, Gerald A., *The Political Integration of Philippine Chinese* (Berkeley, CA: University of California Press, 1995).

McCoy, Alfred W., ed., *An Anarchy of Families: State and Family in the Philippines* (Madison, WI: University of Wisconsin Center for Southeast Asian Studies, 1993).

McCoy, Alfred W., "An Anarchy of Families: The Historiography of State and Family in the Philippines," in *An Anarchy of Families: State and Family in the Philippines*, McCoy, ed. (Madison, WI: University of Wisconsin Center for Southeast Asian Studies, 1993), 1–32.

McCoy, Alfred W., "Rent-Seeking Families and the Philippine State: A History of the Lopez Family," in *An Anarchy of Families: State and Family in the Philippines*, McCoy, ed. (Madison, WI: University of Wisconsin Center for Southeast Asian Studies, 1993), 429–536.

McCoy, Alfred W., *Closer than Brothers: Manhood at the Philippine Military Academy* (New Haven, CT: Yale University Press, 1999; also Manila: Anvil, 1999).

McCoy, Alfred W., *Policing America's Empire: The United States, the Philippines, and the Rise of the Surveillance State* (Madison, WI: University of Wisconsin Press, 2009).

Machado, Kit G., "From Traditional Faction to Machine: Changing Patterns of Political Leadership in the Rural Philippines," *Journal of Asian Studies* 33:4 (August 1974), 523–47.

Machiavelli, Niccolò, *The Prince*, intro. Christian Gauss (New York: Mentor, 1955 [orig. 1532]).

Mackie, Jamie, "Changing Patterns of Chinese Big Business in Southeast Asia," in *Southeast Asian Capitalists*, Ruth McVey, ed. (Ithaca, NY: Southeast Asia Program, Cornell University, 1992), 161–90.

Mackie, Jamie, and Bernardo Villegas, "The Philippines: Still an Exceptional Case?" in James Morley, ed., *Driven by Growth: Political Change in the Asia-Pacific Region* (Armonk, NY: M.E. Sharpe, 1993), 142–60.

Magadia, José J., *State–Society Dynamics: Policymaking in a Restored Democracy* (Quezon City: Ateneo de Manila University Press, 2003).

Magno, Alexander R., *Kasaysayan: The Story of the Filipino People, vol. 9, A Nation Reborn* (Manila: Reader's Digest, 1998).

Magno Torres III, Wilfredo, ed., *Rido: Clan Feuding and Conflict Management in Mindanao* (Manila: Asia Foundation, 2007).

Mangahas, Mahar, "Democracy and Economic Progress: The Filipino People's Perspective," paper for XIII World Congress of Sociology, Germany, 1994.

Mangahas, Mahar, "Pinoy [Filipino] Voters, Incorporated" (Diliman: Social Weather Stations Bulletin, 1995).

Mangahas, Mahar, "Public Opinion about Public Officials" (Diliman: Social Weather Stations Occasional Paper, 1995).
Mangahas, Mahar, "The Government's Pop Charts: Personalities" (Diliman: Social Weather Stations Bulletin, 1995).
Mangahas, Mahar, "Lotto, Jueteng, and Cockfighting" (Diliman: Social Weather Stations Bulletin, 1996).
Mangahas, Mahar, "The Popular Call for Government Spending" (Diliman: Social Weather Stations Bulletin, 1996).
Mangahas, Mahar, "Making a 'True' Filipino" (Diliman: Social Weather Stations Bulletin, 1996).
Mangahas, Mahar, "SWS Surveys on Self-Rated Poverty" (Diliman: Social Weather Stations Bulletin, 1997).
Mangahas, Mahar, "The Divine Word College-Tagbilaran/Social Weather Stations Bohol Poll 1" (Diliman: Social Weather Stations Bulletin, 1997).
Mangahas, Mahar, "Why the Vatican Likes Filipino Catholics" (Diliman: Social Weather Stations Bulletin, 1997).
Mangahas, Mahar, Antonio G.M. La Viña, Steven Rood, Athena Lydia Casambre, and Dennis M. Arroyo, *Monitoring the State of the Judiciary and the Legal Profession* (Quezon City: Social Weather Stations, 1996).
Mannheim, Karl, *Ideology and Utopia: An Introduction to the Sociology of Knowledge* (London: Routledge, 1936).
Mansfield, Edward D., and Jack Snyder, "Turbulent Transitions: Why Emerging Democracies Go to War in the Twenty-first Century," in *Leashing the Dogs of War: Conflict Management in a Divided World*, F.O. Hampson and P. All, eds. (Washington, DC: United States Institute for Peace, 2007), 161–76.
Martinez, Manuel F., *Assassinations and Conspiracies: From Rajah Humabon to Imelda Marcos* (Manila: Anvil, 2003).
Martinez, Manuel F., *More Assassinations and Conspiracies* (Manila: Anvil, 2004).
Marx, Karl, and Fredrick Engels, *Manifesto of the Communist Party*, tr. Samuel Moore (1888) (Beijing: Foreign Languages Press, 1970).
May, Ronald James, *Vigilantes in the Philippines: From Fanatical Cults to Citizens' Organizations* (Honolulu, HI: Center for Philippine Studies, University of Hawaii, 1992).
Melgar, Ma. Teresa R., and Lourdes Gordolan, "Reforming the Ombudsman" and "Credible Reform Against Corruption," *Political Brief* (IPD) 9:2 (2001), 2–27.
Migdal, Joel S., *Strong Societies and Weak States: State–Society Relations and State Capabilities in the Third World* (Princeton, NJ: Princeton University Press, 1988).
Mink, Louis O., "The Autonomy of Historical Understanding," *History and Theory* 5 (1965), 24–47.
Miranda, Felipe B., "A Higher Budget for a Truly More Capable, Modern AFP [Armed Forces of the Philippines]" (Diliman: Social Weather Stations Bulletin, 1995).
Miranda, Felipe B., ed., *Democratization: Philippine Perspectives* (Quezon City: University of the Philippines Press, 1995).
Miranda, Felipe B., "The Philippine Military at the Crossroads of Democratization" (Diliman: Social Weather Stations Occasional Paper, 1996).
Miranda, Filipe B., "Political Economy in a Democratizing Philippines: A People's Perspective," in *Democratization: Philippine Perspectives*, Felipe B. Miranda, ed. (Quezon City: University of the Philippines Press, 1997), 153–228.
Miranda, Felipe B., Temario C. Rivera, Malaya C. Ronas, and Ronald D. Holmes,

Chasing the Wind: Assessing Philippine Democracy (Quezon City, Commission on Human Rights of the Philippines and United Nations Development Program, 2011).

Mitchell, Bernard, and John Ravenhill, "Beyond Product Cycles and Flying Geese: Regionalization, Hierarchy, and the Industrialization of East Asia," *World Politics* 47 (1995), 171–209.

Modina, Rolando B., and A.R. Ridao, *IRRI Rice: The Miracle that Never Was* (Quezon City: ACES Foundation, 1987).

Mojares, Resil B., *The Man Who Would Be President: Serging Osmeña and Philippine Politics* (Cebu: Maria Cacao, 1986).

Mojares, Resil B., "The Dream Goes On and On: Three Generations of the Osmeñas, 1906–1990," in *An Anarchy of Families: State and Family in the Philippines*, Alfred W. McCoy, ed. (Madison, WI: University of Wisconsin Center for Southeast Asian Studies, 1993), 311–38.

Mojares, Resil B., "Making a Turn: Thoughts on a Generation of Philippine Scholarship," Keynote Address at the Philippine Studies Conference, Kyoto, Japan, February 28 to March 2, 2014 (kindly supplied to the author by Norman G. Owen, originally distributed on Facebook by Vicente L. Rafael).

Montes, Manuel F., "The Private Sector as the Engine of Philippine Growth: Can Heaven Wait?" *Journal of Far Eastern Business* 1:3 (Spring 1995), 132–47.

Montinola, Gabriella R., "Parties and Accountability in the Philippines," *Journal of Democracy* 10:1 (1999), 126–40.

Moore, Barrington, Jr., *Social Origins of Dictatorship and Democracy: Lord and Peasant in the Making of the Modern World* (Boston, MA: Beacon, 1966).

Murray, David, *Angels and Devils: Thai Politics from February 1991 to September 1992—A Struggle for Democracy?* (Bangkok: White Orchid Press, 1996).

Murray, Francis J., Jr., "Land Reform in the Philippines: An Overview," in *View from the Paddy: Empirical Studies of Philippine Rice Farming and Tenancy*, Frank Lynch, S.J., ed., *Philippine Sociological Review*, 20:1–2 (January/April 1972), 151–68.

Nery, John, *Revolutionary Spirit: José Rizal in Southeast Asia* (Singapore: ISEAS, 2011).

Nicholas, Ralph W., "Factions: A Comparative Analysis," in *Political Systems and the Distribution of Power*, Michael Banton, ed. (London: Tavistock, 1968), 21–58.

Nowak, Thomas C., and Kay A. Snyder, "Economic Concentration and Political Change in the Philippines," in *Studies in Local Political Change: The Philippines Before Martial Law*, Benedict J. Kerkvliet, ed. (Honolulu, HI: University of Hawaii Press, 1974), 153–242.

Nye, Joseph S., *The Powers to Lead* (New York: Oxford University Press, 2010).

Ordoñez, Rudy, *The Kapampangan Mystique* (Manila: UST Publishing, 2009).

Oshima, Harry T., "Changes in Philippine Income Distribution in the 1970s," *Philippine Review of Economics and Business* 20:3–4 (September/December, 1983), 281–90.

Owen, Norman G., ed., *Compadre Colonialism: Studies on the Philippines under American Rule* (Ann Arbor, MI: Center for South and Southeast Asian Studies, 1971).

Owen, Norman G., *Prosperity without Progress: Manila Hemp and Material Life in the Colonial Philippines* (Berkeley, CA: University of California Press, 1983).

Owen, Norman G., *The Bikol Blend: Bikolanos and their History* (Quezon City: New Day Publishers, 1999).

Owen, Norman G., ed., *Routledge Handbook of Southeast Asian History* (Abingdon: Routledge, 2013).

Owen, Norman G., "Introduction: In Search of Southeast Asian History," in *Routledge Handbook of Southeast Asian History*, Owen, ed. (London: Routledge, 2013).

Pacquiao, Manny, with Timothy James, *Pacman: My Story of Hope, Resilience, and Never-Say-Never Determination* (orig. Nashville, TN: Dunham, 2010; also Manila: Anvil, 2010).

Paez, Patricia Ann V., "State–Civil Society Relations in Policy-Making: Focus on the Legislative," in *Philippine Democracy Agenda*: vol. 2, *State–Civil Society Relations in Policy-Making*, Marlon A. Wui and Ma. Glenda S. Lopez, eds. (Quezon City: Third World Studies Center, University of the Philippines, 1997), 33–80.

Pahilanga-de los Reyes, Romana, and Frank Lynch, "Reluctant Rebels: Leasehold Converts in Nueva Ecija," in *View from the Paddy: Empirical Studies of Philippine Rice Farming and Tenancy*, Frank Lynch, S.J., ed., *Philippine Sociological Review*, 20:1–2 (January/April 1972), 7–78.

Pareto, Vilfredo, *The Rise and Fall of the Elites: An Application of Theoretical Sociology* (New York: Arno Press, 1979; orig. 1901).

Parsa, Misagh, "Entrepreneurs and Democratization: Iran and the Philippines," *Comparative Studies in Society and History* 37:4 (October 1995), 803–30.

Parsons, Talcott, *The Structure of Social Action* (New York: Mcgraw-Hill, 1937).

Parsons, Talcott, *The Social System* (Glencoe, IL: Free Press, 1951).

Parsons, Talcott, *The Theory of Social and Economic Organization* (New York: Simon & Schuster, 1964).

Pasuk Phongpaichit, and Chris Baker, *Thailand's Boom!* (North Sydney: Allen & Unwin, 1996).

Patten, Alan, "Rethinking Culture: The Social Lineage Account," *American Political Science Review* 105:4 (November 2011), 735–49.

Pearse, Andrew, *Seeds of Plenty, Seeds of Want: Social and Economic Implications of the Green Revolution* (Oxford: Clarendon Press, 1980).

Pertierra, Raul, *Religion, Politics, and Rationality in a Philippine Community* (Quezon City: Ateneo de Manila University Press, 1988).

Philippine Center for Investigative Journalism and Institute for Popular Democracy, *Boss: 5 Case Studies of Local Politics in the Philippines* (Pasig City: Philippine Center for Investigative Journalism, 1995).

Philippine Center for Investigative Journalism and Institute for Popular Democracy, *Patrimony: 6 Cases on Local Politics and the Environment in the Philippines* (Pasig City: Philippine Center for Investigative Journalism, 1996).

Philippine Center for Investigative Journalism and Institute for Popular Democracy, *Pork and Other Perks: Corruption and Governance in the Philippines* (Pasig City: Philippine Center for Investigative Journalism, 1998).

Philippine Democracy Agenda: vol. 1, *Democracy and Citizenship in Filipino Political Culture*, Maria Serena I. Diokno, ed.; vol. 2, *State-Civil Society Relations in Policy-Making*, Marlon A. Wui and Ma. Glenda S. Lopez, ed.; and vol. 3, *Civil Society Making Civil Society*, Miriam Coronel Ferrer, ed. (Quezon City: Third World Studies Center, University of the Philippines, 1997).

Philippine Democracy Assessment: Free and Fair Elections and the Democratic Role of Political Parties (Manila: Friedrich Ebert Stiftung, 2005).

Philippine Human Development Report, 2000 (n.p. [Manila]: Human Development Network and UNDP, 2000).

Pinches, Michael, "The Working Class Experience of Shame, Inequality, and People Power in Tatalon, Manila," in *From Marcos to Aquino: Local Perspectives in Political Transition in the Philippines*, Benedict J. Kerkvliet and Resil B. Majares, eds. (Honolulu, HI: University Press of Hawaii, 1991), 166–86.

Pinches, Michael, "Entrepreneurship, Consumption, Ethnicity, and National Identity in the Making of the Philippines' New Rich," in *Culture and Privilege in Capitalist Asia*, Pinches, ed. (New York: Routledge, 1999), 275–301.

Pinches, Michael, "The Philippines' New Rich: Capitalist Transformation amidst Economic Gloom," in *Culture and Privilege in Capitalist Asia*, Pinches, ed. (New York: Routledge, 1999), 105–36.

Pinches, Michael, "The Making of Middle Class Civil Society in the Philippines," in *The Politics of Change in the Philippines*, Yuko Kasuya and Nathan Gilbert Quimpo, eds. (Pasig City: Anvil, 2010), 284–312.

Pingali, Prabhu L., P.F. Moli, and L.W. Velasco, "Prospects for Rice Yield Improvement in the Post-Green Revolution Philippines," *Philippine Review of Economics and Business* 27:1 (June 1990), 85–106.

Polanyi, Karl, *The Great Transformation: The Social and Economic Origins of our Time* (New York: Rinehart, 1944).

Prystay, Cris, "Small Loans and Hard Work Spark Entrepreneurial Spirit," *Asian Business* 32:12 (December 1996), 62–9.

Przeworski, Adam, and Fernando Limongi, "Modernization: Theory and Facts," *World Politics* 49 (January 1997), 159–83.

Pulse Asia, "Presidential Trust Ratings, Presidential Appointments, and Expectations for the First Six Months of the Aquino Administration," *Ulat ng Bayan* press release, July 2010.

Putzel, James, *A Captive Land: The Politics of Agrarian Reform in the Philippines* (Manila: Ateneo de Manila University Press, 1992).

Pye, Lucian W., *Politics, Personality, and Nation Building* (New Haven, CT: Yale University Press, 1962).

Quimpo, Nathan Gilbert, *Contested Democracy and the Left in the Philippines* (New Haven, CT: Southeast Asia Council, Yale University, 2008).

Quimpo, Nathan Gilbert, "The Presidency, Political Parties, and Predatory Politics in the Philippines," in *The Politics of Change in the Philippines*, Yuko Kasuya and Nathan Gilbert Quimpo, eds. (Pasig City: Anvil, 2010), 47–72.

Quimpo, Nathan Gilbert, and Yuko Kasuya, "The Politics of Change in a Changeless Land," in *The Politics of Change in the Philippines*, Yuko Kasuya and Nathan Gilbert Quimpo, eds. (Pasig City: Anvil, 2010), 1–20.

Rafael, Vincente L., "The Cell Phone and the Crowd: Messianic Politics in the Contemporary Philippines," *Public Culture* 15:3 (Fall 2003), 399–425.

Rafael, Vicente L., "Contracting Colonialism and the Long 1970s," *Philippine Studies* 61:4 (2013), 477–94.

Randall, Vicky, "Political Parties and Democratic Developmental States," *Development Policy Review* 25:5 (2007), 633–52.

Ranis, Gustav, Frances Stewart, and Edna Angeles-Reyes, *Linkages in Developing Economies: A Philippine Study* (San Francisco, CA: ICS Press, 1990).

Rawls, John, *A Theory of Justice* (Cambridge, MA: Harvard University Press, 1971).

Reidinger, Jeffrey M., "Everyday Elite Resistance: Redistributive Agrarian Reform in the Philippines," in *The Violence Within: Cultural and Political Opposition in Divided Nations*, Kay B. Warren, ed. (Boulder, CO: Westview, 1993).

Reno, William, "The Politics of Insurgency in Collapsing States," *Development and Change* 33:5 (December 2002), 837–58.

Ressa, Maria A., *Seeds of Terror: An Eyewitness Account of Al-Qaeda's Newest Center of Operations in Southeast Asia* (New York: Free Press, 2003).

Riedinger, Jeffrey M., *Agrarian Reform in the Philippines: Democratic Transitions and Redistributive Reform* (Stanford, CA: Stanford University Press, 1995).
Rivera, Temario C., *Landlords and Capitalists: Class, Family, and State in Philippine Manufacturing* (Quezon City: University of the Philippines Center for Integrative and Development Studies, 1994).
Rivera, Temario C., *Philippines: State of the Nation* (Singapore: Institute of Southeast Asian Studies, 1996).
Rizal, José, *The Indolence of the Filipino*, tr. Charles Derbyshire (Manila: Hard Press, 1913).
Rizal, José, *Noli Me Tangere* (Touch Me Not), tr. H. Augenbraum (New York: Penguin, 2006).
Rizal, José, *The Reign of Greed (El Filibusterismo)*, tr. Charles Derbyshire (n.p.: Dodo Press, n.d.).
Robison, Richard, ed., *Routledge Handbook of Southeast Asian Politics* (Abingdon: Routledge, 2013).
Robison, Richard, "Interpreting the Politics of Southeast Asia: Debates in Parallel Universes," in *Routledge Handbook of Southeast Asian Politics*, Richard Robison, ed. (Abingdon: Routledge, 2013), 5–22.
Rocamora, Joel, "Lost Opportunities, Deepening Crisis: The Philippines under Cory Aquino," in *Low Intensity Democracy: Political Power in the New World Order*, Barry Gills, Joel Rocamora, and Richard Wilson, eds. (Boulder, CO: Pluto Press, 1993), 195–225.
Rocamora, Joel, "From Regime Crisis to System Change," in *Whither the Philippines in the 21st Century*, Rodolfo C. Severino and Lorraine Carlos Salazar, eds. (Singapore: ISEAS, 2007), 18–42.
Rocamora, Joel, "Estrada and the Populist Temptation in the Philippines," in *Populism in Asia*, Mizuno Kosuke and Pasuk Phongpaichit, eds. (Kyoto: Kyoto University Press, 2009), 41–65.
Rocamora, Joel, "Partisanship and Reform: The Making of a Presidential Campaign," in *The Politics of Change in the Philippines*, Yuko Kasuya and Nathan Gilbert Quimpo, eds. (Pasig City: Anvil, 2010), 73–89.
Rocamora, Joel, "Impossible is Not So Easy: Party Building and Local Governance in the Philippines" (essay provided by kind courtesy of the author).
Roces, Mina, *The Lopez Family, 1946–2000: Kinship Politics in Postwar Philippines* (Manila: De La Salle University Press, 2001).
Rodil, Ma., Cristina G., "Philippine Centennial Celebration" (Diliman: Social Weather Stations Bulletin, 1997).
Rodolfo, Kelvin S., *Pinatubo and the Politics of Lahar* (Quezon City: University of the Philippines Press, 1995).
Rodriguez, Edgard, and Albert Berry, "SMEs and the New Economy: Philippine Manufacturing in the 1990s," in *The Role of SMEs in National Economies in East Asia*, Charles Harvie and Boon-Chye Lee, eds. (Cheltenham: Edward Elgar, 2002), 136–57.
Rola, Agnes C., *An Upland Community in Transition: Institutional Innovations for Sustainable Development in Rural Philippines* (Laguna: Southeast Asian Regional Center for Graduate Study and Research in Agriculture, 2011).
Roman, Emerlinda R., *Management Control in Chinese-Filipino Enterprises* (Quezon City: Center for Integrative and Development Studies, UP, 1996).
Rood, Steven, ed., *Assessing People's Participation in Governance: The Case of Itogon Municipality* (Baguio: University of the Philippines College Baguio, Cordillera Studies Center, 1993).

Rood, Steven, "Researching Decentralized Governance," in *Democratization: Philippine Perspectives*, Felipe B. Miranda, ed. (Quezon City: University of the Philippines Press, 1995), 303–24.

Rood, Steven, "Decentralization, Democracy, and Development," in *The Philippines: New Directions in Domestic Policy and Foreign Relations*, David G. Timberman, ed. (Singapore: Institute for Southeast Asian Studies and New York: Asia Society, 1998), 111–36.

Rood, Steven, "Elections as Complicated and Important Events in the Philippines," in *How Asia Votes*, John Fu-sheng Hsieh and David Newman, eds. (New York: Chatham House, 2002), 148–50.

Rose-Ackerman, Susan, *Corruption in Government: Causes, Consequences, and Reform* (Cambridge: Cambridge University Press, 1999).

Ross, Michael L., "The Political Economy of the Resource Curse," *World Politics* 51 (January 1999), 297–322.

Rostow, Walter W., "The Take-Off into Self-Sustained Growth," *Economic Journal* 66 (March 1956), 25–48.

Rueschmeyer, Dietrich, Evelyne Huber Stephens, and John D. Stephens, *Capitalist Development and Democracy* (Chicago, IL: University of Chicago Press, 1992).

Rustow, Dankwart, "Transitions to Democracy," *Comparative Politics* 2:3 (1970), 337–63.

Rutten, Rosanne, *Artisans and Entrepreneurs in the Rural Philippines* (Amsterdam: VU University Press, 1990).

Saito, Katrine Anderson, and Delano P. Villanueva, "Transaction Costs of Credit to the Small-Scale Sector in the Philippines," *Economic Development and Cultural Change* 29:3 (April 1981), 631–40.

Salazar, Lorraine Carlos, *States, Market Reforms, and Rents: The Political Economy of Telecommunications Reform in Malaysia and the Philippines* (Ph.D. dissertation, Australia National University, 2004).

Santiago, Miriam Defensor, *Cutting Edge: The Politics of Reform in the Philippines* (Mandaluyong City: Woman Today Publications, 1994).

Santos, Soliman M., Jr., *Heart and Mind in Bicol, 1975–1993: Forty Selected Activist Writings* (Quezon City: Soliman Santos, 1994).

Santos, Soliman M., Jr., and Paz Verdades M. Santos, *Primed and Purposeful: Armed Groups and Human Security Efforts in the Philippines* (Geneva: Small Arms Survey, Graduate Institute of International and Development Studies, 2010).

Satake, Masaaki, *People's Economy: Philippine Community-Based Industries and Alternative Development* (Kagawa: Shikoku Gakuin University, 2003).

Schaffer, Frederic Charles, "Disciplinary Reactions: Alienation and the Reform of Vote Buying in the Philippines," paper for the American Political Science Association Annual Meeting, 2002.

Schattschneider, E.E., *Party Government* (New York: Farrar & Rinehart, 1942).

Schattschneider, E.E., *The Semi-Sovereign People: A Realist's View of Democracy in America*, intro. by David Adamany (Hinsdale, IL: Dreyden Press, 1975).

Schedler, Andreas, ed., *Electoral Authoritarianism: The Dynamics of Unfree Competition* (Boulder, CO: Rienner, 2006).

Schedler, Andreas, "The Logic of Electoral Authoritarianism," in *Electoral Authoritarianism: The Dynamics of Unfree Competition*, Schedler, ed. (Boulder, CO: Rienner, 2006), 1–25.

Schmitter, Philippe, "Still the Century of Corporatism?" *Review of Politics* 1 (January 1974), 85–128.

Scipes, Kim, *KMU* [Kilusang Mayo Uno]: *Building Genuine Trade Unionism in the Philippines, 1980–1994* (Quezon City: New Day Publishers, 1996).
Scott, James C., "Patron–Client Politics and Political Science," in *The Political Economy of Development: Theoretical Empirical Approaches*, Norman T. Uphoff and Warren F. Ilchman, eds. (Berkeley, CA: University of California Press, 1972), 177–89.
Scott, James C., "The Erosion of Patron–Client Bonds and Social Change in Rural Southeast Asia," *Journal of Asian Studies* 32:1 (November 1972), 6–37.
Scott, James C., *Weapons of the Weak: Everyday Forms of Peasant Resistance* (New Haven, CT: Yale University Press, 1985).
Scott, James C., *The Art of Not Being Governed: An Anarchist History of Upland Southeast Asia* (New Haven, CT: Yale University Press, 2009).
Seagrave, Sterling, *The Marcos Dynasty* (New York: Harper & Row, 1988).
Sermeno, Donna A., *Circumventing Agrarian Reform: Cases of Land Conversion* (Manila: Institute on Church and Social Issues, 1994).
Severino, Rudolfo C., *Where in the World is the Philippines: Debating its National Territory* (Singapore: ISEAS, 2011).
Severino, Rodolfo C., and Lorraine Carlos Salazar, eds., *Whither the Philippines in the 21st Century* (Singapore: Institute for Southeast Asian Studies, 2007).
Shane, Scott A., *The Illusions of Entrepreneurship: The Costly Myths that Entrepreneurs, Investors, and Policy Makers Live By* (New Haven, CT: Yale University Press, 2010).
Shieh Gwo-shyong, *"Boss" Island: The Subcontracting Network and Microentrepreneurship in Taiwan's Development* (New York: P. Lang, 1992).
Shirmer, Daniel B., and Stephen Rosskamm Shalom, *The Philippines Reader: A History of Colonialism, Neocolonialism, Dictatorship, and Resistance* (Boston, MA: South End Press, 1987).
Shue, Vivienne, *Peasant China in Transition: The Dynamics of Development Toward Socialism, 1949–1956* (Berkeley, CA: University of California Press, 1980).
Sicam, Paulynn P., *Understanding Poverty: The Poor Talk about What it Means to be Poor* (Makati: Institute for People Power and Development, 2007).
Sidel, John T., "Walking in the Shadow of the Big Man: Justiniano Montano and Failed Dynasty Building in Cavite, 1935–1972," in *An Anarchy of Families: State and Family in the Philippines*, Alfred W. McCoy, ed. (Madison, WI: University of Wisconsin Center for Southeast Asian Studies, 1993), 109–62.
Sidel, John T., "The Philippines: The Languages of Legitimation," in *Political Legitimacy in Southeast Asia: The Quest for Moral Authority*, Muthiah Alagappa, ed. (Stanford, CA: Stanford University Press, 1995), 136–69.
Sidel, John T., "Philippine Politics in Town, District, and Province: Bossism in Cavite and Cebu," *Journal of Asian Studies* 56:4 (November 1997), 947–66.
Sidel, John T., *Capital, Coercion, and Crime: Bossism in the Philippines* (Honolulu, HI: University of Hawaii Press, 1999).
Sidel, John T., "Response to Ileto: Or, I am Not an Orientalist," *Philippine Political Science Journal* 23:46 (2002), 129–38.
Sidel, John, "Social Origins of Dictatorship and Democracy Revisited: Colonial State and Chinese Immigrant in the Making of Modern Southeast Asia," *Comparative Politics* 40:2 (2008), 127–47.
Sidel, John T., "Economic Foundations of Subnational Authoritarianism: Insights and Evidence from Qualitative and Quantitative Research," *Democratization* (2012), 1–24.
Silliman, G. Sidney, "Human Rights and the Transition to Democracy," in *Patterns of Power and Politics in the Philippines*, James F. Eder and Robert L. Youngblood, eds.

(Tempe, AZ: Arizona State University Program for Southeast Asian Studies, 1994), 103–46.
Sison, A.J.G., "Business and Culture in the Philippines: A Story of Gradual Progress," *Issues in Business Ethics* 13 (1999), 145–66.
Sison, José Ma., and Julieta da Lima, *Philippine Economy and Politics* (Quezon City: Aklat ng Bayan Publishing House, 1998).
Skinner, G. William, *Leadership and Power in the Chinese Community of Thailand* (Ithaca, NY: Cornell University Press, 1958).
Skinner, G. William, "Overseas Chinese Leadership: Paradigm for a Paradox," in *Leadership and Authority: A Symposium*, Gehan Wijeyewardene, ed. (Singapore: University of Malaya Press, 1968), 191–203.
Skinner, G. William, "Chinese Assimilation and Thai Politics," *Journal of Asian Studies* 16 (February 1957), 237–50, reprinted in *Southeast Asia: The Politics of National Integration*, John T. McAlister, ed. (New York: Random House, 1973).
Skinner, G. William, "Change and Persistence in Chinese Culture Overseas: A Comparison of Thailand and Java," in *Change and Persistence in Thai Society: Essays in Honor of Lauriston Sharp*, Skinner, ed. (Ithaca, NY: Cornell University Press, 1975).
Slater, Dan, *Ordering Power: Contentious Politics and Authoritarian Leviathans in Southeast Asia* (New York: Cambridge University Press, 2010; orig. Ph.D. thesis, Emory University, 2005).
Snyder, Richard, "Beyond Electoral Authoritarianism: The Spectrum of Nondemocratic Regimes," in *Electoral Authoritarianism: The Dynamics of Unfree Competition*, Andreas Schedler, ed. (Boulder, CO: Rienner, 2006), 219–30.
Social Weather Stations Staff, "Public Reactions to the August 28, 1987, Coup Attempt" (Diliman: Social Weather Stations Occasional Paper, 1988).
Social Weather Stations Staff, "Public Opinion on Prominent Political Personalities" (Diliman: Social Weather Stations Occasional Paper, 1992).
Social Weather Stations, *Major Research References*, Mahar Mangahas, ed. (compact disk summarizing '25 Years of Statistics for Advocacy') (Quezon City: Social Weather Stations, 2010).
Social Weather Stations, *Silver! 25 Years of Statistics for Advocacy* (Quezon City: Social Weather Stations, 2010).
Sta. Ana III, Filomeno S., ed., *Philippine Institutions: Growth and Prosperity for All* (Manila: Action for Economic Reforms, 2010).
Stauffer, Robert B., *The Political Economy of Refeudalization* [also published as *The Philippines Under Marcos: Failure of Transnational Developmentalism*] (Sydney: University of Sydney Transnational Corporations Research Project, 1983).
Steinberg, David Joel, *The Philippines: A Singular and Plural Place* (Boulder, CO: Westview, 1994).
Stepan, Alfred, ed., *Democracies in Danger* (Baltimore, MD: Johns Hopkins University Press, 2009).
Stone, Lawrence, *The Causes of the English Revolution 1529–1642* (London: Routledge & Kegan Paul, 1972).
Studwell, Joe, *Asian Godfathers: Money and Power in Hong Kong and Southeast Asia* (New York: Atlantic Monthly Press, 2007).
Swidler, Ann, "Culture in Action: Symbols and Strategies," *American Sociological Review* 51:2 (April 1986), 273–86.
Szanton, Cristina Blanc, *A Right to Survive: Subsistence Marketing in a Lowland Philippine Town* (University Park, PA: Pennsylvania State University Press, 1972).

Szanton, David L., *Estancia in Transition: Economic Growth in a Rural Philippine Community* (Quezon City: Ateneo de Manila University, 1971).

Szanton, David L., "Contingent Moralities: Social and Economic Investment in a Philippine Fishing Town," in *Market Cultures: Society and Morality in the New Asian Capitalisms*, Robert W. Hefner, ed. (Boulder, CO: Westview, 1998), 251–67.

Tai Hung-chao, "The Political Process of Land Reform," in *The Political Economy of Development*, Norman T. Uphoff and Warren F. Ilchman, eds. (Berkeley, CA: University of California Press, 1972), 295–303.

Tarrow, Sidney, *Power in Movement: Social Movements and Contentious Politics* (Cambridge: Cambridge University Press, 1998).

Teehankee, Julio C., "Electoral Politics in the Philippines," in *Electoral Politics in Southeast and East Asia*, Aurel Crossant and Marei John, eds. (Bonn: Friedrich-Ebert-Siftung, 2002), 149–202.

Teehankee, Julio C., "Image, Issues, and Machinery: Presidential Campaigns in Post-1986 Philippines," in *The Politics of Change in the Philippines*, Yuko Kasuya and Nathan Gilbert Quimpo, eds. (Pasig City: Anvil, 2010), 114–61.

Tharun, G., "From Waste to Money: Promoting Profitable Bioconversion Technology among Rural Entrepreneurs in the Philippines and Thailand," *Industry and Environment* 17:3 (1994), 30–7.

Thompson, Mark R., *The Anti-Marcos Struggle: Personalistic Rule and Democratic Transition in the Philippines* (New Haven, CT: Yale University Press, 1995; also Quezon City: New Day, 1996).

Thompson, Mark R., "Off the Endangered List: Philippine Democratization in Comparative Perspective," *Comparative Politics* 28:2 (January 1996), 179–205.

Thompson, Mark R., "After Populism: Winning the 'War' for Bourgeois Democracy in the Philippines," in *The Politics of Change in the Philippines*, Yuko Kasuya and Nathan Gilbert Quimpo, eds. (Pasig City: Anvil, 2010), 21–46.

Thompson, Mark R., "Reformism vs. Populism in the Philippines," *Journal of Democracy* 21:4 (2010), 154–68.

Thompson, Mark R., and Philipp Kuntz, "After Defeat: When Do Rulers Steal Elections," in *Electoral Authoritarianism: The Dynamics of Unfree Competition*, Andreas Schedler, ed. (Boulder, CO: Rienner, 2006), 113–28.

Thompson, W. Scott, "Observations on the Philippine Road to NIChood," in *The Philippine Road to NIChood*, W. Scott Thompson and Wilfredo Villacorta, eds. (Manila: De la Salle University and Social Weather Stations, 1996), 54–68.

Thompson, W. Scott, *Trustee of the Nation: The Biography of Fidel V. Ramos* (Mandaluyong: Anvil, 2011).

Tiglao, Rigoberto, "Gung-ho in Manila," *Far Eastern Economic Review* (February 15, 1990), 68–72.

Tilly, Charles, "Processes and Mechanisms of Democratization," *Sociological Theory* 18:1 (March 2000), 1–16.

Timberman, David G., *A Changeless Land: Continuity and Change in Philippine Politics* (Armonk, NY: M.E. Sharpe, 1991).

Timberman, David G., *The 1992 Philippine Elections* (New York: Asia Society, 1992).

Timberman, David G., ed., *The Philippines: New Directions in Domestic Policy and Foreign Relations* (Singapore: Institute for Southeast Asian Studies and New York: Asia Society, 1998).

Tordesillas, Ellen, and Greg Hutchinson, *Hot Money, Warm Bodies: The Downfall of Philippine President Joseph Estrada* (Pasig City: Anvil, 2001).

Torres-Mejia, Patricia, *Peasants, Merchants, and Politicians in Tobacco Production: Philippine Social Relations in a Global Economy* (Quezon City: Ateneo de Manila University Press, 2000).

Tujan, Antonio J., Jr., ed., *Contract Growing: Intensifying TNC* [Transnational Corporation] *Control in Philippine Agriculture* (Manila: IBON Foundation, 1998).

Umehara Hiromitsu, "Green Revolution for Whom?" in *Second View from the Paddy*, Antonio J. Ledesma, Perla Q. Makil, and Virginia A. Miralao, eds. (Manila: Institute of Philippine Culture, Ateneo de Manila University, 1983), 24–40.

Urbanski, C., "Middle Class Exodus and Democratic Decay in the Philippines," *ANU Undergraduate Research Journal* 1 (2009), 71–8.

Van de Walle, Nicholas, "Neopatrimonial Rule in Africa," in *Democratic Experiments in Africa*, M. Bratton and N. Van de Walle, eds. (New York: Cambridge University Press, 1997).

Varshney, Ashutosh, *Democracy, Development, and the Countryside: Urban–Rural Struggles in India* (New York: Cambridge University Press, 1998).

Velasco, Renato S., "Does the Philippine Congress Promote Democracy?" in *Democratization: Philippine Perspectives*, Felipe B. Miranda, ed. (Quezon City: University of the Philippines Press, 1995), 281–302.

Verara, Benito M., Jr., *Pinoy Capital: The Filipino Nation in Daly City* [California] (Philadelphia, PA: Temple University Press, 2009).

Verweij, Marco, Shenghua Luan, and Mark Nowacki, "How to Test Cultural Theory: Suggestions for Future Research," *PS: Political Science and Politics* 44:4 (October 2011), 745–8.

Vitug, Marites Dañguilan, *Power from the Forest: The Politics of Logging* (Pasig City: Philippine Center for Investigative Journalism, 1993).

Warren, Mark E., *Democracy and Association* (Princeton, NJ: Princeton University Press, 2001).

Weber, Max, "Politics as a Vocation," in *From Max Weber: Essays in Sociology*, trans. H.H. Gerth and C.W. Mill (New York: Oxford University Press, 1946), 77–128.

Weber, Max, *The Religion of China: Confucianism and Taoism* (Glenco, IL: Free Press, 1951).

Weightman, George Henry, *Philippine Chinese: A Cultural History of a Marginal Trading Community* (Ph.D. dissertation, Sociology, Cornell University, 1960).

White, Lynn T. III, *Policies of Chaos: The Organizational Causes of Violence in China's Cultural Revolution* (Princeton, NJ: Princeton University Press, 1989).

White, Lynn T. III, *Unstately Power: Local Causes of China's Economic Reforms* (Armonk, NY: M.E. Sharpe, 1998).

White, Lynn T. III, *Unstately Power: Local Causes of China's Intellectual, Legal, and Governmental Reforms* (Armonk, NY: M.E. Sharpe, 1999).

White, Lynn T. III, "Explanations for China's Revolution at its Peak," *Beyond a Purge and a Holocaust: The Cultural Revolution Reconsidered*, Kam-yee Law, ed. (London: Macmillan, 2003), 1–24.

White, Lynn T. III, *Political Booms: Local Money and Power in Taiwan, East China, Thailand and the Philippines* (Singapore: World Scientific, 2009).

White, Lynn T. III, "Temporal, Spatial, and Functional Governance of China's Reform Stability," *Journal of Contemporary China* 22:83 (May 2013), 791–811.

White, Lynn T. III, "Political Mechanisms and Corruption," in *Routledge Handbook of the Chinese Economy*, Gregory Chow and Dwight Perkins, eds. (Abingdon: Routledge, 2014 [forthcoming]).

Wickberg, Edgar, "Notes on Contemporary Organizations in Manila Chinese Society," in *China Across the Seas: The Chinese as Filipinos*, Aileen Baviera and Teresita Ang See, ed. (Quezon City: Philippine Association for Chinese Studies, 1992).

Winters, Jeffrey A., *Oligarchy* (New York: Cambridge University Press, 2011).

Wolters, O. Willem, *Politics, Patronage, and Class Conflict in Central Luzon* (The Hague: Institute of Social Studies, 1983).

Wolters, O. Willem, *History, Culture, and Region in Southeast Asian Perspectives*, rev. edn. (Ithaca, NY: Cornell University Southeast Asia Program, 1999).

Wong, Pak Nung, *How to Guard the Granary? Soft-power Options and Social Changes in the Rural Philippines* (Manila: Yuchengco Center, De La Salle University, Yuchengco Center Occasional Paper Series No. 11, 2009).

Wong, Pak Nung, *In Search of the State-in-Society: Re-Conceiving Philippine Political Development, 1946–2002* (Saarbrücken, Germany: VDM Verlag Dr. Müller Aktiengesellschaft & Co. KG, 2009).

Wurfel, David, "Elites of Wealth and Elites of Power: The Changing Dynamic," *Southeast Asian Affairs, 1979* (Singapore: Institute for Southeast Asian Studies, 1979), 233–49.

Wurfel, David, *Filipino Politics: Development and Decay* (Ithaca, NY: Cornell University Press, 1988).

Wurfel, David, "The Party-List System: Sectoral or National? Success or Failure?" *Kasarinlan* 13:2 (1997), 19–30.

Yashar, Deborah J., *Demanding Democracy: Reform and Reaction in Costa Rica and Guatemala, 1870s–1950s* (Stanford, CA: Stanford University Press, 1997).

Yoshihara Kunio, *Philippine Industrialization: Foreign and Domestic Capital* (Quezon City: Ateneo de Manila University Press, 1985).

Yoshihara Kunio, *The Rise of Ersatz Capitalism in Southeast Asia* (especially the Philippines) (New York: Oxford University Press, 1988).

Youngblood, Robert L., *Marcos Against the Church: Economic Development and Political Repression in the Philippines* (Quezon City: New Day, 1993).

Yuson, Alfred A., *FVR, Sin, Erap, Jawô, and Other Peeves* [F.V. Ramos, Cardinal Sin, Estrada, Jaworski...] (Pasig City: Anvil Publishing, 1997).

Zhou, Kate, Shelley Rigger, and Lynn White, eds., *Democratization in China, Korea, and Southeast Asia? Local and National Perspectives* (Abingdon: Routledge, 2014).

Index

Abra Province 44–5
Abueva, Jose 118
Abu Sayyaf 44
active auxiliaries 34, 37
AFP–NPA conflicts 42
Agrava Commission 108
agricultural productivity 62, 64, 105–7
agricultural technology, in Philippines 105
Aguinaldo, Emilio 19–20, 27, 139
Aguinaldo, Rudolfo 129
Akbayan 142, 147–9, 163
Almonte, Jose 71
Al-Qaeda 44
American colonial regime, in Philippines 20–3, 107, 162
Ampatuan clan, in Maguindanao 30, 33, 43, 159
Anakpawis 148
Anderson, James 78, 220
anti-Arroyo group, of Catholic bishops 128
anti-Chinese pogroms 20
anti-corruption agencies 192–3
anti-corruption program 189, 191
anti-dynasty bill 48
Anti-Graft League of the Philippines 122
anti-Marcos movement 110
anting-anting (protective amulets), power of 29, 212
Anti-Rape Law 166
anti-Sangley discrimination 23
anti-sedition law 20
Anti-Squatting Act 166
Aquino, Benigno S., Jr. 108–9, 122
Aquino, Benigno S., Sr. 139
Aquino, Corazon 33, 36, 43, 45–6, 107–11, 113, 122, 124, 129, 145–6, 158, 187–8
Aquino, Ninoy 139, 142, 144, 146, 158
Aquino, Servillano 208

armed bandits 29
Armed Forces of the Philippines (AFP) 30, 38, 42, 43, 126, 129
arms factories 39
Arroyo, Gloria M. 119–20, 125, 128, 149, 176, 209; main reputation and its results 189–92
Association of Major Religious Superiors of the Philippines (AMRSP) 142
Atlas Consolidated Mining Development Corporation 34
ATM journalism 197
Autonomous Region of Muslim Mindanao (ARMM) 43–4

balance of payments 86
balloting system 142
Banfield, Edward 23
Bangsamoros (Philippine Muslims) 43; Bangsamoro Islamic Freedom Fighters 43
Barangay-Bayan Governance Consortium 147
barangay organizing committees 42
bargaining 83, 137
barkada gangs 29
Bautista, Herbert 169
Bello, Walden 85–6, 137, 149, 163
Berlow, Alan 13, 32, 122
"big people," duties of 13
black propaganda 188
blat 101
"block voting" method, for election of Philippine Senate 164
booty capitalism 5
bourgeois capitalists 67
brain drain 86
bribery 158, 187–8, 192–3
Brion, Arturo 90, 112
Bulacan-Guiguinto-Malolos triangle 140

Bureau of Internal Revenue (BIR) 188–93
Burke, Edmund 50, 179
"buy-and-sell" traders 78, 81

cacique democracy 137
Cala, Cesar 137
capital-accumulating group 67
capital-intensive agricultural industries 65
capital punishment 123
Carandang, Ricky 87, 168
Career Executive Service Officers (CESOs) 75, 92
Cariño, Noel 147, 157
Carothers, Thomas 131, 171
Carroll, John 63
Catholic Bishops Conference of the Philippines (CBCP) 212–13
Catholic social doctrine 212
Cayetano, Peter 186
Certificates of Canvas 157
Chamber of Commerce and Industry 66
Christians Against Communism 36
Citizen Armed Force Geographical Units 37
citizenship laws 69–70
Civilian Home Defense Forces 29, 126
Civilian Volunteer Organizations 37
civil polities 3
Civil Service Commission 119–20, 196, 198, 200
civil societies 4, 142–4
civil society movements 4
clan dynasties' politics 45–9
clan rivalries 28
Clark Air Base 109, 125
class structure, transformation of 107
Coconut Planters' Bank 123–4
Cojuangco clan 110
colonial legacies, in Philippines 23
Comelec 108, 157–60
command voters 156
Commission on Elections 33, 45, 120, 157, 162, 185, 190
Communist Party of the Philippines (CPC) 34, 111, 140
community development funds (CDFs) 169
"*Compadrazgo*" connections 77
Comprehensive Agrarian Reform Program (CARP) 111
Comprehensive Agrarian Reform Program Extension with Reforms (CARPER) 111
confidence, local *versus* national 213–15
confrontational politics 145

Confucian social theory 17
Constitutional Convention 128, 130–1, 168
Constitutional Reform for Development ("Concord") proposal (2000) 72
contesting discourses, hypothesis of 138
Contra Force 36
Cordillera Autonomous Region 44
Cordillera People's Liberation Army (CPLA) 44
corruption 84, 125; action possibilities against 200; agencies against 198–200; Arroyo's main reputation and its results 189–92; Corruption Perception Index 191; development pork and 178–80; Estrada's concept of 218; high-risk low-reward 198; and informal network modernizations 198–200; laws for 195–6; low-risk high-reward 198; manager-entrepreneurs as canaries in 180–3; measurement of 176; muckraking 196–7; non-monetary abuses of power 190; past corruptions and presidents, memories of 187–9; perception of 176–8; of Philippine media 197; in police department 187; post-2010 corruption auditing 183–5; Presidential Commission Against Graft and Corruption (1997) 181; relatively corrupt or clean institutions 185–7; types of 192–5; zero tolerance 200
Corruption Court 198
Court of Appeals 121
crisis of investment 85
Customs Employees' Association 186

Davide Commission 129
dead capital 87
defective democracies 150
deforestation 104, 225
democracies, lessons for 4
Democratic Alliance of Huks and Communists 140
democratic representation, possibilities for 171–2
Department of Agrarian Reform (DAR) 111, 113
Department of Social Welfare 89, 209
despotism of friars 14
"development assistance" funds 183
Development Budget Coordinating Committee 193
De Venecia, Jose 130, 156, 160, 178, 181–2, 190, 217

Drilon, Franklin 72, 89–90
dual-citizens 168

economic: corruption 192–5; democratization 92; export zones 76; globalization 87; inequalities 104, 171; recession 17, 219; stagnancy 209
elections: balloting system 142; electoral campaigns 145, 170; electoral democracy 130, 225; fraud in *see* voting fraud; institution for monitoring 158; as spurs of politics 142–3; violence in 38
electoral authoritarianisms 150
electoral integrity 150
elite and non-elite politics 145–6
elite democracy 137, 150
El Shaddai sect 112
encomiendas system 15
Enrile, Juan Ponce 109, 126, 164
entrepreneurs 63; barriers to industrial unions 81–3; Chinese and Filipino 66–73; culture matters, effects of 79; existential motives of 90–1; and government of business 73–7; immiserating growth 83–6; infrastructure gaps 88–90; as marginal men 77–81; marginal-person 80; multiple occupations 80–1; Overseas Filipino Workers 86–7; pillow and mat capitalist 74; political 137; possibilities against undemocratic wages 91–2
envelopmental journalism 197
Epifanio de los Santos Avenue (EDSA) 88, 125, 127
"ersatz capitalism" 5
Estrada, Joseph Erap 89, 122, 123, 127, 188–9, 217
exit polling 159
extrajudicial killings (EJKs) 38

Fallows, James 4–5
Family and Child Courts Law 166
family planning 212–13
family-scale enterprises 82
fanatical cults 29, 36, 43, 122
farming, violence in 34–5
"Febrev" (February "Revolution" of 1986) 187
Federation of Filipino-Chinese Chambers of Commerce and Industry 69
Feder, Ernest 106
Feliciano Commission 129
Felix, Alfonso, Jr. 121
Ferrer, Jaime 33

"Filipino First" policy 69
Filipino freeway 88
foreign investment 72, 85
Foronda, Marcelino 3
freedom of expression 4, 141
"Freedom of Information" bill (2012) 197
free press 160–1, 196–7

gambling 122, 178; laws against 195; violence in 34–5
Garcia, Carlos 69
Ghost projects 112, 183
Ginez, Jose 167
Gini inequality 220
global competitiveness index 85, 87
Global Transparency Report 218
GMA Network 160
governance and justice: action possibilities for 130–2; problem of 2
governance scores, of Philippines 49
Green Revolution 103, 105
guanxi 101
guns 39–41
Guzman, Arbenz 128

Hawai'i 20, 109, 120
Helica 38
Hodder, Rupert 196, 214
Honasan, Gregorio 124–6, 128, 164, 184
House Appropriations Committee 181
Hukbalahaps 27; campaign against 141; growth of 140
human development index 84
human rights abuses 120–1
Hutchison, Jane 82
hybrid regimes 150

Ilaga Movement 43
Ilaya, Dante 38
Ileto, Reynaldo 136, 220–1
immigrants, legal assimilation of 71
income inequality 219
Independent Commission Against Corruption 200
Indian Administrative Service 75, 92
indigenous communities 43
Indigenous People's Rights Act 166
"Indio" Filipinos 16
industrial unions, barriers to 81–3
informal settlers 89
infrastructure development 75
Integrated Civilian Home Defense Force 29

International Rice Research Institute (IRRI) 102–3
intra-governmental conflict 195

Janet Lim Napoles Group of Companies 183
Japanese occupation, of Philippines 27, 140
JB Management 38
jueteng lords 35
jueteng profits 189, 195
jus sanguinis (law of blood) 69

kalayaan 36, 135, 214
Katipunan secret society 19–20
Kerkvliet, Ben 141, 145
Kilusang Bagong Lipunan (KBL) 165
kinship politics 138
Klitgaard, Robert 198
Kristiana Kontra Komunismo (KKK) *see* Christians Against Communism
kudeta 109–10, 142, 207, 209; anti-Arroyo episodes 125–6; basic causes of 126–9; "God Save the Queen" plot 124; origins of 129; summary list of 124–6
Kuhonta, Erik Martínez 6
Kuratong Baleleng 43

labor-capital division 171
labor supply 212
Lacson, Arsenio 69
Lacson, Panfilo "Ping" 42, 121, 199
land-based conservatism 141
land holdings 100
landlord armies 140
landlord–tenant relationship 28
landownership, issue of 100, 106
land policy, in the Philippines 100
land redistribution 112
lanzadera 157
Lastimoso, Roberto 121
latifundista landowners 106
Laurel, José 139
Laurel, Salvador 108
Law, Jones 21
Lazatín, Vincent 198
leadership, in Philippines 130
Lewis, Arthur 82
lider 142
Lim, Alfredo 218
Local Government Code of 1991 (Republic Act 7160) 146–7, 151
logging, violence in 34–5
Lopezes of Cebu 29
Lopez, Gemiliano 32

Lot Allocation Certificate 113
Luisita, Hacienda 113
Lumads 43
Lynch, Frank 12, 78, 86, 138, 211–12

MacArthur, Arthur 20
McCoy, Alfred 7, 27
Madison, James 222
Magdalo group 127
Magsaysay, Ramon 141
Makati Business Club 66, 72, 141
Makil, Perla 86
Malacañang Palace 188
malakas 101–2, 121, 129–30, 141
Manila Peninsula Rebellion 125
Manila Police Department 47
Manila transport and housing 88–90
Maoist insurgency 41–5
Marcos, Ferdinand 1, 29, 74, 100–1, 145–6, 224; cronies 122; democratic *trapo* stability 106–9; effects of policies on the Philippines economy 103; growth of paramilitary groups 126; human rights abuses 120–1; land non-reform and political fragmentation after 109–13; land reform 102–6; "Masagana-99" ('Prosperity-99') program 102; possibilities against undemocratic landowning 113–14; seed-change reform 105
Marcos, Imelda 121, 146, 163
market voters 156
Marshall, Alfred 105
martial law, decree of 69
"Masagana-99" ('Prosperity-99') program 102
Masses Arise 43
Masses Uprising (*Alsa Masa*) vigilantes (1984) 35–6
militias, types of 31–2
Mindanao: ethnolinguistic and religious divisions in 42–3; Muslim areas of 30; Visayan immigrants 43; Zamboanga Peninsula 44
Mojares, Resil 1, 23
monopolies 76
Moore, Barrington 67
Moro Islamic Liberation Front (MILF) 43
Moro National Liberation Front (MNLF) 43
Moros 41–5
mountain people 41–5
muckraking 196–7
Muslims–Christians conflict 2, 44

Nakasaka 43
National Bureau of Investigation 184, 195
National Citizens' Movement for Free Elections (Namfrel) 108, 158
National Democratic Front 32
National Federation of Labor 82
National Intelligence Coordinating Agency 183
National Police 34–5, 37, 39, 41–2, 121, 183, 185, 194–5, 210
New People's Army 29, 34–5, 39, 41, 43, 128–9, 140–2, 148
non-government organizations (NGOs) 2, 4, 143–4, 222
nonstate militias 29, 32, 35–9, 40
no-strike zone 31

Oakwood Mutiny (July 2003) 125, 127, 129, 210
oligarchic networks 46–7, 108, 137–8
oligopolies 76
Ombudsman 112, 120, 131, 185–6, 189, 192, 195, 198–200
Operation Bawas-Dagdag 170
Operation Quick Count (1986) 158
Organization of the Poor Against Communism 30
Osmeña–Cuenco electoral struggles, in Cebu 140
Overseas Absentee Voting Act 168
Overseas Filipino Workers (OFW) 86–7, 168; emigration of 87; job creation by 87; remittances sent back by 86
Overseas Filipino Workers Family Club 168
Owen, Norman 3, 220

Pacquiao, Manny 216
pakikisama 78, 136, 145
Panganiban, Artemio 218
Parish Councils for Responsible Voting 158
Partido Komunista ng Pilipinas 140
partisan armed groups 44
party disloyalty 163
partyless clientelism, tradition of 165
party-list representatives 147–50, 155, 163, 182, 184
Party-List System Act of February 1995 147
patronage-based state formation 222
patron–client relations 106, 138; in Philippine politics 4, 13, 180
penal justice system, in Philippines 122; imposition of death penalties 123; revision of 126
people power revolution 4, 36, 109, 111, 124, 127, 144, 217
"permit-to-campaign" licenses 34
personalism, proposals against 167–9
Philippine Alliance of Human Rights Advocates 29
Philippine–American War of 1898–1906 27
Philippine Center for Investigative Journalism 45–6
Philippine citizens, sense of nationhood 2
Philippine Commission on Human Rights 38
Philippine Commonwealth, establishment of 22
Philippine Communist Party 140
Philippine Constabulary 15, 36, 121, 126, 129, 140
Philippine Development Academy 75
Philippine Guardian Brotherhood 128
Philippine industrial decentralization 76
Philippine National Police 34–5, 39, 41, 121, 185, 194–5, 210
Philippine political history, democratic evolution of 1
Philippine Press Institute 161
Philippines Benevolent Missionary Association 29
Philippines Commission on Audit 187
Philippines Military Academy 110, 121
Philippines, possibilities for future progress 224–5
Pinches, Michael 5
plebiscites, on autonomy 43–4
PNoy, President 8, 31, 37–8, 40–2, 50, 72, 87, 89, 113, 121, 123, 156, 168, 191, 193, 197, 214; demagogue danger 215–20; election in 2010 146; Liberal Party 166, 184; "open skies" policy 210; policy issues 208–11; position on pork 183; Presidential Anti-Graft Commission 199; presidential campaign 210
political dynasties, in Philippines 48–56
"political ID" cards 169
political non-violence, usefulness of 18
political personalism, traditions of 1
politics: clan dynasties and professionals 45–9; confrontational 145; elections as spurs of 142–3; by other means 32–4
Politics (Aristotle) 66

popular progress, paradigms for 141–2
populism and reformism, issue of 150
pork as policy: allocations to politicians 169–70, 193; "pork" funds 32
poverty: in Philippines 180, 211; Poverty Alleviation Law 166
precinct-count optical scanners (PCOS) 159
Presidential Commission Against Graft and Corruption (1997) 181, 199
Presidential Committee on Human Rights 110
Presidential Social Fund 183
principalia 15, 27, 145
Priority Development Assistance Fund 182–3
private armies 29, 31, 35, 37, 39, 42–5, 122
Procter and Gamble 83
Procurement Transparency Group 189
professionals' politics 45–9
professional squatters 89
Propaganda Movement 19, 139
prostitution, violence in 34–5
public–private partnerships 76
public trust in justice: for better governance 130–2; courts' integrity and 120–4; human rights abuses 120–1; and imposition of death penalties 123; zero tolerance 131
Public Works Act 183
Pulse Asia 159
Puno, Reynato 128

Quezon, Manuel 21, 127–8
Quirino, Elpidio 140, 178

race-based interpretations of development 68
RAMboys 126
Ramos, Fidel 31–2, 45, 126–7, 146, 183, 188
Randall, Vicky 166
rebels, farmers *versus* educated 139–41
reducción, Spanish policy of 15
reformism in Philippines 19–22
Reform the Armed Forces Movement (RAM) 108
remontados 15
Remulla, Juanito "Johnny" 31–2
Reparations and Recognitions of Human Rights Violations Victims Act (2013) 121
Reproductive Health Bill 213

resource allocation 33
"resource curse" 2
Retail Trade Nationalization Act 69
Retirement Service and Benefits System (RSBS) 129
revolts and repressions 137–9
revolutionary tax 34, 74
rice farming 103
right-wing vigilantes 29
Rizal, José 19, 136
Roaring Thunder (marketing company) 161
Robison, Richard 3
Rocamora, Joel 4, 31, 76, 141, 149, 151, 162
Roces, Mina 28
Rock Christ 29
Roman Catholic: Church 28, 158; community 80
Romualdez, Benjamin 20, 112
Romulo, Carlos P. 170
Rood, Steven 147
Rosales, Eta 149
rule of law 32, 130–1

salary taxes, evasion of 193
Samahang Magdalo 127
Sandiganbayan anti-graft court 120, 191–2, 198
Sangleys 16–18, 68
Santiago, Miriam Defensor 48, 137, 149, 161, 164–5, 184, 195, 199
Schattschneider, E. E. 142, 162
semi-feudal tenancy system 140
"September Thesis" of 1988 111
sharecropping 102, 104–5
shari'a law 44
Sidel, John 71, 220
small and medium enterprises (SMEs) 66, 69, 73, 79
small-scale buy-and-sell-dealers 81
"smiling money" 197
Smith, Adam 90
social capital 78, 144, 179
social-class differences 4
social globalization 87
social inequalities 125
social justice 4
social reform laws 166
Social Weather Stations 145, 159
Social Welfare Department 37
socioeconomic development 107
Soldiers Against Communism and for the Oppressed 29

Sotto, Vicente 137, 165
"sovereign" governments 150
Spanish–American War 19
Spanish occupation, in Philippines 20
speed money 192
squatting on land 111
State of the Nation Address (SONA) 128, 185
state–society relations 6
stock redistribution option scheme 111
strategic hypocrites 44, 196
Sugar Development Fund 34
Sukarnoputri, Megawati 189
"*suki*" relationship 77
sustainable reforms, action possibilities for 150–1
Swidler, Ann 79
Szanton, David 80

Table Tennis Association 210
Tadeco 76
Tadtad (rightist religious vigilante group) 36–7, 43
Taft Commission 20
Taft, William Howard 20
Tagalog for "People's Anti-Japanese Army *see* Hukbalahaps
tanod 34, 194
Tanodbayan 120, 191–2, 198
tax and tariff evasions 193
tax compliance 187
technocrats 46, 74–5, 85, 100, 106–7, 166
Technopark 76
Teehankee, Julio 48
tenancy system 105, 140
Thompson, Mark 218
Tordesillas, Ellen 160
trade unions 3, 82–3, 137, 148
Transparency and Accountability Network (TAN) 198
Transparency International 186
trapo clan organizations 49
trapo oligarchs 110
trapos 34, 44, 46–9, 75, 92, 113, 140, 147–50, 221

"trickle down" effect 106
Truth Commission of 2010 198–9
Tuazon, Bobby 48

undemocratic landowing, action possibilities against 113–14
undemocratic wages, action possibilities against 91–2
unemployment 82–4, 91, 105, 225
United Democratic Opposition (UNIDO) 108
United Nations Development Program 84
urban immigrants 89
urban industrial jobs 104
urban–rural division 47

Varshney, Ashutosh 67
Vietnam War 224
violence: action possibilities against undemocratic 49–50; centralization of, by the state 49; electoral 38; in logging, farming, gambling, and prostitution 34–5; political 30, 32–4, 49; against women 35
Visayan immigrants 35, 43
Visayan languages 155–6
vote-buying 139, 157, 158, 169
voting fraud 157–60, 170

wages and births, issues of 211–13
wasta 101
Weber, Max 9, 27
white-collar professions 46
Wildman, Rounseville 19
World Bank 49, 64, 83, 85, 111

Youth Councils, elections of 157
Youth Federation 157

Zamora "municipality" 30
Zheng, Chenggong 16
ZTE Corp. 189

eBooks
from Taylor & Francis

Helping you to choose the right eBooks for your Library

Add to your library's digital collection today with Taylor & Francis eBooks. We have over 50,000 eBooks in the Humanities, Social Sciences, Behavioural Sciences, Built Environment and Law, from leading imprints, including Routledge, Focal Press and Psychology Press.

Choose from a range of subject packages or create your own!

Benefits for you
- Free MARC records
- COUNTER-compliant usage statistics
- Flexible purchase and pricing options
- 70% approx of our eBooks are now DRM-free.

Benefits for your user
- Off-site, anytime access via Athens or referring URL
- Print or copy pages or chapters
- Full content search
- Bookmark, highlight and annotate text
- Access to thousands of pages of quality research at the click of a button.

Free Trials Available

We offer free trials to qualifying academic, corporate and government customers.

eCollections

Choose from 20 different subject eCollections, including:

- Asian Studies
- Economics
- Health Studies
- Law
- Middle East Studies

eFocus

We have 16 cutting-edge interdisciplinary collections, including:

- Development Studies
- The Environment
- Islam
- Korea
- Urban Studies

For more information, pricing enquiries or to order a free trial, please contact your local sales team:

UK/Rest of World: **online.sales@tandf.co.uk**
USA/Canada/Latin America: **e-reference@taylorandfrancis.com**
East/Southeast Asia: **martin.jack@tandf.com.sg**
India: **journalsales@tandfindia.com**

www.tandfebooks.com